A Concise History of Economic Thought

From Mercantilism to Monetarism

Revised edition

Gianni Vaggi
Professor of Economics
University of Pavia
Italy

and

Peter Groenewegen
Emeritus Professor
University of Sydney
Australia

First published 2014 by
PALGRAVE MACMILLAN

Palgrave Macmillan in the UK is an imprint of Macmillan Publishers Limited,
registered in England, company number 785998, of Houndmills, Basingstoke,
Hampshire RG21 6XS.

Palgrave Macmillan in the US is a division of St Martin's Press LLC,
175 Fifth Avenue, New York, NY 10010.

Palgrave Macmillan is the global academic imprint of the above companies
and has companies and representatives throughout the world.

Palgrave® and Macmillan® are registered trademarks in the United States,
the United Kingdom, Europe and other countries

ISBN: 978-1-137-37245-1

This book is printed on paper suitable for recycling and made from fully
managed and sustained forest sources. Logging, pulping and manufacturing
processes are expected to conform to the environmental regulations of the
country of origin.

A catalogue record for this book is available from the British Library.

A catalog record for this book is available from the Library of Congress.

Gianni Vaggi dedicates this book to Paolo, Marco and Anna

Contents

Section V   The 'Golden Age' of Classical Political Economy

PART II   MODERN DEVELOPMENTS, 1870–1960

Section I   The First Generation

Section II   The Development of Marginalist Economics: Distribution and Capital Theory

Section III   Pioneers of Macro-economics

Section IV   Further Developments in Micro-economics

Section V   The Foundations of Modern Macro-economics

List of Figures

Prologue

The question 'why another book on the history of economic thought when the market seems already glutted with texts, some of them of very high quality?', may be posed. The answer to this is straightforward. As teachers and researchers of the subject over many years we think that a new book on the subject can still make a useful contribution, particularly when it focuses on developing the story of how economics evolved by means of a dual division between classical political economy on the one hand, and modern developments on the other, in which a section on Marx concludes the first part while a section on Mill introduces the modern era. The importance of this logic for ordering the subject matter of the book is fully explained in this introduction.

Why a relatively *short* book for assisting students of the history of economics in their preliminary study, also needs some comment. Most of the existing history of economics texts are lengthy affairs, William Barber's venture for Penguin books being one of the few, outstanding exceptions. A shorter book has considerable advantages. Apart from the obvious one of cost (affecting both price for the student purchaser and that of time spent in reading), a shorter book allows a clearer overview of the subject, enabling the reader to see the forest as well as many of the individual trees. Moreover, our focus is on linking the past with the present, and intended to show that an understanding of aspects of classical economics and of post-1848 developments of the subjects assists in grasping the trends of modern, contemporary economics.

Why a book in two parts, specifically devoted to classical economics and what we call, 'modern developments'? To answer this question, our views on the meaning of classical economics and modern developments need clarification. Classical economics for us spans the virtually two centuries from Petty to Marx, in which economists saw the key features for explaining the operations of a modern economy in terms of the requirements for reproduction, the generation of surplus product and the accumulation of capital. Consistent and logical explanation of these key issues for them likewise involved explanation of value and price, of production theory, of accumulation, and of a theory of distribution, in which emphases differed. Thus Smith in his account stressed increasing returns and growth; earlier Quesnay had emphasised the need for balance to secure genuine development of the national economy; Ricardo made distributional issues (what determines wages, profits and rent) the centrepoint of his analysis; Malthus concentrated on population growth and its consequences as well as on the role of effective demand; Marx largely examined the impact of accumulation on wealth, living standards and distribution.

Much of this analysis remains relevant to understanding the present problems of economies. At the same time, it has implications for our method in handling the material.

To maintain our intention to be brief, we adopted a quite specific method for presenting the material. In the first place, our account emphasises the key individual authors and the major topics in economics with which they are generally associated. For example, the section on Adam Smith deals with national wealth, productivity of labour and division of labour; that on Marx with accumulation and crises; that on Marshall with partial equilibrium and useful economics; that on Keynes with the essentials of his new, general theory of employment, interest and money. This way of presenting the development of economics over three centuries or so (from mercantilism to monetarism) avoids the encyclopedic approach adopted in many texts of trying to deal with *all* the contributions of the individual authors. Each little chapter, in short, is devoted to one (or occasionally several) author(s) and the topics most closely associated with them. Each chapter can thereby also present a brief biographical presentation of its key actor (or actors in the case of some chapters) preceding the analysis of their main contributions and suggestions for additional reading drawn from the wide array of literature available. Biography, analysis and major references are, in short, the structural components making up our writing 'recipe'.

Presenting the material in this way likewise has a number of advantages. It permits explicit recognition of the fact that economics is the product of individual minds (up to now, largely from men, though Chapter 29 introduces Joan Robinson, as perhaps the first major woman economist) with backgrounds of which some knowledge generally assists in understanding the key reasons why they made the contributions that they did. Selectivity of topics allows a broad overview of all the key elements of the classical system (Part I) and of the major micro- and macro-economics into which the modern developments examined in Part II are so easily classified. The need to make suggestions for further reading needs little justification in a short book. These suggestions also enable some signalling of those topics where interpretation continues to be controversial by highlighting sources of some of these alternative views.

Organisation of the material: an overview

Our division of labour as authors of this book in part reflects the direction of our published research. Gianni Vaggi has devoted much of his history of economics research to the classical period, in particular to the economics of Quesnay, of the physiocrats, and of Adam Smith; Peter Groenewegen has recently published work on Alfred Marshall in the setting of the marginal revolution and other intellectual developments of the second half of the nineteenth century, including therein the association between Marshall's work and that of Keynes; though he has also worked on the classical period, with special reference to the economics of Turgot, Smith and the early developments of value, production and distribution theory from its formative period after 1650. Moreover, both of us have taught the history of economics for many years at our respective universities of Pavia and Sydney.

The subdivision of the subject matter of this book reflects more than our respective research interests and skills. More significantly, it is predicated on our firm belief that the development of economics took place in two, quite distinct ways. The first of these, that of classical economics, looked broadly at aspects of production and distribution theory, and of the theory of value and price, in order to explain the nature and growth of annual, national wealth in terms of that part of it available as surplus and that part which, as necessary costs of production, had to be devoted to enabling continuous national production and reproduction to take place. Part I of this book is devoted to explaining the development of this type of analysis, which ends with the work of Marx, the last major writer of the nineteenth century to explain the key operations of an economic system in this way.

By the middle of the nineteenth century, however, the classical approach to economics was being gradually abandoned. A greater emphasis on the market, on exchange, on supply and demand, replaced the earlier view that production, reproduction and surplus provided the key to economic understanding. An early tendency to this more recent approach is apparent in the writings of John Stuart Mill, whose work is therefore the first to be discussed in our modern developments segment. It acts as a prelude to the marginal revolution which more systematically developed this type of approach rooted in exchange, on the basis of the unifying principle that the foundation for all economic decision making was to be discovered at the margin of such decisions. Marginalism is therefore the key to the modern developments in analysis which have resulted in the current state of micro-economics; it has influenced aspects in the development of macro-economics secured through that other theoretical revolution of the modern period, the Keynesian Revolution. However, that second revolution, by reopening the door to growth theory as part of the study of output as a whole, also reintroduced features of classical analysis into the modern era. Contemporary economic thinking, in widely varying respects, now draws on aspects of both the older, classical, and the more recent, marginalist methods, one reason why knowing about the historical evolution of these traditions is useful for the current student of economics.

At this stage, a brief overview of the discussion presented into the two major parts of this book may be found helpful by way of introduction, in order to get a clearer feel for the logic of our ordering of the material. This also allows a fuller appreciation of the broad structure of the evolution of modern economics. The overview is presented sequentially, commencing with the classical system.

The classical system

The process of formation of classical political economy is the subject of Part I of this book, though it can also be described as discussing the development of theories of surplus. Part of this development is apparent through the changing perceptions of the surplus: as a favourable balance of trade for the mercantilist; as a surplus over costs for many of the post-mercantilist writers, with the explanations for the existence of surplus ascribed to the productiveness of nature (as especially in the case of the Physiocrats), or to the productivity of labour (as more generally done by the later members of the classical school including Marx). Finally, the development of classical political economy can be seen as a gradual process of refining and clarifying the meanings of concepts such as wealth, value, price, production, capital, labour, wages, profit, distribution.

Part I of this book covers more than two centuries of which the first segment (1620–1776) covers the emergence of classical political economy from mercantilism to the publication of Smith's *Wealth of Nations*. Its three sections cover the mercantilist era, including critics of mercantilism such as Locke and North, as well as Petty; section II looks at early French eighteenth century writings (Boisguilbert, Cantillon, but also at Quesnay); section III covers the 20 years from Quesnay's first economic article to the publication of the *Wealth of Nations*, looking at Hume, Galiani, Steuart, Turgot and ending with Smith's great contribution. Section IV treats the first post-Smithian generation of classical economics: Say, Bentham, Sismondi, Malthus and the major theoretician of this period, Ricardo. The final section examiners post-Ricardian developments in the work of Torrens and Senior, and concludes with the work of Marx. It also links directly with the opening chapters of Part II dealing with J.S. Mill as the last of the classics and, simultaneously, the first of the moderns.

Modern developments

Modern developments in economics from the 1850s to the early 1980s are covered in Part II. The discussion is subdivided into five sections, after an introduction which overviews the main themes of this part in terms of the emergence of marginalism and the rise of modern macro-economics. It examines the notion of the marginal revolution as a historical phenomenon, looks in some detail at the difference between the old and the new (during which Robbins's famous definition of the economic problem is shown to be particularly illuminating on the features of the newer, marginalist economics). Implications of the new marginalism for methodology and for changing the nature of the economics profession are also discussed, as is the question of the extent to which the new economics constituted a major break, or discontinuity, with the past. Not surprisingly, given the earlier discussion of this introduction, the answer is a resounding yes. The major innovations of the Keynesian revolution are then briefly summarised, in order to highlight the reasons why a new macro-economics could be constructed on them. It also draws attention to the fact that some of the foundations for this new macro-economics were laid by a number of writers earlier in the century, of which Wicksell, Fisher and Schumpeter are leading examples discussed in Section III of Part II.

The nature and content of the five sections into which Part II is subdivided also need some introduction. Section I looks at the first generation of writers of the new, marginalist economics, that is, Jevons, Menger and Walras, as well as the contributions of Marshall and, at the start, John Stuart Mill's economics as an important element in the transition from the old to the new. Section II briefly covers work by the second generation of the marginalists, with special reference to the theory of distribution and of capital and interest. As intimated in the previous paragraph, Section III introduces the work of three, turn-of-the-century economists as pioneers on what is now called macro-economics; Section IV looks at further developments in micro-economics such as welfare economics, the cost controversies, the theory of the firm, and the implications of the decline in utility theory. These can all be described as important, preparatory steps in the construction of modern micro-economics. Section V studies the foundations of modern macro-economics provided by the Keynesian revolution (and by its alternative formulation in Kalecki's work) and its continuation and development in the early growth models of Harrod and Domar, and the controversial issues to which they gave rise. It concludes with a discussion of monetarism, expectations theory, and developments in growth theory of the 1970s and 1980s.

Conclusion and epilogue

Is this a history of economics with a difference? We think so. It is concise, clear, informative and, above all, attempts explicitly to link the past with the present. The last objective is achieved in several ways. It is done by linking specific aspects of classical and marginalist thought to current thinking and debates. Treatment by topics as well as by authors, topics which in most cases remain relevant to the subject as it is studied today, also allow easier linkage of past and present. Above all, an overview of the development of economics of the past in terms of its two major strands of development, allows students to recognise more easily the specific heritage left by the great masters on their subject as currently practised. In this way, the past has a useful purpose and, yes, study of the history of economics is important for the contemporary student of economics. If our book has an important role to play in this important process of learning, we will be well satisfied.

Gianni Vaggi thanks the Master and Fellows of St John's College, Cambridge because the writing of Part I began in 1997 when he was Visiting Scholar at St John's.

Sydney   Peter Groenewegen

Pavia   Gianni Vaggi

Preface to the Second Edition

In 2009 we were informed by Palgrave Macmillan that a second edition of our book was warranted, hence enabling us to make some revisions and updating. Given the fact that original publication was only in 2003, the changes we have decided to make are relatively few. Our 'Notes for further reading', appended to each chapter, were an obvious part for introducing additions to the relevant literature made since then. There has been considerable growth in the writings on the History of Economic Thought in both book and article form during the first decade of the 21st century. Textual changes have been fewer. Gianni Vaggi had added to his chapters on mercantilism, and on Quesnay and Smith to incorporate the findings on new material, particularly on Smith, but also on current trends in neo-mercantilism in the chapter on mercantilism, and on issues of agricultural reform in the chapter on Quesnay. I have added a short paragraph to the introduction to Part II on 'economic imperialism' as an important phenomenon for explaining the effectively expanding scope of economics, and added brief remarks on Solow's growth theory and the rapidly declining acceptance in the literature of the findings of the Cambridge controversies in capital theory. I have also commented on the return of Keynes-type economic policies for recovery during the 2008 World Financial Crisis in both the final chapter (Chapter 34) and the Epilogue. These changes have not greatly increased the size of the book. We have, in fact, kept it short, as an important quality of the work for reasons explored in the original prologue.

Gianni Vaggi   Peter Groenewegen
University of Pavia   The University of Sydney
(December 2010)

Foreword

Reading and studying the history of ideas brings many rewards, not least among which are a sense for how life and thought in the present age involves 'standing on the shoulders of giants' of the past, and a humility with regard to the 'truth' claims attached to the ideas of any particular era. Ideas are continually evolving or even changing wholesale – perhaps progressively, perhaps not. Understandings and meanings are historically contingent. Today's grand theory may be but one facet of tomorrow's explanation or even relegated to the dustbin. Through it all though, the past informs our understanding of the present, just as our present knowledge informs our understanding of the past.

All of that having been said, the merits of detailed attention to things historical – especially ideas (as opposed to, say, monuments) – are increasingly subject to question in modern society. This age of rapid technological change, 'instant classics,' worldwide transmission of ideas within seconds, and emphasis on the purely practical, makes that which happened even two years ago seem terribly dated, and even irrelevant. The hottest 'blog' is given far more status in the public conscience than careful, studied inquiry or reflective literature. And, of course, the post-modern turn of recent years has led many to question whether one can properly speak of 'classics' or of a particular set of 'great ideas' of the past.

All of this is true of economics no less than of other fields of scholarly inquiry. The rise of increasingly technical mathematical and statistical modes of inquiry has brought with it the marginalization of certain approaches to and facets of economic analysis, not least among which is the history of economic ideas. 'The wrong ideas of dead men', they say. Non-economists, and economists with historical sensibilities, often ask me how it is that economists can hope to understand the present without a healthy appreciation for the ideas of the past. I would never claim that it is not possible to do economics without an understanding of the history of economic thought; after all, thousands of economists do just that every day. The point, rather, is that the economist and economics benefit from such an acquaintance in the same way that a preacher benefits from the study of the history of theological ideas or modern military commanders benefit from reading the work of Sun Tzu.

It is against this backdrop that Gianni Vaggi and Peter Groenewegen offer us their *Concise History of Economic Thought*. To treat the history of economic thought from 1620 through to 1960 is no mean feat, given the many currents and nuances that characterise the evolution of economic thinking. To cover this same period in 326 pages would seem to be all but impossible. But this is precisely what the authors have done in this wonderful little book. Both Vaggi and Groenewegen have substantial records of scholarly publication in the field, and their respective areas of expertise complement each other in ways that redound to the benefit of the book and its readers.

The book is consciously divided into halves on 'classical' and 'modern' developments and as such gives the reader a sense of the relationships between contributors and contributions over two relatively large epochs. The discussion covers all of the canonical figures in the field, but it also introduces the reader to people like Boisguilbert, Galiani, Steuart, Sismond and Torrens, who made important contributions to specific areas of economic analysis but who one might expect to be passed over in a 'concise' history. And, reflecting the fact that ideas do not arise in a vacuum, but are in part the product of circumstances of place and time, the book also gives the reader a sense of the personalities and the contexts within which these writers made their contributions.

The writers of 'comprehensive' histories worry that they have somehow missed something, and these various 'somethings' are pointed out to them with regularity by readers. Vaggi and Groenewegen's *Concise History* does not pretend to be comprehensive; it intends, rather, to cover the main ideas of the main thinkers. Some will undoubtedly quibble with their decisions as to who fits into the 'main thinker' category. Others will dispute their decisions as to the most significant contributions of this or that individual. The point, though, is that the reader of a book such as this one comes away with an appreciation of the development and evolution of ideas and the persons and circumstances that are part of the story. In this, Vaggi and Groenewegen succeed admirably.

Scholars of the history of ideas are virtually unanimous in their view that there is no substitute for reading the original texts of the past. However, the reader coming to those texts benefits greatly from having an accompanying roadmap, such as that provided here by Vaggi and Groenewegen. Students will enjoy the short chapters (they average less than ten pages) and having each subject's main ideas set out in front of them. The educated lay person, too, will appreciate this aspect of the book. From here, the interested reader can move on to more extensive, detailed, and specialised general treatments of the subject, such as those by Mark Blaug, Samuel Hollander, Mark Perlman and Joseph Schumpter, or even more narrowly targeted works like Vaggi's *Economics of François Quesnay* or Groenewegen's *Soaring Eagle*, a biography of Alfred Marshall. The reader would also do well to peruse a selection of the ample suggestions for further reading provided, with annotation, at the end of each chapter.

The present book is not an end, but a beginning, a window into both past and present. Enjoy.

University of Colorado at Denver   STEVEN G. MEDEMA

PART I

CLASSICAL POLITICAL ECONOMY, 1600–1870

1

Introduction: from Mercantilism to Marx

Part I of this book examines the process of formation of classical political economy, or the evolution of the 'theories of surplus'. The reason for using either of these two terms will emerge from the contents of the book. As for the meaning of classical political economy itself, no further specific definition needs to be provided at this stage.

The starting point of the classical period, mercantilism in the sixteenth century, implies that the story told here largely overlaps with the emergence of the nation states of Europe, in particular with those of Great Britain and France. What were the causes of the wealth of these two countries, the sources of their power and the means for their good governance constitute the subject matter and major objectives of all the 'economic' writers examined in first part of this book.

Notions and their mutual relationships

The contents of this book are divided according to author but this does not imply a mere history of people, facts and dates. More generally, the book aims at providing an overview of the major notions which characterise the thought of each author; the inter-connection between these notions making them theoretical structures; and the evolution of these analytical structures over time.

These points can be elucidated as follows. The first entails telling the story of the modifications taking place in the actual meaning of concepts such as wealth, value, price, production, capital, labour, profit, wages and distribution. These categories and their evolution through time provide a first grid for interpreting the formation of and changes in, economic theories from the early mercantilists to Marx.

The second point emphasises the need to pay attention to the various ways in which these concepts were interrelated by different authors, sometimes giving rise to novel views.

Thus innovation may be regarded as the definition of a concept, or the manner in which an already existing concept or view is related to other aspects of economics in order to present a system of thought.

The third point needs also to be refined. For every author, their notions and their theories are examined as attempts to find answers to the main economic problems of the time. So historical background matters a lot, economic history in particular; and the contemporary distinction between political economy and economic policy becomes a very feeble one for most classical political economists. Considerable attention needs to be devoted to identifying the object of investigation, that is, the problem which worried particular authors. Sometimes, only the selection of the subject matter by different economists identifies aspects of continuity and change. The evolution of the different notions and of their mutual linkages through time is important, but it must always be remembered that for each author there is a background, a stage on which the theory is represented. These settings and visions are provided by history, and sometime by disciplines other than economics.

The separation between micro- and macro-economics of such paramount importance in the twentieth century is much less relevant for classical political economy. The now common stress on individual economic agents had to wait for the second half of the nineteenth century. For the classical economists, the individuals are primarily citizens, with precise rights and duties. Then they have specific interests derived from the social group (or rank, or class) to which they belong. This is clearly relevant to notions of distribution of income and wealth, which are linked to the role each group plays in the production process. This view derives from the idea that human societies are organised according to the principle of the social division of labour. This is particularly true of the civilised, or modern, commercial, capitalist (according to Marx) societies, which were the object of the analysis of the classical authors.

Value and distribution, and wealth

Some of the key concepts for understanding the evolution of classical political economy need now to be examined. In many histories of economic ideas the analysis of the exchange *value* of commodities is regarded as the fundamental element for determining the contributions of various authors to economics, as implied in the work of Sewall, Hollander and Schumpeter mentioned at the end of this chapter. This view is not wrong; the problem of the determination of the relative prices or the theory of the exchange value of commodities is of fundamental importance in writing history of economic thought. However, far too often on acceptance of this approach to the history of economic thought, authors are generally classified into two major groups; the supporters of the view that prices are determined by cost of production on the one side and those in favour of demand and supply explanations on the other. This way of treating the history of economics ideas is unsatisfactory. It concentrates too narrowly on a classification based on a single notion. Value offers a fundamental perspective but by itself fails to grasp the structure of a particular theory, let alone the general visions behind it. Dobb's view that visions and value judgements are as important in the history of economics as the technical evolution of concepts is accepted in the account offered in this book. Moreover, the utility–cost explanation of value is not always satisfactory for analysing contributions of the seventeenth and eighteenth century authors. At a superficial level, the same author may be classified as a supporter of a subjective theory of prices or as having adopted the labour theory of value. Smith is no exception; sometimes he is regarded as a cost of production theorist, while others see him as a forerunner of general equilibrium analysis.

Income distribution, like the topic of value, plays an important role in the classification of the various contributions to economic ideas. Thus theories of distribution are particularly important in reviewing the debate between Ricardo and Malthus at the beginning of the nineteenth century, and in the context of the so called 'marginalist revolution' of the 1870s.

Value and distribution therefore play an important part in this short history. However, these topics by themselves cannot offer a good understanding of the formative period and of the characteristic features of classical political economy; the notion of wealth needs to get into the picture specifically. The inquiry into the nature of wealth and the causes of its growth constituted the major object of investigation of most economic authors in the period bounded by the discovery of America and the industrial revolution.

The substantial change in the definition of *wealth* between mercantilist writings and the works of Quesnay and Smith is emphasised throughout Part I. This has important implications for the policies designed to increase it and thereby improve the prosperity of the nation. As a result of their work, notions of reproduction and surplus, the analysis of capital accumulation in a model of circular production, and the role of productivity and technological progress supersede commerce and the merchant as major determinants of national wealth.

The evolution of the analysis of wealth from the approach of Thomas Mun to that of Quesnay and Smith can almost be described as a change of paradigm. Although less commented on than the change in value theory during the 'marginal revolution', the changed conception of wealth is no less important because it generated much modern economic analysis, as shown in Part I. Wealth evolved from the 'stock' idea of precious metals, (financial reserves in contemporary parlance) to the 'flow' notion of annual produce, net and gross, the direct forerunner of modern GDP. Notions of material production, productivity, the role of circulating and fixed capital, a new definitions of social classes, followed from this change of perspectives on national wealth.

Surplus and reproduction

The reader of Part I can be alerted to another major change at this stage. Mercantilist literature largely emphasised the role of exchange and circulation of commodities in the process of the creation of wealth. The establishment of an orderly circulation systems was also a major concern of authors like Boisguilbert and Cantillon. With Quesnay and Smith the productive powers of nature are discovered, together with those of labour and then of capital. None of this is completely new, but this revolutionised the theory of wealth.

The *Wealth of Nations* may be regarded as a first, detailed explanation of the functioning of modern industrial society. This book also contains appropriate answers, or answers adequate to contemporary sentiments, on matters of organisation of economic policy and on the revenue of industrialising societies at the end of the eighteenth century.

What is the role of surplus in all this? Without a *surplus* of necessaries (wage goods) it is impossible to have a social division of labour. Petty pointed this out as early as 1662. The amount of surplus or net product over capital invested measures the different productivity of various types of investments and productive sectors. A society first of all must reproduce itself, just like an organic body, and that is achieved primarily by preserving the stock of means of production. *Reproduction* then proceeds, but also enables economic *growth* to take place. Over the centuries, capital combined with labour becomes the decisive cause of economic growth and prosperity. Technical progress is embodied in capital accumulation and capital accumulation derives from the reinvestment of profits, a part of social surplus.

Is all the emphasis then on material production? And should circulation be forgotten? Not at all. The theories of value and distribution are indispensibly linked to the analysis of wealth and of enlarged reproduction. Reproduction and growth are the result of the operation of market forces; accumulation takes place via income distribution and price determination. The analysis of circulation re-enters as part of a better articulated system.

For Ricardo, and in a different way for Marx, the theory of relative prices is a necessary step in the determination of the rate of profit. Value and distribution are also essential component in Smith's analysis of the causes of national wealth, and in the work of some of his predecessors. In classical political economy, the theories of value, of distribution and of wealth are fragments of a mosaic depicting the features of economic growth and prosperity.

Linking the analysis of value and distribution to the problem of wealth gives a better appreciation of the modifications which take place in economic theories either due to reasons 'internal' to their analytical structure, or because of the evolution taking place in the economies of Europe from the sixteenth to the eighteenth century.

It has to be mentioned at the outset that in classical political economy, the analysis of income distribution is not only related to those of value, reproduction and wealth, but is also history dependent. By this is meant that the authors refer to actual, real distribution of income and wealth among existing groups, that is classes of people within a specific historical period. Social classes are not given by laws of nature, once and for all, nor are all people alike; social classes are different in different epochs or stages of society. The idea that there are different ways of organising social and economic life was crucial to the age of the Enlightenment; there are primitive, feudal societies and commercial ones and they are regulated by different laws. This view is found in Smith and Turgot, and endured as late as Torrens and Marx. Was the commercial, modern industrial society, or capitalism, the 'end of history'? Some of our authors did take this simplistic and consolatory view. This was certainly not the case with Sismondi and Marx but this point is not discussed in what immediately follows. Instead, attention is drawn to two equally simple points which are distinguishing feature of the method of classical political economy:

(i) societies evolve through time, and their fundamental economic and social structures change accordingly, whether or not modern capitalism is the 'end of history', it is undoubtedly the 'product of history';

(ii) societies are never regarded as simple objects, on the contrary their complexity must be accepted as an inherent feature arising not only from various economic aspects, but from ethics, perspectives on justice and jurisprudence, in short, their evolving civil society.

Finally, investigation of the analytical constructions by the various authors must never overshadow their policy preoccupations. In particular, these stories are always closely related with the history of the nation states of Europe, particularly Britain and France. Classical political economy is a social science with clear policy aims. Its analytical tools were designed to explain the working of market and production mechanisms, thereby gaining insights for improving the conditions of citizens, and possibly mankind. For instance, Quesnay and Smith derived *laissez-faire* from their view that the origin of wealth was to be found in the productive powers of labour and in the modernisation of production, not from the power and control of international trade and colonies.

Needless to say, this did nothing to diminish their analytical apparatus, and this type of consideration does not eliminate the fundamental differences between classical political economy and neo classical economics.

A further corollary flows from the above consideration; wealth and prosperity were designed to help bring about not only well being, but also *peace* among nations. Naive as it may now appear, this was a major purpose of the investigations into wealth of many classical economists, of which they were consciously aware.

An overview of Part I

Part I of this book then covers more than two centuries, a long period when compared to the mere century covered in Part II. It may assist the reader to take the first 11 chapters as the long period 1620–1776, which tells the story of the emergence of classical political economy, particularly of Smith, from the mercantilist era. The remaining two sections then cover less than a century (1776–1870) and deal with the golden age of classical political economy, the period of Ricardo and Malthus, and some aspects of the further evolution of political economy up to Marx.

Although the title of each chapter involves one or two authors and the major issue it examines, they often constitute symbols of a group of writers or even of an epoch. Moreover, the space devoted to Quesnay, Smith, Ricardo and Marx greatly exceeds that given to other economic writers. Although partly unjust to some minor economists, it derives from the fact that this brief history of economic ideas is particularly designed to illustrate the analytical structure of the different theories. For classical political economy, those four authors definitely contributed most to formulating and developing the key notions and their mutual relationship, which together make up the 'theories of surplus'.

For much of Part I, mercantilism is presented as a benchmark or reference-point for the subsequent writers. Chapter 2 evaluates this approach. A proper understanding of classical political economy and of its 'founding fathers', like Quesnay and Smith, is impossible without a due appreciation of mercantilist literature. Chapter 3 then examines two early critics of mercantilist views: Locke and North, who thereby open the way to the analysis of market forces. Chapter 4 highlights the role of Petty, an author who wrote during the height of mercantilism in Britain, but who can be regarded as the first author to put forward key notions constituting the foundations for classical political economy; from the division of labour to the analysis of the permanent causes of value, the concept of surplus and the role of measurement in social sciences.

Section II takes us to France at the turn of the seventeenth century, a Kingdom burdened by huge public debts and incapable of successfully competing with the emerging economic power, England. Two authors, Boisguilbert and Cantillon, towards whom Quesnay and Smith were highly indebted are initially discussed. Both were closely concerned with problems of policy, given the perilous economic situation of France at the time. Boisguilbert analysed the economic system as a circular flow including causes which can lead to its malfunctioning; Cantillon examined the economic role of the farmer–entrepreneur, a point stressed later by Quesnay. Cantillon's analysis of value also followed the lines suggested by Petty and introduced the notion of income distribution among social classes.

Sections III and IV provide essential background to contributions leading to the zenith of classical political economy in the 20 years from Quesnay's first economic works to the publication of the *Wealth of Nations*. Quesnay had provided a system designed to 'solve' the economic problems of the French Kingdom of Louis XV: modernisation of agriculture from accumulation of capital in the hands of the farmers; tax reform, and the commercial policy of *laissez-faire* to produce a price system able to sustain the exchange value of French corn and thereby favour accumulation. The notion of *produit net* was crucial to this analysis; the *Tableau économique* and associated articles by Quesnay were pieces of a complex system of thought, indicating to the monarch the best economic policies, that is, those in accord with natural laws.

Smith provided a new principle of wealth: the division of labour; and the main source of wealth becomes the increase in the productive powers of labour. This combined concepts already present in economic thought with the many novelties in his argument. These sections also show that the formation of classical political economy was not the exclusive achievement of the two masters; they include more 'minor' contributors from Hume to Turgot, Steuart and Galiani, who were all among the brightest intellects of the Enlightenment on both sides of the Channel.

Section V presents the 'golden age' of classical political economy, the period of its maturity. Contemporary debates were at the core of the economic interests of both Ricardo and Malthus. The well-known debate on the Corn Laws at the end of the Napoleonic wars in England provides the background to Ricardo's major contribution, his masterly treatment of the determination of the rate of profit and of income distribution among the three major classes of society, on the basis of a specific doctrine of value.

Malthus proceeds along a similar, but perhaps broader framework; the law of population becomes a pillar of most subsequent investigations. Malthus's preoccupations with the moral and social aspects make him an almost unique example of an author who shares the broad preoccupations of the economists of the second part of the eighteenth century, but also those prevailing in the first half of the nineteenth century; growth and decline of societies on one side, social unrest and confrontation on the other. Chapter 12 deals with Jean Baptiste Say and Sismondi in France, Bentham in England, as authors representing different evolutions of thought and different economic visions.

In Section V post-Ricardian developments in classical economics are covered. Torrens elaborated on Ricardo's thought, while Senior attempted to drive the focus of economic policy away from income distribution and with other authors prepared the way for that change of vision which became the 'marginalist revolution'. This aspect is also visible in the work of John Stuart Mill, the discussion of which is the start for Part II of the book.

Marx further developed the analysis of the relationships between prices and the rate of profit already investigated by Ricardo. At the same time, he went back to the 'grand visions' of the evolution of history which characterised the period of the enlightenment. By the time Marx wrote *Das Kapital*, nineteenth century economics was already taking different directions. The 'individual in society' of Smith was becoming an economic agent and the metaphor of the invisible hand was replaced by that of Robinson Crusoe. Economics itself became more and more self-standing as a science, but the close relationships between economic speculations and practical policies so typical of classical political economy, started to slowly fade away. However, this matter heralds what is covered in the second part of the book.

Notes on further readings

There are many excellent texts to which one could refer for a deeper analysis of classical political economy. J.A. Schumpeter, *History of Economic Analysis* (Allen and Unwin, London, 1954) is a clear example. Specially recommended is the presentation of the evolution of economic ideas provided by M. Dobb, *Theories of Value and Distribution Since Adam Smith* (Cambridge University Press, Cambridge, 1973); this book satisfactorily covers the transition period from Smith and Ricardo into the nineteenth century. D.P. O'Brien, *The Classical Economists* (Clarendon Press, Oxford, 1975) covers more or less the same period of Part I and provides very interesting information and interpretation of the contributions of classical economists to the different branches of economics.

An interpretation of the so called 'analytical core' of classical political economy is presented in P. Garegnani, 'Value and distribution in the classical economists and Marx', *Oxford Economic Papers*, vol. 36, June 1984. It substantially agrees with, and elaborates on Sraffa's interpretation in his famous introduction to the *Works* of Ricardo (1951). A quite different view of classical economics is provided by S. Hollander, *Classical Economics* (Blackwell, Oxford, 1987).

T.W. Hutchison, *Before Adam Smith* (Basil Blackwell, Oxford, 1988) provides a detailed discussion of the different streams of thought and contributions from the early sixteenth century to the *Wealth of Nations*. A less well-known, but very stimulating interpretation of the classical system of prices is J. Cartelier, *Surproduit et Reproduction* (Maspero, Paris, 1976), unfortunately not translated into English. M.N. Rothbard, *Economic Thought Before Adam Smith – an Austrian Perspective on the History of*

Economic Thought, Vol. I (Elgar, Aldershot, 1995) gives an overview commencing with the economic thought of the great Greek philosophers Plato and Aristotle. E. Sewall, 'The theory of value before Adam Smith' (*American Economic Association Publications*, vol. 3, third series, 1901) presents the case for separating authors and supporters of the cost of production view as against the one based on demand and supply. A useful, concise perspective on the evolution of the notion of wealth from mercantilism to Smith is G. Vaggi. 'The theory of wealth, the ancien régime and the physiocratic experiment', *International Journal of New Ideas* (no. 2, 1992). For a general overview of classical political economy, see H.D. Kurz and Neri Salvadori, eds., *The Elgar Companion to Classical Economics*, Cheltenham: Edward Elgar, 1998. A splendid study of the evolution of ideas from ancient thought to Adam Smith is Cosimo Perrotta, *Consumption as an Investment: the Fear of Goods from Hesiod to Adam Smith*, London: Routledge, 2004. See also A. Roncaglia, *The Wealth of Ideas: A History of Economic Thought*, Cambridge: Cambridge University Press, 2005.

Section I
Seventeenth-century Pioneers

2
Thomas Mun, 1571–1641: from Bullion to Foreign Trade

Thomas Mun's grandfather was a provost in the Royal Mint, his father was a Mercer. He himself was a very successful merchant and became a Director of the East India Company in 1615. The East India Company was much criticised because its trade involved the export of bullion (in order to purchase spices). In 1621 Mun wrote a pamphlet, *A Discourse of Trade, from England to East Indies*, in order to defend the Company from the accusation of being detrimental to Britain's prosperity because it exported bullion in order to import goods. In the pamphlet he described the benefits derived from this type of trade.

In 1622 and 1623 Mun was also an important member of a committee of merchants which had been asked by James I to examine the problem of the fall of Britain's exchange rate. His magnum opus, *England's Treasure by Forraign Trade, or the Ballance of our Forraign Trade is the Rule of our Treasure*, which Schumpeter referred to as 'the classic of English mercantilism', was published posthumously by his son John Mun in 1664.

The discovery of the 'new world' of America and the establishment of colonies there by some European States in the fifteenth century resulted in a large flow of gold and silver into Europe from Mexico and Peru. International trade henceforth became more and more important and merchants took on an important role, also in the domestic economy. The rural economy of the feudal period, with its limited markets, concentrated in the fairs in neighbouring cities, and with semi-barter exchanges gradually gave way to a more widespread use of money. The new mercantile bourgeoisie allied itself with the state in order to better exploit the growing possibilities of international commerce. At the beginning of the seventeenth century this alliance culminated in the formation of the first big merchant and trading companies of the modern world: the East India Companies of Holland and England.

Colonial trade and merchant companies increasingly became part of an endless story of wars between the nation states of Europe. England ultimately emerged as the victorious, imperialist country, after the defeats of

Spain and Portugal in the sixteenth century, of Holland in the late seventeenth and of France in the eighteenth century. This pluricentennial story of wars dominated the minds of the founding fathers of political economy during the Enlightenment.

The more important authors of this period were themselves merchants, like Thomas Mun who was a director of the British East India Company. The works of the Mercantilists often consisted of short pamphlets aimed at convincing public opinion or, better still, the government, to implement the policies most favourable to their trading companies. No major theoretical treatises are to be found, at best there are tracts with the practical rules and norms of commerce. For these reasons, it is difficult to speak of a mercantilist school of thought; mercantilism is more a way of approaching and devising solutions for the economic problems of the period.

Nevertheless, the mercantilists gave a tremendous impetus to sever economics from the purely ethical and normative approach of medieval times. Facts, figures, calculations began to enter economic discourse. Mercantilism as a major system of thought disappeared after the harsh treatment it received in Book IV of Smith's *Wealth of Nations* in 1776, but its great merit is to have singled out the fundamental object of economics: the analysis of the causes of the wealth of nations. Many of its policy views have prevailed since then in parts of the world, and continue to prevail.

Finally, it may be noted that mercantilism endured for almost three centuries. Neither classical political economy, nor neoclassical economics has yet experienced such a long life as systems of political economy. This long lifespan can be divided into two periods, more or less covering the sixteenth and seventeenth centuries respectively.

First period: bullionism

During the sixteenth century, the flows of precious metals from the American Colonies of Spain produced high inflation in Europe, but for the mercantilists gold and silver were the substance and the definition of both private and national wealth. Precious metals guaranteed the command over goods, resources and labour all over the world. The power of the state depended on the amount of gold and silver in its coffers, because this international currency made it possible to build ships and to pay armies. 'Bullion' was the name used for the precious metals.

An important feature of the mercantilists' definition of wealth was that this is a stock concept: national wealth is measured by the amount of 'international reserves' at the disposal of the state. National wealth can be increased by bringing more gold and silver within the borders of the state, or by preventing them from flowing out. It is from the balance of payments that changes in national wealth can be evaluated, particularly from the capital account section. Several policies were put forward to favour the increase of the national stock of bullion. Using modern terminology, some of these measures were designed to influence capital movements directly, while other policies operated through the current account balance.

In England, Thomas Gresham and John Hales were representatives of such views. Gresham is well known for his view that 'bad money expels good', because everyone wants to hoard the latter, hence only non precious coins made of copper are in actual use. Thus, in order to favour the inflows of capital from abroad the nation must have a strong currency. This requires that governments must avoid the debasement of money; where the metal value content of the issued coins is diminished with respect to their face value. Frequent debasements reduce the credibility of the national currency as a store of international value. Together with a strong currency, high domestic interests rates favour the influx of capitals (see Rubin 1929, pp. 43–6).

As for the trade part of the balance of payment, the government must favour the sale of raw materials abroad because they will be purchased with precious metals, hence adding to the stock of national wealth (see Rubin, 1979, pp. 29ff.). But for the same reason, imports must be discouraged. Hence all sorts of tariffs and duties need to direct international trade into appropriate directions. Moreover, such taxes are among the easiest ways of increasing the revenue of the state. In the case of Britain, the exports to continental Europe, mainly wool, largely took place from well-defined locations, the so-called staples, where government officials could easily register the volume and the value of the exchanges and charge them with the appropriate duty. So what was good for the merchant seemed to be good for state finances as well, a recurring theme in Mercantilist literature.

At the beginning of the sixteenth century, some important changes took place in the organisation of the economy, particularly in England and in the northern part of Europe. The merchants also became entrepreneurs. Instead of simply buying and selling goods, they began to provide workers with raw materials to be transformed into manufactured products, which were then sold. In particular it was possible to take advantage of the long periods of inactivity in agriculture during the winter; textile industry in England began with the so-called *cottage industry* under the supervision of the merchant–capitalist, who supplied the peasants with the raw materials and often advanced them money.

The extension of manufacturing activities and the need to protect the newly established industry from foreign competitors led to the end of the age of bullion and to a new phase in mercantilist thinking.

Second period: the balance of trade

The sixteenth century is the age of mature mercantilism. The leading writer of the period is Thomas Mun with his two pamphlets *A Discourse of Trade* and, above all, the subsequent *England's Treasure by Forraign Trade*. A change take place in the definition of wealth; money is always the ideal measure of wealth, but in Mun's work, wealth is also considered to consist of produced commodities. Money commands the exchange value and it is the obvious means for employing workers, but no longer is it the only and main form of wealth. In his dispute with Malynes about the effects of a devaluation, Mun distinguished two types of wealth: *natural wealth* consists of primary, mainly subsistence, goods; *artificial wealth* 'consists in our manufactures and industrious trading with forraign commodities' (Mun, 1623, p. 7, see also pp. 71–3).

However, the distinction between wealth as a stock of foreign currency and as a quantity of products is not always clearcut. Much clearer is the fact that the main source of the increase in national wealth is a surplus trade balance. According to Mun, monetary movements and the exchange rate depend on the condition of the trade balance: the inflows of precious metals reflect the existence of a positive balance of trade and vice versa (Mun, 1623, p. 5). The wealth and power of a nation depend on its capacity for international trade. Wealth has its origin in the sphere of circulation, but domestic trade can only redistribute a given amount of wealth. A trade surplus is depicted as the best indicator of a successful country.

Hence, the government needs to guide foreign trade in order to favour the establishment of a positive trade balance. The importance of the new balance of trade view to the analysis of the causes of national wealth becomes clearer when examining the policies suggested by Mun and his followers. The new perspective produced an almost complete reversal of the major measures of the bullionist period.

Mun was in favour of the exportation of manufactured commodities because they have much higher value, (or, in modern terminology, 'value added'), than the raw materials with which they have been produced. Manufacturing employs a larger number of people, hence it has greater employment potential than agriculture. Why then export raw materials which only give the merchants and the workers of Holland and of northern France the chance to enter the process of production and transformation? The export of raw materials needs to be discouraged, contrary to the opinions prevailing during the bullionist period.

On the other hand, it might be convenient to let money flow out of the country in all those cases which in the end assist England's ability to export her products. For instance, the exportation of capital may be useful and even necessary in special circumstances.

'It is not therefore said that then we should add our money thereunto to fetch in the more money immediately, but rather first to enlarge our trade by enabling us to bring in more forraign wares, which being sent out again will in due time much encrease our Treasure' (Mun, 1623, p. 15).

The above is a clear example of the ability to distinguish between immediate and indirect effects. Notice that the different policies do not reflect a real change in the analysis of the causes of wealth, but rather an adaptation of the idea that foreign trade is the major source of wealth to the new economic conditions of the English merchants, who have now become industrial entrepreneurs. National manufactures must be supported and defended; this is the protectionist variant of mercantilist thought.

Value and distribution

With the expansion of manufactures, the successful merchant can no longer think in terms of buying cheap and selling dear, the relationship between production costs, competitiveness and the selling price now enters into the picture. In Mun's work, a rough analysis of the production mechanism and of the components of the price of manufactures can be discovered.

The importation of raw materials at low costs has two highly positive effects on national wealth. First, given the value of exports, the lower that of imports, the higher is the trade surplus. Secondly, raw materials are used as inputs in the production of manufactured goods, hence cheap imports of raw materials favour the exportation of industrial products by making their cost structure more competitive.

Note that according to Mun the sale of domestically produced manufactures at high prices on international markets it is not necessarily a positive thing. It may be more convenient to have low production costs and have moderate selling prices in order to expand the sales of British manufactures on foreign markets all the better. Thanks to low unit costs of production, it becomes possible to increase the market share of Britain and the overall value of her exports. The Mercantilists assumed a high elasticity of world demand with respect to the prices of British manufactures.

However, cost of production also includes the wages of the labourers in the cottage industry and in the small scale factories of the time. Money wages must be kept low in order to favour the competitiveness of British products (Mun, 1623, pp. 8, 12). For the Mercantilist, money wages depended on the price of corn and that of other wage goods, but contrary to Ricardo (see below, Chapter 14) they did not favour a low prices of necessaries. On the contrary, corn must not be too cheap in relation to money wages, because if the workers can easily buy their wage goods then they become lazy and idle. Low wages are argued to stimulate industry and productivity.

Monetary and credit policy no longer resembles that of bullionism. The merchant–entrepreneurs need to borrow money for their investments, the interest rate is the price of capital and it affects the cost of production and the competitiveness of British manufactures. Hence the mercantilists want the government to set an upper legal limit to the rate of interest, and the issue of setting an appropriate maximum legal rate becomes one of the major economic policy issues during the seventeenth and early eighteenth centuries. Merchant contributions to these controversies invariably suggested the lowest feasible interest rate.

The mercantilist notion of capital presents interesting ambiguities. Of course, capital goods must be advanced in the production process and in some cases these advances do not consist just of raw materials and necessaries. But mercantilist writings did not present capital primarily as a physical magnitude, but rather as a sum of money, a stock of financial means which enabled the implementation of the production process. Similarly, the rate of interest for them was the price to be paid for obtaining such financial resources.

The analysis of distribution conveys one of the most famous concept in mercantilist literature: that of profit upon alienation (Mun, 1623, p. 26). This is the gain of the clever merchant when he buys goods at a cheap price and sells them for a higher one. Profit is basically defined as a difference between two market prices. Sometimes unit production costs displace purchase prices, but the first are just a representation of the prices of raw materials and of money wages. The notion of profit upon alienation clearly signifies the idea that wealth is generated in the process of exchange, where there is always someone who loses and always someone else who gains.

But if, in this manner, international trade is only a zero-sum game, the mercantilists maintained that once national wealth had been increased thanks to their activities and to appropriate and supportive government policies, then all sections of the population would benefit. According to Charles Davenant, the inflows of precious metals due to a surplus in the balance of trade will be beneficial to society as a whole. The government budget will receive the tariffs and the duties on imported goods, particularly on foreign manufactures. Lower interest from increased money is also favourably regarded by the landlords, who often are heavily indebted and whose land values rise with a lowering of interest.

The benefits accruing to the money lenders and, above all, to the workers are more dubious. The latter are badly paid, often at no more than subsistence wages, but this was seen as favourable to the expansion of British manufactures. Labourers should therefore be satisfied with having better employment opportunities.

In its mature phase, mercantilism produced a set of notions which, by bringing together theoretical and practical aspects, gave an answer to the problem of increasing national wealth. The main objective of Mun and of the many other mercantilist writers was that of establishing an alliance between the emerging merchant class and the dominant aristocracy, to the detriment of foreign competing nations. Notwithstanding its flaws and shortcomings during the seventeenth century, the mercantilist paradigm was quite successful in sustaining the growth of the British economy, and of its manufactures in particular.

Further developments in mercantilist thought

Important common elements exist in the two phases of mercantilism. First, even after the work of Mun, gold and silver did not cease to be considered as the best approximation to that general command over other goods and over people, or generalised purchasing power. For the Mercantilists, money constituted the essence of wealth.

Secondly, foreign trade was the major source of wealth and prosperity, but the growth of national wealth often took place to the detriment of trading partners. This is illustrated by the well known phrase 'beggar-thy-neighbour' trade policy.

The competitive struggle of the nation states of Europe is part of the history of mercantilism. In England, Cromwell, proclaimed the first Navigation Act in 1651, according to which all trade with Great Britain and with her colonies had to take place on English vessels. This is an obvious way of keeping foreign exchanges under control, but also provides a way of profiting from freights and shipping services and stopping foreign competitors – the Dutch in this case – from supplying such services. The mercantilists discovered that it was the whole current account balance that mattered, not just the exchange of commodities. Services could be as important as goods in achieving the desired surplus in foreign trade.

In seventeenth century France, policies designed to protect its rising domestic manufactures from foreign competitors were implemented by Colbert, the Minister of Finances of Louis XIV. He gave his name to the term *colbertisme*, a shorthand for the policy of protecting infant industries.

It is interesting to note that the recommendation of adopting discriminatory rules in favour of domestic producers and against foreign ones did not always receive unanimous support by mercantilist writers. In 1622, Misselden wrote a pamphlet with the significant title *Free Trade, or the Meanes to Make Trade Flourish*, where he maintained that a prosperous foreign commerce was beneficial to all social groups. Misselden went on to argue that the state should not try to regulate the foreign exchanges. On the other hand, and in the same year, Gérard de Malynes, though not directly opposing free trade, requested the government to control the exchange rate. From Misselden's *The Circle of Commerce or the Ballance of Trade* (1623), this very intriguing passage can be quoted:

> And trade hath in it such a kinde of naturall liberty in the course and use thereof, as it will not indure to be fors't by any .... Natural liberty is such a thing, as the will being by nature rightly informed, will not endure the command of any, but of God alone.
>
> (Misselden 1623, p. 112)

The importance of these words should not be overstated and it would be an exaggeration to regard Misselden as a forerunner of *laissez-faire*.

However, it is interesting to note that discordant voices did arise about the appropriate commercial policies and the role of trade. England had to wait for Hume and Smith to have an alternative view on the formation of national wealth, but it would be wrong to regard classical political economy simply as the theory which defeated Mercantilism. The story is more complicated and richer than that and signs of it are visible in the seventeenth century. The trail to be taken to the period of the Enlightenment, commenced with Mercantilism; a doctrine which had the merit of establishing the main object of political economy: the improvement of national wealth.

Notes on further readings

Reading of the mercantilist writings can be a pleasure. Its literature is made up mainly of little books, full of spirited language and sharp phrases. Major texts are now accessible thanks to reprints. These include Thomas Mun, *England's Treasure by Forraign Trade*, circa 1623 (Thomas Clark, London, 1664; Augustus M. Kelley reprints, New York, 1968). In 1971 Kelley reprinted four other important texts, facilitating the study of the debate between Malynes and Misselden. Mun's *A Discourse of Trade* (1621), Edward Misselden *The Circle of Commerce or the Ballance of Trade* (1623), his *Free Trade or the Meanes to Make Trade Flourish* (1622) and Gérard De Malynes, *The Maintenance of Free Trade* (1622).

The classic text on Mercantilism remains E. Heckscher, *Mercantilism*, 2 vols (Allen and Unwin, London, 1934); also from the 1930s but still quite authoritative is Jacob Viner's discussion of mercantilist thought in his *Studies in the Theories of International Trade* (Allen and Unwin, London, 1937) which draws on an article entitled 'Early English trade theories' published in 1930 in two parts in the *Journal of Political Economy*. A less well-known book on history of economic thought with a very interesting chapter on mercantilism is I.I. Rubin, *A History of Economic Thought* (Ink Links, London, 1979). Mercantilist literature in the different countries of Europe is also investigated at length by M.N. Rothbard, *Economic Thought Before Adam Smith – an Austrian Perspective on the History of Economic Thought*, vol. 1 (Edward Elgar, Aldershot, 1995).

Other useful reading is D.C. Coleman (ed.), *Revisions in Mercantilism* (Methuen, London, 1969), L. Magnusson: *Mercantilism – the Shaping of Economic Language* (Routledge, London and New York, 1994), and Cosimo Perrotta, 'Is the mercantilist theory of the balance of trade really erroneous?', *History of Political Economy* (vol. 23, no. 2, 1991, pp. 301–36).

3
Dudley North, 1641–91 and John Locke, 1632–1704: Early Critical Reactions to Mercantilism

During the seventeenth century, the class of the capitalist entrepreneurs began to be differentiated from that of the merchants. This brought to the fore deficiencies in the universal benefits of mercantilist policies. Reasons for conflicting interests became more obvious and were no longer confined to explaining those between merchants. Increasingly, money lenders and workers found themselves on one side, and landlords and manufacturers on the other, in debates over economic issues.

In 1690, in his *An Essay on the East-India Trade*, Charles Davenant challenged the idea that government intervention in foreign trade will improve the prosperity of England. He believed that with less foreign trade regulation, the overall wealth of England, and that of her trading partners, would increase. Note that the logical relationship producing these effects are still very much rooted in mercantilist's thought. A more liberal foreign trade would increase the exports of England. This implied a larger trade surplus with the consequence that more international currency will flow in. According to Davenant, this increase in the stock of money leads to lower interest rates and to higher prices of land. The increase in the value of landed estates brings about a rise of rent and of tax revenue. As a result of a freer trade every section of the population is better off, but the starting point of the whole story is still the successful export trade of England.

Towards the end of the century, other writers such as Barbon, North and Martyn, underlined the positive role of extensive and unbounded markets for both domestic and foreign trade, as well as the positive impact of consumption on wealth. Wealth itself becomes more and more identified with real commodities capable of improving the standard of living of people and much less with the precious metals.

However, the debate on the legal determination of a maximum rate of interest, best characterises the theoretical discussion of the last decade of the seventeenth century. Both John Locke and Dudley North, amongst others, participated in this debate. It is worth remembering that in England the maximum value of the legally permitted interest rates had been decreasing for over a century. From a 10 per cent rate in 1550, the legal rate fell to 8 per cent in 1600 and to 6 per cent in 1654. At the end of the century, a further compulsory reduction to 4 per cent was ardently debated.

Dudley North: markets

Sir Dudley North was born at Westminster in 1641, the third of five sons of the fourth Baron of Guilford. He died at Covent Garden on 31 December 1691. He was a merchant engaged in the Turkey trade and returned to England in 1680. He was appointed a Commissioner of the Customs in 1683. After a short period as Commissioner of the Treasury, he returned to the Customs where he remained until the 1688 Revolution. In 1691 he anonymously published the essay *Discourses Upon Trade*. The work was summarised in the biography of Sir Dudley published by his brother Roger in 1744.

In the *Discourses Upon Trade*, North supported the view that free trade on international markets brings about benefits to all exchanging parties and that it was wrong to try to put a limit to interest rates. Moreover, government attempts to fix the rate of interest and to regulate markets in general were doomed to fail, because market forces operate which tend to negate state intervention.

North distinguished between the monetary aspect of capital and capital as physical investment. He also shared the mercantilists' preoccupation with high interest rates which increased the cost of capital and discouraged investments. But he realised that the level of interest in credit markets cannot be fixed by law, and on this issue he opposed the views of Culpeper and Child. The rate of interest depended on the availability of loanable funds and saving. Thus trade influenced the rate of interest by increasing the available monetary capital in the country and not the other way round. If trade was prosperous, the system created the necessary quantity of money. Hence the rate of interest was the result of the opposing action of two groups of dealers: those who need to borrow money in order to carry on production and investments, and the lenders. The circulation of money depended on the activities of these two groups of people and on the overall level of economic activity. Such activity invariably overcame state regulations in the credit market.

North's analysis of the working of the credit market identified forces which can be loosely defined as being on the side of 'supply' and 'demand', with the proviso that these terms must not be conflated with the well defined notions of 'demand' and 'supply' in marginalist economics. Similarities in terminology cannot be taken as similarities in the analytical definition of concepts. In North, for example there is no decreasing demand function derived from a diminishing marginal utility of goods, nor an increasing supply function resulting from a process of cost minimisation by firms.

General laws are also at work in the markets for commodities and they cannot be constrained. More strongly, attempts to regulate the markets by means of rules and laws may lead to economic crisis. This is another interesting point of view by North; crises constitute a phenomenon which regularly take place in markets. The forces on the supply and demand side are at work and they are powerful, but there is no self-regulating mechanism and the working of markets can be disrupted. Apart from wrong state intervention, such crises can derive from monopolistic positions which distort market operations. In general, for North, all types of crises are connected with a disruption of the functioning of markets and may lead to a decrease in economic activity with negative effects on both national wealth and the personal income of all social groups. North was also opposed to sumptuary laws, (that is, laws against luxury consumption) which tended to make the nation poorer, because the appetites of men were seen by him as the main 'spur' of trade. Economies are moved by the desire of people to enrich themselves and not by their acceptance of bare necessaries as sufficient for their needs.

John Locke: value

John Locke, the philosopher and author of *An Essay Concerning Human Understanding*, *Two Treatises of Government*, and *A Letter Concerning Toleration*, studied at Westminster School and Oxford. He lectured in Greek and Moral Philosophy, he also studied experimental medicine and later developed an interest in political and economic matters. Notwithstanding his cautious political involvement, Locke spent a short period in exile in Holland during the 1680s until James II abdicated and William and Mary ascended to British throne during the 1688 revolution. In 1695 he contributed to reorganising the Board of Trade.

Locke's first economic essay, *Some Considerations on the Consequences of the Lowering of Interest, and Raising the Value of the Money*, was published in 1691 (but written much earlier). It was an attempt to convince the British Parliament to defeat a Bill designed to lower the legal rate of interest from 6 per cent to 4 per cent. Locke was on the winning side in this debate, and the essay is an important milestone in the history of economic thought. Locke's second major essay, *Further Considerations Concerning Raising in the Value of Money* (1695), was concerned with the issue of recoinage. Thus John Locke is an important author in the history of economics, but also in that of civil law, particularly for establishing the principle of property rights as one of the cornerstones of modern societies.

In *Some Considerations on the Lowering the Rate of Interest and Raising the Value of Money*, Locke reiterated North's view that the government cannot lower the market rate of interest simply by fixing the legal rate at a lower level. In this argument, Locke presented an interesting analysis of the determination of value, even if it was not entirely free of internal inconsistencies. First of all, he distinguished between use and exchange value, a distinction which became familiar to most ensuing economic thinkers. As other authors of the eighteenth century, but with much more clarity, Locke used the air and water paradox to illustrate these two concepts of value:

> The being of any good, and useful quantity in any thing, neither increases its price, nor indeed makes it have any price at all. ... What more useful or necessary things are there to being, or well-being of men, than air and water? and yet these have generally no price at all.
>
> (Locke, 1691, p. 41)

Water is absolutely necessary for life and it has a very high value in use because it satisfies one of the wants of human beings which are fundamental for their survival. But water is free; its price, or value in exchange, is zero.

Locke spoke also of intrinsic and natural value. '... The intrinsic, natural worth of any thing, consists in its fitness to supply the necessities, or serve the conveniences of human life' (ibid., p. 42). This is the use value of a thing, but it does not play any role in the determination of its market price. As a matter of fact, Locke continued the argument as follows:

> That there is no such intrinsic, natural settled value in any thing, as to make any assigned quantity of it constantly worth any assigned quantity of another
>
> (Ibid.)

Locke therefore has a clear notion of relative price, the proportion in which two commodities exchange for one another. But this ratio is the 'marketable value' and can change quite often without any change in the intrinsic value (ibid, p. 43).

The marketable value, or the price of a good on the market, has a loose relationship with its value in use, or with its utility. Value in use does not regulate the price, the value in exchange depends on circumstances which are different from, and only partly related to the particular and specific features of a good, which make it appropriate for satisfying precise human wants and needs. Hence a first interesting element in Locke's analysis of value is the fundamental differentiation between the two notions of value in use and value in exchange; the latter concept became a major analytical feature of all ensuing economic theories. Locke's water example mentioned above is a clear predecessor of the water-diamond paradox in the explanation of value, a metaphor widely used in the eighteenth century.

The second interesting feature of Locke's value analysis is his investigation of the causes which determine the exchange value of commodities. The exchange ratio between two commodities depends on abundance and scarcity of a good relatively to the demand for it; 'this proportion in all commodities, whereof money is one, is the proportion of their quantity to the vent' (ibid., p. 43). 'Vent' is the term Locke used to indicate the actual selling possibilities of a commodity and not just a generic demand for it. Locke explicitly mentions the word 'scarcity' (ibid., p. 31) as the main cause of the price, even if this is particularly the case for commodities which men cannot do without.

It must be noticed that Locke also ascribed an important role to human labour necessary in the production of different commodities; but this was not a labour theory of value. For Locke, it provided the foundations of property rights, which derive from the efforts and energy which have been employed by each individual in acquiring this property.

Locke's analysis of value was likewise applied to the value of money, that is to say, to the interest rate:

> the natural value of money, as it is apt to yield such a yearly income by interest, depends on the whole quantity of the then passing money of the kingdom, in proportion to the whole trade of the kingdom.
>
> (Ibid., p. 46)

Hence the rate of interest cannot be fixed by law, because it depends on the quantity of money in circulation, as well as on the overall amount of trade in the kingdom, that is, the level of economic activity.

Locke's political theory is to be found mainly in his *Two Treatises of Government* of 1690, which also was probably written earlier. The *Treatises* contain Locke's theory of property, and more extensively his views on the organisation of modern civil societies, a theme which had earlier been brought to the fore by Thomas Hobbes.

Mercantilism at the turn of the century

Notwithstanding North's and Locke's criticisms and the new interesting notions they introduced, mercantilist views on wealth and on economic policy continued to dominate the scene at the beginning of the eighteenth century. France was consolidating a policy of protectionism, but even in England the so called recoinage debate during the last decade of the seventeenth century led to the defeat of these early views on free trade. Mercantilism continued to dominate largely because no alternative doctrine of national wealth had yet emerged which was capable of challenging the balance of trade view.

The definition of wealth was, however, no longer closely linked to precious metals: now production and the possibility of increasing productive capacity were viewed as the really important features of wealth. At the end of the century some authors, such as Dalby Thomas, regarded the wealth of a nation as determined by its populousness and in particular by the number of productive workers. The view that the wealth of a nation was made up of its population also appeared much later in Mirabeau's *L'Ami des hommes*, written before his encounter with Quesnay. In France this approach took the name of *populationisme*.

Such an approach provides space for considering value, production and circulation of commodities not simply as more or less successful activities of merchants. The contributions of Locke and North just discussed are good examples of this. However, the idea of wealth as resulting from a surplus in the trade balance is perfectly compatible with a definition of wealth in terms of commodities, or of necessaries, as various of authors, including Davenant, fully realised.

Neo-mercantilist thoughts have never disappeared completely and are resurfacing in the twenty-first century. Many countries view the targeting of the trade surplus rather than domestic demand as the major impulse for enhanced economic growth.

Notes on further readings

J.O. Appleby, *Economic Thought and Ideology in Seventeenth-Century England* (Princeton University Press, Princeton, 1978) provides a useful guide to the economic debates of the late seventeen century both in support of, and against mercantilist practices, and includes a discussion of the role played by John Locke. Both North and Locke receive a chapter each in W. Letwin, *The Origins of Scientific Economics: English Economic Thought, 1660–1776* (Methuen, London, 1964). North's essay was reprinted in 1856, in J.R. McCulloch, *Early English Tracts on Commerce* (Political Economy Club, London, reprinted by Cambridge University Press in 1954).

Locke's works have been frequently collected, e.g. in T. Tegg *et al.*, 1823, *The Works of John Locke* (this is the source used here, as reprinted in 1963 by Scientia Verlag, Aalen, Germany). The role of John Locke in economics and in political theory has been extensively analysed by K.I. Vaughn, *John Locke: Economist and Social Scientist* (Chicago University Press, Chicago, 1980). G. Routh, *The Origin of Economic Ideas* (Macmillan – now Palgrave Macmillan, London, 1975) gives plenty of space to North and Locke. Locke's policy perspective and views on society are discussed in D. Wootton (ed.), *Political Writings* (Penguin Books, 1993) and in the Introduction by P. Laslett to John Locke, *Two Treatises of Government* (Cambridge University Press, Student Edition, Cambridge, 1988).

4
Sir William Petty, 1623–87: Division of Labour and Surplus

Sir William Petty was of humble origins; the son of a clothier. At age 13 he went to sea, but, after a shipwreck on the French coast, studied for a while with the Jesuits in France. After serving in the Royal Navy, Petty went to Leiden and Paris, where he studied medicine (possibly with Hobbes). Back to Britain in 1646 he became a doctor of medicine at Oxford University in 1648. In 1650, he was appointed Professor of Anatomy. However, the following year he moved to London to take the Chair of Music at Gresham College. In 1651 he went to Ireland as medical officer to the English army, and there prepared a topographical survey of Irish lands to be allotted to English soldiers in Cromwell's army. He himself ended up with a remarkably large estate, whose care and management engaged him for the rest of his life. In 1660–62 Petty was among the founding members of the Royal Society.

Some of Petty's main economic works were published after his death and after the Glorious Revolution of 1688. The *Verbum Sapienti* and *The Political Arithmetick*, written between 1671 and 1676, were published posthumously in 1690, *The Political Anatomy of Ireland* in 1691.

In any short outline of the history of economic thought, Sir William Petty deserves a special place, because his contribution developed crucial notions and concepts which a century later helped to create classical political economy as a separate science. The notion of surplus and the idea of division of labour are in Petty's work. In many respects, these concepts provide a theory of wealth quite different from that of the mercantilists. Nevertheless, Petty never specifically rejected mercantilist policies.

Petty's method

In *Theories of Surplus Value*, Karl Marx was the first major author to recognise Petty's fundamental contributions to the formation of economic analysis. A modern commentator (Routh, 1975, p. 35) regards Petty as the father of several notions and branches of economic science; from the labour theory of value to econometrics, from division of labour to national accounting. There may be some exaggeration in this position but certainly also a good deal of truth. For a start, Petty is the first economic writer who explicitly faced the issue of what is the appropriate method for the study of social and economic phenomena. Similar to nature, human societies are characterised by a high degree of interdependence among their component parts. Human science must highlight this mutual relationship between the various parts of society. The forces at work in society can be described by means of general laws, and these laws can be meaningfully used as guidelines for economic policy precisely because they are part of a general system. The answers to the specific problems can only come through the understanding of the working of the general system of society.

Petty's studies and experience as physician certainly influenced his approach to economics and it is not by chance that he was so aware of methodological problems. In his *The Political Anatomy of Ireland* he explicitly presented the metaphor of society resembling a human body. It must also be recalled that he was among the founders of the Royal Society, where he experienced, and contributed to, many methodological debates. Petty was deeply influenced by English empiricism. Science can only be grounded in precise facts and phenomena, scientists must reason in terms of weight, measure and quantity. This is also the case for social sciences, where the measurability of economic and social magnitudes provides a vital starting point. At the same time, Petty was not a naive supporter of the inductive approach. This is useful, but deductive reasoning is equally necessary and the two approaches are largely complementary.

Division of labour and surplus

Like a human body, society is a complex organism in which different groups of people have different roles and functions, all necessary to the functioning of society. This is not a new idea, it goes back to Plato's *Republic*. It can also be seen in Boisguilbert's work (Chapter 5 below), but William Petty clearly introduced this notion into modern economics and indeed it was the starting point of his economic investigation. In his 1662 *Treatise of Taxes and Contributions*, Petty wrote:

> if there be 1000. men in a Territory, and if 100. of these can raise necessary food and raiment for the whole 1000. if 200. more make as much commodities, as other Nations will give either their commodities or money for, and if 400. more be employed in the ornaments, pleasure, and magnificence of the whole; if there be 200. Governours, Divines, Lawyers, Physicians, Merchants and Retailers, making in all 900. the question is, since there is food enough for this supernumerary 100. also, how they should come by it?
>
> (Petty, 1662, p. 30)

Ignoring Petty's specific question for the moment, let us focus on his notion of social division of labour. At least three important aspects emerge from the beautiful passage just quoted.

First, the social division of labour is very strikingly articulated: it identifies at least four major social groups with corresponding economic functions. There are the producers of necessaries, food and clothing; those who produce for export; the producers of luxury goods; and finally the governors, the learned professions and the traders. Then of course there are the remaining hundred men who do not perform any precise activity. Notice that the merchants do not play a particularly important role in Petty's scheme even though it was written at the zenith of mercantilism.

Secondly, Petty does not make any clearcut distinction between productive and unproductive activities, however, he suggests there is a hierarchy between the different tasks performed by each group of citizens. This hierarchy does not depend on their political functions, but mainly on the type of goods and services they produce. The first 100 men produce the necessaries for the entire society; the remaining 900 would not be able to survive without the work of the people employed in agriculture. They are at the core of society, as the workers employed in the production of wage goods, and, more generally, the subsistence for the whole of society.

Then we find the 200 men in the export sector, which contribute to bring commodities and money into the country. For Petty, export activity seems to be more important than the production of luxury goods. The next 400 men are more difficult to classify and include the production of both goods and services, needed for the pleasure and magnificence of life. Here the definition seems to have more to do with the final use of these products than with the material features of their production. These products are not strictly necessary either for domestic consumption or for the nation's foreign trade, they are luxuries in every sense of the word. Petty did not explicitly mention the distinction between goods and services, but most of the producers of public and private services are included in the fourth group. The economic organisation of society is founded on the activity of the people employed in the production either of necessaries or of exportable products.

This brings us the third point. From Petty's analysis of the social division of labour emerges his notion of surplus. Not only are 100 men explicitly indicated as supernumerary, but as shown above, the 100 men employed in agriculture and cloth production clearly maintain the whole population, which implies that they produce a surplus of food and clothing above their own needs. The existence of a physical surplus of necessaries, or of basic goods, is a necessary condition for the division of labour. If agriculture is defined in a broad way, as including the production of clothes, then the division of society into different activities depends on the efficiency of production in this enlarged agricultural sector, or on the productivity of the 100 men working there.

Petty implicitly gave the following reasons as proofs of the existence of a surplus in the agricultural sector. First, the existence of activities different from agriculture is a sign of the existence of a surplus product of wage goods. Secondly, and a variation of the first point, when looking at the number of people in society; if this exceeds the number of agricultural workers, this is proof that the latter produce a surplus. Thirdly, the existence of rent is a further proof that agriculture yields a surplus, without it rent would be zero.

These arguments imply a degree of ambiguity about the best way of measuring surplus. Is rent a measure of surplus, or can it be measured by the 900 people who are not employed in agriculture, or by the quantity of wage goods in excess of the consumption required by the 100 agricultural workers? Petty did not give precise answers, but it is clear that a physical surplus of necessaries is a condition for the social division of labour.

Petty also grasped the idea of technical division of labour. Although it is in the agricultural sector that surplus is generated, it is in manufacturing that the technical division of labour can be most extensively applied. Petty gave several examples, ranging from the specialisation in shipbuilding, to the clockwork industry and to textile manufacture. In *Political Arithmetick* he wrote:

> for as Cloth must be cheaper made, when one Cards, another Spins, another Weaves, another Draws, another Dresses, another Presses and Packs; than when all the Operations above-mentioned, were clumsy performed by the same hand.
>
> (Petty, 1676, p. 260)

The outcome of the application of these techniques is an increase in the productivity of labour.

Value and prices

Petty analysed the causes which influence the exchange value of commodities and he clearly distinguished the permanent from the temporary causes, or as he said 'the imaginary way of computing the prices of Commodities' and 'the real way' (see Petty, 1662, pp. 89ff.) or between prices and values. The temporary causes influence the prices established in a specific day or short period on the market. They appear analogous to what Smith was to call market price, and can exhibit large oscillations from the diverse actions of sellers and buyers. But the value of commodities is much more stable, and it is not linked to what happens on the market at a particular time or place. It depends on permanent causes, or long run forces, which Petty identified mainly within the conditions of production of a commodity.

Petty related value to the production process and to the costs and difficulties incurred in the production of a commodity, but he offered alternative measures of these costs. Sometimes he seemed to support the labour theory of value. For example, he compared the relative price of the silver produced in Peru with that of the silver produced in European mines, the former being much lower. Petty used the concept of 'natural price' to indicate the value corresponding to the labour employed in production, this is the price in a state of society confined simply to commodity producers (see ibid.).

Petty also mentioned the notion of 'political price', which seemed to refer to the specific inputs required in the actual production process of a commodity. He gave numerous examples of the inputs required in the production of various commodities (see ibid.). In this context, he used the inductive method, since from his detailed knowledge of actual production processes he derived general laws. Thus the 'political price' is defined in terms of a precise enumeration of the costs.

Petty also highlighted a relationship between the concepts of political and natural price. For Petty, the former notion referred to the value of commodities in more complex societies, political prices combine market forces, and the sellers and the buyers may well have different bargaining power, with the impact of government regulations, taxes and controls.

Land and labour as the ultimate determinant of value

Petty's work also shows that there is a need for a measure of the relative values of commodities, because of the different types of goods employed as inputs in the production of the various commodities. The heterogeneity of the inputs requires relative prices, and at the same time Petty needs to measure relative values in a way which bears some relation to the production conditions of commodities.

Petty suggested an interesting way to solve this problem. Suppose that for all commodities production take place in yearly cycles, so that the unit period of production is one year. Petty remarked that each production process employs as inputs labour, L_0, natural resources – in short: land – T_0 and commodities which have been produced in the previous year. Call V_0 the value of the inputs different from labour and land. V_0 was produced one year ago by means of labour, L_1, and land, T_1, and by a set of commodity inputs, whose value was V_1. One can reconstruct the process of production over time by moving backwards year after year and decomposing the value of the inputs into labour, land and a smaller residual V. It can be assumed that after a number of years the residual value V_n will be small enough to be ignored, then $V_n = 0$. Then the value p can be represented by the following equation:

$$p = \sum_{0}^{n} L_i + \sum_{0}^{n} T_i \quad \text{with } 0 \le i \le n$$

The value p has been decomposed into the sum of two series which indicate the inputs of labour and land which have been employed in the overall production cycle. L_0 and T_0 are the quantities of labour and land utilised during the last year of production, and can be seen as labour and land. The other values of L_i and T_i are the quantities of labour and land employed in the previous years, (or periods of production); they are hidden into the commodity inputs of the last year and represent the value of these means of production. In modern terminology, this is a description of the production process which is vertically integrated.

Petty remarked that all products are the result of two inputs, natural resources, or land, and labour, or, as he put it:

> That Labour is the Father and active principle of Wealth, as Lands are the Mother.

> (Petty, 1662, p. 68)

Land and labour are the two originals, non produced, elements in each production process.

> all things ought to be valued by two natural Denominations, which is Land and Labour...This being true, we should be glad to finde out a natural Par between Land and Labour, so we might express the value of either of them alone as well or better then by both, and reduce one into the other.

> (Ibid., pp. 44–5)

Hence value depends on cost of production, and cost of production can be represented by the amounts of land and labour, L_0 and T_0 directly, and indirectly employed in production. To sum up: the exchange value of commodities depends on the costs incurred in paying for the subsistence of the workers and for the use of natural resources over the entire production cycle.

The system is quite ingenious, but the problem of comparing the value of different commodities is not really solved, as Petty clearly appreciated. If a unit of good 'a' requires 10 units of land and 1 of labour and 1 unit of 'b' requires 10 units of labour and 1 of land how can we determine their relative value? Petty recognised that in order to have a proper unit of measurement of the value of commodities one must have a single magnitude, either of land or of labour. Thus the problem is that of finding a way for converting labour into land or viceversa; what Petty called the method of the 'par'. But this problem was left to Cantillon to solve (as shown below in Chapter 6).

Gold strikes back

Petty made important innovations relative to mercantilism; the notion of division of labour and of surplus; the role of technology and the analysis of value. He implicitly treated capital not only as a financial magnitude but also as the specific commodities employed as inputs in the production process. Capital is seen as commodities used in further production and particular attention is given to wage goods. The way seems to be open to a new view of the causes of the improvement of national wealth, a view much more linked to the organisation of production rather than trade relationships.

However, Petty only opened the way and did not take all the theoretical steps needed to fully overcome mercantilism. A trade surplus was not regarded as and end in itself but as a way to increase economic activity and employment. However, Petty did not explicitly deny the mercantilist views concerning the causes of the increase of wealth, and in fact sometimes he seemed to share the bullionists' view on the superiority of precious metals. Gold, silver and jewels are the only forms of wealth not subject to deterioration, in contrast to other commodities, hence they are wealth at any time and in any place (see Petty, 1662, pp. 259–60).

These limitations in Petty's analysis have an impact on his views of distribution. The surplus accrues to the landlord as rent, while profits do not receive much attention as a separate income share. The same is true for the role and functions of the capitalist entrepreneur. This was also done by Cantillon, who inherited a rich theoretical and conceptual legacy from Petty which he considerably developed.

Notes on further readings

The works of Petty and some unpublished material are included in the collection: *The Economic Writings of Sir William Petty*, 2 vols, edited in 1899 by Charles Hull (Cambridge University Press, Cambridge, 1899); this is the standard reference to his work. *The Petty Papers* (in two volumes) and *The Petty–Southwell Correspondence*, were edited in 1927 and 1928 by the Marquis of Lansdowne, *A Dialogue on Political Arithmetic*, has been edited by S. Matsukawa in 1977.

The role of Petty in the formation of Political Economy was clearly recognised by Karl Marx in the first volume of the *Theories of Surplus Value* (Lawrence & Wishart, London 1963) A. Roncaglia, *Petty: the Origins of Political Economy* (Sharpe, New York, 1985) provides a very interesting analysis of Petty's economics and in particular of his analysis of value and prices, in which there is an anticipation of the surplus approach to value and distribution. A very good analysis of Petty's contribution to classical political economy is found in A. Aspromourgos, *On the Origins of Classical*

Economics: Distribution and Value from William Petty to Adam Smith, Routledge, London (1996). A brief discussion is in Guy Routh, *The Origin of Economic Ideas,* Macmillan (now Palgrave Macmillan), London (1975), Chapter 2, Section 3, pp. 35–46.

Section II

Developments in French Economics

5
Pierre le Pesant Sieur de Boisguilbert, 1646–1714: France at the turn of the century

The introductory outline presented Pierre le Pesant, Sieur de Boisguilbert, as the most interesting author in a group of economists who worked in France in the last years of the seventeenth century and the first decades of the eighteenth. Vauban, John Law, a Scotsman, and Boisguilbert investigated the French economy at the turn of the century to discover solutions to its many economic problems.

Boisguilbert was born at Rouen in a family of noble lineage and received his education from the Jesuits. In Paris he was trained to become a lawyer, but he initially appeared to be more interested in literary matters. He wrote some successful historical novels. In 1677 Boisguilbert married a very rich woman, and subsequently became a magistrate in Normandy. This put him in touch with the poor and deteriorating conditions of the French economy and the need to reverse this situation through economic reforms.

His first work, *Le Détail de la France* appeared in 1695, with several later editions and changes; in this work, Boisguilbert's preoccupation with the economic conditions of France was already clearly visible. Boisguilbert's other major works include the *Traité de la nature, culture, commerce et interêts des grains* of 1704, a *Dissertation on the nature of wealth, money and taxation* (also of 1704) and *Factum de la France*, which appeared in various collected editions from 1707 onwards.

By crossing the Channel at the turn of seventeenth century, a completely different world is encountered. The French kingdom was vastly dissimilar to Great Britain (and to Holland), where big merchant companies by now were the major economic actors. The France of Louis XIV was an important political and military power, but by the end of the Sun King's long reign could appropriately be described as a stagnant economy. Its social and economic organisation remained predominantly feudal. England had paid a high price for the Cromwell led rebellion and the ensuing Civil War. At the time of the Restoration, however, it began to approximate a constitutional monarchy by, for example, recognising personal and civil rights with *habeas corpus*. Moreover, England at this time began to exhibit precapitalistic economic and social structures. The French monarchy was much more absolute, grounding its legitimacy on divine right. Economic and political power was firmly in the hands of King, and only partially shared with the landed aristocracy, the church and public administrators, who often came from the ranks of landlords themselves. French agriculture had a comparatively low productivity and there were still frequent famines associated with harvest failure. The fiscal system was based on many taxes, both central and local, ranging from poll taxes (*capitation*), to those on trade and transportation (such as *aides* and *gabelles*), to taxes on agricultural output (*taille*), which discouraged investments in cultivation and taxes on labour (like the *corvée* and the *milice*). Aristocracy and Church, the first two estates, had been granted tax exemption. Hence the total burden of taxation fell on the third estate, comprising merchants and rural bourgeoisie, as well as the workers and the large numbers of peasants.

The French fiscal system was also terribly inefficient. Only a small proportion of the tax revenue gathered actually reached the central government, which therefore had major problems in financing the lavish expenses of the Court at Versailles, not to mention the many military adventures in which Louis XIV embroiled Europe during his long reign. The French Kingdom was heavily indebted, and the problem of the huge debt stock and of its management remained a major economic issue in France for the whole of the eighteenth century.

The recommendations of Vauban and Law

The *Maréchal* of France, Sébastien le Prestre de Vauban (1633–1707) in his book *Dîme Royale* of 1707 suggested a major reform of the tax system, based on a single tax on agriculture's net income. This tax was intended to replace all existing taxes. It was to be a fixed proportion, like the *dîme* (tithe) assigned to the upkeep of the Church. However its revenue was to accrue directly to the central government and for this reason it belonged to the king. Hence the name *Dîme royale*. It was an obvious suggestion for simplifying the fiscal system, and Vauban's proposal clearly anticipated the more famous single tax on the net product of land put forward by the Physiocrats half a century later. Both attempts at tax reform were unsuccessful, the French fiscal system of the *ancien régime* was to prove immune to peaceful change.

An alternative way at finding a solution to the already chronic problem of high public indebtedness was attempted by the Scotsman John Law(1671–1729). Law had emigrated to France, where in the second decade of the eighteenth century, he tried to find a solution to the fiscal problem and growing debt of France, not through tax reform but through a novel and, indeed, quite modern financial management of the debt itself.

Law desired to finance the public deficit by issuing bonds and bills. This would make the debt less expensive and more manageable in the long run. Of course, given the financial conditions of the kingdom, such bonds were not very attractive to the potential subscribers. To raise their attractiveness, more interesting collateral had to be found to which to link the value of the bonds, thereby to guarantee their face value, hence reassuring the creditors. Law found such collateral in the shares of the Mississippi Company, a French joint stock trading company which had been granted the monopoly of trade for the valley of this large American river in the then French territory of Louisiana. Such an association would make the government bonds very attractive because if the Mississippi Company did well and made profits , the value of its shares would rise and with it the market value of the collateralised bonds, with substantial capital gains for the subscribers.

In fact, Law had very advanced views on the role of money and credit, whose functions need not be restricted to the mere circulation of commodities. But the time was not ripe for this experiment or, perhaps, Law was too adventurous, if not simply unlucky. In any case, events failed to fulfil his expectations. Share values of the Mississippi Company collapsed and so did the value of the collateralized government bonds. Law's credit system disintegrated and he had to flee France in a hurry.

Law's ideas were extremely innovative. In many respects they anticipated some modern financial instruments and techniques, such as the use of collateral and the possibility of leverage in a credit market. The Mississippi Company crisis shares many features with the 2008 financial crisis.

Law's most famous book is *Money and Trade Considered with a Proposal for Supplying the Nation with Money* (1705), in which he set out the framework for analysing the demand and supply of money, breaking its ties with the production of, and demand for gold. Law introduced a more modern monetary and macroeconomic analysis in which the circular flow of income played an important role. His status as innovative contributor to monetary thought has been bolstered by the discovery (and publication in 1994) of his earlier *Essay on a Land Bank* (1694), which anticipated, and elucidated, much of the 1705 pamphlet.

Boisguilbert and the proper exchange value of corn

Boisguilbert's contribution to economics has often been underrated. However, he deserves to be considered as one of the most interesting precursors of Quesnay and Smith. In 1704, he wrote a *Treatise on the Nature, Cultivation, Trade and Interest of Corn*, a work which in its title introduced another major topic in French economic debates, that of the corn trade. This was also a crucial political problem for a country prone to famine, but in which the King was regarded as the good father of his subjects and hence with responsibility, if not for their well being, at least for their survival. Several economic policy issues were associated with the grain trade issue. These ranged from the management of public granaries, dating back to the Roman Empire and particularly relevant for the provisioning of large cities, the restrictions on exporting corn, and controls on the domestic corn trade. Such policies seemed to be very sensible in a situation of frequent shortages of the necessaries due to regular harvest failure.

In 1704 Boisguilbert published his most important work, his *Dissertation on the Nature of Wealth, Money and Taxation*. The title is fascinating by itself: does it not anticipate the more famous *Inquiry into the Nature and Causes of the Wealth of Nations*? Boisguilbert's title refers to two major economic policy issues of his time: taxes and money, but he did not begin with them. Wealth is the first concept he tackled by focussing on the nature of wealth and how it is defined. Like the mercantilists, Boisguilbert's analysis started from well defined policy problems, but contrary to them he presented his views by means of well-articulated treatises and not by mere pamphlets. Although this practice may reflect a different literary genre, popular in the days of Louis XIV, it is also an indication of the need to ground economic policies and strategies within comprehensive and systematic views on the functioning of the economy.

According to Boisguilbert, in modern societies there are more than two hundred types of economic activity (see Boisguilbert, 1704, p. 18), which can be organised in a sort of hierarchical order according to the goods they produce; for instance, agricultural products are more important than the others. Boisguilbert description of society recalls the social division of labour, as recounted by Petty 40 years before (above, Chapter 4).

But for Boisguilbert the merchants and the workers producing luxury goods also perform productive activities:

> true wealth consists of complete enjoyment, not only of the necessities of life, but of every superfluity which gives pleasure to the senses.
>
> (Boisguilbert, 1704, p. 17)

Merchants perform a useful activity when they support the implementation of orderly exchanges in the markets. The landlords too play a useful role because through their expenditures they generate consumption and employment, an argument which was later taken up by both Cantillon and the Physiocrats. But Boisguilbert also reaffirmed the crucial role of agriculture in a society organised on the principle of division of labour; luxury goods can be produced and sold only because 'the excess supply over necessaries enables us to obtain what is not strictly necessary' (ibid.).

Recall that Petty had also maintained that a surplus product in agriculture was a necessary condition for other activities to arise and for division of labour to take place. This proposition is in fact frequently encountered in Physiocracy, in the work of Cantillon, and even in that of Smith.

A system of orderly exchanges

Boisguilbert emphasised the fact that all the different economic activities are related to one another, hence if one worker suffers damage, this detrimentally influences all others and impairs the orderly system of exchanges. Boisguilbert did not share the mercantilist view that in exchange there are always winners and losers. In such a case the circulation of commodities must not be controlled by a few powerful merchants. A country can become prosperous only if exchanges take place according to the natural order of things, in which all activities are as complementary as the works of a watch (see Boisguilbert, 1704, pp. 30–1).

A nation can become wealthy if there is balance in the circulation of commodities; as is indicated in the following remarks about the need for transactions transferring wealth to be conducted at appropriate prices:

> As wealth, therefore, is only this incessant mixing, as much from man to man, as from trade to trade, from country to country, and even from kingdom to kingdom, it is a frightful delusion to seek elsewhere the cause of the distress which, in the discontinuation of an identical trade, eventuates from a disturbance of proportionate prices which are no less essential to their maintenance than their proper composition.
>
> (p. 27)

An orderly circulation is the essential condition for prosperity; not just for a country but for every country and kingdom which trade with one another. Contrary to the mercantilists' views, the growth of foreign trade benefits all trading countries, provided that markets and exchanges are not disrupted.

But what is an appropriate or orderly system of exchanges? How to prevent the more powerful merchants from imposing prices more convenient for them, but which may bankrupt other traders and then disrupt the markets? Boisguilbert had faced the problem of the causes which determine the exchange value of commodities. Following on from his view of wealth, he believed that all exchange must take place at appropriate prices (p. 29); the prices must be 'in proportion' to one another. This concept of price does not have a precise analytical meaning, it is difficult to understand what precisely Boisguilbert meant by proportion. He seemed to imply that in each act of exchange the gain should be shared in a fair way between the buyer and the seller, so that neither of the two parties makes an excessive profit.

Boisguilbert, however, spoke of the need of prices to be in proportion to the expenses incurred in the production of commodities (see pp. 29, 42–3). Certainly, cost of production plays an important role in the determination of the price of commodities, in the sense that it fixes the minimum acceptable level for the market price. Boisguilbert called this floor to an exchange value, the appropriate price (ibid., p. 19). The idea that for each commodity there is a minimum level of price is particularly relevant in the case of agricultural products (see pp. 27, 29). However, the actual level of market prices was left unexplained in Boisguilbert's work. Quesnay later showed that the expenses of production establish a minimum, sustainable level for the market price (see below, Chapter 7).

Disorders in the circulation of commodities

In his discussion of the fiscal system, Boisguilbert remarks among other considerations that the expenses of cultivation must be exempted from taxation (Boisguilbert, 1704, pp. 12–14). As a matter of fact the production of :

> the fruits of the soil, and principally corn, put every occupation on their feet. Now their production is neither the consequence of chance, nor the free gift of nature. It is the outcome of a continual labour and of expenses paid in money.
>
> (p. 22)

This is still the almost medieval France of Louis XIV, but Boisguilbert had no difficulty whatsoever rejecting the idea of agricultural products simply as a 'gift of nature'. Agricultural output is the result of investments and much labour and care from the cultivators.

Boisguilbert, however, did not provide a clear discussion of the nature of cultivators, nor did he indicate whether they were simple peasants, entrepreneurial farmers or sharecroppers. Nor did he provide an analysis of the distribution of income and of agricultural product. Such argument had to await the work of Cantillon and Quesnay (below, Chapters 6 and 7).

Boisguilbert suggested three reasons for possible economic crises, which all derive from policies and behaviour in conflict with the laws of nature, the observation of which is essential to make a country prosperous. The first type of 'disorder' arises from excessive taxation in agriculture; a fiscal system which burdens the cultivators and their capital outlays has damaging consequences not just for agriculture but for all other activities as well. In such a case, taxation is clearly inappropriate and constitutes a serious disorder to the system.

Secondly, in the system of exchange no one must make excessive gains at the expense of his trading partners, because this made them poor and compelled to abandon their activities to the detriment of the whole country.

Thirdly, even though Boisguilbert did not explicitly condemn the production of luxury goods, he nevertheless saw that excessive expenditure on these commodities would undermine the economy and particularly the producers of basic necessaries and of agricultural commodities. Boisguilbert therefore attempted to link together issues in the production of wealth with those relating to exchange value and circulation. A limitation of his work consists in excessive emphasis on the normative aspects of the price system and an inadequate analysis of the actual causes determining the exchange value of commodities. Nevertheless, he provided several important ideas used later by Cantillon and Quesnay (below, Chapters 6 and 7).

Notes on further reading

The most extensive collection of Boisguilbert's works is *Pierre de Boisguilbert ou la naissance de l'économie politique*, 2 vols, edited by J. Hecht (Institut National d'Etudes Démographiques, Paris, 1966). Detailed papers on various aspects of Boisguilbert's contribution to economics and social sciences can be found in *Boisguilbert parmi nous – Actes du Colloque international de Rouen (22–23 mai 1975)*, edited by Jacqueline Hecht (Institut National d'Etudes Démographiques, Paris, 1989). G. Faccarello, *Aux origines de l'économie politique libérale: Pierre de Boisguilbert* (Anthropos, Paris, 1986) should also be consulted. A summary of the last work is given by T.W. Hutchison, *Before Adam Smith* (Blackwell, Oxford, 1988, ch. 7, pp. 107–15). Boisguilbert *Traité* is available in English as *A Treatise on the Nature of Wealth, Money, and Taxation*, translated with an introduction by Peter Groenewegen (Centre for the Studies of the History of Economic Thought of The University of Sydney, Sydney, Reprints of Economic Classic, Series 2, n. 10, 2000). This is the source for quotations from this work in the text.

On Law and the story of the failure of the Mississippi Company experiment, see Edgard Faure, *La banqueroute de Law* (Gallimard, Paris, 1970). On Law's contributions to economics, and his monetary theory in particular, see Antoin Murphy, *John Law: Economic Theorist and Policy-Maker* (Oxford University Press, Oxford, 1997). For a general overview of the evolution of economic thought in France during the eighteenth century, see G. Faccarello and P. Steiner, 'Interest, Sensationalism and the Science of the Legislator: French 'philosopie économique' 1695–1830', *European Journal of the History of Economic Thought*, 14(1), 2007.

6

Richard Cantillon, 1697–1734: the Entrepreneur in Agriculture and Trade

Richard Cantillon, son of Philip Cantillon of Ballyheigue, was born in Ireland in 1697 (the date is uncertain). The Cantillons went to Ireland during the early Norman period and later became devoted to the Stuart cause. Richard's great-grandfather is said to have become the banker of the Stuart Pretender when the Cantillons went to France with James II. Migration to France and travelling around Europe was a characteristic of this family, so it is no surprise to see the close contacts of Cantillon with the continent, and with Paris in particular.

Between 1716 and 1720 Cantillon was in Paris, where he made a fortune from the operation and collapse of Law's scheme. After a period in Holland, he went back to Paris and then moved to London in 1734. That year, on 14 May, he was robbed and murdered, his body burnt in his townhouse in Albermarle Street, set on fire by the thieves. His manuscripts were destroyed in the fire, so only one work, the *Essay on The Nature of Trade in General*, survives. It was written between 1730 and Cantillon's death, but the first printed edition appeared only in 1755 in French, though the actual printing was done in London. This edition was prepared by persons close to Mirabeau, and it is not known whether Cantillon wrote the book in French or English. Internal evidence in the *Essay* shows that Cantillon wrote a statistical supplement for the book, but this so far has not been discovered.

In many ways, Cantillon's work represents a crucial link between the work of Petty and Boisguilbert, and that of Quesnay, Turgot and Smith. There are particularly close connections between Cantillon's *Essay* and Petty's writings. They reveal major analytical similarities, particularly on value theory. Secondly, the two writers gave clear descriptions of some concepts which were to be extensively used in classical political economy. However, neither Petty nor Cantillon 70 years later, totally rejected mercantilist policies and practices. Notwithstanding their theoretical achievements, something was still missing in their construction of an alternative theory of wealth.

Cantillon's analysis of value 'solved' Petty's measurement problem; he emphasised the role of the entrepreneur and that of profits, his analysis of the circulation of commodities anticipates that of Quesnay. Cantillon's *Essay on the Nature of Commerce in General*, larger than a pamphlet and a title with a mercantile flavour, profoundly influenced the Physiocrats and in fact, political economists in every part of Europe.

Wealth and the division of labour

The first chapter, 'On Wealth', begins as follows:

> The Land is the Source or Matter from whence all Wealth is produced. The Labour of man is the Form which produces it: and the Wealth itself is nothing but the Maintenance, Conveniences, and Superfluities of Life.
>
> (Cantillon, p. 3)

The book therefore starts with a definition of wealth, in terms of the goods and services needed for survival and for making life more pleasant. Land and labour are the two sources of wealth, a clear debt to Petty. Like Petty and Boisguilbert, Cantillon described society according to the principle of the division of labour. In particular, he shared with Petty the view that people employed in producing the necessaries of life maintain the entire population, thus making the production of other goods possible. Cantillon posits the example of a society of 100 people, in which 25 provide the basic goods for the others (p. 87), while the remaining 75 can be employed in the refinement of goods, or in any other activity. However:

> if all the others are busied working up by additional labour the things necessary for life, like making fine linen, fine cloth, etc. the State will be deemed rich in proportion to this increase of work.
>
> (p. 87)

Hence all types of labour are seen as being productive by Cantillon, irrespective of whether they are employed in agriculture, in manufacturing, in trade or in the production of luxuries. Again following Petty, Cantillon suggested that the wealth producing capacity of the different activities is not the same. There is a sort of hierarchy, depending on the characteristics of the goods produced. This is confirmed in a later passage where Cantillon mentions the 25 workers producing luxury goods. If they should be employed instead on producing durable objects and instruments of production:

> permanent commodities, to draw from the Mines Iron, Lead, Tin, Copper, etc ... the State will not only appear to be richer for it but will be so in reality.
>
> (p. 89)

Cantillon also emphasised the role of land in sustaining all other activities, because it is from land that the whole of society derives its nourishment. Even those employed in the direct exploitation of other natural resources, like fisheries, need the products of land for their survival. Thus Cantillon stressed in particular the role of land rather than that of natural resources in general; from land come the raw materials to be transformed into usable commodities.

Intrinsic value and the 'land theory of value'

Cantillon distinguished the market price, or simply the price, from the value of a commodity. Here again, Petty's distinction between the contingent and the permanent causes of value is drawn upon. Cantillon used the term intrinsic value to indicate the latter forces. More precisely, the intrinsic value of a commodity depends on the material costs incurred in its production, or, in Cantillon's own words:

> intrinsic value of a thing is the measure of the quantity of Land and of Labour entering into its production.
>
> (p. 29)

Commodities are not always sold in the market at this value. The market value depends on the 'Humours and Fancies of men'. In the second part of the *Essay* Cantillon offered a further analysis of the Market Prices which depend on 'the quantity of Produce or of Merchandise offered for sale, in proportion to the demand or number of Buyers' (p. 119). Hence actual, effective demand and supply are the main forces behind the market price of a commodity. But Cantillon continued the argument 'that in general these prices do not vary much from the intrinsic value' (p. 119). There is therefore a need to investigate the causes which determine this latter value, and possible ways of its measurement.

Cantillon argued that land and labour are the common and original elements in all productive activity. However, he solved Petty's measurement problem and found, though under certain assumptions, a 'par equation' which allowed the conversion of quantities of labour into quantities of land. Cantillon did not take labour as the basis for value in this approach to the problem of measurement; unlike the subsequently well known labour-value theories of Ricardo and Marx in the nineteenth century. Cantillon's solution is that of converting labour into land, because:

> the value of the day's work has a relation to the produce of the soil, and that the intrinsic value of any thing may be measured by the quantity of Land used in its production and the quantity of Labour which enters

into it, in other words by the quantity of Land of which the produce is allotted to those who have worked upon it.

(p. 41)

Cantillon assumed that the wage rate is given and that it consists entirely of the products of land. This is not difficult when the idea of a subsistence wage is accepted, as he in fact did.

It is then possible to establish equivalence between a given amount of labour, say for one day, and the daily subsistence wage in terms of agricultural products, say, a basket of corn. Given the techniques employed in agriculture, the production of one basket of corn requires, for example, one hundredth of an acre of land, thus the value of one day labour is equal to one-hundredth of an acre. The intrinsic value of a commodity is thus given directly by the amount of land or, indirectly, by the wages of the labour employed in its production.

The 'land theory' of value seems a funny one, but it is based on the simple idea that agriculture, a land using activity, maintains the people employed in all other activities, from its capacity to produce a surplus of wage goods over the necessities of the agricultural workers. Cantillon's view of the predominance of agriculture probably influenced Physiocracy and, in any case, resembles it strongly (see Chapter 7 below).

The farmer and the 'three rents'

An essential, and at the time quite novel aspect of Cantillon's economics is his emphasis on the role of the farmers in agricultural production. The farmer is seen as a true entrepreneur, he is in charge of the production process, decides what to produce and he therefore gains the revenue from the sale of its product. Above all, farmers determined the methods of cultivation and they needed to be sufficiently wealthy to employ the best available, most productive, techniques, as English farmers were said to do (see pp. 121–2). In these passages of the *Essai* the farmer has all the features of a modern entrepreneur, who organises production and carries the risks involved (as Murphy, 1986, pp. 255–7, has indicated). However, the economic role of the entrepreneur is not limited to agricultural activities, it can also be found in trade.

Cantillon's notion of the farmer-entrepreneur has important consequences for his analysis of distribution. Cantillon argued that the product of agriculture accrued entirely to the farmer but must then be divided into 'three rents', each part being one third of the total value. 'The first rent must be paid to the Landowner in ready money' (Cantillon, p. 123).

That the first rent should be paid to the landlords is not surprising. The other rents are to be used by the farmer to buy all the necessary instruments and raw materials to carry on cultivation as well as to guarantee the necessaries of life to the labourers by paying them their wages. The farmer may reinvest any excess portion of his two rents once they have replaced the wage goods and the means of production.

Cantillon's 'three rents' theory is probably a stylised view, simply intended to illustrate the component parts of agricultural output. And, it must be emphasised, Cantillon is the first author to suggest that profits are a regular share of output, at least at the macro-economic level.

The praise of the farmers, who play such an important role in Cantillon's depiction of economic life, needs to be balanced with some evaluation of the basic functions of the landlords. Cantillon indicated that they have a fundamental role in deciding the composition of production, and on the way in which land is used. This is not done directly but through their decisions about the nature of their expenditures. In short, landlords through their expenditures determine the composition of aggregate demand and hence the structure of national output.

Profits and capital

Cantillon's view of distribution is extremely important, but his notion of profit still contains significant ambiguities. Apart from hinting at the size of these profits in his three rents doctrine, Cantillon gave no clear indication about what determines them. The farmer has to obtain a profit basically because of the risks incurred in production and the uncertainty which is characteristic of all entrepreneurial activity. Such risks may therefore derive from difficulties in selling his products, as was the case for merchants. And indeed, Cantillon occasionally associated the activity of farmers with that of merchants. In short, his notion of profit is a mixture between the mercantilist view of profit upon alienation and the idea of wages of superintendence (e.g. p. 27). The size of the farmer's profits in Cantillon's *Essay* is nowhere related to the amount of capital invested in his farm, but to the uncertainties and risks farmers face in the production and sale of commodities. Cantillon did have a very interesting view of capital, which later influenced Smith and Ricardo. In fact, wages are made up of agricultural products and apart from raw materials, which also directly come from the land, they are the only other 'original' inputs in every production process. Hence when capital is looked at from the macroeconomic point of view, as a magnitude in national accounting, as Cantillon also did for profits, capital is made up of the subsistence wages paid to the workers (it is a capital, or fund, of wage goods) or rather of purchasing power over wage goods. The way was thereby opened for the wage fund notion of capital which was later elaborated by Smith, Ricardo and, especially by J.S. Mill. This followed from Petty's and Cantillon's notion that the goods which constitute fixed and circulating capital can be represented by the quantities of land and labour employed in their production. Hence at the macroeconomic level, in terms of national accounting, the wage bill and raw materials represent the value of capital (see below, Chapters 11, 14 and 18).

Cantillon largely took an aggregate view of capital and did not develop Petty's idea that capital must first of all be regarded as the actual inputs of each production process. The last was done more clearly by Turgot (see below, Chapter 10).

Cantillon's economics straddles classical political economy and mercantilism

The 'three rents' theory was an important anticipation of the classical view of the distribution of national income into wages, profits and rent. But Cantillon's analysis of value and theory of distribution still had major flaws.

First of all, there was no clear analytical relationship between the 'three rents' view and the notion of intrinsic value. Rents were part of the value as the price of land, wages were 'transformed' into a quantity of land, but it was not shown how profits did arise from the value of agricultural products. Moreover, the intrinsic value was seen as a stable magnitude, dependent on the techniques of production, on subsistence wages and on rent. But the farmers were said to receive their profits because of the uncertainties and risks which characterise their activity, and the size of their profits was by definition highly unstable. In short, while the intrinsic value was a 'long run' magnitude for Cantillon, his approach to farmers's profits was much more 'short term' and temporary.

Apart from such flaws in the relationship between value and distribution analysis, Cantillon's limitations arose from the following. His view of capital was more that of generic purchasing power over commodities, particularly wage goods, rather than the specific inputs used in the production process. Cantillon considerably advanced the analysis of the process of circulation of commodities in his description of the economy as a system of circular flows, but he failed to grasp the essential aspects of the process of reproduction and the crucial role of capital accumulation for the growth of wealth.

Cantillon, in fact, was still very much influenced by mercantilist ideas, particularly when formulating policy recommendations. For Cantillon, foreign trade remained an essential way of increasing national wealth and the size of the population. The exportation of manufactured goods had to be favoured, because they embodied much labour and few raw materials, thus having a higher value added. The imports of foreign manufactures must be discouraged and it had to take place in British vessels. Speaking of gold and silver, Cantillon wrote that:

> the comparative greatness of States is their reserve Stock above the yearly consumption...And as Gold and Silver can always buy these

things, even from the Enemies of the State, Gold and Silver are the true reserve Stock of a State.

(pp. 89–91)

Precious metal is the measure of a nation's wealth *par excellence*, even if wealth itself is made up of commodities.

However, a nation which relied solely on foreign trade for increasing its wealth had also some important weaknesses. In fact, the inflows of precious metal deriving from a surplus in the trade balance led to an increase in prices and in domestic consumption, 'and this will, by imperceptible degrees, ruin the work and manufactures of the State' (p. 235).

Cantillon anticipated Hume's presentation of the money specie flows of two decades later (see Chapter 8 below) but unlike Hume, Cantillon did not explicitly present this as a critique of mercantilist policies. Cantillon also indicated that mercantile success need not endure:

States who rise by trade do not fail to sink afterwards…But it is always true that when the State is in actual possession of a Balance of Trade and abundant money it seems powerful, and it is so in reality so long as this abundance continue.

(pp. 235–7)

Foreign trade was a risky and defective way for increasing national wealth, but a nation stayed rich and powerful so long as it succeeded in its commercial activities.

Despite such sentiments, Cantillon's work was an important anticipator of classical political economy. The 'three rents' theory, the intrinsic value concept, the wage fund notion and the description of the role of the farmers provided important legacies for Quesnay and Smith, as did much of Cantillon's work on trade, circulation and money. He was the economists' economist of the eighteenth century, whose work influenced almost every major economic writer in the third quarter of the eighteenth century.

Notes on further readings

The *Essai* is enjoyable to read. The best edition is *Essai sur la Nature du Commerce en Général* edited by Henry Higgs (Royal Economic Society/Macmillan, London 1931), which produces both a French and English text, and a useful introduction by the editor on the 'Life and Work of Richard Cantillon'. Other commentators have provided useful insights into Cantillon's contribution to economics, for example, J.J. Spengler, 'Richard Cantillon: first of the moderns', *Journal of Political Economy* (vol. 62, 1954), and more recently, Antoin Murphy, *Richard Cantillon: Entrepreneur and Economist* (Oxford University Press, Oxford, 1986). The links between Cantillon and subsequent economic writers also presented in considerable detail by A. Brewer, *Richard Cantillon: Pioneer of Economic Theory* (Routledge, London, 1992).

Cantillon's land theory of value and his model of circular flows are analysed by A. Brewer 'Cantillon and the land theory of value', *History of Political Economy*, vol. 20, 1988 and see also A. Aspromourgos 'Cantillon on real wages and employment: rational reconstruction of the significance of land utilization', *European Journal of the History of Economic Thought* (vol. 4, no. 3, 1997, pp. 417–43).

Section III

Towards a Mature Classical Political Economy

7
François Quesnay, 1694–1774: Reproduction and Capital

Quesnay was born at Mère, Seine-et-Oise. He came from a family of humble origin, the eighth of thirteen children. In 1711, he went to Paris for formal training in medicine and surgery. In 1717 he married Jeanne-Catherine Dauphine who gave him four children, two of whom survived. He began his career at Mantes, a small town not far from Paris, and in the 1720s and 1730s he made his reputation as a surgeon. In 1736 he published the *Essai physique sur l'oeconomie animale*, his first major work. In 1750 and 1751 Quesnay published the last of his medical works and became a member of the French Académie des Sciences and of the Royal Society in London.

In the early 1750s Quesnay became interested in economics and, in particular, in agricultural matters. He wrote several articles for the French *Encyclopédie* of Diderot and D'Alembert: *Evidence* (published in 1756) and *Function de l'âme* (never published because the *Encyclopédie* was by then proscribed by the government). In 1756, he also wrote and published his first economic essay (*Farmers*). In 1757, Quesnay wrote further articles for the *Encyclopédie*: *Grains* was published in its seventh volume in 1757; *Hommes*, *Impôts* and *Intérêt de l'argent* were published much later, two of them posthumously (respectively by Etienne Bauer in 1908, and by Gustave Schelle in 1902).

In 1757 Quesnay met Victor Riqueti, Marquis de Mirabeau, who became the most faithful propagator of his ideas. Their first meeting is often taken as the effective beginning of the Physiocratic school. Quesnay was the undisputed master of the Physiocrats and produced the main analytical innovations in Physiocracy. Apart from Mirabeau, Quesnay's followers included Pierre Samuel du Pont de Nemours, the *Abbé* Baudeau, Mercier de La Rivière and Le Trosne.

In the winter of 1758/59 Quesnay published the three early editions of the *Tableau économique*. In 1763, Mirabeau published the *Philosophie Rurale* which contained alternative versions of the *Tableau*; Quesnay in fact revised this entire work and contribted some chapters. After producing *Le droit naturel*, the *Mémoires sur les avantages de l'industrie et du commerce*, or the *Dialogues sur les travaux des artisans*, Quesnay in 1766 published his final version of the *Tableau*, *Analyse de la formule arithmétique du Tableau économique*, in the *Journal de l'agriculture*.

By 1768 the cultural and political impact of Physiocracy had begun to wane. Henceforth, Quesnay's theories were frequently criticised. He spent his last years studying geometry. He died in December 1774 at Grand-Commun, a place not far away from Versailles, where he had resided from the 1750s as the personal physician of Louis XV's mistress, Madame de Pompadour.

The France of the *ancien régime* and the Physiocrats

The France of Louis XV at the middle of the eighteenth century experienced economic problems similar to those of his predecessor, and the French kingdom continued to lose economic ground relative to Britain. The fiscal problem had not been solved, and the kingdom's finances were on the verge of collapse. All sorts of taxes and duties, (*aides, taille, dîme, gabelle, capitation*) both of the central government and of the provinces, hampered the production and trade in agricultural products. The first two estates (nobility and church) continued to enjoy the privilege of tax exemption, thus leaving agriculture and other productive activity to bear the full burden of taxation. Moreover, the system was still based on tax farming (or leasing the right to collect taxes by private interests) which was strongly attacked by Mirabeau in his *Théorie de l'Impôt*.

However, in the eyes of the Physiocrats, the major French economic problem remained rurally based as shown by the fact that its primary sector was much less productive than English farming. The techniques of production and of social organisation of cultivation were still predominantly feudal. Share-cropping, or *métayage*, prevailed in French agriculture (with exceptions confined to the northern provinces with their more modern, capital using system of agriculture based on independent farmers). This situation produced regular famines, responsible for sporadic declines in French population. Physiocracy as a doctrine must be evaluated with this historical background in mind. Its major purpose was to suggest remedies for restoring French prosperity and power to a level comparable to that of Britain.

With Smith, Quesnay can be hailed as the founder of classical political economy based on notions of surplus and reproduction. Both for Smith and Quesnay, the causes of the wealth of a nation were the major object of investigation, and both authors saw capital accumulation and raising labour productivity as the major sources of wealth. Physiocracy gave the final analytical blow to the mercantilist view that wealth was made up of precious metal and, above all, that a positive balance of trade was the only source of national wealth.

It is convenient to separate the economic writings of Quesnay into two groups: those written between the years 1756 and 1760 and those belonging to the period 1763–68. During the first period Quesnay presented his economic ideas mainly through articles prepared for the *Encyclopédie* of Diderot and D'Alembert; it is the formative period, to which the early 'zig-zag' versions of the *Tableau économique* belong. The second period opens with *Philosophie Rurale*, a joint work with Mirabeau and characterised by the maturity of the school, by its successes, but also by the need to defend the major propositions of Physiocracy from numerous, and growing attacks. Other work appeared in articles published in the *Journal de l'Agriculture* and in the *Ephémérides du citoyen*, both periodicals under the control of the Physiocrats. The *Tableau économique* has not only a special place among the works of Quesnay but also in the history of economics. This original and ingenious scheme struck Quesnay's contemporaries as an item of great novelty for depicting the workings of an economy, profoundly influenced Marx, and went on to exert its influence on modern economics in the form of Leontief's input–output analysis (Leontief, 1951, p. 9). The fame of the *Tableau* is such that it sometimes is regarded as a general summary of Physiocratic economics. This is inappropriate; it is more suitable to examine the *Tableau* in the context of, and therefore as an essential part of, Quesnay's other economic writings.

Farmers and increased agricultural productivity through the accumulation of capital

The 1756 article *Fermiers* is the starting point for examining Quesnay's theory of growth and prosperity. Quesnay considered productive every activity which produced a surplus over the necessary expenses of production. However, for an activity to be productive, it was not enough simply to be part of the primary sector, the net product of agriculture was not a *free* gift of nature. Indeed, Quesnay introduced the distinction between two types of production in agriculture: *la grande* and *la petite culture*. The first was visible in the large scale cultivation of the northern provinces of France where tenant farming was the dominant mode of production, and was sharply contrasted with the second form, that is, the poor cultivation by share-croppers which dominated the rest of France. Rich farmers invested a lot of money in cultivation and provided every instrument and tool it required. Hence only they could use the most advanced techniques of cultivation, characterised by the use of horses instead of oxen, because the former allowed a more extensive tillage of land and the utilisation of the iron ploughshare, as opposed to the wooden plough used with oxen. (Quesnay, *Farmers*, in INED, pp. 438–41). Horses were more expensive than oxen and were regarded by Quesnay as a form of fixed capital. Capital accumulation enabled technical progress which clearly was of an endogenous type. This is the central element for understanding Quesnay's analysis of development and growth. A similar analysis was also advanced by Turgot (below, Chapter 10).

According to Quesnay, only large scale cultivation earned a surplus, because it permitted adoption of more advanced methods of production. The less advanced, if not feudal methods of small scale cultivation prevailing in France did not leave much net product over expenses; only an appropriate stock of capital guaranteed the productiveness of agriculture. In short, the problem of France derived from the low productivity of most of its agriculture, the result from deficient investment and capital, particularly fixed capital. Hence the French kingdom would only achieve prosperity and wealth through transforming the primitive, feudal conditions prevailing in most of its countryside into modern, efficient agriculture based on wealthy farmers, more typical of Great Britain and confined to some northern provinces in France.

The problem of modernisation of French agriculture was strongly linked to Quesnay's view of capital and of accumulation. Quesnay described capital as *avances*, that is, as means of production which had to be advanced in order to carry out the process of production most effectively. He distinguished several types of capital advances in the context of large scale cultivation. Annual advances (*avances annuelles*) were made up of wages (at subsistence level) and raw materials. Smith was to call them circulating capital. Original advances (*avances primitives*) were durable instruments of production (spades, carts, but also horses, stables) which Smith called fixed capital. Aggregate advances (*reprises*) were defined as the inputs necessary to continue cultivation (see Quesnay, *Analyse* in INED, pp. 794–96). Satisfactory *reprises* guaranteed the regular reproduction of the economy over time.

Note that in many developing countries the problem of food scarcity is still related to low agricultural productivity due to lack of capital and advanced cultivation techniques.

Quesnay noted that a modern agriculture, which adopted the most productive techniques of cultivation, is characterised by a ratio of net product to annual advances of 100 per cent. However, this ratio was only achievable if circulating capital was applied with the requisite amount of fixed capital (which in the example of *Fermiers* included the horses). This for him was the key element for enabling adoption of a modern farming techniques. The growth of the French economy depended on this accumulation of capital, of fixed capital in particular, in agriculture. Hence in *Farmers*, Quesnay outlined the concepts of capital, net product and reproduction, which were at the core of his analysis in the *Tableau économique*.

The sterility of trade and manufacture

According to Quesnay, wealth cannot originate in an act of exchange, because commerce is just an exchange of commodities of equal value

(Quesnay, in INED, p. 897). Wholesale trade was a sterile activity, and also one that caused damage since it implied artificially high prices given the excessive power of the merchants. Nobody before Quesnay had so explicitly denied the ability of trade, including foreign trade, to contribute to raising national wealth. This was then still an important novelty in the economics of the eighteenth century, but it was part of the process of revision of mercantilist doctrine which had begun with Locke and North (see above Chapter 3). This aspect of Physiocracy greatly irritated the merchants, but was far more acceptable to agricultural thinkers. Quesnay's statement that manufacture was sterile was much more controversial. Industry only reshaped the products of nature from the primary sector without adding anything to their value. As Quesnay put it: 'the idea of *production*, or of *régénération*, forms here the basis for the distinction between the classes of citizens' (in INED, pp. 886–7, Quesnay's italics). The artisans simply transformed the subsistence goods and the raw materials they received from agriculture without creating a physical surplus. Quesnay's criteria for regarding an activity as productive was its ability of creating a surplus over necessary inputs: 'One must distinguish an *addition* of different items of already existing wealth ... of things which existed before this kind of increase, from the generation or creation of wealth, which form a reproduction and a real increase of new wealth' (ibid., p. 890, Quesnay's italics).

Another aspect is worth noting in Quesnay view of the sterility of industry. He considered manufacture as being mainly small scale: shopkeepers and artisans, who employed almost no fixed capital and were thus unable to raise their productivity and earn a surplus.

Quesnay clearly indicated at which stage of the process of circulation national wealth could be measured. Wealth was of course not a stock concept, as in mercantilist literature; it became an annual flow of agricultural products for Quesnay, whose values constituted national output. In order to measure this annual output, prices established in the first act of exchange needed to be used, that is, those taking place between the farmers, the direct producers, and the merchants. He called these prices 'prix de la première main' (price at first hand) (Quesnay, in INED, p. 750). Hence value and new wealth were created up to this first act of exchange, or up to the wholesale market. All remaining exchanges for Quesnay were only circulating products whose value had already been determined and which did not add anything to national output.

Value and prices

How are 'first hand prices' determined? In his analysis of value, Quesnay used several concepts. Like Petty and Cantillon before him, Quesnay distinguished day to day market price from the long term value of the products, which he called 'fundamental price'. This was the unit cost of production to the direct producer of commodities, including his overall expenses.

Hence below this level, producers incurred a loss (see INED, p. 555) and the condition for reproduction for the economy as a whole were not met.

The fundamental price of the products of industry covered the subsistence wage of labour and the value of the raw materials used up. The same items were part of the fundamental value of agricultural commodities, but in the case of large scale cultivation, the amortisation of fixed capital needed to be added. However, in order to continue cultivation, farmers needed also to pay rent to the landlord, a further cost to be included among their annual expenses: 'But it is necessary to include in the fundamental price the taxes and the rent of land' (in INED, p. 752 and cf., pp. 861–4).

The fundamental prices for the productive and sterile sectors, p_g and p_m, can then be represented as follows:

$$p_g = [(w_g + m_g) + aK] + R$$
$$p_m = w_m + m_m$$

where w_i and m_i are respectively the values of wages and of raw materials consumed in sector 'i'; a is the rate of amortisation, K is the value of fixed capital, R is the annual rent. All magnitudes are expressed per unit of output.

The value of manufactured products, p_m, is a pure physical cost of production; the value of the product of land (p_g) is the sum of two main elements:

(a) the physical production costs, in square brackets, which are made up of:
   a_1, circulating capital (*avances annuelles*) in round brackets,
   a_2, the amortisation of fixed capital (*avances primitives*);
(b) rent, which is a cost for the farmer, but which is part of the net product of the economy.

Only the elements of a_1 are common to both sectors. Those of a_2 are confined to large scale cultivation as practised exclusively by rich farmers.

The physiocratic concept of fundamental price of primary products depends on two sets of conditions and hence satisfies them:

(a) the technical conditions for the physical reproduction of the inputs, that is, the replacement of the capital stock;
(b) the rule for distributing surplus prevailent in that particular society.

Relative prices are then closely related to the techniques of production on one side and to the distribution of net product on the other. This way of analysing the role of prices of production was revitalised two centuries later by Piero Sraffa in his book, *Production of Commodities by Means of Commodities*.

Quesnay's condition (b) suggests that the landlords received most of the agricultural surplus in the form of rents, hence prices for him were linked immediately to the process of reproduction and to income distribution.

Quesnay also introduced two types of market prices: p_v, sellers' price and p_a buyers' price (in INED, pp. 531–3, cf. pp. 462, 474). These prices referred to wholesale and retail markets respectively, as indicated by Quesnay's own numerical examples: p_v is the price paid for produce by the merchant to the farmer, while p_a is the price paid by final consumers to merchants (cf. Vaggi, 1987, pp. 60ff.). The profit of the merchant was the difference $(p_a - p_v)$, hence a profit upon alienation. The profit of the farmer was likewise a difference, that between the seller's price and the fundamental price $(p_v - p_g)$.

Quesnay was concerned about the low level of p_v in France, and its sizeable oscillations. These were seen as very damaging because they discouraged farmers from long-term investments in fixed capital. Once more, England appears as Quesnay's model economy. It had much higher and far more stable values of p_v in exchanges at 'first hand'. This enabled introduction of a further, and famous, physiocratic notion of price, that of *bon prix*. This price at 'first hand' is sufficiently high for guaranteeing substantial profits to the farmer, thereby encouraging further capital investment in cultivation. Increased investment embodied technical progress and enabled large scale methods of cultivation. A virtuous path to prosperity was then triggered.

The *Tableau Economique*

In the winter of 1758–1759, Quesnay wrote three versions of the *Tableau économique*, the so-called *zig zag tableau*, because of the descending lines which intersect each other and describe the economic exchanges among the three classes (Figure 7.1 shows the third version).

Its three columns represent three classes or sectors: landowners, the productive class (agriculture) and the sterile class (manufacturing). The descending lines indicate inter-sectoral circulation of commodities which demonstrate that at the end of the year (harvest cycle) this ensures reproduction of the advances, enabling production to continue the following year. The diagrams contained some explanatory text but this was not always easy to understand. *Philosophie Rurale* (1763) provided a simpler version of the *Tableau*, in summary form. In 1766, the scheme of the *Tableau* was reformulated completely (see Figure 7.2). This contained a concise description of the components of capital, a neat definition of net product and a clear analysis of the necessary conditions to enable reproduction of the economy in the following year. The *Tableau* of the *Analyse* described the circulation and reproduction of commodities in an ideal economy, which had implemented all the major physiocratic policies. Its

64

TABLEAU ÉCONOMIQUE[1]

Objects to be considered: (1) three kinds of expenditure; (2) their source; (3) their advances; (4) their distribution; (5) their effects; (6) their reproduction; (7) their relations with one another; (8) their relations with the population; (9) with agriculture; (10) with industry; (11) with trade; (12) with the total wealth of a nation.

PRODUCTIVE EXPENDITURE relative to agriculture, etc.	EXPENDITURE OF THE REVENUE after deduction of taxes, is divided between productive expenditure and sterile expenditure	STERILE EXPENDITURE relative to industry, etc.
Annual advances required to produce a revenue of 600^l are 600^l	Annual revenue	Annual advances for the works of sterile expenditure are

600^l produce net ········one-half goes here········ 600^l one-half goes here   300^l

Products one-half goes here   Works, etc.

300^l reproduce net ····one-half goes here···· 300^l one-half goes here ····300^l

150 reproduce net ·one-half, etc.····150 ·one-half, etc.····150

75 reproduce net ········75 ········ 75

37···10^3 reproduce net········37···10 ········37···10

18···15 reproduce net········18···15 ········18···15

9····7····6^d reproduce net········9····7····6^d ········9····7····6^d

4····13····9 reproduce net········4····13····9 ········4····13····9

2····6···10 reproduce net········2····6···10 ········2····6···10

1····3····5 reproduce net········1····3····5 ········1····3····5

0···11····8 reproduce net········0···11····8 ········0···11····8

0····5···10 reproduce net········0···5···10 ········0···5···10

0····2···11 reproduce net········0···2···11 ········0···2···11

0····1····5 reproduce net········0···1····5 ········0···1····5

etc.

TOTAL REPRODUCED......600^l of revenue; in addition, the annual costs of 600^l and the interest on the original advances of the husbandman amounting to 300^l, which the land restores. Thus the reproduction is 1500^l, including the revenue of 600^l which forms the base of the calculation, abstraction being made of the taxes deducted and of the advances which their annual reproduction entails, etc.

Figure 7.1   Quesnay's *Tableau économique*
Source: Quesnay's *tableau économique*, edited by M. Kuczynski and R.L. Meek, Macmillan (now Palgrave Macmillan), London, 1972.

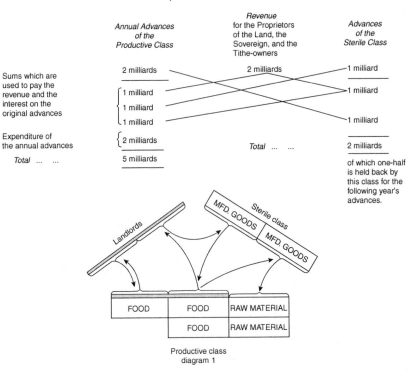

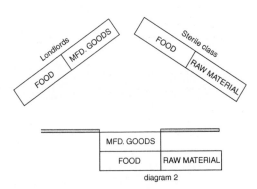

Figure 7.2   Formula of the *Tableau économique*
Sources: R.L. Meek, *The Economics of Physiocracy*, Allen & Unwin, London, 1962, p.158; Paul Sweezy, *Theory of Capitalist Development*, Dennis Dobson, London, 1949, pp. 366–7 (this is, in fact, an appendix prepared for Sweezy by Shigeto Tsuru).

opening page reveals that Quesnay in fact assumed a large kingdom with an advanced agricultural sector, with free external trade of corn and hence with stable prices (in INED, p. 794).

The various exchanges taking place in this *Tableau* are as follows. They are presented to show the *Tableau's* conformance with Quesnay's price notions, already discussed. The start of the analysis is the end of the production cycle, after the harvest. Gross product equals 5 milliards in agriculture and 2 milliards in manufacturing:

1. The first act of exchange implies a pure monetary transaction: the payment of rent by the farmers to the landowners, 2 milliards of *livres* (R).

   Henceforth money acts only as a medium of exchange, and for each exchange of commodities, there is a movement of money of equal value in the opposite direction.
2. The landlords buy 1 milliard of primary commodities for their subsistence from agriculture.
3. The landlords spend the other 1 milliard of their rent to buy 1 milliard worth of manufacturing goods, for their luxury consumption.
4. The manufacturers buys 1 milliard of subsistence goods from the primary sector (w_m).
5. The farmers buy 1 milliard of manufactures for their consumption and also for the maintenance of their fixed capital (aK).
6. The manufacturers buys 1 milliard of raw materials to be transformed into manufactured products (m_m).

The distribution of commodities and money stocks by the three sectors before and after the process of circulation can then be summarised as follows (as shown in the two diagrams provided at the lower half of Figure 7.2):

At the end of production and before circulation

Agriculture	Manufacturing	Landlords
Corn 5	Manufactures 2	–
Money 2	–	–

After circulation

Agriculture	Manufacturing	Landlords
Corn 2	Corn 2	Corn 1
Manufactures 1	–	Manufactures 1
Money 2	–	–

Several points should be emphasised:

Reproduction. The 2 millards *livres* in money have returned to the farmers, and agriculture and manufacturing have both recovered their advances so that a new production cycle can commence.

The net product. Manufacturing has used up 2 milliards of primary commodities and transformed them into 2 milliards of manufactures, without adding any surplus product, the reason why Quesnay considered the sector as sterile. By contrast, agriculture employed 3 milliards inputs, (1 milliard in manufactures) and produced 5 milliards of corn leaving a net product of 2 milliards. At the end of the process, the entire net product is transferred to the landlords as their rent.

In short, the circulation of gross output in an ideal economy needs to satisfy two conditions:

(a) the two producing sectors must secure the inputs necessary for continuing production in the next period as specified by technology, that, reproduce their capital advances;
(b) the net product must accrue to the landlords, because they create the social and political rules regulating the requisite income distribution in society which ensures reproduction.

It has already been indicated that Leontief later saw the *Tableau économique* as an anticipation of his input-output tables; Phillips (1955) first presented Quesnay's *Tableau* as an input–output table, in the manner of the following table:

	Agriculture	Manufacturing	Landlords	GDP
Agriculture	2	2	1	5
Manufacturing	1		1	2
Landlords	2			2
Gross National Income	5	2	2	9

The first two rows and two columns show the intersectoral inputs. The third row (rent) may be interpreted as a kind of value added, which lifts gross national income to 9 milliards. The first two rows of the third column show the composition of net final demand equal to the net product.

Ironically, the presentation of the *Tableau* in input–output form indicated that manufacturing provided an essential 1 milliard of input to agriculture. It was therefore wrongly described as sterile, because it indirectly contributed to the creation of the 2 milliards of net product emerging from agriculture.

Subsequently, Quesnay used the 1766 *Tableau* to investigate various policies measures such as free trade in corn, alternative taxation forms and different consumption patterns by landlords (see Eltis, 1975 for a detailed discussion).

From *laissez-faire* to accumulation and growth

For Quesnay, French national wealth could only be increased through substantial investment in agriculture, this depended on securing a *bon prix* for French produce, especially for corn. The free export of corn was designed to achieve this goal: foreign demand would sustain the French corn price, and competition from foreign merchants checked the power of French dealers. The widening market also extended effective demand, stabilising corn prices at levels which secured high profits for French farmers. In *Philosophie Rurale*, Mirabeau described the price effects from a free corn trade as benefiting not only French agriculture but the whole kingdom including landlords. (Mirabeau, 1764, II, pp. 366–7).

Free trade in corn enabled the creation of a virtuous circle or reproduction, where high profits produced high investments, yielding increasing returns, reduced unit production costs, and led to potential increases in rents and profits, even with lower retail prices. Hence consumers benefited as well from free trade in food stuffs.

In this scheme, merchants bear the entire burden from reforms through the income redistribution required for raising farmers' profits which trigger the investment growth. This redistribution occurred through the increased wholesale price secured by free export of French corn which benefited farmers incomes.

Quesnay supported free trade in so far as it was necessary for sustaining the sale of French primary products. He opposed free imports of foreign manufactures. The landlords, who only have access to a genuinely disposable income, have to buy the products of French agriculture (*luxe de subsistance*) but not luxury imports (*luxe de décoration*)

From end 1763 to July 1764, Finance Ministers Bertin and de l'Averdy introduced partial freeing of the corn trade (see Weulersse, vol. II, pp. 222–4). This was, in fact, the only implementation of policy which followed Physiocratic prescriptions. Increasing corn prices ensued, but failed to induce the predicted capital accumulation in agriculture, French dealers retained most of their power. Public opinion believed free trade in corn to be the cause of its dearness and an Edict of 1770 removed the free trade in corn during the *ancien régime* (with the exception of a brief period in 1775–76 when Turgot was Finance Minister; see below, Chapter 10, and Weulersse, pp. 591 ff.).

The political views of physiocracy

A further reason why Physiocracy offended enlightened spirits during the second half of the eighteenth century arose from their political vision. They favoured legal despotism, a kingdom governed by the landed aristocracy and by a King. In his article, 'Natural Right', Quesnay spoke of absolute monarchy as benign authority (in INED, pp. 737–42). He added that good governance by an enlightened monarch is essential for securing prosperity. There was no invisible hand in Physiocracy which inevitably led to a prosperous society. For Quesnay, appropriate policies needed to be implemented, giving substantial scope for intervention by the sovereign, the 'visible hand' of the natural order. In the France of the *ancien régime*, Physiocracy was seen as a conservative movement by reformers such as Voltaire and Diderot (cf. Fox-Genovese, 1976, pp. 238–42). Moreover, Physiocracy *de facto* opposed the interests of manufacturers and merchants, groups which were emerging as a potentially politically powerful French bourgeoisie, whose political instincts were largely liberal.

After 1770, Physiocracy rapidly lost ground in France, for analytical as well as for such political reasons. Quesnay's economics disguised contradictions between landlords and capitalist farmers (see Vaggi, 1987, pp.179ff.), reflected in the ambiguity of the physiocratic concept of profit. Farmers' profits were the source of accumulation, technical progress and growth; they clearly formed part of the net product in Quesnay's early articles but do not feature as such in the later *Tableaux*. The *Philosophie Rurale* sometimes treated farmers' profits as a temporary phenomenon, lasting only until leases were renewed, usually after every nine years. Renewed lease contracts then gave landowners the entire net product or surplus (Mirabeau, 1764, vol. I, pp. 37–9). This involved a striking contradiction: although profits were the source of accumulation, modernisation and development in agriculture, they were, nevertheless, not a permanent component of the long term, fundamental prices elaborated by Quesnay. The very existence and size of farmers' profits depended on the wholesale price and its oscillations, revealing profits as a temporary unstable magnitude in Quesnay's analysis. Profit remained partly linked to the mercantilist notion of profits upon alienation, hence were inadequate for supporting a theory of the growth of national wealth based on capital accumulation and increasing productivity.

Despite these limitations, and for the first time in the history of political economy, Quesnay had produced a theory of wealth capable of fully challenging mercantilist explanations of wealth in terms of a positive balance of trade. Quesnay's analysis of reproduction, capital, productivity and the role of prices in the process of circulation and distribution, established foundations of a logical structure for elaborating a theory of surplus. As such, they were fully appreciated, and used, by his eminent economic successors, Turgot and, especially, Adam Smith.

Notes on further readings

The edition largely used as source for quotations in the text, is *François Quesnay et la Physiocratie*, ed. L. Salleron, 2 vols (Institut National d'Etudes

Demographique (INED), Paris, Presses Universitaires de France, 1958), the standard edition of Quesnay's works. A new expanded edition of Quesnay's works, *Oeuvres économiques complètes et autres texts*, edited by Christine Théré, Loïc Charles and Jean-Claude Perrot, Paris: Institut national d'études démographiques, 2005, is now available. Quesnay's 1758–59 *Tableaux* are reprinted in a Royal Economic Publication Society (edited by M. Kuczynski and R.L. Meek, as *Quesnay's Tableau économique*, Macmillan – now Palgrave Macmillan, London, 1972). R.L. Meek, *The Economics of Physiocracy* (Allen and Unwin, London, 1962) provides analysis and translation of much of Quesnay's work while *Farmers* has been translated by Peter Groenewegen (University of Sydney, Department of Economics, Reprints of Economic Classical Series 2, No. 2, 1983). Mirabeau's works are available only in French: *Théorie de l'Impot – Pour servir de Suite au Traité intitulé l'Amis des Hommes* (1760), *Philosophie Rurale, ou Economie Générale et politique de l'Agriculture* (1764), (both reprinted by Scientia Verlag, Aalen, 1972).

A detailed economic and intellectual history of France at the time of Physiocracy is G. Weulersse, *Le mouvement physiocratique en France (de 1756 à 1770)*, 2 vols (Felix Alcan, Paris, 1910). More recent accounts are E. Fox-Genovese, *The Origins of Physiocracy – Economic Revolution and Social Order in Eighteenth Century France* (Cornell University Press, Ithaca and London, 1976) and G. Vaggi, *The Economics of François Quesnay* (Macmillan – now Palgrave Macmillan, London, 1987).

The intricacies of the *Tableau* have been extensively examined by many authors. Reference should be made to A. Phillips, 'The *Tableau Économique* as a simple Leontief model', *Quarterly Journal of Economics*, 69, pp. 137–44, 1955). W.A. Eltis, 'François Quesnay: a reinterpretation. 2. The theory of economic growth', *Oxford Economic Papers*, vol. 27, no.3, 1975, reprinted in Walter Eltis, *The Classical Theory of Economic Growth*, London, Macmillan (now Palgrave Macmillan), 1984.

An interesting analysis of corn price policies in France at the time of Physiocracy is L. Charles, 'From the *Encyclopedie* to the *Tableau économique*; Quesnay on freedom of grain trade and economic growth', *European Journal of the History of Economic Thought*, vol. 7, no.1, 2000; see also Loïc Charles, 'The visual history of the Tableau Economique', *European Journal of the History of Economic Thought*, 10(4), Winter 2003.

8
David Hume, 1711–76 and the Scottish Enlightenment

This chapter illustrates further aspects in the formation of classical political economy of special relevance to the writing of the *Wealth of Nations*. The contributions of the various authors mentioned are evaluated relative to Smith's achievement in the *Wealth*.

This chapter covers the 1750s, revealing in part the powerful impetus given to natural and social sciences by the phenomenon now known as the Enlightenment. The contributions are grouped into three sections. The first examines the stadial view of history or the 'four stages theory'. Secondly, the academic tradition which was dominant in Scotland when Smith was a student and a young teacher, that is, aspects of the Scholastic and Natural Law approach, is examined. Thirdly, the chapter concludes with David Hume, a leading intellectual figure in Europe and a man to whom Smith, and the Enlightenment as a whole, owed a great deal. This is why his name is invoked in the title of the chapter.

The 'four stages theory'

Both Smith's *Wealth of Nations* and his earlier *Lectures on Jurisprudence*, and Turgot's essay *On Universal History* describe the evolution of human society as a sequence of specific stages. This view was not confined to these writers; to the contrary, it appears to have been widely diffused both in Great Britain and in France. Several predecessors can be found in England, for example, in Locke's theory of property presented in his *Two Treatises on Government*. In France, and closer to the hey day of the Enlightenment, it occurs in Montesquieu's famous book *L'esprit des lois* (1748). This argued for a definite relationship between the social and political laws of a country and its material and natural conditions in the economic aspects of life. Montesquieu exerted a major influence on most authors of the Enlightenment with respect to the method for analysing the evolution of societies. Human societies are a complex and difficult subject of investigation; and in attempting to explain their evolution, the notion that specific stages of organisation have prevailed in particular periods of history can be very helpful. The most advanced discussion of these four stages is, however, in works by Turgot and Smith, not published during their lifetime.

These stages are: hunting, pasturage, agriculture and finally the commercial stage. They are characterised by the different ways the procurement of subsistence is organised by a society, or by the different 'mode of producing subsistence'. Hence economic and property relations come to the fore. The mode of producing subsistence is argued to affect all other aspects of social organisation: politics, law, religion, customs and habits.

During the hunting stage, people subsist by directly exploiting nature and its resources: wild animals and the fruits of land and forest. Only a very limited division of labour is possible, mainly derived from physical characteristics such as gender and age. The dominant occupation is that of warrior and hunter. Chief and high priest are the only conceivable roles of distinction. There is no private property, natural resources are a common heritage and capital is confined to a set of instruments for the hunt (spears, knives, bows and arrows) which everyone knows how to fashion with varying degrees of skill. The chief upholds the law, and oral tradition is more than sufficient to transfer the technical knowledge required for the continual reproduction of society. Barter is sufficient for exchanging, the tribe is nomadic, because it has to follow the animals from which it depends for subsistence through the hunt, or because the natural fruit of the forest have been completely gathered and it is time to seek fresh sources of supply in other forests. The social organisation derives from the consumption of the tribe, surplus is virtually non-existent, population remains stable. In the eighteenth century, American Indians were considered to be a typical society in the hunting stage, which also represented the original, first stage of all human societies (Meek, 1976, pp. 37ff.).

The second stage, or the stage of shepherds, is characterised by pasturage. It grows naturally out of the hunting stage, as it is realised gradually that much work in the future is saved by holding on to part of the catch, and keeping it as a certain source of food supply. It is represented by the great Tartar tribes of central Asia or by the biblical patriarchs who founded the people of Israel (see for instance Smith, 1762–63, vol. V, i, b, 7). The breeding of domestic animals is now the fundamental economic activity and the wealth of a tribe depends on the size of its herds. The social division of labour is still limited and herds are often common property, but considerable private property can exist in a society of shepherds in the form of livestock, implements, moveable dwellings and ornaments. Surplus is the natural increase of the live stock, the main form of private property.

The third stage is that of agriculture which implies major modifications for society. It develops naturally from the pastoral stage. Tilling the soil for food for man and beast removes the uncertainty and trouble from a never-ending search for new natural pasture. Society is no longer nomadic, because the cultivation of land, requiring settlement, becomes the main source of subsistence and wealth. Techniques of production in agriculture gradually become more refined, and give rise to steadily rising surplus. Hence cities arise, where fairs and markets can develop, and the social division of labour becomes more complex. Artisans and merchants separate their activities from those of peasants and farmers (see above, Chapter 4). The king becomes the centre of society and power. He can even be regarded as a god, as was the case with the Egyptian Pharaoh, but the functions of government are increasingly undertaken by specialised persons: administrators and judges, priests and warriors. Property in land is the dominant form of property and needs support from suitable legislation. The vastly superior surplus obtainable from agriculture enables population to increase, despite frequent wars, famines and other natural disasters.

The fourth and last stage is that of commercial society. The need for merchants and artisans by farmer eventually becomes so large that they begin to dominate society in the growing towns and cities. Exchange now dominates the mode of subsistence, and manufactures in particular become a major part in the standard of life. The social division of labour becomes more and more complex and, more specifically takes on the advanced form of technical division of labour. Technology, productivity and capital accumulation are now the key sources of wealth; in exchange and production contracts become the basic economic relationship in the sphere of circulation. Laws must then be more refined and cover virtually every aspect of individual and social life. The landed aristocracy gradually loses its dominance in political power; the new bourgeoisie comprising merchants and entrepreneurs initially claims a growing share of government, and eventually becomes the dominant class.

This description of the evolution of human society appears to be an economic interpretation of history, in which the mode of subsistence governs the other aspects of society. But at least for Smith, this approach, though considered important for illuminating the evolution of human societies, is not fully deterministic (cf. Meek, 1976; Skinner, 1982). In fact, the four stages need not necessarily follow one another precisely in the order described above. Some stages may be skipped, for example.

The importance of the fours stages theory then rests on the following: firstly, it provided a method for analysing complex societies; secondly, it clearly recognised that all societies evolve in the course of history, and are therefore frequently not static because they contain forces making for change.

In his *Biographical Memoir* of Adam Smith, Dugald Stewart described this type of argument as 'Theoretical or Conjectural History, an expression which coincides pretty nearly in its meaning with that of Natural History, as employed by Mr. Hume' (Stewart, 1793, p. 34).

Leaving aside the question of whether or not Hume would have shared Stewart's judgement of his work, it is often argued (for example, by Taylor, 1930, pp. 226–31) that Smith adopted a strictly deterministic approach to the analysis of human societies. This is highly debatable, since it is easily shown that this approach was not an essential part of his methodology.

Adam Ferguson similarly rejected a strictly deterministic view of the evolution of societies, but his (1767) *An Essay on the History of Civil Society* is a clear orientation towards the idea that men are guided by very simple and basic instincts, without preventing human progress and the construction of organised societies, of nations and states. Ferguson believed that individual decisions do not play a significant role in the determination of the history of human societies, because a law of unintended consequences predominates, hence the results are often quite different from the motivations of the individuals and from their original design:

> Mankind, in following the present sense of their minds, in striving to remove inconveniences, or to gain apparent and contiguous advantages, arrive at ends which even their imagination could not anticipate...
>
> Like the winds, that come we know not whence, and blow whithersoever they list, the forms of society are derived from an obscure and distant origin; they arise, long before the date of philosophy, from the instincts, not from the speculations, of men.
>
> (Ferguson, 1767, p. 119)

Ferguson was a friend of Hume and may have influenced him, but Hume apparently did not like Ferguson's *Essay*.

The scholastic tradition and the Scottish Enlightenment

As a professional teacher and scholar, Adam Smith belonged to an academic tradition which had its roots in the thoughts of Aristotle and Thomas Aquinas. The more modern revival of their theories owed much to the Dutchman, Hugo de Groot (1583–1645), better known as Hugo Grotius, whose *De jure belli et pacis (The Law of War and Peace)* was published in 1625. The major object of investigation of this book was the historical and legal foundations of societies in which natural law was taken as the spring from which actual societies derive and to which they should conform. Positive laws have to conform to natural ones, so that a normative approach prevails.

This was also the approach of Samuel von Pufendorf (1632–88) in Germany in his 1672 *De jure naturae et gentium (The Law of Nature and Nations)*, a text used at Glasgow University when Smith was a student there. Both authors attacked economic problems from a normative perspective, by treating just price, a just rate of interest and just salaries as major issues for discussion.

For Pufendorf, all goods need to have a value in use in order to have a positive exchange value. The former is a kind of 'prerequisite' of the latter, but does not determine it:

> The foundation of price in itself is the aptitude of a thing or action, by which it can either mediately or immediately contribute something to the necessity of human life, or making it more advantageous and pleasant.
>
> (Pufendorf, 1672, p. 676)

People are simply not interested in things which have no specific utility for them, a proposition necessary but not sufficient for explaining price or the exchange value of goods.

Pufendorf's analysis of value used several concepts of price, thereby providing an interesting indication of the state of scholastic value theory. 'Yet in organized states prices are fixed in two ways: One way is by a decree or law of those in authority, the other by general valuation and judgement of men.... Some are accustomed to call the former legal, the latter common or natural price' (ibid., p. 686).

Pufendorf shows more interest in the concept of natural price and indeed this proved to be a useful concept for economics. In addition, he used the famous and important concept of 'just price':

> a just price which is commonly set by those who are sufficiently acquainted with both the merchandise and the market.
>
> (Ibid., p. 687)

In an ideal world, various common, just, natural, and even the legal price, should be equal. The exchange value was influenced by the two main forces of scarcity and cost of production. Scarcity is one of the causes of the exchange value of a commodity (p. 680), but so are the difficulty and the effort employed in obtaining it:

> in fixing the common price consideration is to be given to the labour and expenses which merchants undergo in importing and handling their wares.
>
> (p. 687)

Gershom Carmichael (1672–1729) brought the influence of Grotius and Pufendorf to Scotland. In 1718 he prepared an English edition of Pufendorf's *De officio hominis et civis* of 1675. Francis Hutcheson (1694–1746) succeeded Carmichael as Professor of Moral Philosophy in Glasgow and was one of Smith's favourite teachers, 'the never to be forgotten Frances Hutcheson' as he later described him. In 1747 Hutcheson published *A Short Introduction to Moral Philosophy*, the more detailed *A System of Moral Philosophy* appeared posthumously in 1755.

Hutcheson followed Pufendorf's argument by describing value in use as a necessary condition for exchange value:

> The natural ground of all value or price is some sort of use which goods afford in life; this is a prerequisite to all estimation.
>
> (Hutcheson, 1755, Vol. II, p. 53)

The price of a good or its exchange value however, depended on two sets of circumstances:

> we shall find that the prices of goods depend on these two jointly, the *demand* on account of some use or other which many desire, and the *difficulty* of acquiring, or cultivating for human use.
>
> (Hutcheson, 1755, p. 54, italics in the original)

The second cause can be expressed by the great labour or toil of the workers producing the commodity, but 'rarity or scarcity' plays an important role as well (Hutcheson, 1755, p. 54).

When subsequently discussing the determination of wages and the foundations for merchants' profits Hutcheson provided an interesting view of the component part of price:

> In matters of commerce to fix the price we should not only compute the first cost, freights, duties, and all expenses made, along with the interest of money employed in trade, but labours too.
>
> (Hutcheson, 1755, p. 63)

This interesting list seems to anticipate the contents of Smith's famous chapter 'Of the Component Parts of the Price of Commodities' in the *Wealth of Nations*.

Hutcheson's analysis of profits (again having in mind the later contribution by Smith) is another interesting aspect of his work. The 'ordinary profits of merchants' are justified because of their care, attention and labour, 'on which account merchants can justly demand a higher price in selling, than what answers all that was expended upon the goods' (ibid.).

Mercantile profits, derive from the difference between the sale price and the purchase price plus additional expenses, a notion of profit quite similar to the mercantilist concept of profit upon alienation, as also held by Quesnay (Chapter 7 above).

Hutcheson was quoted by Smith in his *Theory of Moral Sentiments*, where he appears as the founder of an ethical system which regarded benevolence as the leading passion in influencing people's action. Smith placed Bernard de Mandeville (1671–1733) and his famous *Fable of the Bees: or Private Vices, Publick Benefits*, at the other side of the spectrum: it maintained that selfishness is the main feature of human nature, and that, only by leaving men free to act according to their private interest was it possible to achieve the common good. Contrary to popular belief, this view was not fully endorsed by Smith.

Both the analysis of value and the analysis of wealth did not undergo major modifications in the scholastic tradition. Moreover, notwithstanding their many differences, both Hutcheson and Mandeville shared the view that national wealth is increased through a positive balance of trade (see Hutcheson, 1755, vol. II, p. 318).

Such background assists in appreciating the innovations of Smith's *Wealth of Nations*. But Smith had also been deeply influenced by debates on natural law and natural order, where ethical, administrative and technical aspects were continuously interrelated.

Hume on men, money and trade

Hume was born in 1711 in Edinburgh, Scotland. His father died when he was three years old and the family was not wealthy; he lived with his mother at Ninewells and subsequently studied at the University of Edinburgh. In 1734 he went to France where he stayed for three years and where began to write the *Treatise of Human Nature*, published in London between 1739 and 1740. In England Hume tried to enter the legal profession and also tried commercial activity before spending some time as a tutor. He then went abroad, for many years as secretary to the British Embassy in various parts of Europe. In the meantime he published *An Enquiry Concerning Human Understanding* (1748) and *The Political Discourses* (1752). In addition, he published a major history of England.

In 1763 he went to France as the secretary of the Ambassador Lord Hertford, return to England with Rousseau in 1766. In 1767, he was appointed Under-Secretary at the Ministry of Foreign Affairs. He retired in Edinburgh in 1768 and died there in 1776. Hume never held a university chair, but had tried unsuccessfully both in Edinburgh and Glasgow to obtain one.

Hume was a major figure in the Enlightenment, with an interdisciplinary approach to social sciences and wide cosmopolitan interests. This implies correctly that he was influential both in England and France, making him a sort of intellectual 'bridge' across the Channel.

His 1739 *A Treatise of Human Nature* advanced the idea that utility was the fundamental passion guiding the behaviour of men, providing the foundations of human judgement and of virtue, a view not shared by his friend Smith (Smith, *TMS*, Part IV, chapter II). In his *Treatise*, Hume also supported the use of both the inductive and experimental methods.

For the historian of economic ideas, Hume is particularly remembered for his *Political Discourses*, a collection of nine essays in which he analysed some of the main economic problems of the time, and made very significant contributions to economic thought. In some of these essays, *Of Money, Of Interest, Of commerce* and *Of the Balance of Trade*, Hume explicitly criticised mercantilist views and policies, including their erroneous notion of wealth.

Most essays echo Hume's views on utility already advanced in the *Treatise*; where he established utility as the main passion in the human mind. In fact, some argue he came close to establishing the principle of diminishing marginal utility. In *Of Commerce*, he wrote:

> A too great disproportion among the citizens weakens any state. Every person, if possible, ought to enjoy the fruits of his labour, in a full possession of all the necessaries, and many of the conveniences of life. No one can doubt, but such an equality is most suitable to human nature, and diminishes much less from the *happiness* of the rich than it adds to that of the poor. It also augments the *power of the state*, and makes any extraordinary taxes or impositions be paid with more cheerfulness.
>
> (Hume 1752, p. 102, italics in the text)

This passage is quite interesting for other reasons as well. First, human happiness is related to the power of the state and the taxation system therefore resembles a quid pro quo. Secondly, Hume sounds very egalitarian, particularly when he relates equality of wealth to human nature. Thirdly, the whole passage shows Hume's main preoccupation to be with the cohesion and wellbeing of society, which is linked by him to the distribution of wealth.

Hume subsequently made it clear that 'where the riches are in few hands', concentration of power emerges and this places the entire burden of taxation on the poor, 'to the discouragement of all industry' (ibid.). Such sentiments on undue concentration can also be found in Smith. Hume's plea for free trade is likewise an attack on concentration of wealth and power in the hands of rich merchants and mercantile companies. Moreover, his economic arguments (taxation, industry) are always closely linked to political ones, an important feature both of Hume's work and that, more generally, of Enlightenment thinkers.

Hume used the quantity theory of money to challenge the mercantilist view that money constitutes wealth. For Hume, national wealth is given by the quantities of goods and of labour available in a country. An increase in the stock of money has no long run effects on them; it is only a sort of accounting device. The opening sentences of *Of Money* state:

> Money ... is one of the wheels of trade: It is the oil which renders the motion of the wheels more smooth and easy ... the greater or less plenty

of money is of no consequence; since the prices of commodities are always proportioned to the plenty of money.

(see Hume, 1752, p. 115)

Later in the essay, his view is restated:

It seems a maxim almost self-evident, that the prices of everything depend on the proportion between commodities and money.

(ibid., p. 121)

Hume also used the quantity theory of money for analysing international trade, enunciating the famous international species flow mechanism of monetary distribution. A surplus in the balance of trade implies a net inflow of money (gold and silver) into the country. This gradually induces a proportional increase in the level of prices and wages which will make domestically produced products less competitive. Hence there is an automatic tendency for the trade surplus to disappear.

However, Hume distinguished the equilibrium condition making prices proportionate to money supply which eliminated the possibility of a permanent trade surplus from the process which adjusts the price level to money stocks. When there is an inflow of money, wages and prices do not rise immediately, since there is a intermediate phase during which economic activity, the industry of people and employment may increase, and with these, national wealth. A once-for-all increase in the domestic money stock soon exhausts its positive effects and national wealth falls back to its previous level.

This was an important concessions to mercantilism on Hume's part; maintaining a constant inflow of money makes it possible to sustain a spirit of industry among workers, thereby increasing wealth. In short, money is not wealth but its continuous and gradual increase represents a useful economic policy when there are underused resources. Hume fell short of an explanation of the origin of wealth alternative to that of mercantilism.

For Hume, the rate of interest depended on two circumstances: the demand and supply of credit and the profits in trade. The second cause is particularly interesting because it shows that for Hume the profitability of merchants' activities had clear implications for the price of borrowing. However, a precise notion of a rate of return or of the rate of profit on capital invested is missing. It has already been mentioned that in the essay *Of Commerce*, Hume argued that inequality in distribution and in the command over resources should avoid extremes, because the people rejected such excessive inequality. But this essay also indicated that commerce can bring power and wealth to the nation as well as happiness and freedom for the individuals. This resembles Montesquieu's notion about 'sweet commerce', according to which trade and exchange contribute to smoother relationships between individuals and nations (see Hirschman, 1977, p. 70).

Hume's analysis of international trade and growth is extremely interesting because he introduced two themes to economic argument which marked the rest of the eighteenth century and the initial stage of the next.

The first of these is the so called 'rich country-poor country' debate, visible in *Of Commerce* and *Of Money*. Hume maintained that commerce will benefit all trading countries, and that poor nations benefit from the wealth of rich neighbours. He even added an argument in favour of convergence and catching up by poor countries, since thanks to lower prices of necessaries and labour, poor nations are more competitive in the markets of rich nations:

> Manufactures, therefore, gradually shift their places, leaving those countries and provinces which they have already enriched and flying to others, whither they are allured by the cheapness of provisions and labour.
>
> (Hume, 1752, p. 116)

The second issue suggests that due to the competitive potential of poor countries from cheap, abundant labour, a limit has been set to increases in rich countries' wealth. There is a ceiling to growth, a check to the opulence of each rich country. Both issues have implications for the rise and fall of nations, a subject previously broached by Cantillon and, in the political sphere, by Machiavelli.

Hume wrote a further short essay, with the appealing title *Of the Jealousy of Trade* in 1758. This explicitly attacked the mercantilist view of international trade as a zero sum game. All nations can gain from free trade, thanks also to the fact that 'Nature, by giving a diversity of geniuses, climates, and soils, to different nations, has secured their mutual intercourse and commerce' (Hume, 1752, p. 151). However, Hume's argument rests more on the fact that rich states provide a market for each other's products, than on differences in natural endowment, and complementarities in domestic and foreign demand.

The rise and fall of nations was a recurring theme for authors of the Enlightenment, given their interest in the causes of prosperity, and in the evolution of societies over time. This is visible in Book III of the *Wealth of Nations*, and in Gibbon's history of *The Rise and Fall of the Roman Empire*, which also appeared in 1776. For Hume, the true wealth of a nation is the *spirit of industry* of her people, something able to postpone its decay and an expression which recurs in many places in his *Essays* (see for instance pp. 120, 152).

Hume's modernity is particularly evident in his view of the individual and of the open nature of national economies, always bargaining and trading with each other. In this and other respects, his work embodies typical features of the Enlightenment. These include their cosmopolitan character (Enlightenment authors were curious about different societies, and investigated them) while the notion of an economic argument confined to a closed economy was never taken as a serious option; the opposite holds in fact, it was regarded as great error. Secondly, history was invariably present and history means evolutionary process. Nothing in society and in its economic organisation is static. Hume's model of the evolution of societies is both complex and imperfect, but its methodology is clear. This created a benchmark for successive economists well into the next century, and fully integrates his *History of England* within the rest of his work.

Notes on further readings

On the history of the four stages theory, see R.L. Meek, *Social Science and the Ignoble Savage* (Cambridge University Press, Cambridge, 1976) and Andrew Skinner, 'A Scottish Contribution to Marxist Sociology?' in *Classical and Marxian Political Economy* (edited by I. Bradley and M. Howard, Macmillan, London, 1982). Parts of the Smith's Glasgow Lectures can also be recommended, as can Adam Ferguson, *An Essay on the History of Civil Society* (Cambridge University Press, Cambridge 1995).

Reading Francis Hutcheson provides a good example of the state of value theory in Scotland prior to *Wealth of Nations*, that is, F. Hutcheson (1747), *A Short Introduction to Moral Philosophy* (second edition, R. and A. Foulis, Glasgow 1753), and the more detailed *A System of Moral Philosophy* (R. and A. Foulis, London 1755), both available in reprints. Hume has been quoted in the text from the handy edition by K. Haakonssen, *David Hume – Political Essays* (Cambridge University Press, Cambridge, 1994); the standard edition remains that by T.H. Green and T.H. Grose (*The Philosophical Works of David Hume*, 4 vols, London 1874–75). Hume on international trade and growth is treated in Istvan Hont 'The 'rich country–poor country' debate in Scottish classical political economy', in I. Hont and M. Ignatieff, *Wealth and Virtue* (Cambridge University Press, Cambridge, 1983). This book also provides a good discussion of the British Enlightenment. Equally useful is K. Haakonssen, *Natural Law and Moral Philosophy – from Grotius to the Scottish Enlightenment* (Cambridge University Press, Cambridge, 1996).

Hume's economic writings were collected by D. Rotwein (*David Hume's Writings on Economics*, Nelson, London, 1955). A.O. Hirschman, *The Passions and the Interests* (Princeton University Press, Princeton, 1977) provides a vivid interpretation of the formation of economic and political thought in the seventeenth, and especially the eighteenth century. On the evolution of monetary views from Hume to the nineteenth century, see A. Arnon, *Money, Credit and the Economy*, Cambridge: Cambridge University Press, 2010.

9
Ferdinando Galiani, 1728–87 and Sir James Steuart, 1713–80: Real Value and Corn Trade

Galiani and Steuart share some similarities in the process of formation of economic science. Both were contemporaries of Hume, Quesnay, Turgot and Smith and were part of the Enlightenment. They were, however, much less successful among their contemporaries, though Galiani was extremely popular in Paris. They both travelled extensively in Europe, and were especially familiar with France. In the history of economic thought, Galiani has been overshadowed by Quesnay, and Steuart's *Principles of Political Oeconomy* by the *Wealth of Nations*. Both authors also suffered political misfortunes, though Galiani's recall from Paris back to Naples is incomparable to Steuart's long exile. With respect to their economic analysis, they played a small role in development of classical political economy, even though their work contains interesting hints and notions. The line running from Petty to Cantillon and then to Quesnay and Smith, is much thinner in the case of these two authors. Occasionally they oppose, sometimes for very good reasons, the emerging surplus approach. Partial neglect of their contributions is now being remedied. Although the economics of Steuart and Galiani appears to have little in common, they share a concern for reality, for the actual effects of specific policies and, for problems of administration. This caused them to treat wide ranging generalisations or the application of identical theories to different historical situations with suspicion. Both Steuart and Galiani also show a strong taste for policy and for history.

Ferdinando Galiani, money and methodology

Galiani was born at Chieti, Italy, on 2 December 1728 and died in Naples on 30 October 1787. At the age of seven he was sent to Naples, where he received a classical education. Galiani was a prodigal child, as a youth he was in close touch with Neapolitan cultural circles of the time and, early on was introduced to the study of economics. In 1745 he took religious orders.

His extensive monetary studies began when at 15 he translated Locke's *Some Considerations of the Consequences of the Lowering of Interest and Raising the Value of Money* and Locke's writings on money into Italian. They culminated in the publication of *Della moneta* (1751), his major work. In 1759 he was appointed Secretary to the Neapolitan embassy in Paris where he lived, almost continuously, for the next ten years. At the end of his Paris period he wrote, between the end of 1768 and June 1769, eight *Dialogues* on the grain trade, which attacked major tenets of Physiocracy. Diderot and Mme d'Epinay published The *Dialogues* in 1770 when Galiani had already returned to Naples. There Galiani held several high positions in the civil service, in particular that of Counsellor to the Chief Magistrate of Trade and published essays in fields other than economics. Galiani was influenced by earlier Italian economic writers (such as Montanari and Davanzati) and contemporary Neapolitan authors such as Antonio Genovesi, but his works also contain traces of that of Giambattista Vico, and, less surprising given his church education, of Thomas Aquinas.

Galiani's two economic texts are quite distinct. The first contains a most interesting analysis of value and prices. Its second chapter of Book I discussed principles of value in general, not only the value of money. He used the well known paradox of value, which he illustrated by air and water on one side and a 'basket of sand from the shores of Japan' on the other. Galiani introduced notions and terminology often seen as anticipating a subjective theory of value and the explanation of value in terms of scarcity and utility.

First of all, value is described as a process of estimation, and is, therefore, a subjective notion.

> The value of things...is defined by many authors as the appraisal men make have of them.
>
> (Galiani, 1751, p. 38)

That we are talking of a state of the human mind is made clear a few lines later:

> appraisement, that is value, is *an idea of proportion between the possession of one thing and that of another one in the concept of a man.*
>
> (Ibid., p. 39, italics in the original)

For Galiani, the value of things is a relative concept, it suggests a comparison, as in a ratio of exchange between two commodities, as Galiani illustrates in an example dealing with corn and wine (see ibid.). Hence value can only be discussed in relative terms, not as absolute value, and it depends on individual tastes given by human nature and on the resources of those who wish to purchase goods.

In his discussion of the value of money and, especially, that of the precious metals, Galiani did use the expression, 'intrinsic value', but this seems to reflect a general consensus among people who use these metals, gold in particular, in their exchanges (ibid., p. 58). He thereby wished to establish the principle that gold and silver are generally accepted as money for a definite reason, and not by mere chance.

But to return to Galiani's analysis of the principles of value:

> Then value is a ratio; and this ratio is the result of two other ratios expressed by the names Utility and Scarcity.
>
> (Ibid.)

Both utility and scarcity need explanation. Galiani's discussion of utility is particularly interesting because he clearly indicates that everything can be regarded as useful, both necessities and the pleasures of life. Utility is happiness for Galiani, it is the satisfaction of a passion (ibid., pp. 39, 40). All this is perfectly in line with his perception of value as both subjective and relative. The paradox of value is easily resolved from this standpoint. For Galiani, the world has been so marvellously designed by Providence that for each commodity:

> generally speaking, utility never meets with scarcity; but on the contrary, the more primary utility is high, the more there is abundance, and for this reason the value cannot be high.
>
> (Ibid., p. 44)

Scarcity is defined as 'the proportion between the quantity of thing and the use of it' (ibid., p. 46). In this context, Galiani also mentions labour and toil, as elements affecting the value of a commodity, but relative scarcity is considered to be the most influential among these elements. Galiani illustrated this with an example of the increase in the price of wine in a country due to the sudden arrival of an army(see ibid.,, p. 53). The example also hints at the notion of effective demand or the actual purchasing power over commodities. But more generally Galiani is quite firm in holding that notwithstanding the importance of utility and scarcity, 'value does not derive from a single principle, [but] from many, which join together to form a composite ratio' (ibid, p. 43). He therefore criticised Davanzati and all those who, like him, failed to appreciate:

> that *more useful* and *less useful* are relative terms, which are measured according to the varying condition of individuals.
>
> (Ibid., italics in the original quotation)

This cautious relativistic approach to science is a hallmark of Galiani's approach, and appeared more than 20 years later in the *Dialogues*. The young Galiani generally refrained from assigning a unique role to a single principle; he invariably stressed complexity and the potential for variation (as also illustrated in his critique Petty's political arithmetic, in ibid., p. 61).

Chapter III of *Della Moneta* deals with the value of money. Money has an intrinsic value which depends on the value of the metal embodied in the coin, without such value, money and coins cannot be used as means of payment. However, the value of the precious metals themselves derives from the estimation of those involved in their trade:

> there is no other way to know with certainty the price of gold, than by asking how much it is commonly evaluated with respect to all other commodities.
>
> (Ibid., p. 58)

And later:

> they are used as money because they are highly valued, but are not highly valued because are used as money.
>
> (Ibid., pp. 58–9)

The intrinsic value of money is essential because money is needed for commerce and exchange. Only trade and exchange have ensured the progress of society and money is the 'principal drive' of trade (ibid., p. 90, see also p. 87). Exchange cannot flourish under barter conditions. Hence money has two features; first, it is the universal measure of all prices; second, it can buy everything, it is general purchasing power over commodities (see ibid., pp. 68–9).

Book III of *Della Moneta* examined the question of 'raising the value of money', that is, its debasement or depreciation. As a general principle, Galiani neither opposed nor favoured this practice, which increased the face value of coins relative to their intrinsic value. It could be useful in certain circumstances, but must never be abused by the prince. Galiani fully understood that debasement benefited debtors (ibid., p. 209–ff.) and hence the rulers and governments which issue the money. This aspect is clearly explained by Galiani as follows:

> Debasement of money, *is a profit, that the prince and the State obtain due to the slowness in which the multitude of people change the connections of their ideas about the prices of commodities and money.*
>
> (Ibid., p. 188, italics in the original)

Ordinary people tend to adapt slowly to new monetary values but this does not last indefinitely.

The Dialogues sur le commerce des blés

Galiani's *Dialogues* are a powerful pamphlet on one of the most important contemporary policy issues, that of liberalising the domestic and foreign corn trade. Initially Galiani favoured this process of liberalisation, but he later changed his mind. Galiani's pamphlet was a violent blow to physiocracy, particularly because of its brilliant use of the literary form of the dialogue, filled with wit and biting satire.

First of all, methodological considerations make for doubts about the opportunity to liberalise corn trade in the France of Louis XV according to Galiani. Every policy measure needs time to reveal its actual consequences, and during this time it is quite possible that initial conditions of the economy change, thus leading to results different from those predicted by the theory:

> Nothing is so true than the fact that free trade will bring corn wherever there are money and consumers; nothing is so true in theory.
>
> (Ibid., p. 153)

In practice, however, there are lags and delays, it takes time for arranging to supply corn to everyone, 'and if this time is of fifteen days, and you have provisions only for a week, the city is left without bread for eight days' (ibid.). As Galiani concluded in a delightful epigram: 'Therefore the theorem goes well, the problem goes quite badly' (ibid.).

But apart from the problem of time, there is a second reason why theoretical prediction may not work out in reality. All policy recommendations need to consider the specific conditions of a country and not rely on the abstraction of theory. Climate, soil, means of communication, money may vary substantially in different countries. What is good for Rome may not be good for France (Galiani, 1770, p. 11). Galiani objected to Physiocratic examples of corn trade in England, because 'France and England are not at all alike' (p. 12). Moreover, conditions change over time, so past situations cannot be invoked to support today's policies: 'Because today France no longer looks like the France of Colbert and Sully' (ibid., p. 13).

The *laissez-faire* for the corn trade suggested by the physiocrats might work *if* France already had a class of wealthy farmers capable of quickly taking advantage of the rise of the price of corn. But in reality, the French class of agricultural entrepreneurs is quite small; the economic policy of Physiocracy assumed the ideal economy described by the *Tableau économique*; it ignored the actual political and social conditions of the *ancien régime*. According to Galiani, liberalisation of the corn trade and raising the price of corn would raise taxes and rent. There is no clear benefits for French farmers.

Galiani also criticised the physiocratic doctrine of the exclusive productivity of agriculture and sterility of industry; for him manufacturing had some clear advantages over agriculture and not vice-versa. In industry, output tends not to be affected by the vagaries of good and bad seasons, 'there are neither good nor bad years of harvesting in manufacturing' (ibid., p. 30). Hence output and prices are more stable than in agriculture. Manufacturing had also a far greater potential for growth.

Moreover, manufactures sustain the activities of agriculture, through the consumption of the workers they employ. Galiani tended implicitly to favour balanced growth for the two productive sectors. However, Galiani's dislike of agriculture also derived from his view that an agricultural country is often characterised by despotism and superstition.

Sir James Steuart

James Steuart was born on 10 October 1713 in Edinburgh, Scotland. He was the only son of Sir James Steuart, Solicitor General of Scotland and a Member of the London Parliament after the Union. He succeeded to his father's title in 1727 and after travels in the Continent between 1735 and 1740, became a leading advocate of a Jacobite Restoration. He helped to draft Prince Charles Edward's manifesto in 1745 and was a member of his Council. He was sent to Paris just before the Pretender's abortive march to Derby with a brief to negotiate full-scale assistance from the French. After the annihilation of the Stuart army at Culloden, he was forced to live abroad until 1763. Shortly after his return from exile, he published *An Inquiry into the Principles of Political Oeconomy* (1767), the work on which his reputation as a political economist is based. His participation in the 1745 Rebellion was not fully pardoned until 1771. This enabled him to become an adviser to the East India Company, for whom he wrote *The Principles of Money Applied to the State of Coin in Bengal* (1772). He died on 26 November 1780.

Steuart's *An Inquiry into the Principles of Political Oeconomy* is in five books, of which the first two deal with the most theoretical aspects. The other three books are devoted to policy recommendations, advice and practical rules. Steuart's title may have prevented Smith from using 'political economy' in the title of his own book published nine years later.

Steuart starts his work by discussing the evolution of human societies through three stages, which closely resemble the four stages of Turgot and Smith (see below, Chapters 10 and 11) a matter on which Steuart also was influenced by Montesquieu. The first two stages are combined into a single one by Steuart: that of nomadic and savages populations, the agricultural stage then follows and finally that of manufacturing. The evolution of societies and states through the various stages is visible through a particular indicator: the ratio of population to necessaries, which is one of Steuart's main preoccupation in the early parts of his book.

However, the similarities between Steuart and Smith do not go much beyond this, as can be easily seen by comparing the tables of contents of their treatises (that of Smith is given in Chapter 11 below). Steuart's *Principles* open with his main preoccupation: population and its needs and wants and with the problem of how is it possible to employ everyone, quite different from the first chapters of the *Wealth*, where division of labour is the centre of attention.

Book II contains an analysis of value and prices. Steuart introduced the notion of real value of commodities which depended on their cost of production, or, essentially, upon the expenses incurred for wages and raw materials. The price, however, depends upon many other circumstances, which Steuart analysed by means of a description of the forces at work on the market; the forces of competition between buyers and sellers. When there are several people in each group, the situation conforms to what Steuart called 'double competition'. When a type of equilibrium is established between the two parties, then for Steuart this is a situation of *balance of work and demand* (Steuart, 1767, 1966, pp. 189–92). Thus the price depends on a relationship between supply, work, and demand, and Steuart describes the existence of an inverse relationship between price and demand (ibid., pp. 171, 182). However, Steuart did not relate demand to a notion of marginal utility. He looked on demand as effective demand, the demand of buyers who can afford to pay for the commodity they wish to buy (ibid., p.151). This notion provides an upper limit to the price of the commodity, a limit which depends upon the purchasing power and the will to pay of the potential buyers (ibid., pp. 164–5, 169–70). Steuart refers also to a *common rate of demand*, and when the quantity offered for sale falls below this threshold, the price rises (ibid., p. 153). Generally speaking, therefore, the movements of prices on the market depends on supply and demand.

However, in Steuart the link between demand, supply, price and competition is more fully articulated than what can now be found in the neo-classical concepts of excess demand and supply. In fact, it approximates much more closely the relationships highlighted by Smith in the *Wealth of Nations*. The effective (effectual) demand depends upon historical circumstances (such as, habits, tradition), but also on the wealth of potential buyers, and in some case this demand even depends on the price of the good (ibid., pp. 349–50). Given this demand, the relationship between demand and supply on one side and the market price on the other depends upon changes in output. According to Steuart, the merchant-sellers adjust the quantity produced to the usual level of demand, but they also take into account the ability to pay of the buyers (ibid., p. 162). Therefore, the sellers may decide both the output and the supply price resulting from the relationship between supply and demand.

However, in order to determine the market price of a good, another extremely important element needs to be added: competition. Steuart distinguished between a strong demand and a strong competition; the former makes it possible to have large production and sales, the latter increases the price of the sale (ibid., pp. 152–3). Competition displays its effects through the continuous changes and 'vibrations' of the prices. In this way the market forces lead to the determination of market and equilibrium price, which Steuart denotes as intrinsic value, and which generally exceeds the real value because it includes a 'consolidated profit' (ibid., pp. 192–5, 202, 204). Steuart also adopts other notions of price: intrinsic worth (ibid., p. 312), useful value (ibid., p. 318), fundamental price (ibid., p. 340–41), but none of these notions plays an analytical role as relevant as that of real and intrinsic value:

> I have, in the fourth chapter, observed how necessary a thing it is to distinguish the two constituent parts of every price; the value, and the profit. Let the number of persons be ever so great, who, upon the sale of a piece of goods, share in the profits; it is still essential, in such enquiries as these, to suppose them distinctly separate from the real value of the commodity; and the best way possible to discover exactly the proportion between the one and the other, is by a scrupulous watchfulness over the balance we are now treating of, as we shall presently see.
>
> (Ibid., p. 189)

The profit 'consolidates' with the value of a commodity because it is an essential element to induce the producer to manufacture it. If the price did not guarantee this consolidated profit over and above the expenses, the commodity would not be produced. Merchants and producers get used to obtaining a certain profit and incorporate it in what they regard as the minimum acceptable price of commodity.

Steuart's analysis of value and profit is interesting because it shows that contemporary developments were sufficiently advanced to enable profits to be considered as an essential part of the value of commodities. However, the concept of profit Steuart used retains similar features to the mercantilist notion of 'profit upon alienation'. For Steuart, the size of the consolidated profit depended entirely on the market price of commodities. Variations of price are directly translated into changes of profit. Thus, given the effective demand, the profit depends on the quantity of the commodity supplied and on the degree of competition among the buyers. Hence the consolidated profit derives from, and follows, the 'vibrations' of competition and has no particular relationship with the size of capital invested.

The prices of subsistence goods are seen by Steuart as regulated by the same causes which determine the prices of all other commodities (ibid., pp.183, 187–8). This is also true for the price of labour which depends on the number of people looking for a job and on the intensity of the competition between them (ibid., pp. 251, 265, 269–71). Wages can also vary because of different dexterity of workers.

Steuart's treatise contains other interesting considerations. For instance, he believed that the introduction of machines would not induce a reduction of employment but rather a decrease of prices (ibid., pp. 255–6). He also examined the problems of returns in agriculture and said that there are decreasing returns due to natural limits to cultivation. Finally, Steuart criticised the quantity theory of money, which had been more or less formalised by Montesquieu and by Hume, because prices depend upon competition, on demand and on the quantity produced, and not only on the amount of money existing in a country (ibid., pp. 345, 350, 355).

Steuart introduced several notions and aspects of economic analysis which can also be found in Smith. Moreover, examining these notions indicates that nine years before the *Wealth of Nations* was published, theoretical relationships between value and distribution on one side, and production and market on the other remain to be clarified. Smith's, and subsequently, Ricardo's solutions of these problems will become the real legacy for classical political economy. Problems in the determination of the 'consolidated profit' arise from the fact that the analysis of market forces occupied a large part of Steuart's work, and that his sellers look much more like merchants than capitalist-entrepreneurs. On the other hand, his notion of effectual demand opens the way to Smith's analysis of market prices. Steuart remains a halfway house between mercantilism and classical political economy, in some respects he is the last of the mercantilists, no matter how advanced part of his work is.

Notes on further readings

The works of Galiani are quoted respectively from *Della Moneta* (Feltrinelli, Milano, 1963) and the *Dialogues sur le commerce des blés*, from a collection: *Mélanges d'Economie Politique*, ed. E. Daire, vol. II (Guillaumin, Paris, 1848). *Della Moneta* has been translated by P.R. Toscano, as 'On Money', Ann Arbor, Chicago, University Microfilms International; F. Venturi 1972, 'The Position of Galiani between the Encyclopaedistes and the Physiocrats', in *Italy and the Enlightenment* (New York University Press) presents an interesting discussion of Galiani's place in the Enlightenment. For some modern commentaries on various aspects of Galiani's work see F. Cesarano, 'Monetary theory in Ferdinando Galiani's *Della Moneta*', *History of Political Economy*, 1976, vol. 8 no.3, and the special issue of the *Journal of the History of Economic Ideas*, 2002, devoted to the Subject. The process of composition of the *Dialogues* is carefully described by Philip Koch in his edition of *Dialogues sur le commerce des blés* (V. Klostermann, Frankfurt am Main, 1968).

The edition used of Steuart's *Inquiry* is the 1966 edition for the Scottish Economic Society by Andrew Skinner *An Inquiry into the Principles of Political Oeconomy*, 2 vols (Edinburgh: Oliver and Boyd) from which all the quotations are taken. The reading of Skinner's *Introduction* to his edition is strongly recommended. In particular, it contains a detailed analysis of Steuart's stages theory. Also interesting articles are G.M. Anderson and R.B. Tollison 1984, 'Sir James Steuart as the apotheosis of mercantilism and his relation to Adam Smith', *Southern Economic Journal*, n. 51, and W. Eltis, 'Sir James Steuart's corporate state', in *Ideas in Economics*, edited by R.D.C. Black (Macmillan – now Palgrave Macmillan, London, 1986).

For a more recent evaluation of Steuart's contribution to economics see H.S. Yang, (1994), *The Political Economy of Trade and Growth: an Analytical Interpretation of Sir James Steuart's Inquiry* (Edward Elgar, Aldershot), and Ramón Tortajada (ed.), *The Economics of Sir James Steuart* (Routledge, London, 1999), which provides a general overview of Steuart's work by an international group of scholars.

10
Anne Robert Jacques Turgot, 1727–81: Investments and Returns

Anne Robert Jacques Baron de L'Aulne Turgot was born in Paris, the third son of a Norman family with a long tradition in the French administration and *magistrature*. He was destined originally for a career in the church, entered the Seminary of Saint-Sulpice and from June 1749 to 1751 was a student at the Theological Faculty of the University of Paris. After his father's death, Turgot received an inheritance which provided him with sufficient income to set out on an administrative career, thus avoiding taking final church vows. During the 1750s, Turgot took up appointment to some judicial positions. He also engaged in much intellectual activity, and had time to travel extensively throughout France in the company of Gournay, the Indendant of Trade. His contributions to the *Encyclopédie* spread his fame as a philosopher, and he became a friend of Voltaire.

In 1761 he was appointed *Intendant* of Limoges, a position he held for 13 years. He introduced reforms of the still existing feudal *corvée* and *milice* and established public workshops to assist a destitute population during the severe famine of 1769–72. In the 1760s he wrote most of his economic writings, in particular his most famous work: the *Réflexions sur la Formation et la Distribution des Richesses*. He also wrote many memoranda on public administration, often setting out the theoretical principles on which they were based. When Louis XVI succeeded to the throne in 1774, Turgot became member of the Royal Council, first as Minister of Navy and then as Minister of Finance, a position he was forced to resign in 1776 when the public failed to accept his reforms, the factor that made court intrigue against him successful. He died in Paris in March 1781.

Social classes: some revisions of physiocracy

Turgot is often considered to be a Physiocrat, may be because during 1774–76 when he was Finance Minister of Louis XVI, he introduced measures to liberalise the corn trade and abolished some taxes. Notwithstanding his close relationship with the Physiocrats, and the important influence of Quesnay's economics on his own work, Turgot never accepted their view of the exclusive productivity of agriculture and the sterility of industry. In a letter (February 1766) to Du Pont, Turgot wrote that the Physiocrats should stop calling industry sterile and thereby humiliate this class of honest men, because, while appearing to be the enemies of industry and trade, in reality their doctrines supported them (Turgot, 1992, p.4). Turgot also argued that the Physiocrats neglected 'distinguishing between the enlightened merchants who only desire freedom and... the petty, ignorant, greedy traders' (ibid., p. 5).

Moreover, Turgot abhorred the atmosphere of a closed group, or the sectarian spirit which characterised the Physiocrats. His friend, Du Pont fully accepted that Turgot was not a real Physiocrat (see Schelle, 1913, vol. II, no.1, p. 75). Finally, Turgot did not share the political views of the Physiocrats and, in particular, their idea of *legal despotism*. He emphasised that the principle of the enlightened monarch cannot be regarded as one of the pillars of the organisation of modern societies; that it was much better to adopt the simple principle of complete freedom (see the letters to Du Pont, February 1766, and to Tucker, December 1773, in Turgot, 1992, pp. 3–4, 50–1). Furthermore, Turgot disagreed with using expressions such as 'laws of natural order' as was often done by the Physiocrats (see ibid., p. 33). Above all, Turgot suggested that Physiocrats should insist more on the 'principle of competition and free trade, which follows immediately from the right to private property and from the special quality which *each individual has in knowing his own interests better than anybody else*', and that they should only oppose monopolies and exclusive privileges (Turgot, 1992, pp. 4–5, emphasis added in quote).

Turgot's remark combined two major criticisms of Quesnay's doctrine: his erroneous view of the sterility of manufacture and trade and the restricted role ascribed by the Physiocrats to individual motivations and choice.

It is interesting to note that Turgot wrote his major economic works the *Reflections* in the space of few months in 1766, though it was not published until 1769–70. Its ostensible purpose was the occasion of the visit to Paris of two Chinese students, who wanted to know more about the new science of society, brought about by the Enlightenment. The *Reflections* is a relatively short text, organised into a hundred dense, and sometimes extremely concise paragraphs.

The different qualities of land and its unequal distribution is one of the causes favouring the social division of labour, giving rise to an exchange economy. As in Petty, Cantillon and Quesnay the existence of a surplus in agriculture is essential for enabling increased specialisation or division of labour.

Turgot followed Quesnay in envisaging three major social classes; the *productive class*, which produces wage goods and raw materials, in short agriculture; the manufacturing or stipendiary class, and the landlords or disposable class. The people employed in industry are maintained by those occupied in agriculture, but Turgot did not view their activities as sterile. It is important to note that within the two producing classes, Turgot separated the employees from those who organise and direct the production, the capitalist farmers in agriculture and the master–entrepreneurs in industry. Apart from stating that agriculture is no longer the only productive activity, Turgot's emphasis on the role and figure of the entrepreneur, constitutes a further departure from physiocracy. The two main productive sectors, are therefore themselves subdivided into wage earning employees and profit making entrepreneurs.

The main characteristic of the landlords is the fact that they are the only class in society who can freely choose how to employ its revenue, which is, therefore, described as fully disposable. In particular, the landlords can decide which commodities to buy; they are the source of aggregate demand and they also determine the composition of final outputs. This view, likewise, owed much to Cantillon and Quesnay (see above, Chapters 6 and 7).

A final point on Turgot's view of society it worth noting: contemporaneously with Smith, Turgot had a four stage theory to describe the evolution of societies (see Chapter 8, above).

The distribution of output, profits and interest

It has just been indicated that Turgot's view of society suggested the existence of three major classes, of which two are sub-divided into employers and employees. How is the product distributed among these classes? First of all, Turgot clearly distinguished the surplus product of a country from the capital it used in production. Hence the overall product is initially divided into two parts, the portion essential for securing reproduction, and one that is 'disposable' or free. The 'free gift' of nature accrued to the landlord. A passage by Turgot from a letter to Hume of March 1767 dealt with this key principle of the new science of wealth. In it, Turgot examined the concepts of net product and reproduction, which he described as follows:

> the total product is divided into two parts: one destined for the reproduction of the following year, which includes not only that part of the product which is consumed in kind by the entrepreneur-farmers, but also what they use to pay the wages of all the different types of workmen... it also includes their profits and the interest on their advances. The other part is the net product which the farmer gives to the proprietor.
>
> (Turgot, 1992, p. 17)

This remark clearly indicates Turgot's position. 'Net product' is the share of the proprietor, this can be taken as equivalent to rent. Unlike the Physiocrats,

Turgot did not associate landed improvements (*avances foncières*) of the land-lords with the origin of property in land and the entitlement to rent (see two letters to Du Pont of February 1770 in Turgot, 1992, pp. 33, 38).

Turgot resolved the problem of farmers' profits by including them in the items necessary for reproduction and leaving them out of the disposable part of the net product. Hence profit are not disposable income suitable for taxation. The farmer is, therefore, not free to do what he wants with his profits, he has to reinvest them. This is why profits cannot be taxed. Aspects of this position clearly derive from Quesnay; however, in Turgot's work, profit is much more precisely differentiated both from the wages of superintendence of the cultivator and from the interest on his original advances, the fixed capital. Turgot's position is much closer than that of Quesnay to the concept of profit in proportion to the capital invested (as is further discussed in the next section of this chapter).

In a letter to Finance Minister, Terray, Turgot explained why landlords obtain the entire net product. Before the renewal of the leases, the whole net product over wages and the other expenses of cultivation goes to profits; but when leases are renewed, competition among the farmers trans-fers such profits to increase the rents of landlords. For Turgot, part of the increase in surplus is explained by a rise in the price of corn. Turgot spoke occasionally of primary *profit* as that part of an increase in surplus which follows directly from higher prices. Secondary *profit* is reserved for an increase in the net product, deriving from an increase of output and the accumulation of capital (Turgot, 1770, pp. 322, 327). However, Turgot emphasised that the farmers retained part of the net product as profits and in any case had the whole of the surplus until the renewal of the lease. On average, over the production cycle, farmers enjoyed a profit which was part of the net product (see ibid., pp. 301–4).

The passage quoted at the beginning of this section may give the impres-sion that Turgot considered the surplus of agriculture as a 'gift of nature'. This is not really true. For Turgot, the main cause of the productivity of land and hence of its physical surplus is not nature, but the use of appro-priate technology in cultivation. In a short essay of 1766, *Sur la grande et la petite culture*, Turgot indicated that the productivity of land was dependent on applying methods of production typical of large scale farming, only made possible by a requisite quantity of capital and advances to the farmers (see Turgot, 1766b, pp. 28–9). As for Quesnay, capital accumulation by wealthy farmers embodied the best available technology and was the main cause of labour and land productivity in the rural sector.

Returns and investments

Although Turgot adopted the concepts of 'advances', and saw capital as a physical input, in other passages he described 'capital' as general purchasing power, as an amount of monetary value which can be employed in different activities. He emphasised the fact that income, saving and investment constitute monetary flows. This view of capital stressed the existence of monetary circulation and opened the way for investigating the different possible ways in which capital can be employed, a topic of Turgot's economics which is of considerable importance.

According to Turgot, a monetary capital can be invested in five different ways (clearly described in sections 58, 59, 62, 66, and 71 of his *Reflections*). They can be used to buy a piece of land, so that the investor becomes a landlord; alternatively, the funds can be used to finance advances for manufacturing, and the investor becomes an entrepreneur. They can also be invested in agriculture, the investor then becomes a farmer; or use them in trade, the investor thus becoming a merchant; while finally money can be lent to others at interest. The interesting aspects of this analysis is that precisely because capital is a kind of 'movable wealth', it can move between these different types of employment according to the remuneration it obtains in them. The different types of investments have different rates of return depending mainly on the varying degree of risk attached to the different activities. In this way, the purchase of a landed estate yields the lowest return, a loan yields a higher return, while the 'the money invested in agricultural, manufacturing and commercial enterprises is bound to bring in more than the interest on money placed on loan' (Turgot, 1766, in Groenewegen, 1977, p. 86).

For Turgot, it was clear that the products 'of these different employments mutually limit one another, and in spite of their inequality are kept in a kind of equilibrium' (ibid., p. 172). The underlying idea is that there are interest rate differentials among the different employments of capital. These remain more or less constant, because 'as soon as the profits resulting from one employment of capital, whatever it may be, increase or diminish, capitals either turn in its direction and are withdrawn from other employments, or are withdrawn from it and turn in the direction of other employments' (ibid. p. 86).

As shown in Chapter 11 below, this discussion of capital circulation resembles Smith's analysis of the tendency towards a uniform rate of profit in conditions of free competition. In the analysis of the circulation of capital Turgot ascribed a particular role to money lending, because the rate of interest on money appeared to fix a minimum level for the returns on the other four possible types of investments. Moreover, Turgot conceived the interest on loans as a 'thermometer' of the relative abundance and scarcity of capital. Turgot added that interest should not be taxed, because it was an essential element of the advances in every type of employment of capital.

Finally, it is worth noting that in the analysis of the circulation of capital among the different types of employment, Turgot clearly used the concepts of interest, or profit, as a ratio, not as an absolute value, and this conception of profit as a rate subsequently became the prevailing one in economics.

A further important aspect of Turgot's economics is his analysis of the laws of returns with respect to agriculture, the clearest expression of which can be found in his *Observations on a Paper by Saint-Péravy*. Good agriculture tends to adopt techniques of production, requiring the substantial advances of the *grande culture*. This leads initially to increasing returns to scale and per unit of capital employed. With more advances, the produce will 'increase in a much larger proportion than the expenditure', but only up to the point 'at which the produce would be as large as possible relative to the advances. Past this point, if the advances are still further increased, the product will still increase, but less so, and continuously less and less until an addition to the advances would add nothing further to the produce' (Turgot, 1767, in Groenewegen, 1977, pp. 111).

Turgot made clear that production must not stop at the point in which the yield per unit of advance is highest, because in such a case, no advantage is taken of the increase in the overall net product of the soil that continues even when further increments of advances do not yield as much as previous increments (Turgot, 1767, p. 112).

Hence in agricultural production, several phases can be singled out: first, there are increasing returns; when accumulation continues the output does not increase in proportion and eventually there are diminishing returns. This analysis did not relate variations in productivity to different qualities of land but highlighted the returns on the intensive margin, a problem which received much attention in the early nineteenth century. According to Turgot, the cultivator must not cease investing when highest return per unit of advances is reached; but he must continue to invest as long as the increment of advances yield a satisfactory return as compared to other investment yields.

Value and prices

Turgot's analysis of value is interesting, but poses problems of interpretation: he may be seen either as a follower of Quesnay, or as a forerunner of the type of subjective theory of value which emerged during the nineteenth century (below, Part II introduction). On some occasions, Turgot used the notions of current and fundamental price in a similar way to Quesnay. In the *Reflections*, the current price is defined as the ordinary market price determined by demand and supply (Turgot 1766, in Groenewegen, 1977, pp. 136–7). In a letter to Hume (1767), Turgot indicated that the fundamental value, by contrast, is the permanent and stable value of the market price of commodities. Hence there are two concepts of price: 'the current price which is determined by the relationship of supply and demand; and the fundamental price which for a commodity is what the thing costs the workman' (Turgot, 1992, p. 18).

The fundamental price invariably includes the workman's wages, or the costs of his subsistence but the workers also need to obtain a certain extra for unexpected events, otherwise they will not continue production. But 'in a nation where commerce and industry are free and active, competition settles this profit at the lowest possible rate' (ibid.). Turgot identified a very precise relationship between current and fundamental price; 'althought the fundamental price is not the immediate basis of the current value, it is, however, a minimum below which it cannot fall' (ibid.). In short, fundamental price is a kind of floor to prices, clearly implying that reproduction would cease if the current exchange value is unable to cover the overall expenses inclusive of a moderate profit.

Turgot went on to state that there is an equilibrium between the two notions of price; he illustrates this by the metaphor of liquid in communicating vessels, where it might take some time to achieve this equilibrium, but that, nevertheless, it will inevitably be achieved (ibid., pp. 18–19). Turgot also described fundamental price a kind of 'natural resting point' (ibid., pp. 19).

The same notion of fundamental value appeared in a footnote to his *Observations on a Paper by Saint-Péravy*, where Turgot stressed the relative stability of fundamental value, and that this concept of price covered expenses for raw materials, wages and interest on the advances (Turgot 1767, in Groenewegen, 1977, p. 120). Moreover he reiterated that market value continuously tended to approach the fundamental value, and could not permanently move away from it. The notion of the need for standard interest on the advances of the farmer also appeared in the 1770 *Letters to Abbé Térray on the Corn Trade* (Turgot 1770, in Groenewegen, 1977, pp. 172–4).

In an unfinished paper of 1769, *Value and Money*, Turgot provided what appears as a different analysis of the exchange value of commodities. Two points need to be stressed in this context. First, Turgot spoke of *valeur estimative*, by which he seemed to imply the fundamentally subjective nature of value, because it was an evaluation of the individual (an isolated individual at the start of the paper). Value, therefore is the degree of appreciation that man ascribes to the different objects he desires (Turgot, 1769, in Groenewegen, 1977, p. 139). In this context, Turgot referred to Galiani's *Della Moneta* (see above, Chapter 9).

Later in the paper, Turgot described an exchange of commodities against commodities, corn against wood, and that an exchange will take place only if the two contracting sides have different evaluations for the commodities exchanged. In fact, it is essential that the valeur estimative should be different because 'it is thus always equally true that each gives a equal value to receive equal value' (ibid., p. 142, italics in the original). Hence, goods exchanged have the same exchangeable value so that differences in esteem value make exchanges possible. Those buying wood in exchange for corn, need to assign to the quantity of wood they obtain a higher value than what they give to the quantity of corn they forego, and vice versa for the other party in exchange.

Another interesting point to note concerns the method adopted by Turgot to illustrate the price determination mechanism and hence to answer the question: how is the exchange ratio between corn and wood fixed? Turgot proceeds with a series of examples in a process of successive approximations from what he considers the simplest act of exchange, that taking place between two isolated individuals, to more complicated models, involving four exchangers, two on each side and so on.

Unfortunately, the paper on *Value and Money* was not finished and its contents are rather difficult to reconcile with Turgot's notion of fundamental value. However, Turgot did leave some room also for the role of costs in value. In fact, the essay may not have been completed because of the difficulty of building a theory of value on the notion of utility. Alternatively, Turgot only mentioned esteem value as a factor influencing market price, and not fundamental value, in which case there is no contradiction. What is extant of *Value and Money* does not mention fundamental value or costs of production, but allows for labour costs as potential influences on esteem values.

Notes on further readings

The most complete edition of Turgot's works is that of G. Schelle, *Oeuvres de Turgot et documents le concernant* (Félix Alcan, Paris, 1913–1923) including much correspondence, relevant documents and a detailed biography.

Various English translations of Turgot's writings are available: these include *Sur la grande et la petite culture* (1766), Reprints of Economic Classics, series 2, Number 2, University of Sydney, *Extracts from His Economic Correspondence, 1765–1778*, Reprints of Economic Classics, series 2, Number 6, University of Sydney (1992). These are quoted here as Turgot (1766b) and (1992) (P.D. Groenewegen, *The Economics of A.R.J. Turgot*, Martin Nijoff, The Hague, 1977) provides translation of Turgot's major economic work, with an introduction and editorial notes. All references in the text are to those translations. Groenewegen, 'A Reinterpretation of Turgot's Theory of Capital and Interest', *Economic Journal*, vol. 81, June, 1971, remains a useful discussion of Turgot on this topic. Turgot's use of a stages theory of history is discussed at length in R.L. Meek (ed.), *Turgot on Progress, Sociology and Economics* (Cambridge University Press, Cambridge, 1973) which also translates his *On Universal History*, and the *Reflections*. On the economic and social situation in France in the time of Turgot, reference can still usefully made to D. Dakin, *Turgot and the Ancien Régime in France* (Methuen, London, 1939).

Section IV

The First Full Systems of Classical Political Economy

11
Adam Smith 1723–90: National Wealth and the Productivity of Labour

Adam Smith was born on 5 June 1723 in Kirkcaldy, Scotland. He was the son of the Clerk to the Court martial and Comptroller of Customs in the town. Smith attended the High School in Kirkcaldy and in 1737, and at the early age of fourteen, proceeded to Glasgow University. In 1740 he left Glasgow for Oxford as a Snell Exhibitioner at Balliol College to begin a six-year period of postgraduate study. Although, the atmosphere of the college was Jacobite and anti-Scot it gave Smith easy access to the excellent libraries of this ancient university.

Smith left Oxford in 1746 and returned to Kirkcaldy without any definite plan for a career. However, in 1748 he was invited to give a series of public lectures in Edinburgh, these gained Smith a reputation as a lecturer. In 1751, he was elected to the Chair of Logic at Glasgow University and in 1752 he was appointed to its Chair of Moral Philosophy, a position he preferred. During this period, he published his first major book, the *Theory of Moral Sentiments (1759)*.

In 1764, Smith resigned his chair to accept the post of tutor of the young Duke of Buccleuch, about to set out on his European grand tour. This included Paris (where Smith met Quesnay and Turgot) and Geneva (where he met Voltaire). Smith returned to London in 1766, then stayed at Kirkcaldy for about six years. During this time he prepared his major work, *An Inquiry into the Nature and Causes of the Wealth of Nations* (here after WN), published in 1776. In 1778 he was appointed Commissioner of Customs. Smith worked hard both for the Commission and at new editions of his books until his death on 17 July 1790. He never married and during the last years of life, enjoyed very poor health. His will instructed two of his friends, Joseph Black and James Hutton, to burn most of his papers. Some of the papers specifically exempted from this instruction were published in 1795 as *Essays on Philosophical Subjects*.

Smith did not have a particularly exciting life, but his *WN* represents two fundamental milestones in the history of economics. It is the first work which explicitly destroyed the mercantilist conception of wealth; secondly, it provided a benchmark for almost all further development of economic analysis and debate, becoming the major source of inspiration for many in the subsequent generations of economic writers. *WN* is a real turning point in making economics a separate science. However, the role of Smith in the development of economic theories is also subject to much controversy: first, some commentators regard Smith as a mere collector of already existing concepts and theories, who often failed to mention his predecessors (for example, Schumpeter, 1954 and Rashid, 1998). In a sense this is true, and the preceding chapters of this book testify to the many important concepts and theories already available in the Europe of the Enlightenment.

One of the reasons for the greatness of Smith is precisely the way in which he organised these views and concepts into a system. Moreover, the success of *WN* is also explained by the fact that it provided answers to many major contemporary problems of economic policy. History, theory and policy all play important roles in Smith's work and form an essential element of classical political economy.

Since the late 1960s, and in particular following A. L. Macfie (1967), investigation of Smith the economist draws more attention to ethical and methodological aspects; a practice especially adopted by Andrew Skinner and Donald Winch. This revision has renewed interest in the question of the relationships between Smith's early works and his *WN*, revitalising a debate initiated by German scholars of the nineteenth century, called *Das Adam Smith Problem*. Are there conflicting views on the fundamental principle of human behaviour in Smith's major books, that is, an altruistic one in his *Theory of Moral Sentiments*, and a selfish one in his *WN*?

There are also opposing views about whether Smith's economics belongs to the so-called surplus approach or to the tradition of efficient allocation of resources based on the market mechanism of 'supply and demand' (see, for example, Napoleoni, 1975 and Hollander, 1973 as leading representatives of these opposite views).

Finally (and the final major issue of content for this chapter): Smith's works can be divided into two different periods; first is the material produced before his journey to France, the other the preparation of his *WN* which came after that event. But how much does his *WN* owe to physiocracy? Which notions can be found in the writings of the fifties and early sixties and which ones were adapted from the physiocrats, or, more specifically, from Turgot?

Before *WN:* with special reference to *Theory of Moral Sentiments*

The most interesting of Smith's *Philosophical Essays* is the *History of Astronomy*, which reveals the influence on Smith of natural science, and in particular of the views thereon of Bacon and Newton. It also provides interesting indications of Smith's method. These indications can also be found in his *WN* where there are passages in which he seems to establish a very strong link between the natural order, or nature, and a well-organised civil society. Institutions and men can disturb the natural course of events (see *WN*, III.i.4), but the laws of nature seem to be powerful enough to overcome the effects of misgovernment:

> The wisdom of nature has fortunately made ample provisions for remedying many bad effects of the folly and injustice of man.
>
> (*WN*, IV.ix.28)

However, Smith did not take a naive approach to the study of organised society; he cannot be regarded as a strict determinist for whom civil laws and human societies are simply a copy of the natural order. The *History of Astronomy* provides an example of a careful and non-deterministic methodology, even if it contains the first use of the expression 'invisible hand' (see *Astronomy*, III.2). Other examples of Smith's prudence in embracing drastic generalisations can be seen in his *WN* (I.xi.m.12).

The same is true for Smith's view of human behaviour. Recent debates on the *Theory of Moral Sentiments* have shown that Smith's analysis of civil societies is far more complicated than the simple self-interest plus free competition model often attributed to his economic work. In the *Theory*, the principle of sympathy dominated all other human passions; this is the ability of men to share in some degree the sentiments of other people, a fellow-feeling, which provides the cement for every society. Men can be more or less virtuous, ranging from self-love to benevolence, but each man has the possibility to form his own judgements as if he were an impartial spectator. The impartial spectator is a metaphor Smith used to enlighten what he saw as an ideal rule in the behaviour of the individual in societies. This meant that each man should view 'himself in the light in which he is conscious the others will view him'; in this way:

> the impartial spectator may enter into the principles of his conduct [and he will] humble the arrogance of his self-love and bring it down to something that other men can go along with.
>
> (*Theory*. II.ii.2.1)

However, society also needs obedience to the rules of justice, or positive laws. This obedience is a more modest approach to virtue, but without it society would be destroyed by continual fighting: 'justice ... is the main pillar which upholds the whole edifice' (see ibid., II.ii.3.4). Note that the metaphor of the invisible hand also appears in the *Theory of Moral Sentiments* (see ibid., IV.i.10).

That Smith did not consider men to be fundamentally selfish is clear from his comments on the other systems of ethics in Part VII Section II, Chapter IV of his *Theory of Moral Sentiments*, where he strongly opposed the view of Mandeville, and also of Hume, that in different ways emphasise the role of utility in guiding the actions of mankind. However, it must be noted that Smith likewise disagreed with his predecessor in the Chair of Moral Philosophy at Glasgow, Frances Hutcheson, who believed men's actions were fundamentally guided by benevolence.

For Smith, the study of individual behaviour is a central aspect of his theory of the prosperity of society and of liberty; there is a continuous interaction between social norms and individual behaviour in which both terms are shaped and transformed. This view of man in society is part of the process of the liberation of individuals from the bondage of the feudal system and opens the way to the notion of the modern state.

The Lectures on Jurisprudence

Smith's *Lectures on Jurisprudence* are made up of two sets of notes taken by Smith's students at Glasgow during the academic years of 1762/63 and 1763/64. These *Lectures* contain more extensive economic material than his *Theory of Moral Sentiments*. Several important notions which later appeared in the *Wealth of Nations* give an idea of the state of Smith's elaboration of economic material before his journey to France. The *Lectures* also seem to be the first attempt at the history of jurisprudence to which Smith refers at the end of his *Theory of Moral Sentiments*; at the same time they attempt to explain the history of civil societies. Smith used the four stages theory in order to explain the emergence of the commercial stage (see *Lectures*, i.27–35). Other economic arguments from the *Lectures* contain the social division of labour, which depends on the ability of agriculture to produce subsistence goods for the artisans, the technical aspects of the division of labour, whose analysis resembles that of the pin factory example in *WN* (see ibid., vi.29–30), the identification of three specific causes of improvements in productivity (see WN.,vi.38), the fact that the division of labour depends on the extent of the market (see WN., vi.63–4), and an indication of the several disadvantages which the division of labour also entails.

The analysis of price formation is likewise already well advanced in the *Lectures*. In particular, the *Lectures* contains notions of natural and market price, and the tendency of market price to gravitate towards natural value (see Lectures., pp. vi.67–86). There is also an analysis of the circulation of capital within a competitive system, but this mechanism was much more clearly described in the later *WN*. The *Lectures* lack any real analysis of the composition of the capital stock of society, the distinction between gross and net product and that between productive and unproductive labour.

An Inquiry into the Nature and Causes of the Wealth of Nation (1776)

What are the major merits of this book, so revered in the history of economics? First, the title of the book emphasised Smith's view about the object of political economy, a science which for him needed to generate a theory of the growth of national wealth. As he stated in Book II: 'But the great object of the political oeconomy of every country, is to encrease the riches and power of that country' (*WN*, II.v.31). Book IV praised Quesnay because he provided the definition of 'Political Oeconomy, or of the nature and causes of the wealth of nations' (*WN*, IV.ix.38). Although national wealth had previously been discussed with merit by Boisguilbert; in Cantillon's *Essay* and (in his opening chapter) was analysed in some detail by Turgot, none of these authors organised their entire economic argument and its presentation around the theme of nature and causes of the *Wealth of Nations*.

Secondly, it is sufficient to look at the table of contents of *WN* to appreciate that the order of presentation of the various economic topics is rather novel with respect both to Smith's previous work in the *Lectures* and to that of all of his predecessors. (A comparison of the economic contents of Smith's *Wealth of Nations* and that of Sir James Steuart's *Principles of Political Oeconomy* illustrates this particularly well). In Book I, a major cause of productivity, the division of labour, is followed by chapters on money and value, including discussion of the relationship between market and natural price, and concluded with chapters dealing with the three distributive categories: the rate of wages, profits and rent. Book II deals with the second great cause of labour productivity and growth of wealth: accumulation of capital or the proportions of productive and unproductive labour in society. No such emphasis given to the division of labour as the main principle of national wealth was ever repeated in later volumes of economic principles.

At the end of the *Introduction*, which contains a summary of the entire work, Smith included a definition of wealth: 'the real wealth, the annual produce of the land and labour of society'. Smith repeatedly used the expression 'annual produce' to indicate the wealth of a country, sometimes he used the term revenue as synonymous. At other times, wealth appears to be equated with annual consumption. Although such variations in terminology and the reference to consumption have created doubts about the adequacy of Smith's position on national wealth and on his distinction between net and gross revenue based on wages (see for instance *WN*, II.ii.5), two points are clear: first, wealth is made up of commodities and not of precious metals and these, generally speaking, are the outcome of productive processes; secondly, wealth is a flow concept and 'annual produce' resembles today's GNP to a remarkable extent.

The division of labour

Following his customary method of analysing and explaining major problems by reference to simple principles, Smith immediately presented his major explanation for the growth of national wealth. This is the division of labour. Both gross and net revenue of society depend upon it. The first three chapters of Book I illustrate why the social and technical division of labour are a major cause of the improvements of the productive powers of labour. It is clear from Book I that Smith wished to stress his own explanation of prosperity, which sharply contrasted with that of the mercantilist notion of surplus in the balance of trade. Book IV is therefore largely devoted to criticising Mercantilism and its policies, as one of the wrong systems of political economy, the other being physiocracy.

The existence of a physical surplus of subsistence goods, of food (*WN*, I.xi. Part I.2), favours the division of labour (see *WN*, I.xi.c.7, III.i.2). This surplus produce of land is what remains after the consumption of cultivators and proprietors has been deducted (see *WN*, IV.ix.17). The size of the surplus produce of agriculture enables the emergence first of manufacture and then of domestic and foreign trade (see *WN*, IV.ix.22). The wealthier societies are characterised by a more complex social division of labour, which means that people can specialise in the production of a single commodity and then increase their productivity. Smith emphasised the superior productivity of agriculture (*WN*, II.v.12, IV.ix.30), but also stated that there is more scope for the application of the division of labour in manufacture than in agriculture (see *WN*, I.i.4, IV.ix.35). More generally, Smith indicated that application of the division of labour was limited by the extent of the market (*WN*, I, iii), since the increased output, and subsequently, revenue, itself increased the extent of the market. Smith's vision of growth was therefore that of a cumulative process, an optimistic view which contrasts with the later pessimistic growth models of Malthus and Ricardo (Section V).

An extensive social division of labour facilitates a more extensive technical one. The pin- example illustrated the advantages of reducing a complex production to a number of simple operations. Three reasons explain the subsequent improvement in productivity (see *WN*, I.i.6–8): first, the repetition of the same simple operation improves the dexterity of the worker; secondly, time is saved in not having to move from one operation to others; thirdly, the simpler the operations to be undertaken, the easier it is for the workers to introduce small innovations and to invent machines which facilitate production. Smith remarked that the division of labour also had some negative effects. For example, by always repeating the same operations, individual workers lose involvement in the whole process, and tend to become dull, if not, ineffective operators (see *WN*, V, 1). At the end of the eighteenth century, several other authors appreciated this problem.

The picture of the division of labour drawn by Adam Smith implies an explanation of increasing return to scale with reference to the number of productive workers. However, achievement of this requires an accumulation of capital, enabling the employment of more workers. Before turning to this issue in Book II of *WN*, Smith dealt with value and its measurement, price determination and the distribution of the annual produce among the various orders of society.

Value theory and the notion of natural price

A monetary economy, which must facilitate exchange, greatly favours the diffusion of the division of labour (see *WN*, I.iv). The exchange value of commodities can be represented in various ways; money is usually adopted as measurement unit in exchanges and when commodities are expressed in money terms they are said to be given a nominal price (see *WN*, I.v). In addition, Smith introduced a notion of real price, that is, the quantity of labour that a commodity can buy, or command, at the current wage rate. The use of 'labour commanded' for evaluating commodities was relevant to the theory of accumulation, because it immediately indicates the number of new workers which can be employed by a particular set of commodities, whether in the form of the existing stock of capital, or of the physical surplus of wage goods.

How did Smith determine the relative value of commodities? 'In that early and rude state of society which precedes the accumulation of stock and the appropriation of land, the proportion between the quantities of the labour necessary for acquiring different objects' (see *WN*, I.vi.1) is the only rule for determining exchange value. This labour theory of value is illustrated by Smith's famous example of the two hunters. If two days are required to kill a beaver and only one is necessary for a deer, then the only possible price is two deer for one beaver (see WN, I.vi.1); for any other exchange ratio one of the two hunters will find it more convenient to search directly for the good.

The primitive rule for a society of hunters is no longer appropriate for a more advanced state of society, where the means of production and natural resources have accumulated in the hands of particular persons and have become private property. In the commercial stage of society, the price of commodities must include also profits for the capitalist entrepreneur and rent for the owners of land (see *WN*, I.vi.5–10):

> When the price of any commodity is neither more nor less than what is sufficient to pay the rent of the land, the wages of the labour, and the profits of the stock employed in raising, preparing, and bringing it to market, according to their natural rates, the commodity is then sold for what may be called its natural price.
>
> (*WN*, I.vii.4)

The natural price is the cost for the producers when inputs are paid at their natural rates, that is, under competitive conditions. If the natural price is measured in real terms, as labour commanded, it needs to be higher than the labour embodied, because now the exchange value also includes profits and rent. This can be illustrated as follows:

Let r be the uniform rate of profit, r_e and w rent and wages per unit of land and labour respectively; L, T and K respectively the quantities of labour, land and capital directly and indirectly employed in the production of one unit of a commodity: the natural price may be described as follows:

$$p_n = wL + r_eT + rK$$

When inputs, and in particular capital, can circulate freely among the productive sectors of the economy, the natural price depends on two sets of elements: first, the techniques of production, described by the unit coefficient of production; second, the distribution of income between wages, profits and rent. With a precise indication of its component parts, the notion of natural price provides a link between value and distribution, and profits have become an essential and permanent component of the value of commodities. Subsequently, natural price is also elegantly related to market price.

In order to examine the market price of a commodity Smith introduced the concept of 'effectual demand ... the demand of those who are willing to pay the natural price of the commodity' (*WN*, I.vii.8). If the quantity produced and brought to the market is below the effectual demand, competition ensues among buyers and market price exceeds natural price. Market price is therefore a short term price depending on 'greatness of the deficiency or of the excess' of output relative to demand on the strength of the competition. In a competitive economy, characterised by capital mobility and free entry of resources into each productive sector, all market prices in the long run 'gravitate' towards their natural level.

For smooth operation of this competitive mechanism, capitalist-entrepreneurs need not know in advance the natural rate of profit or the natural price. They need only to be well informed about profit rates in general and base their investment decisions on profit rate differentials.

The natural price is a fundamental concept in classical political economy. Long run values and the profitability of investments for classical economists do not depend on short-term market fluctuations. The part of the surplus destined for the accumulation of capital, that is to say profits, depend exclusively on technology and on the overall characteristic of income distribution.

Distribution and the rate of profit

The natural rates of wages, profits and rent depends 'partly on the general circumstances of the societies, their riches or poverty, their advancing, stationary, or declining condition; and partly on the particular nature of each employment' (*WN*, I.vii.1).

Nations experience, in Smith's view, a sort of long-run economic cycle. The size of their capital stock, and especially the rate of its accumulation, are the key determinants of the particular phase in which the economy and the distribution of income are placed. When profits are vigorously reinvested, demand for labour tends to sustain the value of wages, as happened in England during the previous century (see *WN*, I.viii.35). However, the process of capital accumulation entails a gradual reduction of profitability (see *WN*, I,.ix.10), and a declining rate of interest (see *WN*, I.ix.11). A subsequent slowdown of accumulation leads to a phase of stagnant wages and low profits.

In Smith, profitability is firmly anchored in the ratio of profit to capital invested, and completely disassociated from differences between selling and buying prices as in the now discredited mercantilist concept of 'profit upon alienation'. The rate of profit depends upon the stock of capital and competition among capitalists. Nor is profit a form of wages of superintendence, or a compensation for entrepreneurial risks.

Smith presented a notion of the subsistence wage in which:

> the money price of corn regulates that of all other home-made commodities. It regulates the money price of labour, which must always be such as to enable the labourer to purchase a quantity of corn sufficient to maintain him and his family.
>
> (*WN*, IV.v.a.12, see also II.iii.7)

In addition, wages are influenced by the demand for labour and can vary from country to country. Smith was also aware that competitive forces in the labour market are limited and unevenly balanced, because entrepreneurs invariably exhibit much stronger bargaining power than workers.

Smith's analysis of rent is sometimes seen as somewhat confused. Part of his long account on the subject suggests the idea of an absolute rent of a feudal kind (*WN*, I.vi.8). Elsewhere, rent is shown to depend on the prices of necessaries and considered to be residual, on other occasion, agricultural surplus is equated to rent (*WN*, I.xi.Part 1.2). There are also hints at an association between the size of rent and differential fertility and locational advantage.

The accumulation of capital and productive labour

Smith sharply distinguished the capital of a country from its revenue (*WN*, II.iii.4). The existence of adequate revenue induces accumulation of capital when revenue is saved and invested, in turn generating improvement in industry (*WN*, IV.ii.13). Accumulation of capital arises from savings out of surplus, particularly profits (*WN*, IV.ii.13). In short, saving, or parsimony, are key determinants of capital accumulation.

Technical progress is part and parcel of capital accumulation. Hence, capital accumulation is the key to productivity growth and wealth (see *WN*, II.iii, in particular 8, 13–18, 32) and, 'the accumulation of stock must, in the nature of things, be previous to the division of labour' (*WN*, II, 'Introduction', p.3). Accumulation therefore produces 'this great improvement in the productive powers of labour' (ibid., p. 4), which leads to increasing returns (see *WN*, II.ii.7).

Smith therefore identified two main causes of economic growth: first, improvements in dexterity of productive workers, associated with division of labour; secondly, an increase in the numbers of productive workers relative to unproductive ones, synonymous for Smith with the accumulation of capital. Equipped with a theory explaining growth from capital accumulation and endogenous technical progress, Smith easily avoided the Physiocratic error of ascribing exclusive productivity to agriculture (see *WN*, IV.ix.29). Nevertheless, in Smith, the existence of a physical surplus in the primary sector is a crucial prerequisite for the social division of labour, and there is a positive, dynamic interdependence between manufacturing and agriculture, because during growth, each sector fosters the expansion of the other (see *WN*, III.iii.20).

Smith did not devise a single, clear-cut criterion for distinguishing between productive and unproductive activities. Sometimes he saw labourers employed in the production of material goods as productive, labour employed in services as unproductive. On other occasions, he considered activities leading to output growth and a surplus which can be accumulated, as productive. Smith also analysed the different components of the national capital stock, and likewise distinguished fixed from circulating capital. Fixed capital for him included all inputs which enabled a profit without themselves having to be exchanged. Smith considered wages as being part of the circulating capital of a country (*WN*, II.ii.25, 37). Wages, as an element of 'provisions', were part of the 'stock reserved for immediate consumption' (*WN*, II.i.23, cf. *WN*, V.ii.k.43, V.iii.53).

Commodities entering capital need to be measured according to their natural prices. Hence the value of produced means of production is given by the wages, profits and rents which have been paid out to produce them. Thus the Gross National Product of a country is likewise measured by the sum of the three types of income: wages, profits and rent. Smith therefore had a theory of surplus over wages (see O'Donnell, 1990, pp.34ff.), where the wages portion of national output represent the overall capital, profits and rent the surplus portion.

Extension of the market and of international trade

The close interdependence between the theories of wealth and international trade is clear in the very title of chapter III of book I 'That the

Division of Labour is limited by the Extent of the Market'. For Smith, the effectual demand, that is to say, the purchasing power of the domestic market may act as a possible limit to capital accumulation, and hence to both the social and the technical division of labour. For every country, free trade opens a way for gaining all the advantages of the division of labour and hence for raising labour productivity. Foreign trade, enabling output sales in excess of domestic consumption thereby favours productivity growth. This is so-called 'vent for surplus' problem (see *WN*, II.v.34, IV.i.31).

Volumes have been written about Smith's liberalism, but he was never a naive supporter of free trade. Foreign trade, as just shown, was to the mutual advantage of all trading nations. Such benefits are essentially dynamic phenomena, arising as they do from increasing returns. The static advantages from more efficient resource allocation according to natural endowments were only a very small aspect of such benefits from free trade for Smith.

Moreover, when dealing with the relationships between rich and poor nations, Smith did not take the view that the latter ones will invariably benefit from free trade (see Myint, 1977, pp. 246–8). Hume had earlier discussed issues of trade between rich and poor countries, and Smith's so-called *Early Draft of the Wealth of Nations* (probably written before his journey to France) includes some interesting remarks on this subject. These deny automatic mechanisms guaranteeing catching up or convergence of the poorer countries towards income levels of rich ones. On the contrary, wealthy nations have a greater interest in trading among themselves, because of their rich markets, than with poor countries (see Smith, 1763, p. 578). Poor countries hence experience great difficulties in the international market, because, 'it is easier for a nation, in the same manner as for an individual, to raise itself from a moderate degree of wealth to the highest opulence, than to acquire this moderate degree of wealth' (ibid., p. 579).

The first step is therefore the most difficult one, there seems to be a threshold in the process of development. Why this difficulty? For Smith, the reasons lie in the very essence of the process of economic growth. Quite frequently, a poor country did not have the resources to adopt production techniques in use among richer nations. Smith's list of the impediments facing poor countries in their first steps into a development process given in this draft is fascinating. They are:

'the extreme difficulty of beginning accumulations and',
'the many accidents to which it is exposed',
'The slowness and difficulty with which those things, which now appear the most simple inventions, were originally found out'; the fact that 'a nation is not always in a condition to imitate and copy the inventions and improvements of its more wealthy neighbours'; that their

'application of these frequently requiring a stock which is not furnished'; while in addition,

'oppressive and injudicious governments to which mankind are almost always subject, but [are] more especially [prevalent] in the rude beginnings of society'.

The initial lack of capital is the really crucial one among these impediments. For Smith, the fundamental issue was not lack of knowledge, but lack of the necessary capital, because introduction of new technologies generally requires more capital. Productivity increases and technological progress therefore depend on the accumulation of capital, a process which is difficult to trigger in the countries which are late-comers in international markets, or, to use the contemporary phrase, the global economy.

There may also be negative effects for a rich country, in particular lack of competition. For instance, Smith vigorously opposed monopoly in colonial trade which fosters high rates of profit because such high rates destroy a spirit of parsimony (see *WN*, IV.vii.c.61).

Book V is dedicated to the role of government and to public economics. This includes his famous three tasks of government: defence, justice and public works and public institutions. It is worth noting that among the latter item, Smith included education; and the advice that it was essentially the responsibility of the state to counter the negative effects of the division of labour on process workers through education.

Concluding comments

Smith believed that human society is capable of moving along a path of progress and that there are some fundamental principles facilitating such progress. These include principles in human nature: self love, sympathy and self command; principles in nature such as the invisible hand; principles in the relationship between nature and men such as technology and the division of labour. But the manner in which these principles combine in an actual society is not easy to predict. The 'system of natural liberty' describes a model to which societies must tend to conform, but it cannot be taken simply as an *actual* economy.

Smith's fame largely and appropriately rests on his economic analysis. He completed a process of revision and innovation in theories of national wealth which had begun with Petty more than a century before the publication his *Wealth of Nations*.

However, both in Smith's view of man and society, and in his economic analysis, there are unresolved issues. In particular, there is a flaw in Smith's determination of the rate of profit. The concept of natural price failed to provide a satisfactory link between Smith's analysis of surplus and his theory of the rate of profit and of accumulation. Something is missing between his notion of a physical surplus and the way in which it is distributed, and in particular the way in which the rate of profit is determined (see O'Donnell, 1990).

The profit rate is assumed to be known when natural prices of commodities are determined, a fundamental step for measurement of gross output, capital and wages. But the profit rate itself cannot be determined until profits and aggregate capital are known, since it is calculated from profits per unit of capital invested. This logical flaw was overcome by Ricardo and Marx (as shown below in Chapters 14 and 16).

Notwithstanding such limitations, it is difficult to find another economic writer with such a wide and deep perspective on the analysis of society. Perhaps only Marx attempted a similar task, but he never managed to complete it. Moreover, Smith's merits flow from this ability to present arguments which proved useful in interpreting the then new commercial and industrial stage of history, and enormously inspired the next generation of political economists in England, in France, and in fact in all countries where the economy was studied and debated.

Notes on further readings

The number of books and articles dedicated to Smith is immense. Hence only major readings are suggested. The best edition of the works of Smith, the so-called Glasgow edition, was initiated in 1976 by Oxford University Press on the occasion of the bicentenary of the *Wealth of Nations*. The classical biography of Smith is that of his friend Dugald Stewart, *Account of the Life and Writings of Adam Smith, LL.D.* (1793), in Smith (1795); see also the book by John Rae, *Life of Adam Smith* (Macmillan– now Palgrave Macmillan, London 1895) and more recently I.S. Ross, *The Life of Adam Smith* (Clarendon Press, Oxford, 1995). All references in the text are given to the Glasgow editions of the works, and the introductions to them provide useful insights on Smith's works.

On the *Lectures*, see Cannan's Introduction to his 1896 edition and that by Meek, Raphael and Stein in the Glasgow edition. Hirschman (1977) gives a fascinating description of the process which led to the breakdown of feudal society and of the role played by commerce in it. A negative view of Smith's originality in economics is in S. Rashid, *The Myth of Adam Smith* (Edward Elgar, Aldershot, 1998).

The new approach to the interpretation of Smith's two major published works, *Theory of Moral Sentiments* and *The Wealth of Nations* owes much to the research of A.L. Macfie, *The Individual in Society – Papers on Adam Smith*, London: Allen and Unwin, 1967.

On the theories of growth of Smith and Quesnay see W. Eltis (1984). A further comparison of the theories of Quesnay and Smith is in G. Vaggi, 'The limits of physiocracy and Smith's fortune', *Economies et Sociétés – Série*

Oeconomia, Histoire de la Pensée économique, 1995, P.E. nos 22–3, 29(1–2). See also A. Brewer, *The Making of the Classical Theory of Economic Growth*, London: Routledge, 2010.

On the relationship between Turgot and Smith, see Groenewegen (1969) and Meek (1973). On Smith's view of free trade, consult the famous essay by J. Viner (1928), 'Adam Smith and laissez-faire', in *Adam Smith, 1776–1926* (Augustus M. Kelley, New York 1966) and D. Winch, 'Adam Smith: The Prophet of Free Enterprise?', *History of Economics Review*, no. 16, Summer 1991. An important collection of essays on Smith is T. Wilson and A. Skinner (eds), *The Market and the State* (Oxford University Press, Oxford, 1976), a companion edition to the bi-centenary edition of the works. Perceptive accounts of the division of labour are P.D. Groenewegen, 'Adam Smith and the division of labour: a bicentenary estimate', *Australian Economic Papers*, vol. 16, no. 29, 1977; S. Rashid, 'Adam Smith and the division of labour: a historical view', *Scottish Journal of Political Economy*, no. 33(3), August, 1986, pp. 292–7.

On Smith's moral philosophy see J. Evensky, *A Historical and Contemporary Perspective on Markets, Law, Ethics and Culture*, Cambridge: Cambridge University Press, 2005. Smith's contributions to economics are comprehensively analysed in A. Aspromourgos, *The Science of Wealth. Adam Smith and the Framing of Political Economy*, London: Routledge, 2009. Useful collections of important contributions to the understanding of Smith's views are K. Haakonssen, ed., *The Cambridge Companion to Adam Smith*, Cambridge: Cambridge University Press, 2006 and Jeffrey T. Young, *The Elgar Companion to Adam Smith*, Cheltenham: Edward Elgar, 2009.

12

Jean-Baptiste Say, 1767–1832 and Jean-Charles Simonde de Sismondi, 1773–1842: Value, Revenues and Crises

Between Smith and Ricardo there is a period of transition characterised by important changes both in the main economic themes and in the way of analysing them. The French Revolution and the Napoleonic wars left a deep mark on economic debates. England was horrified by the events of the French Revolution and by the period of the so called 'terror', especially the beheading of Louis XVI. In his *Reflections on the Revolution in France* (1790) Edmund Burke put forward an interpretation of Smith designed to oppose the thought of the author of the *Wealth of Nations* to the liberal and radical views of the revolutionary leaders. The economic debates during the final decade of the eighteenth century are succinctly described in Winch (1996, especially chapters 5 and 7).

The new century, in short, opened with a reaction to the more liberal and egalitarian interpretation of Smith and of contemporary French thinkers. The general mood therefore became quite different from that of the Enlightenment. This perspective on the period helps appreciation of the gradual emergence of concepts and views that ultimately led to Marginalism. Several other important figures characterise this epoch, but the two authors chosen, Say and Sismondi, clearly contrast one another on the possibility of generalised economic crises. Moreover, the two writers indicate the different directions that economics is beginning to take already in the first two decades of the nineteenth century. On one side, Say provides an original reading of Smith and in some ways distanced himself from the Scottish author and from Quesnay. On the other hand, Sismondi highlights the dynamic forces of the capitalist economic system, its continuous evolution and intrinsic instability. Both authors were from continental Europe but the story commences a bit earlier in England with Jeremy Bentham, and with the views of Malthus (reserved for Chapter 13, below).

Jeremy Bentham, 1748–1832 and the principle of utility

Bentham was born in London. Most of his life was spent in writing on questions concerning government and its institutions. Much of this was not published during his lifetime; and some writings were published in French by his pupil, Etienne Dumont.

Bentham began his work when Smith was still alive and in his *Defence of Usury*, written during a visit to Russia between 1783 and 1785 and published in 1787, he criticised Smith's views on usury, revealing Turgot's influence in its construction. He had previously published *A Fragment on Government* in the year of publication of the *Wealth of Nations*; this pamphlet criticised Blackstone's authoritative *Commentaries on the Laws of England*. But his most famous work is *An Introduction to the Principles of Morals and Legislation* of 1789. With Malthus (chapter 13, below), Bentham left the most important marks on economic and social debate for much of the nineteenth century. The origin of the movement later known as *Utilitarianism* was largely inspired by him. It became the title of a major work by John Stuart Mill (see Part II, Chapter 18).

In the 1776 *Fragment on Government,* Bentham acknowledged his debt to Hume as one of the first authors to suggest that the principle of utility was the foundation of human action (Bentham, 1776, p. 51). In its opening page, Bentham declared the 'fundamental axiom', providing both the main rule of justice and chief guide to the behaviour of people and governments alike, as:

> it is the greatest happiness of the greatest number... [that is] the measure of right and wrong.
>
> (Ibid., p. 3, italics in the original)

The actions of men are ruled by two principles: pain and pleasure. The search for pleasure or utility, Bentham claimed to be the determinant of what is right and wrong. It was, in his view, impossible to oppose this fundamental principle of human nature, because it was part of natural law. The legislator had to accept the principle of utility and devise laws capable of establishing situations which can lead to felicity or happiness. Later in the *Fragment*, Bentham was even more explicit on the all-sufficient nature of the principle of utility:

> Now this *other* principle that still recurs upon us, what other can it be than the *principle* of UTILIY? The principle which furnishes us with that *reason*, which alone depends upon any higher reason, but which is itself the sole and all-sufficient reason for every point of practice whatsoever.
>
> (Ibid., pp. 58–9, Bentham's emphasis)

The *volte-face* with respect to Smith's classical political economy is large, and potentially opens the way for a subjective foundation of value. In fact, Bentham's principle of utility also governed the exchange value of commodities for him, and enabled him to criticise Smith's use of the water and diamond paradox and the related distinction between value in use and value in exchange. For Bentham, value is a subjective magnitude, which has four dimensions: 'intensity, duration, propinquity and certainty', to which 'extent' was added. Only the last four elements are measurable, according to him. Bentham also appears to suggest the possibility of an inverse relationship between the quantity of a commodity consumed, and its utility. The use Bentham made of his utility principle was far reaching, but cannot be further pursued here.

Say on exchange value and utility

Jean-Baptiste Say, born into a Protestant family, received a sound education and spent two years in England. He then joined an insurance company, was a supporter of the French Revolution, and took part as a volunteer in the 1792 military campaign. In 1799, Say was appointed a member of the Tribunate under the Consulate, but his disapproval of Napoleoni's regime led to his dismissal in 1803. He moved to a small town in northern France to set up a cotton-spinning plant, and in 1813, after the fall of Napoleon, he returned to Paris.

The restoration of the Bourbon monarchy enabled him to teach at the Athénée what was probably the first public course of political economy. In 1815 he published his *Catéchisme d'économie politique*. Two years later, the government created a chair of industrial economy for him and finally, in 1830, he became professor of political economy at the Collége de France. His most famous work is his *Traité d'économie politique* of 1803; in 1828/29, he published the *Cours complet d'économie politique practique*. In France, Say was considered by himself as *the* interpreter and *the* moderniser of Smith's thought. On the question of value and distribution Says shows some elements of continuity with the approach of Quesnay and Smith, but he also reveals important differences with the surplus approach. In fact, in the *Histoire abrégée de l'économie politique*, in an appendix to the *Cours*, Say acknowledged his theoretical debts towards his eighteenth century antecedents, Quesnay, Hume and Smith.

In analysing value, Say argued that prices depend both on cost of production and on utility, but emphasis is on the role played by the last. For Say, value did not depend on some intrinsic feature of the commodity, like labour, but was a relative notion, an exchange ratio, because the value of commodities derived from the aptitude of goods and services to satisfy wants and to procure utility. The creation of useful objects is the same thing as the creation of value, and hence the creation of wealth:

Then there is a creation, not of material objects, but of utility; and in the way in which this utility affixes to them the quality of value, there is a *production of wealth.*

This is the way in which the word *production* in political economy must be interpreted, and in the whole of this work [the *Traité*], production is not a creation of a material object, but a creation of wealth.

(see Say, 1803, p. 51, his italics in the text)

However, utility alone cannot determine the price of a commodity. This can only happen in the process of exchange. Exchange takes place if sellers and buyers have different subjective evaluations of the utility of the goods they respectively want to buy and sell. Different subjective utilities are the necessary condition for generating an exchange of goods, as is the case in barter, but exchange in fact is conducted in money terms, the introduction of which greatly facilitates the circulation of commodities. For monetised exchange to take place, each good needs to have a well established and accepted evaluation on the market, so that its value can be easily grasped. Say called the monetary value of a commodity its current price (see ibid., p. 50) and this was independent from the evaluation process of the two specific contracting parties. In order to have an exchange value, many dealers and frequent exchanges are needed.

To describe the workings of the market, Say used the metaphor of the balance. Demand and supply constitute the two arms, and the price is the position of equilibrium. Of course, price varies in the same direction as demand, and in opposite direction to supply. Cost of production did play a role because it is a benchmark for the current price, which Say sometimes, following Smith, called natural price. Like Smith, he also appears to have considered cost of production as a kind of benchmark around which the current, or market, price may fluctuate (see ibid. pp. 328, 364).

Say's law and income distribution

The *Traité* indicates the extent to which Say departed from classical political economy, even if he admitted a role for cost of production in the determination of exchange value. However, the value of a consumption good depended basically on demand and supply for it and the order of causation is not from cost, or labour to price, but rather from utility to the value of the productive services of the three elements of production. Utility, or desire, is indicated as the true origin of the exchange value of a commodity, and the value of the productive agents derives from two circumstances: the value of the good in whose production they are employed and their importance in the production process. The prices of inputs reflect those of the final products.

Say singled out three main elements of production: labour, or *industrie*, capital goods, and natural resources. These three elements need not belong to the same persons, but their use in production must be compensated. The problem of distribution in Say's work is the pricing of the production services of the agents of production. 'Those who dispose of one of these three sources of production are merchants of this good that here we call productive services' (ibid., p. 354). Social and historical circumstances influence the measure of compensation for each of these three elements, but supply and demand determines the value of productive services (see ibid., pp. 326, 355).

Say separated profits from interest; the functions of owners of capital are distinguished from those of the entrepreneur. The latter is in charge of the organisation of production and the profit the entrepreneur receives is depicted as a compensation for his difficult work and for the risks he incurs. The same person may play both the roles of investor and entrepreneur, of course, but the two functions are clearly separated by Say and their rewards arise from different considerations. Interest is justified as part of the cost of production because capital derives from frugality. Nassau Senior later gave a similar justification for interest (as earlier had been done by Turgot and, following him, Bentham).

The revenues of the productive agents enter the cost of production but do not determine it; the value of output independently determined in the market goes entirely to the owners of the productive services. The above consideration lead to the formulation of Say's law and to the view that the sum of all distributed revenues is equal to that of the value of total output. The production of a good implies the creation of a demand of equal value, through the revenues of the owner of the three elements of production:

> The sum of the revenues of all the individuals which make up a nation makes up the *revenue* of that nation. It is equivalent to the *gross value* of all her products.
>
> (Ibid., p. 359; see also p. 327)

Goods are of course exchanged for money and not directly for other goods. It is also true that individuals are anxious to get rid of money in order to obtain commodities, money is just the way in which value is expressed and the medium of exchange. Some sectors may experience difficulties in selling their products, but there can be no generalised crisis due to lack of purchasing power in the overall economy. The most convincing description by Say of the impossibility of a general lack of purchasing power is found in the famous chapter (XV of Book I) entitled, *Of Markets*. This reiterates money's intermediary role in exchanges of products and that in fact, 'the purchase of a product cannot take place that with the value of another product' (ibid., p. 140). Various consequences derive from this 'important truth'; of which the most relevant is the first one: 'the more numerous are producers and products, the easier, the larger and the more variegated are the sales' (ibid.).

Hence the possibility of a general glut is ruled out. The other two consequences of the law of markets are equally calming; all individual interests are harmonious and no interrelated conflicts can arise in international trade because foreign imports induce the sale of domestic exports (see ibid., p. 145). General harmony therefore seems to prevail, but Say also indicated that in order to stimulate development of an industrial sector, consumption and the development of tastes has to be fostered.

Jean-Charles Léonard Simonde de Sismondi, 1773–1842, and the possibility of crises

Sismondi was born in Geneva, the son of a wealthy Italian family which had lost part of its wealth during the Swiss upheavals which followed the French revolution. The original surname was Simonde, it was only later that he depicted himself as a descendant of the Genoese Sismondi family. During the political riots in Switzerland of the 1790s, he was himself imprisoned and then exiled to Italy. In 1803 he published a first economic book with the title *De la richesse commerciale* which both exposited Smith's theory and exposed it as false. The book was not successful. In 1819, Sismondi published the *Nouveaux Principes d'Economie Politique*, his most famous work, but it did not bring him the fame as a major contributor to economic thought he had expected.

In the *Nouveaux Principes d'Economie Politique*, Sismondi maintained that general crises due to an excess of productive capacity were both possible and likely. The main cause of the crisis is found in the separation of exchange values of commodities from the needs and wants of people which is a characteristic of societies in which production take place for resale in the market of goods (exchange value) and not for individual direct use. In societies where use and production are not separated, production and consumption decisions are directly linked. By contrast in societies were producers aim at the exchange value, needs do not directly influence production decisions.

Although the needs and wants of people are almost unlimited, many of those in need of commodities often do not have the means to buy them (*Nouveaux Principes*, pp. 217ff.). Thus a glut of commodities derived not from a general saturation of men's wants and desires, but from a maldistribution of income which caused a glut of commodities from insufficient demand. This disproportion may appear to be concentrated in only a few sectors of the economy, but it cannot be solved by re-adjusting demand and supply in various markets. The general causes of crisis are inherent in the process of commodity production and the drive for exchange value in the market.

Sismondi makes other interesting observations concerning economic crisis. First, information tends to be incomplete and this is particularly true for workers, who are invariably uncertain about their incomes. Producers too have only partial information about their markets and especially about the decisions of other entrepreneurs, as indicated in Book IV, chapter 2, significantly entitled 'On Knowledge of the Market':

> Such revolutions in the markets are difficult to know with precision, difficult to calculate; and their obscurity is greater for each individual producer, because he but imperfectly knows the number and means of his rivals, the merchants, who are to sell in competition with him.
>
> (Sismondi 1819, p. 255)

The producer is only aware of his own price and that of his possible buyers, but since all producers behave similarly, there is a tendency to over-production. All producers, 'ignorant of the extent of the efforts of their rivals, almost always overshoot the goal they had set themselves' (ibid.).

This is one cause of excessive output. Production should increase in proportion to needs and demand, but this, according to Sismondi, is not normal behaviour. His criticism of Say's views of the subject are particularly clear in the three articles which are now included as appendices to his major work. Moreover, according to Sismondi, overproduction is not a phenomenon limited to the domestic market, or to a closed economy: on the contrary, the possibility of crisis is visible at the international level (ibid., pp. 276ff.). In particular, there are many British products which remain unsold both in Europe and abroad. Note that in a letter to Malthus in 1820, Say contradicted this view, by stating that in Europe there was no lack of purchasing power. The problem was that the Italians did not produce enough goods to buy English products and that English law discouraged imports from Italy. Say reaffirmed the general principle that no crisis can arise because the overall value of demand is always equal to that of output (cf Routh, 1975, p. 146).

In addition to his views of crises, Sismondi was probably the most lucid forerunner of Marx among the early critics of capitalism. Sismondi criticised classical political economy, which wanted to explain everything with a few principles, but which never took into account the particular historical and social features of society. Moreover, Sismondi pointed out that the causes of exploitation lie in the separation of the workers from the product of their labour, that this was a typical feature of contemporary society in which production takes place for exchange rather than for use.

Sismondi distinguished three different types of commodities: those destined for the poor, luxury goods, and capital goods. His argument resembled that later adopted by Marx in his reproduction schemes (see below, Chapter 16); there may be a mismatch both between the overall production and aggregate demand and also within the three main sectors of production (see Sismondi, 1819, Book II chapter 6, pp. 101ff.). Finally, Sismondi clearly differentiated fixed from circulating capital, and capital from revenue. These are the three items making up national wealth (see ibid., Book II, chapters 5 and 6), and despite being conceptually different, are continuously linked to one another. Sismondi's distinction between short and long run phenomena suffers from a lack of clarity, but he had the great merit of being well aware of the interdependence of the different economic magnitudes. Sismondi tried to provide a theory which is analytically rigorous, and at the same time of relevance to the explanation of the operation of actual economies.

The debate on productive and unproductive labour

The distinction between productive and unproductive labour was an important aspect of the economics of Smith and Quesnay. Subsequently, Ricardo and Marx also employed these notions. By the beginning of the nineteenth century, however, whether such a distinction was meaningful was increasingly questioned. Garnier, a French editor of the *Wealth of Nations*, in footnotes to his 1803 edition, maintained that the Smithian distinction between productive and unproductive activities was meaningless, because all labourers produce utility and pleasure, including servants and others employed in the service sectors.

The notion of productive labour gained some unexpected defenders. For instance, Say agreed that the foundation of value and wealth was utility and not labour, and that therefore non-material products such as services are useful. But he added that the distinction between material and immaterial goods is a useful one because only the former type of goods can be conserved through time and hence become part of the process of accumulation.

Even if for him, unproductive consumption was important and need not be condemned. Malthus (see chapter 13, below) also thought that Smith's distinction was a useful one, if only because it is often difficult to measure the value of services.

In 1815, Storch suggested that the criterion of material permanence cannot be used to rank different goods. The final blow to the notion of productive labour came from Ganilh. In 1821, he rejected Malthus' arguments that goods are wealth only because of their exchange value and not from their physical characteristics, hence any kind of labour producing a good with a positive price must be regarded as productive. But a good is produced *only if* it has a positive exchange value, hence all types of labour are productive. This view derived from the principle that it is exchange which gives value to commodities, not production itself.

The debate on productive and unproductive labour continued in subsequent decades with the contributions from John Stuart Mill and Senior, who both believed that there is a difference between the goods utilised in immediate consumption and those required for further accumulation. However, in Ganilh's arguments, there are elements for a general theory of value founded on utility, along the lines described by Bentham, as indicated in the opening of this chapter.

Notes on further readings

The writings of Bentham have been republished in *The Collected Works of Jeremy Bentham*, (University of London, The Athlone Press and later by Clarendon Press, Oxford, 1970–99); Bentham's *An Introduction* ... is the first volume of 1970 and was edited by J.H. Burns and H.L.A. Hart; this edition includes all his major economic works. A paperback edition of J. Bentham, *A Fragment on Government* (Cambridge University Press, Cambridge, 1988) is available. W. Stark has edited the economic works in *Jeremy Bentham's Economic Writings*, 3 vol (Allen and Unwin, London, 1953–54).

J.B. Say's *Traité d'économie politique* (Calmann-Lévy, Paris, 1803) has been used in this chapter for the analysis of Say's contributions, particularly, for his Say's law of markets. There is an English translation. See also the entries by Thomas Sowell in the *New Palgrave Dictionary of Economics*; by Philippe Steiner in *The Elgar Companion to Classical Economics* (edited by H. Kurz and N. Salvadori, Cheltenham, 1998) and his 'J.B. Say: the *Entrepreneur*, the Free Trade Doctrine and the Theory of Income Distribution', in G. Faccarello (ed.), *Studies in the History of French Political Economy* (Routledge, London, 1998). More accessible is W.J. Baumol 'Say's (at least) Eight Laws, or What Say and James Mill Really Have Meant', *Economica*, vol. 44, 1977, pp. 145–62.

Sowell has also written the entry on Sismondi in the *New Palgrave*. The standard French edition of the *Nouveaux Principes d'Economie Politique*, 1819, is that by J.C. Delaunay, Paris 1827. The English edition used here is *New Principles of Political Economy – of the Wealth in Its Relation to Population*, edited by R. Hyse (Transaction Publishers, New Brunswick, 1991).

Section V

The 'Golden Age' of Classical Political Economy

13
Thomas Robert Malthus, 1766–1834: Population and Effectual Demand

Malthus was born in the county of Surrey, England. His father Daniel himself had literary and scientific interests. The Malthus family library is now in Jesus College, Cambridge. Notwithstanding his father's considerable reputation, Malthus did not share many of his father's philosophical views. In 1783, he studied briefly at the Dissenting Academy at Warrington, in the north-west of England and, later that year became a private pupil to Gilbert Wakefield, a Unitarian minister and a member of the staff of the Academy. In November 1784 Malthus entered Jesus College University of Cambridge as an undergraduate, graduating in 1788. His course of study was largely in mathematics. In 1789 he entered the Church of England, in 1791 he was ordained and in 1803 he was appointed as Rector of Walesby in Lincolnshire.

Malthus married in 1804 and had three children. In 1805, he was appointed to the East India College as its first 'Professor of History and Political Economy'. During this period and through the publication of several articles on monetary issues, he began a correspondence with David Ricardo. In 1807, Malthus participated in public debate on the Poor Laws and in 1814–15 in that on the Corn Laws. He was one of the original members of the Political Economy Club, formed in London in 1821.

Malthus's first published work – *An Essay on the Principle of Population* – appeared anonymously in 1798 and was republished in five, very much expanded, editions during his lifetime. The intention to be involved in public debates was again evident in his second work, *An Investigation of the Cause of the Present High Price of Provisions* (1800). His *Principles of Political Economy* appeared in 1820 (second edition, 1836). In 1823 he published *The Measure of Value Stated and Illustrated*, in 1827 *Definitions of Political Economy* and in 1830 *A Summary View of the Principle of Population*, his final publication.

The decades from the end of the eighteenth century up to 1825 in England were marked by several economic crises. From the mid-1790s, these combined with several bad harvests. In 1797, the Bank of England suspended the convertibility of the currency (which was only restored in 1819–21) thereby initiating the so-called 'bullion controversy'. This in fact debated the extent of devaluation of the inconvertible pound with respect to gold. Much of this period also experienced economic problems caused by the massive military expenditures generated by the French wars on the continent and British involvement therein. Their end in 1813 and 1815 generated financial depression, but prices of foodstuffs fell dramatically, partly because of very good harvests. Revenues of farmers and landlords declined, as did the profits in the export sector and money wages. Unemployment however rose with terrible consequence for the living standards of many workers.

Malthus on population

The above supplies some of the historical background against which Malthus started to write. It assists in explaining his pessimistic approach to social facts, and clarifies his belief that political economy is a discipline much closer to politics than to mathematics. Malthus as moralist and as propagator of a 'christian political economy' also deserves emphasis (see Winch, 1996). This chapter examines the major aspects of Malthus' economics, only his contributions to the 'Corn Laws' debate are left for the next chapter, where they are discussed in the context of Ricardo's contribution.

As previously indicated, the first edition of the *Essay on Population* appeared in 1798 as a rather brief pamphlet. The second edition of 1802 was greatly enlarged, and eliminated from its title all reference to Godwin and Condorcet, whose views on progress had inspired much of the first edition. In his 1793 *Political Justice*, Godwin had ascribed human misery to particular political and economic institutions, especially private property, while nature if left to itself would have produced general opulence. For Malthus, however, there are severe limits to the increase of prosperity because, as stated in the first chapter of the *Essay*:

> the power of population is indefinitely greater than the power in the earth to produce subsistence for man.
>   Population when unchecked, increases in a geometrical ratio: Subsistence increases only in an arithmetical ratio.
>   (Malthus, 1798, pp. 13–14)

Malthus provided a numerical illustration of his argument (see ibid., pp. 25–6). Natural resources cannot therefore keep pace with population increases but, according to Malthus, there were natural checks to population, including 'misery or vice', which invariably resulted from a rapidly growing population (see ibid., pp. 37, 100). In fact, most of the first seven chapters of the first edition of the *Essay* were devoted to the analysis of these 'preventive and positive checks' derived from excessive increases of population.

As had been emphasised previously by Smith, when real wages increase, men can 'multiply enormously', but this bring in its wake increased infant mortality, famines and even plagues, which inevitably reduce population to the previous, lower level. There are less tragic checks than famines and pestilence such as refraining from, or delaying, marriage, because of the costs and troubles entailed by having a large family (see ibid., pp. 63ff.). These types of moral restraints were regarded by Malthus as the most acceptable way of controlling the size of population. It may be noted that Cantillon, Hume, and other eighteenth century writers had anticipated aspects of Malthus' view on population (see Routh, 1975, p. 108), which was not very original apart from its startling comparative statement on the powers of increase of population relative to resources in terms of arithmetical and geometrical progressions.

Misery and poverty thereby became part of nature's design to limit the size of mankind. According to Malthus, men should resort to moral restraints in order to avoid an excessive rise of population and its terrible consequences. But why is there a limit to agricultural production? Malthus's essays written in 1814 (*Observations on the Effects of the Corn Laws*) and 1815 (*An Inquiry into the Nature and Progress of Rent and the Principles by which it is regulated*) explicitly introduced a clear statement of diminishing returns in agriculture, and via this work; and later that of Ricardo, diminishing returns in agriculture entered the analytical structure of classical political economy. In Malthus' opinion, the existence of diminishing returns in agriculture provided powerful support for the view that foodstuffs cannot increase indefinitely. Malthus further investigated the limits to a process of economic development in works after 1815, of which his *Principles* stress the possibilities of general gluts, or the economic causes of crisis and general stagnation.

The notion of a general glut and unproductive consumption

The *Principles of Political Economy* (1820, and a second enlarged edition, 1836) contained ideas rooted in the Smithian tradition of exploring long run problems in the process of growth of the economy (O'Brien, 1975, p. 214). Malthus departed from Smiths's (and Ricardo's) opinions on the long run forces of economic growth by suggesting that the process is accompanied by frequent crises, which periodically affect the economy for considerable periods of time and not as haphazard, or accidental phenomena.

To understand Malthus' view of crisis, his concept of wealth needs to be examined, which is not given by a physical stock of commodities, but by their value. The wealth of a country and its capacity to command labour, that is to generate employment, depends on the value of production.

Excessive accumulation of capital in the past, inducing an increase in wages above their subsistence level, may also lower incentives to employ labour. In addition, it causes profits to fall, further weakening the stimulus to accumulate. For Malthus, economic crisis may arise from different causes, but they are all invariably reduced to difficulty of sustaining the value of output, because of lack of demand:

> General wealth, like portions of it, will always follow effective demand. Whenever there is great demand for commodities, that is, whenever the exchangeable value of the whole mass will command more labour than usual at the same price, there is the same kind of reason for expecting a general increase of commodities, as there is for expecting an increase of particular commodities when their market-prices rise.
>
> (Malthus, 1820, p. 371)

The reverse is equally true, and declining effective demand generates a decrease in the overall level of activity. Although Malthus was aware of the opinion of 'some very able writers, that although there may easily be a glut of particular commodities, there cannot possibly be a glut of commodities in general' (ibid., pp. 303–4), that is, Say, James Mill and above all Ricardo (see ibid., p. 308), contrary to them Malthus saw a general glut as a real possibility because the demand of those employed in productive activities 'can never alone furnish a motive to the accumulation and employment of capital' (ibid., p. 302).

A crisis is then the consequence of a fall in the value of the goods produced, which implies low profits and stagnation due to the lack of incentives to invest. In a letter to Ricardo of 1821, Malthus wrote:

> that under all common circumstances, if an increased power of production be not accompanied by an increase of unproductive expenditures, it will inevitably lower profits and throw labourers out of employment.
>
> (Malthus, 1821, pp. 10–11)

Over time, a balance between production and consumption is required, but the consumption of the productive workers and of the capitalist by themselves cannot secure the necessary level of effectual demand to match a continuously rising productive capacity. Hence consumption by the landlords has a positive role to play because their predominantly luxury expenditures tend to sustain overall demand. But workers employed by landlords in the so-called unproductive sectors, are likewise crucial to the process, precisely because they are not employed in material production. These workers therefore do not add new commodities to national output, while nevertheless adding to overall consumption. In order to avoid a general crisis, the forces of production on one side and unproductive expenditures on the other need to grow proportionately. Malthus posited a distinction between productive and unproductive workers, because the last consume without producing, a distinction introduced at the very beginning of his *Principles* (Section 2 of chapter I, entitled '*On Productive and Unproductive Labour*' (see *Malthus*, 1820, p. 15). Hence to avoid a general glut, 'it is absolutely necessary that a country with great powers of production should possess a body of unproductive consumers' (ibid., p. 421). And, Malthus claimed, there is a 'certain proportion', a balance, between productive and unproductive classes 'which yield the greatest value' (ibid., p. 436).

Malthus adopted two criteria for defining productive and unproductive labourers. One relied on the material existence of the product of the worker, the argument advanced by Adam Smith (see ibid., pp. 18, 22). This emphasised the physical characteristics of products, people providing personal services are unproductive, while productive labour includes those employed in the production of material, transportable commodities, whose value can be ascertained independently of the labourer.

The second criterion suggested that a labourer is productive if value is added to the object on which he works. As a different way of expressing the same concept, Malthus distinguished between output employed as capital, and output consumed as revenue. The difference between these two ways of using a product depends on the different types of labour, only productive labour can reintegrate and increase the capital which has been used in production. Therefore, Malthus' objective in distinguishing between the two types of labour relates to capital accumulation: the labour employed in the process of production in view of the valorisation of the capital invested is productive, while the labour engaged in activities for consumption is unproductive (ibid., pp. 17ff.)

Malthus on value

How are the value of a commodity to be measured? And what are the causes of value? Malthus' answer to the first question endorsed Smith's notion of labour commanded as the most appropriate measure of exchangeable value. Labour commanded is the amount of labour that each commodity can buy, and provides an appropriate way of measuring both the gross and net revenue of a country:

> the quantity of labour of a given description (common-day labour, for instance) which it can command, it will appear to be unquestionably the best of any one commodity, and to unite, more nearly than any other, the qualities of real and nominal measure of exchangeable value.
>
> (Ibid., p. 89)

Malthus used the term, 'common-day labour', to indicate standard labour, the unit required for representing labour commanded. Labour commanded is not a perfect measure, because it entails that the value of commodities is divided by the money wage, something varying from country to country, but it is nevertheless the best available measure for him.

Malthus views on determining relative prices are more articulated. Like Smith, Malthus regarded profits as well as wages as an essential component of prices (ibid., p. 43). The cost of production is the sum of all incomes and greatly influences the value of commodities, particularly in the long run. However, supply and demand also enter the picture:

> the relative values of commodities in money, or their prices, are determined by the relative demand of them, compared with the supply of them; and this law appears to be so general, that probably not a single instance of a change of price can be found which may not be satisfactorily traced to some previous change in the causes which affect the demand or supply.
>
> (Ibid., p. 37)

However, Malthus was not a supporter of utility as the foundation of value. For example, in the *Definitions of Political Economy* of 1827 he accused Say of confusing use and exchange value, and in the same work criticised Samuel Bailey for his support to the view that value depends on utility.

Rent and wages

The net revenue is distributed between wages, profits and rent, but Malthus saw no conflict of interests between workers, landlords and capitalist, so long as a high effectual demand guaranteed high selling prices. Under these conditions, the distribution of value depends on demand and supply in the different markets of labour, land and capital.

Malthus strongly defended the role of landlords in production and their right to obtain a share of the product in the form of rent:

> rents are neither a mere nominal value, nor a value unnecessarily and injuriously transferred from one set of people to another; but a most real and essential part of the whole value of the national property, and placed by the laws of nature where they are, on the land, by whomsoever possessed.
>
> (Ibid., p. 127)

In the long run, rent will rise because of the scarcity of fertile land and the increase in the amount of capital invested in cultivation. Malthus also accepted the idea of a subsistence wage which is needed to guarantee the reproduction of labourers, a corollary of his population theory. This method of determining wages presented a very long-run view, influencing much of the treatment of wages in the rest of the nineteenth century. According to Malthus the natural price of labour was:

> that price which, in the actual circumstances of the society, is necessary to occasion an average supply of labourers, sufficient to meet the average demand.
>
> (Ibid., pp. 228)

In fact, in the *Principles*, Malthus also maintained that wages are determined by the supply and demand of labour (see ibid., p. 224); thus the natural wage is the one which 'equilibrates' supply to demand. Moreover, under certain conditions, mainly those of a growing economy, the market wage rate can stay above the subsistence rate for a long time; while the composition of the customary subsistence level can change over time, rising as perceptions of customary living standards rise. Finally, as a policy overcome the inevitable depressions from a lack of demand, Malthus suggested it would be useful to use the unemployed workers in road construction and other public works. Apart from alleviating the hardship for the unemployed, such measures helped to sustain effectual demand. Malthus views on this subject turned him into a hero for Keynes during the 1930s (see below, Chapter 31).

Notes on further readings

For population theories before Malthus see J. Bonar, *Theories of Population from Raleigh to Arthur Young* (London, 1931). The Malthus editions used here are T.R. Malthus, *An Essay on the Principle of Population as It Affects the Future Improvement of Society, with Remarks on the Speculations of Mr. Godwin, Mr. Condorcet and Other Writers* (first edition, 1798; reprinted Kelley, New York, 1965) and Malthus, *Principles of Political Economy, Considered with a View to Their Practical Applications* (Murray, London, 1820) in Ricardo, *Works and Correspondence*, Sraffa ed., vol. II, *Notes on Malthus's Principles of Political Economy*. Malthus's *Observations on the Effects of the Corn Laws* (1814), *An Inquiry into the Nature and Progress of Rent and the Principles by Which It Is Regulated* (1815) are included in *The Pamphlets of Thomas Robert Malthus* (Kelley Publishers, New York, 1970). Malthus' *Letter to Ricardo* of 7 July 1821 is quoted from Ricardo *Works and Correspondence*, Sraffa ed., vol IX.

   A particularly useful analysis of Malthus' contributions to history of ideas and to politics is in D. Winch, *Riches and Poverty: An Intellectual History of Political Economy in Britain, 1750–1834* (Cambridge University Press,

Cambridge, 1996). This also provides a useful discussion of the prevailing economic conditions of the first decades of the nineteenth century. William Petersen, *Malthus* (Heinemann, London, 1979), presents a good overview of his life and work with special reference to his demographics.

14
David Ricardo, 1772–1823: the Rate of Profit

Ricardo was born in London and died at his country estate of Gatcomb Park. Both his father and his mother belonged to Jewish families and his father was an affluent stockbroker. David was the third of seventeen children. At the age of fourteen he began working with his father and subsequently made a large fortune as an independent stockbroker. When he was twenty-one he married Priscilla Ann Wilkinson, a Quaker. By the age of twenty-five, Ricardo turned his attention to scientific subjects, chiefly mathematics and geology. In 1799 he became interested in economics, attributed by him to a reading of the *Wealth of Nations*. A first economic article 'The Price of Gold' appeared in 1809 in the *Morning Chronicle*; *The High Price of Bullion, a Proof of Depreciation of Bank-Notes* was published a year later and made a remarkable impact. Ricardo's participation in the Bullion Controversy led to his acquaintance with James Mill, Malthus and a number of less well known economics writers.

In 1815, when the question of Corn Laws came up for debate in Parliament, Ricardo published his *Essay on the Influence of a Low Price of Corn on the Profits of Stock; Shewing the Inexpediency of Restrictions on the Importation of Foreign Corn* (known as *Essay on Profits*). By this time he had decided to abandon his business in the Stock Exchange and started to transfer his money into landed estates. In 1817 he published his main work, *Principles of Political Economy and Taxation*. In 1819 he entered Parliament as an independent member. The last of his works he prepared for publication was a *Plan for the Establishment of a National Bank* (1823); it was published posthumously in 1824. Ricardo's death came suddenly in September 1823 as a consequence of an ear infection. But even in the last weeks of his life he continued to be puzzled by the problem of the measure of value and was working at a paper on absolute value, first published in the Sraffa's edition of Ricardo's collected works as *Note on 'Absolute value and Exchangeable Value'* (Ricardo, 1951–73, vol. IV).

There have been many, often contradictory interpretations of Ricardo's thought and work. The publication in 1951 of the first volume of Sraffa's edition of *The Works and Correspondence of David Ricardo* which contained a general introduction on his major economic ideas by the editor, provided impetus for a better understanding of Ricardo's economics as well as for vigorous controversy. The debates are still far from settled. A huge number of works has appeared (for example, Hollander, 1979; Peach 1993; De Vivo, 1996). In spite of this controversy, the 1951 *Introduction* by Piero Sraffa to the first volume of his edition of Ricardo's *Works* still provides a very sound description of Ricardo's economic system, and should be the starting point for any serious student of Ricardo. As already mentioned, Ricardo took part in the 'bullion controversy'. He believed that the depreciation of the pound with respect to gold was a clear indication of the over issue of paper money in Britain. He essentially accepted the quantity theory of money in these debates. The economic issues which later captured the attention of Ricardo were raised by the debates on the renewal of the 'Corn Laws', which protected English farmers from foreign imports of corn unless there was a dearth from domestic harvest failure. During the Napoleonic wars, the 'continental blockade' has produced sharp increases in the price of corn in England. At their conclusion in 1815, a debate commenced about the future of the 'Corn Laws'. Ricardo favoured abolition and free transportation of corn. A duty discouraged the importation of corn, artificially increased its price and those of necessaries thus leading to an increase in money wages and rent, but reduction of the profit rate. Since profits were the spur to accumulation, maintaining import duties on corn slowed investment and growth.

Malthus opposed this view. As shown in Chapter 13, rent had positive effects on effective demand and hence on the production of manufactures and on profits. The conflicting views of Ricardo and Malthus mirror the opposing interests of the landed aristocracy, to whom high prices of corn and high rents were beneficial, and of the industrial middle class, who desired low prices of necessaries to avoid pressure on money wages while maintaining real wages at the level necessary for subsistence.

The *Essay on Profits* and the theory of rent

Ricardo's arguments in favour of free trade in corn were grounded on his analysis of the determination of the rate of profit and rent, first put forward in the 1815 *Essay on Profits*. It introduced the 'Ricardian theory of rent', although three other authors had contributed such a theory in that very same year: Malthus in his *An Inquiry into the Nature and Progress of Rent*, Sir Edward West in his *Essay on the Application of Capital to Land* and Robert Torrens in his *Essay on the External Corn Trade*. Moreover, in 1777 James Anderson had already presented a theory of differential rent. Ricardo himself always ascribed the theory of rent to Malthus (see Ricardo, 1951–73, vol. IV p. 6).

Ricardo's definition of the rate of profit

Ricardo's analysis rested on four assumptions:

1. In the long run, Say's law operates, that is, there can be no general lack of effectual demand or general glut in the market.
2. Initially, there is no fixed capital but only circulating capital made up of wages advanced by the capitalists to the workers.
3. Wages are at subsistence level; Ricardo accepted Malthus theory of population and its implication that market wages are constantly restored to their natural level, that is, that which guarantees the subsistence of workers and their constant number.
4. Wage goods only consist of agricultural products.

In addition, Ricardo implicitly assumed that in sectors of the economy other than agriculture, techniques of production are given and do not change. On these assumptions, agriculture is the only productive sector in which output and inputs are the same commodity, corn. Hence surplus product can be measured directly in physical terms, without the need to use relative prices. This is the Ricardian 'corn model'. It can be illustrated using the following symbols: w is the wage, in terms of corn, per worker, L is the number of workers employed in the cultivation of corn, Y is agricultural output. Then: wL is the aggregate capital employed in agriculture, $(Y - wL)$ is net product, or surplus, also in corn. The rate of profit can then be defined as follows:

$$r = (Y - wL)/wL = [(Y/L) - w]/w = (\pi - w)/w \qquad \text{or} \qquad (14.1)$$
$$r = (1 - wl)/wl$$

where π is the productivity of labour in corn production, or corn product per unit of labour and $l = L/Y$ is the labour necessary to produce one unit of corn.

The rate of profit then depends on two magnitudes: the real wage rate, w, that is to say the quantity of corn annually required for the subsistence of a worker; and secondly, the productivity of the labour employed in the cultivation of corn $\pi = 1/l$. The rate of profit therefore varied directly with changes in productivity and inversely with real wages. This is a fundamental Ricardian theorem.

The rate of profit of agriculture determines that for the whole economy

In non-agricultural sectors, product and its means of production are different commodities, hence relative prices are necessary in order to measure the surplus and the rate of profit. Take the textile sector, for example, which produces cloth. Its rate of profit is given by the expression:

$$r_c = (p_c Y_c - w L_c)/w L_c = (p_c - w l_c)/w l_c \tag{14.2}$$

where 'c' indicates the production of cloth and p_c is the price of one unit of cloth in terms of corn.

A numerical example shows why the rate of profit in the textile sector needs to be equal to that already determined in agriculture by equation (14.1). Suppose the subsistence wage, w equals 10 units (bushels) of corn. Each sector employs one worker, 10 metres of cloth is the output per unit of labour in textiles and 12 bushels of corn is that in agriculture. The rate of profit in agriculture is 20 per cent.

In order to calculate the profit rate in textiles, the exchange value between cloth and corn needs to be given. Suppose $p_c = 1.3$, that is, 1.3 bushels of corn are required to obtain 1 metre of cloth. From equation (14.2), these data imply that $r_c = 30$ per cent.

Ricardo accepted Smith's analysis of the natural and market prices, and his view of a tendency to a uniform rate of profit over all sectors of the economy (see above, Chapter 11). When $r_c > R$, as implied in the above argument, capitalists will leave agriculture and invest in textiles, where the rate of profit is higher. But as long as the techniques of production, and hence π, do not change, the rate of profit in the production of corn will not change. The only way of attaining a uniform rate of profit is by a fall in r_c and, since technology is given, this can only occur from a decrease of p_c to 1.2 units of corn for one unit of cloth. From (14.1) and (14.2) a value which ensures uniformity of the profit rate is easily derived. This is $p_c = l_c/l$. In the simple scheme of the 1815 *Essay*, relative price movements equalise profit rates across sectors.

The rate of profit with different types of land

Ricardo used this type of model to examine the effects on the profit rate of a duty on the importation of corn. Table 14.1 encapsulates Ricardo's numerical example (from Ricardo, 1815, p. 17). The real wage rate stays constant at 10 bushels of corn per annum. In period I, only the most fertile lands, call them A, are cultivated. On A lands 10 workers produce 300 bushels of corn per year, total capital employed including the wage bill is 200 bushels, and the surplus is 100. Suppose initially that *lands A are not scarce* in the sense that, given the productivity of labour in agriculture, this land is more than enough for producing the quantity of corn required to satisfy total domestic demand. If lands A cannot satisfy total domestic demand, but there are no restrictions on importing foreign corn, all additional corn needed for the subsistence of the population can be imported from abroad and the situation remains as described for period I. It has to be assumed that foreign producers of corn, in the northern provinces of France, for example, also employ land of the better quality; or that the techniques of agricultural production in England and France are the same.

Under these circumstances, the entire surplus accrues to the capitalists. If a landowner wants a rent for the use of his land, the farmer/entrepreneur will abandon that estate and go to another, since there is no scarcity of similar quality land. Since every landowner desires to obtain a rent, however low it may be, they compete against each other by offering the use of their lands at lower rents. In the situation described above, competition among landlords leads to zero rent and a profit rate of 50 per cent.

In Period II, population (and domestic corn demand) has increased, or an import duty on corn makes its importation more expensive and more difficult. Then more English land has to be cultivated in order to substitute domestically produced corn for the previously imported one. Inferior land B now enters cultivation, inferior because 21 workers are required to produce the 300 bushels of corn, which in Period I was freely imported. As land B initially is not scarce, the 90 bushels of surplus accrue entirely to the farmers and the profit rate declines to approximately 43 per cent. Of course, farmers now try to cultivate A-land, were the profit rate is higher and hence offer to pay a rent to the owners of lands A, who now that their land is scarce, have an advantage in this competition. But since 86 bushels of profits on A-land give the same rate of profit of B-land, this rent cannot exceed 14 bushels. The uniform profit rate now is lower than in period I, because productivity of labour is less on lands of inferior quality, or 'marginal lands' where no rent is paid. When more corn must be produced at home, because population (demand) further increases, even more inferior C-land comes into cultivation and the rate of profit declines further, as shown in Table 14.1.

For Ricardo, the uniform rate of profit is determined on 'marginal lands', and does not depend on relative prices, so long as the real wage and the

Table 14.1   Rent theory

	Lands	L	w	Y	wL	Surplus	Rent	Profits	r(%)
Period I	A	20	10	300	200	100	–	100	50
Period II	A	20	10	300	200	100	14	86	43
	B	21	10	300	210	90	–	90	43
Period III	A	20	10	300	200	100	28	72	36
	B	21	10	300	210	90	14	76	36
	C	22	10	300	220	80	–	80	36

productivity of labour in the production of wage goods on the least productive land are given. The introduction of an import duty on corn, the typical wage good, lowers the productivity on the 'marginal land', (by forcing recourse to poorer quality land), leading to a decrease of the rate of profit in agriculture which governs the profit rate for the economy as a whole.

A positive rent only arises because the best quality lands, given techniques, are scarce, and insufficient to satisfy national demand for corn. This is a 'differential rent' concept, since rent varies according the quality of land in use. In a closed economy, or at world wide level, increased population gradually entails the cultivation of inferior quality land, hence there is tendency for the rate of profit to fall. In his *Principles*, Ricardo presented this view as follows:

> whether the increased productions, and the consequent demand which they occasion, shall or shall not lower profits, depends solely on the rise of wages; and the rise of wages, excepting for a limited period, on the facility of producing the food and necessaries of the labourer.
>
> (Ricardo, 1817, p. 292)

Continuous technical progress in agriculture can delay this tendency by raising the productivity of labour in corn wage goods production, hence postponing recourse to less fertile land. The *Essay on Profits* implies a precise theory of distribution. A given physical quantity of output, Y, is divide between wages, profits and rent, but the nature of this distribution provides for conflict between the three major social groups for the appropriation of a higher share of output. Since wages are given at subsistence level, rent and profits vary in opposite direction. The theory makes it impossible to increase both shares at the same time. As for rent, Ricardo remarked that:

> rent then is in all cases a portion of the profits previously obtained on the land. It is never a new creation of revenue, but always part of a revenue already created.
>
> (Ricardo, 1815, p. 18)

Ricardo took a definite stand in favour of agricultural entrepreneurs and against landowners. He went even so far as to indicate 'that the interest of the landlord is always opposed to the interest of every other class in the community' (ibid., p. 21). Moreover, with given techniques in the production of wage goods, real wages can only rise at the expenses of the rate of profit (see Ricardo, 1817, p. 111).

The *Principles* and the 'labour-theory' of value

The theory of the rate of profit of the *Essay* rests on the crucial assumption that wages consist entirely in corn, so that in agriculture the output and its means of production are the same commodity and no relative prices are required to calculate the profit rate. Of course, this assumption is not a very realistic one. The importance of this for Ricardo's argument is easily illustrated. If the labourers also consume cloth (say 5 bushels of corn and 5 meters of cloth), then the real wage contains two different goods. The value of the wage rate expressed in corn units is then $5 + 5p_c$, where p_c is the price of a unit of cloth in terms of corn. The value of w now depends on this relative price and so does the rate of profit.

Nothing changes in the data of Table 14.1, if it is assumed that p_c does not vary when B-lands come into cultivation. But this is a rather unrealistic assumption. It implies that a change in the conditions of production of corn does not affect its relative price. It seems far more reasonable to assume that a decline in the productivity of labour in corn production requires the corn price to increase with respect to cloth, where productivity has remained unchanged. Hence p_c falls. But by how much? It is easy to show for Period II that the profit rate either rises or falls with respect to period I, depending on the size of the change in the price of corn.

Let w^* be the corn value of the wage rate which leaves the rate of profit of Period I unchanged at the value r = 50%. w^* can be derived from (14.1) as follows:

$$w^* = \pi_m/(1 + r)$$
with $\pi_m = 300/21$ as the productivity on B-land

If the wage rate is w^*, approximately 9.52 bushels in our example, the price of cloth in terms of corn (p_c^*) must fall to approximately 0.905, as can be seen from $w^* = 9.52 = 5 + 5p_c^*$. (any value of p_c below p_c^* (0.905) implies $w<w^*$, ensuring that in Period II the rate of profit increases). This indicates that with more than one commodity it is impossible to determine the rate of profit without a theory of relative prices: the title of the first chapter of the *Principles* is *On Value*. Ricardo looked for a theory of value which satisfied two essential requirements for his theory of distribution. Firstly, it must enable measurement of output, Y, and wage rate, w, independently of the profit rate r, which is the dependent variable. Secondly, it must relate changes in relative prices to alterations in techniques of production, or the difficulty of producing the commodities. Ricardo therefore distinguished two types of commodities at the outset of the argument: scarce commodities and reproducible ones (Ricardo, 1817, pp. 7–9).

The prices of non-reproducible commodities, such as works of art, rare books, and so on, can only be determined by their quantity relative to the demand for them (see ibid., p. 12). The vast majority of commodities, however, can be reproduced. Hence their natural prices depend on the conditions of production and on the values of wages, profits and rent, as Smith had stated. But contrary to Smith, Ricardo believed that the labour theory of value can explain the relative prices of reproducible commodities even with positive rent and profits, and not only in the primitive stage of society as Smith had argued (see ibid., pp. 14–17).

Take two commodities 'a' and 'b', in whose production no rent is paid; their prices, p_a and p_b respectively must include the wages of the workers and profits of the capitalists who have advanced the wages at the beginning of production. The two prices can be described by the following equations:

$$p_a = wl_a + rwl_a = wl_a(1 + r)$$
$$p_b = wl_b + rwl_b = wl_b(1 + r) \tag{14.3}$$

where l_a and l_b are the quantities of labour directly and indirectly required in the production of one unit of each commodity, and as before, p_a and p_b are the prices w is the wage rate and r the profit rate.

Now if it is assumed that: (i) both sector have the same wage rate and the same rate of profit; (ii) the capital employed in production is made up of wages only; (iii) the period of production has the same length, say one year, for both products, then for equation (14.3), by dividing each side of the first equation by the corresponding side of the second one, we obtain: $p_a/p_b = l_a/l_b$. The relative price of the two commodities is determined by the ratio of the quantities of labour required in their production. This is the labour theory of value.

Ricardo himself realised that the second and third assumptions were particularly restrictive, hence admitting two types of 'exceptions' to the labour theory of value. First, production periods may differ; secondly, the two production processes may employ instruments and equipment as capital and not just wages, and in quite different proportions (see ibid., p. 23).

If, for example, it takes two years to produce commodity 'a', then its relative price will be $p_a/p_b = (1 + r)l_a/l_b$, that is, it includes the rate of profit and no longer depends only on labour embodied. The same holds if the two commodities are produced with different ratios of means of production (or capital) per worker. If the production of 'b' requires the use of a commodity produced last year with $l_b/2$ units of labour plus $l_b/2$ units of labour directly employed this year, then its price is:

$$p_b = [(wl_b/2)(1 + r) + wl_b/2](1 + r). \tag{14.4}$$

and the relative price p_a/p_b depends on the rate of profit. The two commodities have been produced by the same quantity of labour embodied, but the labour theory of value no longer holds. Ricardo was fully aware of such 'exceptions' to the labour theory of value, which he largely attributed to the different proportions in which fixed and circulating capital are employed in the production of different commodities(see Ricardo, 1817, pp. 30, 53–6).

The distribution of income

If these 'exceptions' to the labour theory of value are ignored, then the quantity of labour embodied can be used for measuring capital and output, and income distribution between workers, landlords and capitalists is determined as before. A problem might arise in the case of commodities produced with techniques characterised by different labour productivity and hence with different quantities of labour embodied. In that case, price is determined by labour embodied in the less productive technique.

Assume that in Table 14.1, one unit of cloth is also produced by employing just one worker and that the value of commodities is measured by the labour embodied. What then determines the distribution of output in Period II? The overall value of output (Y) equals 43 years of labour, but the labour actually embodied is only 42 years (20 workers on A-land, 21 on B-land and 1 in textiles). In fact, all corn is valued as if it had been produced on B-lands, where the labour embodied is higher, hence the value of agricultural output Y is higher than the labour actually embodied (L). The difference $Y - L$, (43 − 42, or 1 in our example) denotes the value of aggregate rent. The value of output net of rent is L, that is, the total number of productive workers employed in the economy during the period of production, say, one year. The rate of profit (r) is

$$(L - wL)/wL = (1 - w)/w, \text{ similar to equation 14.1}$$

Therefore r depends on the physical quantities of wage goods; and secondly, the productivity of labour in the production of wage goods. It is obvious that the technical conditions of cloth production now also influence the rate of profit, because cloth has become a wage good. But as was the case in the *Essay*, r can be determined without having to know the relative prices of commodities. Moreover, the rate of profit still shows a tendency to fall when productivity falls in the production of wage goods, which of course continue to include a substantial proportion of agricultural products:

> profits depend on the quantity of labour requisite to provide necessaries for the labourers, on that land or with that capital which yields no rent.
> (Ricardo, 1817, p. 126; see also pp. 48–9)

This is a conclusion quite similar to that of the *Essay on Profits*.

Comparative advantage

Ricardo contributed to the theory of international trade with the so-called doctrine of 'comparative advantages'. Ricardo's famous example is given in Table 14.2, where England and Portugal exchange wine and cloth; the

Table 14.2   Ricardo's comparative advantage

	Cloth	Wine
England	100	120
Portugal	90	80

numbers represent the labour embodied in one unit of the two commodities for each country (see ibid., pp. 135–6).

Portugal has an absolute advantage in the production of both goods, because it employs less workers to produce a unit of each. However, Ricardo shows that it is equally beneficial for Portugal to specialise in the production of wine and import cloth from England. In England, the relative price of wine to cloth is 1.2, while in Portugal it is only 0.88 and as long as the domestic price of wine is lower than the foreign one, it is profitable to export wine and to import cloth. England finds it appropriate to export cloth to Portugal where the price is 1.25, higher than the British domestic price of 0.83. The model therefore assumed constant costs for all commodities and continuous full employment of all resources.

Ricardo's examples assume that in international trade there is no unrestrained capital mobility as is the case in domestic trade, hence at least at the beginning of trading, the values of commodities are not given by labour embodied:

> the same rule which regulates the relative value of commodities in one country, does not regulate the relative values of commodities exchanged between two or more countries.
>
> (Ibid., p. 188)

This is due to the fact that capital is not perfectly mobile across countries, because 'most men of property' prefer a lower rate of profit at home to investing abroad (see ibid., pp. 136–7). Of course, if capital were able to flow freely among countries, there would be a uniform rate of profit everywhere and commodities internationally traded would have their value determined in terms of embodied labour. Hence, at least initially, international trade implies the existence of a trade surplus in one country and a deficit in the other. As a consequence, international currency, or precious metals, flow to the surplus country, increasing its money prices, and lowering them in the deficit country, a mechanism which resembles that outlined by Hume (see ibid., pp.139–40 and Chapter 8, above). But since each country produces a single commodity, there is an international relative price change. This produces a tendency for the two different initial domestic relative prices to converge to a single one, which also indicates the terms of trade between the two countries.

Value and machines in the third edition of the *Principles*

Two interesting pieces of new material appeared in the third edition of the *Principles* (of 1821). First, in Section VI of chapter 1, on value, which has the title *An Invariable Measure of Value* (see Sraffa, 1951, p.lv), Ricardo revealed his dissatisfaction with labour embodied as a measure of value, because it enabled the determination of relative prices, independently of the rate of profit only under very restrictive conditions. He looked therefore for alternative units of measurement; a commodity whose production always required the same amount of labour (for example, Ricardo, 1821, p. 27), or a commodity whose ratio between the labour directly used and that employed in its means of production reflects an average of the different ratios for the different products.

In his unfinished paper on 'Absolute value and exchangeable value' (Ricardo, 1951–73, vol. IV p. 357ff.) Ricardo tackled the problem again and indicated that in reality no commodity can ever be an ideal unit of measure. To him, the best approximation to an ideal unit of measurement is a commodity produced not by labour alone but by labour and capital goods, the value of which is made up of both profits and wages, and the commodity itself produced according to some kind of average production conditions (see ibid., pp. 371–3).

The more important new material of the *Principles* involved the effects of the introduction of machines in production. Previously, Ricardo had not been pessimistic about the impact of mechanisation on workers; the third edition revealed he had changed his mind on the matter:

> I thought that the labouring class would, equally with the other classes, participate in the advantage, from the general cheapness of commodities arising from the use of machinery... but I am convinced that the substitution of machinery for human labour, is often very injurious to the interests of the class of labourers.
>
> (Ricardo, 1821, p. 388)

In 1817, John Barton had published a pamphlet, *Observations on the Condition of the Labouring Classes*, in which he maintained that the introduction of machines lowered employment (see Sraffa, 1951, p. lviii) more than generally thought. Mechanisation benefits capitalists because it lowers the labour content of commodities, but the output of wage goods decreases, because more workers are needed to produce machines. Ricardo's chapter 'On machinery' gave rise to a debate on the effects of technical progress on employment. This remained a highly controversial issue over the ensuing decades, which witnessed considerable mechanisation in British manufacturing.

Notes on further readings

The standard edition of Ricardo's works is *The Works and Correspondence of David Ricardo*, edited by Piero Sraffa with the collaboration of Maurice Dobb (11 vols, Cambridge University Press, Cambridge, 1951–73). This includes the *Essay on Profits* as Ricardo 1815, and the first and third edition of the *Principles* as Ricardo 1817 and 1821, as well as the unfinished paper on value (Ricardo 1823) to which reference was made in the text; Sraffa's interpretation is given in the general introduction to the work (in Volume I). This has been strongly debated. In favour of Sraffa's views, see G. de Vivo, 'Ricardo, Torrens and Sraffa: a summing up', *Cambridge Journal of Economics*, vol. 20, 1996. H. Kurz and N. Salvadori, 'The Standard commodity' and Ricardo's Search for an 'invariable measure of value' in M. Baranzini and G. Harcourt (eds), *The Dynamics of the Wealth of Nations: Growth, Distribution and Structural Change: Essays in Honour of Luigi Pasinetti* (St. Martin's Press, New York, 1993); P. Garegnani's 'On Hollander's Interpretation of Ricardo', *Cambridge Journal of Economics*, vol. 6, 1982. Opponents of Sraffa's views include S. Hollander, *The Economics of David Ricardo* (Toronto University Press, Toronto, 1979) and T. Peach, *Interpreting Ricardo* (Cambridge University Press, Cambridge, 1993). M. Morishima, *Ricardo's Economics: a General Equilibrium Theory of Distribution and Growth* (Cambridge University Press, Cambridge, 1989) takes a more neutral position. A useful mathematical presentation of Ricardo's thought is L.L. Pasinetti's 'A mathematical formulation of the Ricardian system', *Review of Economic Studies*, vol. 27, 1960. M. Milgate and S. Stimson *Ricardian Politics* (Princeton University Press, Princeton, 1991) provide an overview of the political debates in Ricardo's times.

On the 'corn model' interpretation of Ricardo see the debate between Terry Peach, Samuel Hollander and Giancarlo de Vivo in the *Cambridge Journal of Economics*, 25(5), September 2001. On technical change and capital accumulation in Ricardo, Smith and Marx, see Heinz Kurz, 'Technical Progress, Capital Accumulation and Income Distribution in Classical Economics: Adam Smith, David Ricardo and Karl Marx', *European Journal of the History of Economic Thought*, 17(5), December 2010.

15
Torrens, Senior and the Aftermath of Ricardo

In the period from the death of Ricardo to the debates on the Poor Laws of 1836 and 1837, many different developments and lines of thought are visible in economics, produced by many authors. For all of these authors Smith and Ricardo presented obvious points of reference. The post-Ricardian period includes strong supporters of Ricardo, such as James Mill and John McCulloch; authors who attempted to combine the economics of Ricardo with more equity and social justice (the so-called Ricardian Socialists) while thirdly, there are economists who did not accept Ricardo's approach on value and distribution, such as Bailey, Lloyd and Longfield.

There is no clearly outstanding figures in this period. It was a period of either transition, awaiting the emergence of a treatise writer such as John Stuart Mill in the 1840s (see below, Part II), or perhaps new theoretical advances, such as those of Marx and of the Marginalist approach. This chapter is therefore selective, paying special attention to Robert Torrens and Nassau Senior as two of the more interesting economists from this period. As was done above in Chapter 12 with Say and Sismondi, Torrens and Senior strikingly represent different streams of thought emerging in the 1820s and 1830s. Torrens provided rather interesting analytical contributions and amendments to Ricardo's position; Senior, because the criticisms of Ricardo and other notions he introduced present a clear move away from classical political economy and a move towards the later, neoclassical vision. Some material on the Ricardian socialists is wedged in between these two segments of the chapter.

Robert Torrens, 1780–1864, and the structure of capital

Torrens was born in Ireland and died in London. During his lifetime he was successfully engaged in many occupations. He was a Colonel in the Royal Marines, he was a newspaper proprietor of *The Globe*, and promoted schemes for the colonisation of Australia. In 1821, he was among the founders of the Political Economy Club and took the chair at its inaugural meeting. This Club used to hold meetings on economic policy issues every first Monday of each month from December to June. From 1831, Torrens was also a member of the House of Commons.

Torrens had an extensive literary output, which was not limited to economic treatises. He wrote two novels, for example. His more important works are *An Essay on the External Corn Trade* (1815) and *An Essay on the Production of Wealth* (1821). Torrens was also a strong supporter of the so-called Currency School in the fierce debates of the 1830s and 1840s against the supporters of the Banking School on the restoration of the full convertibility of the British pound. In 1848, he wrote *The Principles and Practical Operations of Sir Robert Peel's Act of 1844* on this subject.

Robert Torrens brought several objections to Ricardo's approach, but these criticisms are of a different order to those examined in the previous chapter. In *An Essay on the Production of Wealth*, Torrens refuted Ricardo's labour theory and instead proposed a cost of production theory of value. He admitted that wealth was fundamentally the result of human labour, however, contrary to the theory of Ricardo, he held that the value of commodities in the capitalist system was not regulated by the quantity of labour employed in production but depended also on the amount of capital. To establish the foundations of value, Torrens examined a variety of cases from the simplest to the most complex examples of social and economic organisations. 'In that early period of society which precedes any permanent establishment of the divisions of employment' (Torrens, 1821, p. 17), the exchange value cannot be precisely ascertained and is determined by the respective inclinations to the object of their purchase by the two exchangers (see ibid., p. 18). Then, after the division of employment takes place and exchanges become more frequent, the exchange rate between two commodities will be determined by the quantities of labour necessary for their production (see ibid., pp. 19–21). Subsequently, society evolves even further and in particular 'the labourer and the capitalist become distinct persons' (see ibid., p. 22), ensuring that the labour theory of value no longer holds.

Torrens highlighted the new principle of the determination of the relative value of commodities as follows:

> after the community divides itself into a class of capitalist and a class of labourers, the results obtained by the employment of equivalent capitals or equal quantities of accumulated labour, will be equal in exchangeable value.
>
> (Ibid., pp. 28–9)

Torrens therefore indicated that capital is now the appropriate measure of all things, but by this term he meant labour which had been used to produce instruments of production, as is clear from the above quotation and as is repeated over and over again in his 1821 *Essay*. He distinguished labour into a component directly used up in production, and one which has been accumulated (for example, Torrens, 1821, pp. 25, 34).

Torrens' notion rested on the proposition that no one is prepared to pay for a commodity more than what is required to produce it by using capital. Hence prices are regulated by a sort of opportunity cost in terms of the alternative employment of capital, and they are determined in a system of reproduction in which Torrens emphasised the relationships between output and inputs, between the products and the commodities employed as capital goods in their production. Moreover, Torrens stated that different commodities have different time periods of production, 'different degrees of durability' (ibid., p. 29), hence the periods of employment of labour are different and this means that different sectors use different quantities of capital. This is one of the reasons why prices cannot be in proportion to the labour embodied in production.

With Torrens, therefore, the complexity of the notion of capital came to the fore, and with it, its relationship with the problem of value. Given the nature of capital as previously produced commodities, no easy solution exists to Ricardo's problem of the measurement of value. Following Ricardo, and anticipating Marx, Torrens highlighted a possible case in which exchangeable value is proportionate to the quantity of labour employed in production. This is an 'extremely rare occurrence ... when equal capitals or quantities of accumulated labour, happen to give employment to equal quantities of immediate labour' (ibid., p. 38). This anticipates what Marx was to call the organic composition of capital (see below, Chapter 16), and in a way Torrens therefore opened the way to Marx's analysis of 'prices of production'.

An Essay on the External Corn Trade was published on the very same day, 24 February 1815, as Ricardo's *Essay on Profits*. It included an analysis of the causes determining the rate of profit similar to that described by Ricardo (see above, Chapter 14), 'when the cultivation of inferior soil increases the productive cost, and consequently the exchangeable value, of food and the materials of wrought necessaries, it is quite obvious that manufacturing profits must fall' (Torrens, 1815, pp. 110–11).

Torrens is also particularly clear on the other general causes affecting the profit rate besides 'the quality of the soil'. These include 'the degree of skill with which labour is applied. and the quantity of the productions of labour absorbed as wages' (ibid., p 117).

He therefore also opposed the imposition of duties on the imports of wage goods, but supported duties levied on luxury products. Of course, rents varied inversely to profits when external trade is regulated with import duties on primary products. Hence Torrens shares with Ricardo the notion of comparative advantages in international trade, a theme with which the 1821 *Essay* dealt at length. Its chapter VI examined the question of colonies, which Torrens proposed were beneficial to the mother country.

The Ricardian socialists

The term 'Ricardian socialists' refers to a group of authors who used the labour theory of value as an instrument for advocating social justice and a more egalitarian society. On the basis of the fact that labour creates all values, they asked for a major redistribution of income in favour of the working class. It must be recalled that during this period, British factories had appalling working conditions for women and children as well as for adult males.

In his *Labour Defended Against the Claims of Capital* (1825), Thomas Hodgskin (1787–1869) maintained that capital is unproductive, as are all landlords. Hence the entire social output must accrue to labour. Together with William Thompson, (see next paragraph) he used the labour theory of value to demonstrate the exploitation of the labourers by the capitalists. But as a measure of value, Hodgskin preferred labour commanded, and this enabled him also to derive an inverse relationship between wages and profits.

In 1821, Robert Owen published a *Report to the County of Lanark*. This proposed a remedy for overcoming the exploitation of the labourers through introducing a co-operative system. This question was taken up also by William Thompson, but in a broader and more articulated perspective, within his two major works: *Inquiry into the Principles of the Distribution of Wealth Most Conducive to Human Happiness* (1824) and *Labour Rewarded* (1827). For Thompson, the exploitation of labour is inherent in a capitalist society. He suggested the establishment of a large number of enterprises under workers' self-management in order to overcome the disharmony from the unjust income distribution inherent in the present capitalist system. These self-organised production activities would also avoid excessive power by capitalist-entrepreneurs over their employees.

Other reactions to Ricardo

Torrens' criticism of Ricardo's labour theory of value stayed in the tradition of classical political economy and the same can be said of Malthus' critical perceptives on Ricardo's work. But the situation became different for the criticisms of Ricardo advanced by authors after 1825 and during the early eighteen thirties. These directly challenged both the analysis of value and that of distribution, in particular the Ricardian explanation of profit, thereby attacking the very core of Ricardo's economics.

In 1825, Samuel Bailey published *A Critical Dissertation on the Nature, Measure and Causes of Value* in which he maintained that commodities do not have intrinsic or absolute value. There is no need to distinguish between nominal and real value. The only meaningful notion of value is that of a relative value; exchange value is a relationship between things.

Moreover, value is the expression of an evaluation which derives from the feelings of individuals, hence he subscribed to the idea of a subjective value (cf. Dobb, 1973, pp. 99ff.).

In *A Lecture on the Notion of Value* (1833) W.F. Lloyd distinguished total utility from marginal utility, and more clearly than Bailey, argued that the exchange value of goods depended on marginal utility. Mountifort Longfield is another author who tackled the problem of value in his *Lectures on Political Economy* (1834). Initially, in a non-Ricardian manner he seems to have followed the classical economists and maintained that cost of production of a commodity strongly influences its price. But he subsequently suggested that the cost of production of goods only regulated their supply, while their demand is determined by considerations associated with their utility. Longfield focussed attention on the notion of 'intensity of demand', and in his investigations came close to the concept of a declining demand function, and to the view that market price largely depends on marginal utility (O'Brien, 1975 pp. 103–4).

Longfield introduced also the idea that profit derives from the efficiency of the last item of capital employed. According to him, efficiency decreases with the increase of the amount of capital, and this is an anticipation of the idea that the marginal product of capital determines the rate of profit. Such a theory (as shown in Part II, Chapters 23 and 24) did not come into general acceptance until much later on the nineteenth century. The above mentioned some English forerunners of marginalist economics; the work of von Thünen on agriculture, and of Dupuit, Cournot and Gossen on value and price determination anticipated aspects of the marginalist view in different ways (discussed briefly in Chapter 17 below).

Nassau William Senior, 1790–1864: value and abstinence

Nassau Senior commenced with legal studies for the London Bar. He became the first Drummond Professor of Political Economy at Oxford (1825–30), being elected to a second term later in his life (1847–52). In 1831, he was appointed Professor of Political economy at King's College, London, but he had to resign this position because of his support for the view that some Church in Ireland revenues should be passed to the Roman Catholic Church. Between 1832 and 1834, he was in charge of writing the Report of a Commission appointed to inquire into the Administration and Operation of the Poor Laws. In 1841, Senior wrote the Report of the Commission on the condition of Unemployed Hand-loom Weavers. Senior was elected to membership of the Political Economy Club in 1823, remaining a member for the rest of his life, except for the period 1848–53. In 1821, Senior published an article on the Corn Laws in the *Quarterly Review*; from 1821 to 1859 he was a regular contributor to the *Edinburgh Review*. His major contribution to economics in book form is his *Outline of the Science of*

Political economy (1836). Other significant writings of economics are his *Two Lectures on Population, with a Correspondence between the Author and T.R. Malthus* (1829) and *Two Letters on the Factory Acts* (1837).

There are at least two reasons for Senior's importance in the economic discussion of the 1830s. First, he made important contributions anticipating concepts which later became part of marginalist economics. Secondly, Senior was deeply involved in economic policy debates of the period, in particular those concerning the Poor Laws and in legislation to limit the working hours in British factories.

In 1828, at the beginning of his career, and while Drummond Professor at Oxford, Senior wrote *Two Lectures on Population with a Correspondence between the Author and T.R. Malthus*, in which he criticised Malthus' views on population on the ground that the subsistence wage should be defined in social term, and not purely in physical ones (Winch, 1996, pp. 372–3). What was thought to be socially necessary tended to include more and more goods not strictly necessary, given the increase of wealth and luxuries from rising productivity (Senior, 1829, pp. 34–5). Torrens shared this view in the Appendix to *An Essay on the External Corn Trade* (Torrens, 1829, pp. 473ff). Moreover, the fear of workers on reducing their quality of life, was a strong preventive check, inducing a spontaneous limitation of births, a theme he took up again in his *Outline of the Science of Political Economy* (Senior, 1836, pp. 30ff).

In this work, Senior identified three main productive principles: labour, nature and abstinence where the last referred to an essential condition for securing the material capital necessary for production. The concept of abstinence is a good example of the nature of Senior's contributions to economics. He defined it as follows:

> *By the word Abstinence, we wish to express that agent, distinct from labour and the agency of nature, the concurrence of which is necessary to the existence of Capital, and which stands in the same relation to Profit as labour does to Wages.*
>
> (Senior, 1836, p. 59; italics in the original)

Hence profit is clearly justified, because it is a necessary and just reward for the decision to abstain from consumption and enjoyment. Profit was no longer conceivable as an unearned surplus or the result of exploitation of the workers. With minor modifications, the principle of abstinence was present in the works of John Stuart Mill (see below, Chapter 18). The explanation of profits as a saving from present income in order to increase production and consumption in the future, became particularly successful in neoclassical economics (see Part II, Chapter 24 on Böhm-Bawerk).

When abstinence was justification for the existence of profits, the value of the rate of profit came to depend also on the average period of production, and hence on the length of the period of anticipation of capital. As a matter of fact, capital was made up from wages which had to be advanced, while the unit wage depended on the demand and supply of labour. Explaining the demand for labour was another interesting aspect of Senior's economics, in fact this demand depended on the existing wage-fund, a notion achieving considerable success during the middle of nineteenth century. (The wage-fund was the amount of consumption goods, not augmentable in the short period.) Contrary to Ricardo, the wage rate for Senior was no longer given at subsistence level. What is fixed is the overall wage bill, or wage fund, that is the amount of goods available to the workers as wages. With a given wage fund, any increase in the unit wage will inevitably reduce employment, since fewer workers can be supported from the fund.

In his analysis of value, Senior stated that value is determined by demand and supply. Demand depends on utility, which in turn is related to the intensity of the pain or pleasure obtained by the consumption of a commodity and by its scarcity (see Senior, 1834, pp. 14–15). Therefore, value is strictly dependent on the subjective evaluations of the parties involved in exchange because different persons have different evaluations of the same good, the reason why exchanges take place is explained. Senior did not omit cost of production from consideration, but this only affects value in so far as it helped to explain the relative scarcity of a commodity. Ultimately, cost of production, which for Senior also included entrepreneurial profits, only determined the minimum price a producer could accept.

Senior is also well-known for his formulation of the so-called four postulates of economic science. According to him, these propositions derived from common sense observations of fact, and had to be accepted as the necessary foundations for any economic theory and policy. The four postulates are summarised as follows (see ibid., p. 26):

1. Every person seeks the largest achievable addition to his wealth, with the least possible sacrifice.
2. Population is limited only by moral and physical evil, or by the fear of a lack of subsistence goods.
3. The productive powers of labour and of all the instruments of production may be indefinitely increased by using their outputs as inputs in further production processes.
4. With a given technology and given skill, there are decreasing returns to scale for labour employed in agriculture.

These propositions represent a good description of the state of economics by the middle of the 1830s. Some of Senior's 'postulates' denoted already well accepted principles, such as Malthus' population theory, and the existence of decreasing returns in agriculture. The first proposition may also be regarded as a rather obvious, and hence trivial, statement, but it also anticipated the later principle of utility maximisation under constraints. The third 'postulate' too can be seen as a trivial observation, but it introduced the problem of the duration of the period of production and the idea of *roundaboutness* as fundamental features of all the processes of production which employ capital. (The last was used heavily in the capital theory of Böhm-Bawerk; see below, Chapter 24).

Senior on the Poor Laws and the working class

In the economic policy debates of 1830s, Senior gained a reputation as a staunch conservative. The first cause for this arose from his views on the *Poor Laws*, a system which provided for the compulsory assistance to the very poorest of society through local workhouses and parish relief. The system had been introduced as far back as 1536, and over the centuries its administration had become extremely costly (Routh, 1975, pp. 151–2). Senior was a member of the Commission which in 1832 began investigation of the system. Senior was in fact largely responsible for drafting the final bill, approved in 1834. This bill proposed reform of the system by which subsidies and assistance were to be confined to poor people working in workhouses, but general parish support for the poor, so-called 'outdoor relief', was abolished (O'Brien, 1975, pp. 281–2).

By way of justification for the Bill, Senior indicated that wages had to be proportionate to the actual service rendered by workers, and not to their actual needs. Poor Laws providing too generous benefits risked producing laziness in workers, because either they obtained a living without having to work, or they were able to accept low wages in exchange for little devotion to their work.

The other big policy issue of the time in which Senior was involved, was the debate on the 'Ten hours Bill', which proposed to reduce the maximum number of daily working hours for the people of less than eighteen years of age in the textile industry from twelve hours to ten. The first Factory Act of 1802 had set a limit of twelve working hours a day for the young, a regulation confirmed in 1819 for all workers of less than sixteen years of age. In 1831 the law was extended to cover all workers below the age of eighteen. Senior was totally opposed to such a limitation. According to him:

> a reduction of the hours of work in cotton factories, to ten hours a day, would be attended by the most fatal consequences, and that evil would fall first on the working class.
>
> (Senior, 1837, p. 4)

It may be noted that use of the term, 'labouring poor', as used by Adam Smith, had evolved into the term 'working class' by the mid-nineteenth century. Senior's worries about reducing the hours of work rested on his view about the origin of industrial profit, 'Now, the following analysis will show that in a mill so worked, the whole net profit is derived from the last hour' (ibid., p. 12).

Net profit, which according to Senior only was ten per cent, was entirely earned during the last hour of work. Hence, the textile industry would be unable to undergo the reorganisation of its productive processes required by the compulsory reduction of working hours, even if only for the youngest workers. In particular, a reduction by an hour and a half per day would have implied a reduction of both gross and net profits and made it impossible to replace the wear and tear of fixed capital (see ibid., p. 12).

In the first volume of *Capital*, Marx made sarcastic comments on Senior's position with regard to this problem, but history has opposed Senior on this issue as well. In 1837, the *Ten Hours Bill* was rejected by the English Parliament. However, it was approved ten years later, without the dire consequences which Senior, and others, had predicted.

Notes on further readings

For Torrens, quotations come from R. Torrens (1821), *An Essay on the Production of Wealth* (Kelley Reprints, 1965), and R. Torrens (1815), *An Essay on the External Corn Trade* (Kelley, New York, 1972) which is based on the 1829 fourth edition. On the relationship between Torrens' analysis and that of Ricardo, see G. de Vivo, 'Robert Torrens and Ricardo's "corn ratio" theory of profits' (*Cambridge Journal of Economics*, 1985). See also the C. Benetti's entry on Torrens in the *The Elgar Companion to Classical Economics* (edited by H. Kurz and N. Salvadori, Edward Elgar, Cheltenham, 1998). A standard interpretation of Torrens is L. Robbins, *Robert Torrens and the Evolution of Classical Economics* (Macmillan – now Palgrave Macmillan, London, 1958).

Senior's most well-known work is his 1836 *An Outline of the Science of Political Economy* (Reprints of Economic Classics, Augustus M. Kelley, New York, 1965). The same publisher has reprinted all the other works in N.W. Senior, *Selected Writings on Economics – a Volume of Pamphlets 1827–1852* (Augustus M. Kelley, New York, 1966) a very interesting collection of pamphlets and public letters. Among other works, this edition includes *Two Lectures on Population, with a Correspondence between the Author and T.R. Malthus* of 1829 and *Two Letters on the Factory Acts* of 1837. A classic commentary on Senior's contribution is M. Bowley, *Nassau Senior and Classical Economics* (Allen and Unwin, London, 1937). The story of the debate over the tenth hour of work is told in O. Johnson 'The "last hour" of Senior and Marx', *History of Political Economy* (autumn 1969).

On the Ricardian Socialists, see A. Ginzburg's entry in the *New Palgrave Dictionary of Economics*. On the main economists of the 1820s and 1830s who followed the age of Ricardo, and in particular the first major dissenters from his value and distribution theory, see M. Dobb, *Theories of Value and Distribution since Adam Smith* (Cambridge University Press, Cambridge, 1973, ch. 4). A different perspective on that period is D. Winch, *Riches and Poverty: an Intellectual History of Political Economy in Britain*, 1750–1834 (Cambridge University Press, Cambridge, 1996). On the debates following Ricardo's death, see also S. Hollander, 'The post-Ricardian discussion: a case study on economics and ideology', *Oxford Economic Papers* (November 1980). Reference can also usefully be made to D.P. O'Brien, *The Classical Economists*, Clarendon Press, Oxford, 1975, chapters 4 and 10 especially.

16
Karl Marx, 1818–83: the Critique of Political Economy

This chapter concludes Part I of this study in the history of economic thought. Apart from dealing with Marx's contributions, it provides a more general summary view on theories of surplus.

Karl Heinrich Marx was born on 5 May 1818, the son of a Jewish rabbi and lawyer, Heinrich Marx. Marx studied first at the gymnasium in Trier, and then at the universities of Bonn and Berlin. His doctoral thesis on natural philosophy was accepted at the University of Jena in 1841. Two years later (1843) he married Jenny von Westphalen, the daughter of a prominent Prussian civil servant.

On completing his formal studies, Marx took up journalism, both to spread his ideas and to earn his living. In 1842, he became editor of the *Rheinische Zeitung*, a liberal newspaper of Cologne. He became more and more attracted to political and social questions, which he increasingly treated in a radical way.

The 1844 *Economic and Philosophical Manuscripts* show that by then Marx had become a proponent of collective ownership of the means of production. To escape the Prussian censorship, he emigrated to Paris, where he lived from 1843 to 1845 and met his lifelong friend Friedrich Engels, the wealthy son of a Birmingham manufacturer. In 1847, he published *The Poverty of Philosophy* as criticism of a book by the French anarchist, Proudhon, called the *Philosophy of Poverty*. In 1848, with Engels, he wrote the *Manifesto of the Communist Party*, one of his most famous works.

Marx was expelled from France in 1845 and migrated to Brussels. During the 1848 revolution, he was also expelled from Belgium, going first back to France and then to Cologne. In 1849, on the triumph of the Prussian counterrevolution, Marx was expelled from Prussia. Marx emigrated to London where he lived, with only short interruptions, for the rest of his life. He never had a permanent job, though in 1851 he became the European correspondent of the *New York Daily Tribune*. This collaboration (which ended in 1861) and financial support from his friend Engels kept Marx and his family alive, though only three of their seven children survived. For fifteen years, Marx dedicated his efforts in London mainly to economic studies. From 1852 to 1859, he wrote a rough draft of this economic system, published a hundred years later as the *Grundrisse*. In 1859, he published his *Contribution to a Critique of Political Economy*, the two chapters of which were based on the *Grundrisse* material. The First International Association of Workers met in London in 1864, in which Marx participated as delegate for the German workers. The first volume of *Capital* was published in 1867. In 1871, Marx passionately defended the Paris Commune, but the divisions inside the International Association of Workers induced a split in the worker's movement with the anarchists led by Michael Bakunin. Marx's final years were increasingly marred by bad health. His wife had died in 1881, and Karl Marx did not survive her for long: he died in London in 1883. The second and third volumes of *Capital* were therefore posthumously published by Engels in 1885 and 1894 respectively. During the early 1860s, Marx had also been working on a historical review of previous political economy for a fourth volume called *Theories of Surplus Value* (see Dobb, 1973, p. 165) which in 1905 was published under this name by Karl Kautsky.

Three major philosophical strands influenced Marx's thought, German idealism, and Hegel as presented in particular by Feuerbach were the first. Secondly, were socialist ideas, gaining pace in Europe from the times of the French Revolution in an enormous range and variety. Thirdly, and most important for this book, was 'classical political economy', and in particular that of Ricardo, which he studied especially in London from the late 1840s. Dobb remarks that Marx was the first person to use the term 'classical political economy' (Dobb, 1973, p.142; cf. Schumpeter, 1954 p. 390).

The 'modes of production' and the laws of social movement

To be better equipped for reading *Capital*, it is useful to start with the content of works immediately preceding it, and in particular with *Contribution to a Critique of Political Economy* and its famous *Preface*. According to Marx, the British classical economists had erred by confusing the laws of development of the economy and, more generally that of societies, with laws of nature, thus failing to realise that such regularities were specific to a particular phase in the history of mankind. Marx defined these economists as 'bourgeois', while economists dedicated to capitalist apologetics were called 'vulgar' economists. For Marx, each society was characterised by some general economic features: production, exchange, distribution and consumption which, however, found their concrete expression at a specific time and place in history. These general common features, or general laws, have to be distilled from the features of specific historical periods, but simultaneously, this approach implies that many specific features of society are ignored, at least temporarily, as a necessary form of simplification. The social scientist needs to be aware of what is left out from the analysis. This is the method of abstraction and determination, that is explained in Marx's famous *Introduction to the Contribution to a Critique of Political Economy* (1859) and in the opening pages of its predecessor, the *Grundrisse* (or draft).

This methodology informs the study of the laws of motion of history and, especially, that of capitalism. The basic objective of Marx's wide and complex analysis, in part at least, is reminiscent of the approach of Enlightenment scholars, especially Smith. For Marx, the starting point is the fact that there is no unique and universal way of organising economic relations among individuals. Feudalism was superseded by capitalism, which in turn, and due to its own internal contradictions, would give rise to another form of social organisation. The laws of motion of capitalism are a major target of analysis for Marx, but the intricacies of this large and complicated object are difficult to disentangle.

The complex system of relations among the individuals characterising society at a given time is called a social formation. Marx first established a distinction between the 'structure, or 'economic base' of society, and its 'superstructure' (see Marx, 1859, Preface). The former includes the four general elements in which economic relationships can be divided, the latter encompasses remaining aspects arising from politics, religion, art, ethics, etc. Marx acknowledged the existence of an interaction between 'structure' and superstructure', but in order to understand the evolution of human societies, the modifications taking place in their 'economic' base need to be particularly studied. This is what the materialistic interpretation of history is all about. There are clear similarities between Marx' approach and the eighteenth century 'four stages theory' (outlined in Chapter 8, above).

Even so, the 'structure' remains extremely complex. As a matter of fact, there are several ways in which the four general economic relationships between individuals can be shaped, that is, there are several 'modes of production'. In turn, each mode of production includes two different elements: first the development of the productive forces: labour, natural resources, means, instruments and techniques of production; second, the social relationships of production, that is, the specific ways in which the productive forces are related to one another. Marx described three major examples of mode of production:

1. *The ancient mode of production*, which is based on private property in labour, that is, on slavery. Labour, the most valuable of the productive forces, is completely restricted both in the sphere of circulation and in that of production.
2. *The feudal mode of production*, based on property in land and natural resources. Labour is partly the property of the feudal lord, and there also

are personal obligations to the state, such as the corvée. However feudal labourers can partly decide how to employ their own labour when landlords do not need them. This partial freedom facilitates the rise of free manufacturers.

3. *The capitalistic mode of production*, in which there is private property of all the means of productions. In the sphere of circulation, the labourers are legally free to seek employment in any capitalist firm, but once they have become salaried workers and entered the sphere of production, then they are completely restricted. Once they have sold their labour power, they cannot influence decisions about which commodities to produce, their quantity and, above all, production techniques. The classical economists failed to see this particular aspect of capitalist production, that is, that the system based on private property of the means of production only offers a partial liberty, because there is no freedom for workers in the production process. On the contrary, the system is based on the alienation of labour, both in the sense that labour has become a commodity which is being sold, or alienated, on the market, and in the sense of the distance which exists between wage workers and the product of their labour. They are estranged from the result of their efforts, since they no longer can take decisions about production.

Each society is normally characterised by the coexistence of more than one mode of production. One of these may *dominate* the other ones, in which case it gives its name to that particular society, or phase of history. Thus capitalism is the social formation in which the capitalist mode of production dominates. Domination means that the mode of production in question imposes its laws, and in particular the law of value, on every other mode of production: for instance international prices are established according to the capitalistic mode of production even if the same good is also produced in pre-capitalistic conditions. The dominant mode of production enlarges its sway over the productive forces and in particular over labour; thus peasants for example, are transformed into wage workers.

When no mode of production clearly dominates the others there is a phase of *transition* in which the economic elements of two or more mode of production coexist. For instance, in Europe the passage from feudalism to capitalism took several centuries to complete. It was a long transition. Each mode of production promotes the development of its productive forces, also through the use, or expropriation, of nature. For Marx, however, at a certain point, the social relationship of production no longer provide this economic improvement, but on the contrary becomes a barrier to the further development of the productive forces. A phase of recurrent crisis opens and history shows that in the end each mode of production is overcome by the next one. This had been the case in the transition from feudalism to Capitalism, but the latter likewise is not a universal and eternal form of organisation of the economic sphere of society.

Marx provided only very quick sketches of the future forms of social organisations. Socialism is the name of the phase in transitions commencing when the dominance of the capitalistic mode of production is being challenged. But socialism is not an independent mode of production. That position is reserved for the communist stage (mode of production) in which each individual receives according to their needs and not according to their productive efforts. Moreover, private expropriation of labour will cease to exist under communism, as Marx predicted.

The essential scientific task for Marx was not so much that of detailing the characteristics of future society, but of analysing the essential mechanism of the capitalistic mode of production. What are the forces determining the motion of both the structure, and of the totality of society? In particular, Marx wanted to show that capitalism is not everlasting, because of its inherent contradictions. This was the purpose he set himself in writing *Capital*.

The capitalist mode of production and the labour theory of value

Capital analyses the laws which regulate the capitalist mode of production when they are reduced to their essence, to the specific social relationship of production which characterises this mode of production. The analysis is in simplified abstract terms, for example, in the sense that only two classes exist in society, the salaried workers and the capitalists. The opening sentences of Marx's work introduce the definition of wealth:

> the wealth of those societies in which the capitalist mode of production prevails, presents itself as 'an immense accumulation of commodities'.
>
> (Marx, 1867, p. 43)

Marx had already used this expression in the *Contribution to a Critique of Political Economy*, and undoubtedly commodities are the visible sign of wealth. However, this does not imply that commodities are the essence of wealth and value. In fact, Marx dedicated the entire first section of Book I exploring the relationship between value, exchange and commodities.

Establishing the true origin of value and the causes for the increase of wealth in the capitalist mode of production constitutes the essence of Marx's problem. In section II, as a preliminary step, the relationship between money, commodities and capital is explored. Here Marx highlighted another mode of production, that of *simple commodity production*, where labour is free both in the sphere of circulation and in that of production. There is common property in both the means of production and natural resources and exchange of commodities is regulated by the labour theory of value. Production and exchange take place on the basis of the use value of commodities and money is just an intermediary; thus the typical exchange relationship is Commodity–Money–Commodity (or C–M–C). This is, 'the simplest form of the circulation by contrast of commodities' (ibid., p. 146). In the capitalist mode of production, on the other hand, production takes place on the basis of exchange value and not their use value. The typical reproduction cycle now becomes Money–Commodity –Money (or M–C–M) or rather M–C–M' where M' > M, because it 'would be absurd and without meaning if the intention were to exchange by this means two equal sums of money' (ibid.). What matters to the capitalists, is the opportunity for the invested capital, M, to reproduce its exchange value with an additional surplus value, M'–M: 'this increment or excess over the original value I call 'surplus value' (ibid., p. 149). This surplus value constitutes the true essence of value and wealth in the capitalist mode of production. Each capitalist operates only to gain surplus value. This necessitates explaining the origin of this magnitude and the causes affecting its size.

In their analysis of the capitalist system, according to Marx, the classical economists had overlooked the fact that the true origin of surplus value was to be found in the way in which the process of production is organised, and not in an act of exchange. In order to present this view in the first book of *Capital* in a simple way, Marx assumed that the prices of commodities were determined by the quantities of labour embodied in their production. However, in the sphere of circulation of commodities, values can only be exchanged for values of equal dimension; no addition to value is possible in such circumstances (ibid., pp. 158–9). Hence, another concept is needed to explain the origin of value. Marx discovers this concept in labour power, a unique commodity, because it alone is capable of the creation of value. He defined labour power as follows:

> By labour-power or capacity for labour is to be understood the aggregate of those mental and physical capabilities existing in a human being.
>
> (ibid. p. 164)

In the generalised capitalist mode of production, it is this general productive capacity of labour which is crucial to valorisation of capital; not the specific abilities of the actual workers. The labour force is itself a commodity, which represents the average productive power of labour. Its value, v, or *variable capital*, is given by the labour embodied in the means of subsistence necessary for its reproduction. The process of production of a commodity, of course, also required raw materials and means of production such as machinery. The labour embodied in their production takes the name of *constant capital*, c. Marx described this as 'dead labour', which only acquired a value in so far as raw materials and means of production are combined with labour power, the living labour, the only thing capable of transforming dead labour into value. Once the productive powers of labour are bought for a wage, their specific use depends on the capitalist and on the way in which he decides to combine the labour force with other productive forces. This production process contains the origin of surplus value, s (ibid., ch. VII, pp. 173ff).

The overall value of a commodity (m) is defined by Marx as $m = c + v + s$. Here c does not refer to the stock of physical capital but to the flow of capital services used up to produce m. This is raw materials used up plus depreciation of the plant, fuel, power and so on.

Suppose a legal working day of 8 hours. Only 5 hours are needed to reproduce the goods necessary for the subsistence of the labourer, or the variable capital $(v = 5)$. Assume $c = 5$ as well, the total capital used up and required for the day, is $c + v = 10$. However, living labour is active, purchased for 8 hours, which exceeds v by 3. The surplus value is 3 in this case. It constitutes the unpaid part of the working day, or the surplus value s, in fact a surplus labour. The overall value $(m) = 13$, s/v Marx defined as the rate of exploitation, or rate of surplus value, in this example $3/5 = 60$ per cent.

Marx emphasised that surplus value does not depend on an act of unequal exchange on the labour market, but on the necessary obligations of workers in the process of production according to the rules of the game of the capitalist system. The capitalist has full control of the production process. He therefore also continually tries to increase his surplus. He can do this in two ways. First, he can try to lengthen the duration of the working day which determines $v + s$, or he can attempt to give fewer wage goods to the worker (lower v). Both strategies increase s. Marx gave a special name to surplus from the first strategy. 'The surplus-value produced by prolongation of the working day I call *absolute surplus-value*' (ibid., p. 299).

The working day cannot of course, be extended to infinity. It has physical, moral and legal limitations but no precise limit can be set for the minimum length of the working day (see ibid., ch. X pp. 222ff.). It, however, needs to be sufficient to produce the commodities which make up the subsistence of the workers, v. Marx dedicated many pages to discussing the length of the working day, within a brilliant historical description of the social and political history of England's manufacturing in the nineteenth century. He also made much fun of Senior's opposition to the ten-hours bill during the 1836 debate on the Factory Act (see ibid., pp. 215 and above, Chapter 15).

Moreover, Marx rejected Malthus' explanation of the tendency of wages to approach physical subsistence. For Marx, the subordinate condition of the worker in the labour market was not due to their excessive reproduction, but to the fact that by introducing new machines and new production techniques, the capitalists continuously recreated a mass of unemployed people, what Marx called the 'progressive production of relative surplus-population or industrial reserve army' (see ibid., pp. 589ff.). This is one of the essential elements of the 'general law of capitalist accumulation' (ch. XXIII) and a crucial part of the first volume of *Capital*.

Absolute surplus-value is therefore, however, difficult to achieve. There is another, much more effective way of increasing the rate of exploitation: lowering the value of variable capital v, 'the surplus-value arising from the curtailment of the necessary labour-time, and from the corresponding alteration in the respective lengths of the two components of the working-day, I call *relative surplus-value*' (ibid., p. 299). New machines and new technology tended to increase the productivity of the labour employed in the production of wage goods, thus the same physical bundle of wage goods had a lower value v. This result strongly resembled Ricardo's analysis of the causes of the rate of profit (see above, Chapter 14). But Marx clarified that while the increase in the surplus value appears to be the result of technology and physical capital, it was due in fact to increase in the productivity of labour.

The reproduction schemes and crises

In Book II of *Capital*, which appeared after his death in 1885, Marx investigated the conditions of reproduction of the capitalist system. This was done in so-called 'reproduction schemes', abstract representations of the economy. Such reproduction schemes are particularly clearly described in Sweezy's *Theories of Capitalist Development*. They derived directly from the *Tableau Economique*, in which according to Marx, Quesnay provided a superior treatment of the reproduction problem to that given by Smith (see Marx, 1885, pp. 363–4; see also Marx, 1905, vol. I, p. 308). The economy was assumed to consist of two sectors, or 'departments' (ibid., p. 399); the first produced commodity 1 which includes every segment of constant capital c; the latter produced commodity 2, that is to say the wage goods or 'v'. Both the wage goods and the means of production are advanced by the capitalists at the beginning of the production process.

c_1 and c_2 are the constant capital in sectors 1 and 2 respectively, v_1 and v_2 are the values of variable capital and s_1 and s_2 are the surplus values created in sectors 1 and 2.

The reproduction scheme can then be represented as follows:

$$c_1 + v_1 + s_1 = m_1 \qquad\qquad 16.1$$
$$c_2 + v_2 + s_2 = m_2$$

First, Marx analysed what he described as *simple reproduction*, in which the surplus is entirely consumed and there is no net investment (see ibid., pp. 398–9). The output of constant capital is equal to the quantity which is used in production as input, $m_1 = c_1 + c_2$ and, of course, $m_2 = v_1 + v_2 + s_1 + s_2$.

For the economy to be able to reproduce itself on an unchanged scale, it is necessary for sector 1 to buy wage goods from sector 2, and this latter sector has to buy the means of production from sector 1. Therefore, the structure and size of capital establishes the technical conditions of reproduction, which are satisfied by the exchange ratio $c_2 = v_1 + s_1$.

In the case of expanded reproduction, part of the surplus is invested and hence becomes new capital, that is, additional to the amount strictly necessary to replace the inputs used up in production. Now $m_1 > c_1 + c_2$, and part of commodity 2 needs to be set aside to enable the requisite increase in the variable capital. There is now no longer any simple exchange ratio which secures the reproduction of the economy. In particular, the input structure of production is no longer sufficient to determine the relative price between the two commodities.

Throughout the whole of volume II, Marx highlighted the possibility that the process of reproduction of capital generates major problems in the form of crises. The process of reproduction developed crises of various types. A possible cause of crisis is disproportionate development of the two sectors, for instance, there is an excess in production of constant capital because there is not enough variable capital to combine with it. These kind of crises are characterised by an excess of output in one sector with a concomitant deficiency in the other.

Another type of crises is that of general over-production or under-consumption, a phenomenon not limited to a particular sector of the economy, but according to Marx, a feature of the long run dynamics of the capitalist mode of production. This point was also explored at length in volume III. It also signalled one of the major criticisms by Marx of what he called bourgeois economics, including that of Smith and Ricardo. In fact, Marx maintained that they were especially wrong in ruling out the possibility of a generalised crisis (see Marx, 1905 vol. II, ch. XVII). There, he particularly criticised Ricardo; the chapter sub-title being 'the very nature of capital leads to crises' (Marx, 1905, p. 470). In order to obtain surplus value, capitalists must not only increase the rate of exploitation (s/v) but must also successfully sell their products on the market. But the exploitation of the workers squeezes their purchasing power and hence their ability to consume, thereby creating the potential for a lack of effective demand. Clearly, Marx rejected Say's law (Dobb, 1973, p. 164). Commodities were sometimes sold below their value and then surplus value was not realised. Production and consumption decisions were then no longer in harmony. Capitalists could try various methods to secure the valorisation of their capital: new techniques and new products, the establishment of cartels, take-overs and mergers, collusion with the State. According to Marx, however, capitalists were in vigorous competition against each other and all these methods in the end cannot prevent the occurrence of increasingly frequent crises. These represent the internal contradiction of the capitalist mode of production, which requires growing exploitation in order to increase surplus value, but by so doing endangers the conditions for the realisation of the surplus value itself. The deficient demand aspect of Marx's analysis of crises was developed by Rosa Luxembourg in her *The Accumulation of Capital* of 1913. The 2008 financial crisis had many features of an overproduction crisis, the outcome of the very high investment ratios applicable to some East Asian countries during the last forty years. Some productive sectors appear close to saturation while many emerging economies are trying to preserve their cheap natural resources.

The accumulation of capital and the fall of the rate of profit

The process of capital accumulation entails a tendency to decrease the share of output going to the labourers, who become poorer and poorer and thereby generate under-consumption crises. However, in the long-run, the accumulation of capital has also a direct negative impact on the rate of profit, r, which is defined by Marx as the ratio of surplus value to the total capital (see Marx, 1894, p. 42):

$$r = s/(c + v) \text{ and dividing by } v:$$
$$r = (s/v)/(c/v + 1). \qquad\qquad 16.2$$

c/v was what Marx called the organic composition of capital, and s/v is, as already explained, the rate of exploitation.

What (in Marx, 1867, ch. XXIII) Marx called 'the general law of capitalistic accumulation', can now be examined. In order to increase surplus value, capitalists try to reduce the value of labour, the wage rate, v through the introduction of new techniques and new machines. This implies a decrease of v with respect to c and hence an increase in the organic composition of capital, which, as already explained, has a negative effect on the rate of profit. The rate of exploitation cannot increase indefinitely, because v cannot fall to zero and there is an upper bound to the length of the working day. But there is no such a limit for constant capital, c, on the contrary, its value increases continuously precisely because each capitalist is interested in pursuing a labour saving strategy and to introduce machines, able to displace labour.

This is a further major contradiction of the capitalist mode of production, in which accumulation of capital is needed in order to generate surplus value and profits, while the very same process of accumulation, by increasing c, lowers future profitability. The capitalist mode of production, therefore, has an in-built conflict between the fundamental social relations of production and the development of the productive forces; as for all the previous mode of production, the capitalistic model will be subject to an irreversible crisis and will thereby pass out of history.

It is likely that Marx viewed this as a very long-run tendency in capitalist development. Marx in any case recognised that there were situations capable of slowing down the actual fall of r. Apart from changes in absolute and relative surplus value, two other factors were identified as capable of delaying the fall in the rate of profit. When faced with declining profitability, the capitalist in an open economy can invest abroad. The most effective way of postponing the fall of r, however, seems to be technical progress in the production of new machines. By increasing the productivity of labour in sector 1, this reduces the labour value of c, consequently raising the rate of profit.

The transformation of values into prices of production

Marx was painfully aware of the fact that in a capitalist economy with free circulation of capital and a uniform rate of profit, labour embodied can be used as a measure of relative prices only under very special conditions. Examining equations (16.1) once more, where the labour theory of value is in operation and all the magnitudes are measured in terms of units of labour, two profit rates can then be calculated in the following way:

$$r_1 = (s_1/v_1)/(1 + c_1/v_1);$$
$$r_2 = (s_2/v_2)/(1 + c_2/v_2).$$
16.3

With free competition, the wage rate and the length of the working day are identical in both sectors, as is the rate of exploitation. But in order to have $r_1 = r_2$ it is also necessary to have $c_1/v_1 = c_2/v_2$. The second requirement implies that the value of capital per employee is the same in all sectors, and that all productive processes use an identical technology for uniform profit rates to prevail. This is a highly unrealistic situation, as Marx accepted in *Capital*, vol. III, chapter VIII (Marx, 1895, pp. 142ff.). Of course, Marx was not able to accept the existence of different profit rates because it violated his competitive economy assumption. Therefore, in order to have both a uniform rate of profit and different techniques of production, the labour embodied as a measure of value had to be abandoned and could not act as the unit of measurement for the magnitudes, c, v, s and m.

Marx tried to resolve this problem in *Capital*, volume III, Part II. His concept of prices of production was directly derived from labour values, but satisfied the condition of uniformity of the profit rate; then prices are calculated by applying the same rate of profit to the capital invested in the two sectors (Marx, 1894, p. 164):

$$(c_1 + v_1)(1 + r) = p_1$$
$$(c_2 + v_2)(1 + r) = p_2$$
16.4

p_1 and p_2 are the values of output measured as prices of production; the relative price of the two commodities depends on the labour values which appear as input in their production and on the rate of profit r which is the average rate of profit of the system:

$$r = (s_1 + s_2)/(v_1 + v_2) + (c_1 + c_2)$$ 16.5

Because of competition among capitalists, the surplus value in this case is not necessarily appropriated by the capitalists of the sector in which it originates, but according to where the capital has been invested. Thus a sector with a lot of capital may obtain more surplus value than what was directly generated in that sector.

If, in general, profits and surplus values do not coincide in production sectors, Marx was nevertheless able to show that two conditions hold: first, the aggregate profit of the system is equal to the aggregate surplus value and (16.4) the value of output measured at prices of production is equal to its aggregate labour embodied. The labour theory of value is not an appropriate theory of relative prices, but presumed useful for solving problems at the macro level. For instance, GDP can be measured by the number of people annually employed. Likewise, the labour theory of value can continue to act as a theory of exploitation for the economy as a whole. On aggregate, profits are derived from surplus labour, reflecting the fundamental contradiction of a capitalist mode of production: that between wage labour and capital in the sphere of production where the exploitation dimension is determined. The fact that this surplus value then circulates among capitalists according to the rule of a uniform rate of profit reflects another, but less important conflict in Marx's view, that among capitalists themselves.

However, the process of transformation as presented by Marx was flawed. In system (16.4), the two commodities are exchanged according to the prices of production when they are regarded as outputs, but they are evaluated at their values when used as inputs. In fact, sector 1 buys wage goods from sector 2 paying them v_1, that is, they are bought at their labour value. The same is true for the other inputs. The problem can also be examined by taking equation (16.5); how can the rate of profit be measured in labour values if commodities must be exchanged at prices of production? Marx seemed to realise that his solution was incorrect; but no further improvements to the argument were made by him.

In 1907, Ladislaus von Bortikievicz, a Polish economist, first provided a correct 'transformation' of labour values into prices of production (see Bortikievicz, 1907). It takes into account that both outputs and inputs have to be transformed into prices of production, so that system (2) has to be rewritten as follows:

$$(c_1 x_1 + v_1 x_2)(1 + r) = m_1 x_1$$ 16.6
$$(c_2 x_1 + v_2 x_2)(1 + r) = m_2 x_2$$

where x_1 and x_2 are the prices of production of one hour of labour employed in the production of sector 1 and 2 respectively. If the labour theory of value applies, then $x_1 = x_2$.

When $x_2 = 1$, the system presents two equations and two unknowns, r and x_1. The rate of profit is now determined simultaneously with the relative price and not before, as was the case in Marx's argument. Most importantly, the rate of profit is different from the average profit rate as calculated by Marx in equation (16.3). The two equalities of total labour and the value of output, and of total profit and surplus value, no longer hold. Even at the macro level, profit may be higher than surplus value, hence it is impossible to represent all profit as value surplus, as a kind of aggregated demonstration of exploitation along the lines of Marx's original argument.

What are the consequences of Marx's transformation problem for his general theory of the capitalist mode of production? In 1896, Böhm-Bawerk was the first author to stress the existence of an inescapable contradiction between Book I and III of *Capital* and to suggest that this undermined the entire Marxian system. Many other economic writers have since then demonstrated inconsistencies in Marx's argument and tried to 'solve' the transformation problem. This is extensively documented by Sweezy (1942, Part II). The debate was revitalised by the publication of Piero Sraffa's *Production of Commodities by Means of Commodities* in 1960. There have also been partial vindications of Marx's aggregate demonstration of the exploitation theory. Two Japanese economists, Morishima (1973) and Okisio (1961) for example, have shown that the following two propositions are mathematically sound:

- the rate of profit is positive if, and only if, there is a positive rate of exploitation;
- there is a strict increasing monotonic relationship between these two magnitudes.

This result has sometimes been put forward as the 'fundamental Marxian theorem'. To many interpreters, however, it is not sufficient for saving Marx's analysis of exploitation. Commentators such as Steedman (1977) treat the theory of value as the core of Marx' study of capitalism; without it, his conclusions about the falling rate of profit are also no longer valid.

Other authors believe that Marxian analysis can benefit from various results of Sraffa's theory of prices. In particular, the inverse relationship between the rate of profit and the wage rate in Sraffa's analysis, in a mathematically rigorous way, reiterates a class conflict between workers and capitalists (see, for example, Garegnani, 1981). Other commentators, for instance Napoleoni (1975) argue that Marx's real mistake was pretending that it was possible to present mathematical explanations of exploitation and of the capitalistic mode of production, which by their very nature are characterised by such internal contradictions.

Marx's followers

Among several themes taken up from Marx's economics by his followers, the causes of crises and the future of capitalism have undoubtedly had a special place. The two major types of crises envisaged by Marx, those of disproportions, and those of overproduction and under consumption, became a crucial issue dividing Marxists into separate theoretical and political camps at the turn of the nineteenth century. Tugan-Baranowski was convinced that capitalistic crises depend on different rates of capital accumulation in the two major sectors of the economy, those producing variable and constant capital respectively. The new capital may not be invested in the two sectors in proportion to the existing stocks (discussed in Sweezy, 1942, Part I, chapters VIII–XII). Crises are an inevitable aspect of the process of capital accumulation and are due to the inherent anarchy in the capitalist decision-making process, but they do not imply the collapse of capitalism, because the crises themselves are a way of correcting the disproportionate increase of the capital stocks in the different sectors. Tugan's view of crises became a crucial foundation of social democratic thought and of so called revisionism, of special relevance to political outcomes in the Second International. Kautsky, Marx's intellectual heir on the death of Engels, at first criticised Tugan'analysis of crises and his interpretation of Marx, but later himself became the leader of the reformist social democratic wing, thereby forsaking the revolutionary mission of a true Marxist party.

On the opposite side, Rosa Luxembourg believed in the inevitable collapse of capitalism, because of the inherent contradiction between use and exchange value. This, for her, was the true cause of crises. Continual intensification of this contradiction came for her from the increasing poverty of workers relative to capitalists and hence from an increasing tendency to deficient effective demand and domestic purchasing power. There was, therefore, a chronic tendency to under-consumption in the system, which prevented the full realisation of surplus value, and ultimately caused capitalism to collapse. The ideas of Rosa Luxembourg influenced the Third International, and for some time the communist political movement, while in 1919 she herself died together with Karl Liebknecht in the revolutionary cause in Germany.

At the turn of the century, there were other debates inside the under-consumptionists camp on the role of the state in the development of capitalism. Apart from Rosa Luxembourg's work, this debate included contributions from Lenin and Bucharin. To overcome under-consumption crises, the capitalists world used the state as an instrument for assisting the realisation of the value of capital. The nation state then becomes the ideal ally of large capitalist firms, which must always conquer new markets for their products and find new sources of cheap raw materials. This later phase of capitalism was called 'imperialism' by its protagonists, and was seen by them as the highest stage of capitalism.

During the 1950s, the ideas of Rosa Luxembourg were taken up by Joan Robinson, particularly in her *The Accumulation of Capital* (1956) and by Baran and Sweezy in their *Monopoly Capital* (1966). Baran and Sweezy particularly emphasised the tendency of capital accumulation to destroy competitive conditions and hence encouraged the formation of large monopolistic capitalist groups. In her book on the *Accumulation of Capital*, Joan Robinson, by contrast, provided a skilful blend of Marxian and Keynesian views.

Interpretations of Marx of this type gave different degrees of stress on the role of the laws of motion of capitalism in his thought and on his material-istic approach to economic argument. On the one hand, the view persists in some circles that such general laws bind both the destiny of individuals and systems, leading to inevitable outcomes as described either by Marx or by his followers. Capitalism necessarily evolves through well-defined phases until its final collapse. This is the view of dialectical materialism: societies, as well as nature, are characterised and guided by universal laws. Other authors conceive of Marx' analysis as a method of investigation of history than as an actual prediction of the future course of human societies; this view has been called, historical materialism.

Smith, Ricardo, Marx and political economy

At the end of this chapter, which also concludes Part I, a brief review of the major classical authors is appropriate. Theories of surplus owe much to Quesnay, to Smith, to Ricardo and to Marx. It is worth repeating that there are important analytical similarities in the works of these authors as well as differences. Similarities include concepts such as division of labour, productivity, surplus, capital, distribution and profit and characterise each individual contribution. These suggest a gradual evolution of a common approach from Quesnay's 1756 article *Farmers* to the 1894 third volume of *Capital*. The major difference between their views is that the first three authors mainly aimed in politics at social and economic reforms, as against the revolutionary change of society advocated by Marx. Similarities also exist between Smith's historical method of analysis and that of Marx, which may be mentioned at this stage. Such comparisons can provide a better understanding of the role and meaning of political economy in the classical framework.

Another issue concerns the wide and complex object of investigation as envisaged by these economic writers. In fact, the recognition of the *complexity* of human societies is another distinguishing characteristic of both Smith and Marx. Smith's Newtonian method and the 'determined abstraction' of Marx are ways to examine this complex entity. Both authors defined political economy to include this fundamental dimension of societies: their complexity. Simplification is a necessary scientific step, but should not lead to reductionism. The last would be an unforgivable mistake because societies are ever changing, dynamic organisms, always capable of generating surprise through unexpected outcomes.

Third; all these authors emphatically dealt with the society in which they lived. For Smith, Ricardo and especially for Marx, this was contemporary British society, because it represented the most advanced economy in the world. For Quesnay and others, it was contemporary France and its problems.

Fourth; the immense power of transformation inherent in changing *technology* and the importance of the actual processes of production (captured in terms like productivity) played a major role in the work of all four authors and, undoubtedly, remains very important today.

Notes on further readings

As for all the major authors, the importance of actually reading the original texts needs to be stressed; all the more so in the case of Marx. For an indication of the different editions existing of his works, see the entry 'Marx' by Ernest Mandel in the *The New Palgrave: a Dictionary of Economics*. The following editions have been used in this chapter: K. Marx:

(1859) *Contribution to the Critique of Political Economy* (Lawrence & Wishart, London, 1971)
(1867) *Capital Vol. I* (Lawrence & Wishart, London, 1954)
(1885) *Capital Vol. II* (Lawrence & Wishart, London, 1956)
(1894) *Capital Vol. III* (Lawrence & Wishart, London, 1959)
(1905) *Theories of Surplus Value*, 3 Vols (Lawrence & Wishart, London, 1963, 1968, 1971 respectively).

The debates on the labour theory of value were opened by E. von Böhm-Bawerk (1896), *Karl Marx and the Close of this System*, edited with an introduction and major commentaries (including L. von Bortkievicz, 1907) by Paul Sweezy (Kelley, New York, 1996). See also M. Dobb, *Political Economy and Capitalism-Essays in Economic Tradition* (Routledge, London, 1940) and C. Napoleoni, *Smith, Ricardo, Marx* (Blackwell, Oxford, 1975).

On the analytical and technical aspects of Marx's theory of value and price determination, see M. Morishima, *Marx's Economics: a Dual Theory of Value and Growth* (Cambridge University Press, Cambridge, 1973), N. Okisio, 'Technical change and the rate of profit', *Kobe University*

Economic Review, 1961, vol. 7 and I. Steedman, *Marx after Sraffa* (New Left Books, London, 1977).

On the laws of motion of capital and the evolution of the capitalist mode of production see J. Robinson, *An Essay on Marxian Economics* (Macmillan – now Palgrave Macmillan, London, 1942); and P. Sweezy, *The Theory of Capitalist Development* (Monthly Review Press, New York, 1942) and P. Baran and P. Sweezy, *Monopoly Capital* (Monthly Review Press, New York, 1966).

A good biography of Marx, is David McLelland, *Karl Marx: His Life and Thought* (Macmillan, London, 1973); a detailed study of the construction of *Capital* is Roman Rosdolsky, *The Making of Marx's Capital* (Pluto Press, London, 1980). The standard life remains Franz Mehring, *Karl Marx* (Allen and Unwin, London, 1936).

Rosa Luxemburg, *The Accumulation of Capital*, with an introduction by Joan Robinson is of interest as a Marxist underconsumptionist text (Routledge and Kegan Paul, London, 1953). Her life is brilliantly told by Paul Frölich, *Rosa Luxemburg* (Gollancz, London, 1940). The Marxist theory of imperialism is given in V.I. Lenin, *Imperialism: the Higher Stage of Capitalism* (Lawrence & Wishart, London, 1950).

A recent interpretation of Marx's contribution to economics is Samuel Hollander, *The Economics of Karl Marx – Analysis and Application*, Cambridge: Cambridge University Press, 2008.

Part II

MODERN DEVELOPMENTS, 1870–1960

17
Introduction: the Coming of Marginalism and Macro-economics

The second half of this history of economics is called modern develop-ments because it covers the period during which the foundations were laid for much of the contemporary mainstream theory of economics, both in its micro-, and in its macro-parts. The essentials of modern micro-economics can be said to have emerged from the theoretical developments which took place during the 'marginal revolution' of the 1870s, which were consoli-dated and expanded during the closing decades of the nineteenth century. Sections I and II are specifically devoted to describing the highlights of this process by way of looking at some of the major contributions in Europe and across the Atlantic from the early 1870s onwards. Macro-economics, the theory of aggregates such as output and employment as a whole, the price level, rather than the individual decision-making which is the focus of micro-economics, was developed as a specific and direct consequence of the Keynesian revolution of the 1930s. The history of economics to be covered in Part II is therefore clustered around two major 'revolutions' in economic thought, the so-called 'marginal' and 'Keynesian' revolutions. This introduction briefly explores the meaning of these terms.

The marginal revolution

The marginal revolution has now become part of the language of the history of economic thought. It is generally identified with the almost simultaneous *but independent* discovery of the marginal utility theory of value which was published in three different countries (England, Austria and France) in the early 1870s (1871–75), that is, in Jevons's *Theory of Political Economy* (1871), Menger's *Principles of Economics* (1871) and Walras's *Elements of Pure Economics* (1874–77). Hence a multiple discovery is involved in the phenomenon. This raises the question, what precisely did Jevons, Menger and Walras discover together?

The answer generally given is the marginal utility theory of value. This creates an immediate problem. The marginal utility theory of value was discovered independently and almost simultaneously as early as 1834 (by the Oxford economist, W.F. Lloyd, and the Irish economist, M. Longfield) and in 1836 by Nasau Senior (see Chapter 15 above). It subsequently kept cropping up at intervals of approximately ten years: Dupuit in 1844; Gossen in 1854, Jennings in 1855; Jevons in 1862 when he first announced his discovery in a paper read to Section F of the British Association for the Advancement of Science. Although emphasis on marginal utility is clearly a feature of the work of Jevons, Menger and Walras, this part of their work did not make the marginal revolution such a significant event in the history of economics.

When the focus shifts to the adjective, 'marginal' in 'marginal revolution', there are other problems. In 1838, the French mathematician, Augustin Cournot, had brilliantly demonstrated the usefulness of marginalist techniques in his *Mathematical Researches into the Theory of Wealth*, doing so, moreover, while explicitly rejecting the usefulness of utility as a factor in demand analysis. A group of French engineers in the 1830s and 1850s including Dupuit, were using marginal analysis in their assessment of the benefits of specific public works, such as bridges, roads and railways. Furthermore, an eccentric German landlord and social reformer, von Thünen, employed the marginal method in his *The Isolated State* (published in parts over 1826–63) thereby unwittingly discovering the rudiments of the marginal productivity theory of distribution. The latter theory had several co-discoverers, the Irishman Longfield is one, well recognised instance.

Even 'marginalism' as a name was slow to creep into the language, as was the term, 'marginal'. Wicksteed was one of the first to use it in England. He was followed by Marshall who claimed to have derived the terminology himself from von Wieser's usage of the German equivalent, *grenze*. Marginalism was coined as a derogatory term by the English economic heretic, J.A. Hobson, early in the twentieth century.

What was the difference between the new and the old?

This important question can be answered in terms of three factors: (i) scope; (ii) method; (iii) institutionalisation of the economics profession. The differences under these headings constitute a qualitative change of tremendous significance. Donald Winch, for example, has argued,

> 1870 witnessed the demise of political economy and the birth of economics . . . attention shifted . . . towards the narrower and more precise inquiry into the determination of relative prices. Economics became a quasi-mathematical science in which the important problems were posed as scarcity or choice problems involving the maximisation or minimisation of strategic economic quantities under specified conditions.
>
> (Winch, 1971, p. 63)

More recently, a collection of essays on the foundations of economics (Baranzini and Scazzieri, 1986) has characterised the difference between the old and the new as that between an economics focusing on production (the classical approach) and that focusing on exchange (the marginalist, or as it later became known, neo-classical economics). The remarks by Winch will be illustrated in the subsequent two sections dealing with the early generations of marginalists. The differences made by the new marginalism to scope, method and the organisation of the profession need also to be briefly looked at.

Scope

In his very influential *Essay on the Nature and Significance of Economic Science*, Lionel Robbins argued that the new, post-1870 economics required a new definition of the scope of economic science. He proposed the following definition: 'Economics is the science which studies human behaviour as a relationship between ends and scarce means which have alternative uses'. This definition implies four necessary (and sufficient) conditions for making human action susceptible to economic analysis:

(1) ends are multiple;
(2) ends can be ranked in order of priority;
(3) means to achieve the ends are limited;
(4) means to achieve the ends have alternative uses.

This 'economic problem' was illustrated in the early books of marginalist economics by the allocation of a given stock of corn (homogenous and perfectly divisible) among its various alternative uses by a Robinson Crusoe for whom this stock was fixed until the next harvest. Ranked in order of priority, these uses include basic food such as bread, luxury food such as cakes, feed for animals, brewing of beer, distilling of spirits after that required for seed corn had been set aside. Others used the example of allocating a limited stock of water among drinking, washing, bathing, watering plants and gardens, and so on. Such examples cannot easily be found in the writings of the classical economists whose work was explored in Part I. For the new marginalist economics with the concept of marginal utility at its command, the problem was easily solved by equating the marginal utility of corn (water) in all of its alternative uses. An early solution, and posing, of this problem can be found in the pioneering work of Gossen, an anticipator of much marginalist economics from the 1850s.

A slightly different manner of depicting the change in scope was given by Joan Robinson (1953, p. 22) in a remark with quite wide implications:

> Marshall did something much more effective than changing the answer. He changed the question. For Ricardo the theory of Value was a means

of studying the distribution of total output between wages, rent and profit, each considered as a whole. This is a big question. Marshall turned the meaning of Value into a little question: why does an egg cost more than a cup of tea? It may be a small question but it is a very difficult and complicated one. It takes a lot of time and a lot of algebra to work out the theory of it. So it kept all Marshall's pupils preoccupied for fifty years. They had no time to think about the big question, or even to remember that there was a big question, because they had to keep their noses right down to the grindstone, working out the theory of the price of a cup of tea.

Hence, for Joan Robinson, the question was changed. The marginalists (and Robbins) worked out the theory of optimum resource allocation under static conditions which required, as she put it, a detailed elaboration of the theory of a price of a cup of tea. Ricardo's question had been the distribution of output among the various classes in a growing economy. Smith had inquired into the growth of the wealth of nations. These are very different questions. For some decades after the 1870s they disappeared from much of the economic research agenda.

Robbin's economics of scarcity and 'economic imperialism'

Robbins himself (1934, 16) described his 'economics of scarcity' as almost unlimited in scope. So long as a topic involved issues associated with limited resources, the subject had an economic dimension, and was amenable to economic analysis by using the tools of modern economics. Hence economics has spread its wings to embrace the analysis of education, of art galleries, of social welfare and, in fact, of every issue under the sun in which choice and scarcity are part of the problem. It emphasises the rational, maximisation aspects of economics, its inevitable search for equilibrium outcomes, and the need to check the efficiency attributes of such equilibrium outcomes.

Method

Robbins's definition also had methodological implications visible in the work of the marginalists (as is illustrated in subsequent sections). Robbins made this explicit in his *Essay:*

(1) Economics is a highly deductive science in which mathematics, especially the calculus, initially played a major part. The calculus was of course ideal for solving marginalist problems, as shown already in Cournot's work and as illustrated in many of the writings of the early marginalists, the Austrians excepted. The new marginalists, generally speaking, did not consider economics to be a factual science. The existence of different ends is all that is required, so Robbins argued, to

deduce a rigorous theory of value which can act as a vehicle for an optimum allocation of resources for households, consumers, and producers.

(2) The emphasis on mathematics became a qualitative change in economics. By the end of the nineteenth century, mathematical economists constituted the majority of the leading theoreticians. There were warnings of the dangers of over-reliance on mathematics by some leading marginalists (especially Marshall) but these tended to be ignored by the profession.

(3) Since ends were assumed to be given, economics also became a positive or value-free science with no policy axes to grind. Given the ends and their ranking, and the available means with alternative uses with which to achieve them; the economist could work out ways of achieving the most important ends. This neglected any interdependence of ends and means, or their inseparability, and hence was an over-simplified way of presenting the nature of the economic problem. However, Robbins's separation of ends and means allowed him to portray economics as a positive science in which value judgements did not enter (these were left to the politicians who ranked the ends in order of priority). This was one reason why the old name of political economy was frequently discarded and the new name of economics was so rapidly adopted.

Institutional changes in the economics profession

The marginal revolution coincided with significant changes in the nature of the economics profession. The following aspects are particularly noteworthy and reinforce the notions of change which the new economics brought in its wake.

(1) Economics became a clear specialisation separated from other subject areas such as political and moral philosophy, history, sociology and more generally, the moral sciences.

(2) Economics tended to rely increasingly on specialist skills and specialist language so that the subject became more difficult to grasp by the intelligent layman. The age of the amateur economist was coming to an end, and the textbook of economic principles increasingly was directed at a specialist audience of students and practitioners.

(3) Economics became more academic. The end of the nineteenth century was the period when chairs in economics began to proliferate. The ten major early marginalists identified by Stigler (1941) with the exception of Wicksteed all held chairs in economics during their lifetime. By the middle of the twentieth century there were few leading theoreticians or economic thinkers outside the university.

(4) Specialist journals in economics began to be published in the English-speaking world (initially the *Quarterly Journal of Economics* of Harvard

and the *Economic Journal* of the Royal Economic Society) though such journals had a longer history in parts of continental Europe (the *Revue d'économie politique* in France and the *Giornale degli economisti* in Italy). Professional associations were also formed. Apart from the Royal Economic Society in the United Kingdom, already mentioned, there was the foundation of an American Economic Association and the revitalisation of similar organisations in continental Europe.

These factors enabled more rapid consolidation of the new economics, standardisation of the principles of the discipline, and the emergence of a certain conformity which was not always helpful for the evolution of the subject.

Continuity or discontinuity in the development of economics

Are the differences between the old and the new sufficiently great to warrant the view that there was a significant break in the development of economics caused by the marginal revolution? There is no general consensus on the matter. For the school of thought which argues that the resource allocation problem was always at the heart of economics, there is clearly no break between the old and the new. This perspective relies on interpreting the work of Smith as concerned with optimal resource allocation through the achievement of free trade; and seeing Ricardo's analysis of a uniform competitive wage and profit rate in terms of the resource allocation role of a competitive price system. If greater reliance on supply and demand as explanators in economic argument is depicted as a major characteristics of the new, then continuity can be argued in terms of the recognition of the importance of supply and demand in the work of Smith, and even more that of John Stuart Mill.

Both arguments in favour of continuity are controversial, and can be rejected on fairly good grounds. (The resource allocation problem as depicted by the marginalists in terms of distributing a given stock of resources with alternative uses to greatest effect among the competing ends was quite distinct from the classical recognition of the reallocation properties of a competitive market; the theory of supply and demand in Smith and Ricardo plays quite a different role from that accorded by the new economics.) In fact, the specific marginalist portrayal of the allocational problem can be seen as a major difference, because it played no part whatsoever within the classical system. Likewise, the disappearance of dynamic questions about growth and distribution from the economist research agenda (as noted by Joan Robinson) marks another major discontinuity. Discontinuity is likewise implied for those authors who distinguish an older, production-based tradition from a newer, exchange-based tradition.

Explanations for the 'Marginal Revolution' are likewise problematic. Endogenous explanations rely on the inevitability of a marginal revolution because classical value and distribution theory had lost coherence and acceptability. Its labour/cost of production theory of value lacked generality (it could not deal with joint products, for example). With the demise of the wages fund doctrine in the 1860s, classical economics also lacked a theory of wages. Such problems could be overcome by concentrating more on developing the theory of supply and demand, as John Stuart Mill had in fact been doing, and more particularly, by emphasis on, and explanation of, neglected aspects of demand theory, both in the commodity and in the factor market. Unfortunately, although aspects of this story have relevance to the work of Jevons, they do not fit in well with the case of Menger in Austria, or that of Walras in France. Other endogenous explanations lack persuasiveness. The revival of hedonism and its pleasure/pain calculus of maximising pleasure (satisfaction) with least pain (cost) can only be associated with Jevons (as well as with other English writers, such as Sidgwick, Edgeworth, and Marshall); it does not fit the case of Menger in Austria or Walras in France. Depicting the new economics as the economic theory of a leisure class (which the Russian Marxist, Bukharin (1919) did), or as a critical response to Marx's *Capital*, likewise do not easily match the circumstances surrounding the work of Menger, Jevons or Walras, even though the second generation of marginalist economists (Wicksteed, von Wieser, Böhm-Bawerk and Pareto) produced strident criticisms of Marx's theoretical system. But although the phenomenon is difficult to explain (a case for dehomogenenising, or separating, the individual contributions of Jevons, Menger and Walras) the significance of the event for modern economics cannot be underestimated. The foundations for much of today's microeconomics are visible in the work of the early marginalists, aspects of whose work are briefly discussed in the first two sections of Part II.

The Keynesian revolution and the rise of macro-economics

In many respects, the notion of a Keynesian revolution and its impact on the development of a 'macro-economics' is far less controversial. The later Nobel Laureate and econometrician, Lawrence Klein, coined the phrase, Keynesian Revolution as the title for a book on the subject he published in 1948; Laurie Tarshis, a student of Keynes at Cambridge in the mid-1930s, recorded his version of the 'Keynesian Revolution' for the *New Palgrave Dictionary* (Tarshis, 1987). What constituted the Keynesian revolution, nevertheless, remains a matter of dispute in the literature, as is the interpretation of the vehicle by which the revolution was made, Keynes's *General Theory of Employment, Interest and Money* (1936). The story is made even more complex by the need to carefully distinguish the post-war development of Keynesian economics from the actual economics of Keynes (Leijonhufvud, 1968) and the seemingly overwhelming acceptance of the Keynesian message for policy and other applied purposes in the 1950s and

1960s and its equally rapid demise in what was perceived to be the changed economic climate of the 1970s. From the early 1970s, high unemployment frequently co-existed with high inflation as the result of a variety of factors, some of them quite specific to the period (oil price shocks, the financing of the Vietnam war, and so on). The notion of a Keynesian revolution also deserves a brief discussion. Inflation since then has continued to be a problem in many countries of the world, as has unemployment.

Study of the *General Theory*, the vehicle through which the revolution was first made, inspired a variety of reactions of what the revolution was all about. It is generally admitted that one revolutionary aspects of Keynes's book was the theory of effective demand it developed. This theoretical contribution was also described by many of Keynes's followers as the development of a theory of the level of output as a whole. Keynes found the key variables for this analysis needed new explanations. Hence he developed a theory of consumption (and saving) dependent on the level of income and a psychological propensity to consume; a theory of investment dependent on expectations about its future returns and the rate of interest; and a theory of interest determined by liquidity preference (demand for money) and the money supply determined by the monetary authorities. From this theoretical apparatus, a number of novel ideas were produced, which were contrary to the findings of conventional or, 'classical economics', as Keynes himself misleadingly called it.

Keynes's first novel proposition was that deficient demand would generate output levels too low to induce full employment at the current wage rate and that, in the absence of increased effective demand (and hence higher output) such unemployment levels could persist for a long period. This justified reference to what Keynes called the possibility of unemployment equilibrium. Secondly, the argument showed that interest rates were essentially a monetary phenomenon rather than the real (non-monetary) price determined in the capital market by the 'supply' of savings and the 'demand' for investment. This led to a third, 'revolutionary' proposition: saving and investment were not brought into equality by variations in the interest, but by changes in the level of income. Via the multiplier (or, more generally, the argument which became later known as Mr. Meade's relation), changes in investment produced changes in income which, with a given propensity to save of the public, produced the savings requisite to finance that investment. Investment therefore became the key variable in income (and employment) generation. Private investment deficient in terms of its ability to generate full employment, could be supplemented by additional government spending (including public investment) to generate the additional income needed for more employment. The theory therefore questioned the ability of a free market system (price variations) to clear the labour market (through wage changes) and the capital market (through variations in the rate of interest). These were revolutionary theoretical principles, with equally revolutionary implications for policy because they questioned the ability of the market system to automatically generate the desired employment (output and income) outcomes.

The extent to which these propositions constituted a 'revolution' has been almost continuously debated since the publication of Keynes's *General Theory* in 1936. The ability of the economic system to generate a long term unemployment equilibrium has often been questioned, thereby implying that what Keynes has really modelled were possibilities for disequilibrium or temporary equilibrium situations in the labour market. Defenders of the beneficent outcomes of market processes argued that Keynes's conclusions about wages and unemployment, interest rates and savings-investment equality, rested on perceptions of frictions operating in real market adjustments which hampered the ability of wages, prices and interest rates to achieve the predicted outcome of conventional theory by restricting their flexibility. The debate on these propositions and their many and varied logical offshoots, continues making Keynes's *General Theory*, directly, and indirectly, the most discussed economics book of the twentieth century. This by itself is sufficient to talk of a Keynesian revolution even if it fails to tell the whole story about its essentials. Section V broaches major aspects of the new theory, including its independent discovery by Kalecki and its relevance for growth theory as developed by Harrod and Domar. This follows the discussion in Section III of what are called some of the macro-economic (pre-Keynesian) pioneers: Wicksell on monetary stability, Fisher on capital and interest, and Schumpeter on growth and business cycles.

Notes for further reading

The notion of revolutions in economic theory is explored in detail by T.W. Hutchison in his collection of essays, *On Revolutions and Progress in Economic Knowledge* (Cambridge University Press, Cambridge, 1978, esp. chs 4–7). The marginal revolution as an intellectual and historical phenomenon was explored in detail at its centenary (1971) conference organised by a group of economists associated with *History of Political Economy* (and published in its vol. 4, no. 2, Autumn 1972). It is still worth studying and includes the paper by Winch quoted in this chapter. The same applies to Warren Samuels' introductory chapter to *Neoclassical Economic Theory 1870–1920* (Kluwer Academic Publishers, Boston, 1990). The materialist explanation by Nikolai Bukharin (*The Economic Theory of the Leisure Class*, International Publishers, New York, 1927) makes interesting reading, as does the discussion of the rise in marginalism in relation to Marx's political economy by De Vivo (1990, esp. pp. 42–4). Robbins, *The Nature and Significance of Economic Science*, Macmillan (now Palgrave Macmillan), 1934, chapters 1–2, presents the methodology implications of the marginal revolution. Joan Robinson, (*On Re-reading Marx* in *Collected Economic Papers*, Blackwell, Oxford, 1973, Vol. IV, Part III) gives a humorous discussion of the difference between the old and the new. A more academic discussion is in M. Baranzini and R. Scazzieri (eds), *Foundations of Economics*, Blackwell, Oxford, 1986, esp. chapter 1. See also Lazear, Edward P. (2000), 'Economic Imperialism', *Quarterly Journal of Economics*, 115 (Feb.), 99–146; Medema, Steven G. (2009) *The Hesitant Hand: Taming Self Interest in the History of Economic Ideas*, Princeton and Oxford: Princeton University Press.

The making of the Keynesian Revolution is well presented by Peter Clarke, a Cambridge historian (*The Keynesian Revolution in the Making, 1924–36*), Clarendon Press, Oxford, 1988, esp. chs 11, 12). Lawrence Klein's book, *The Keynesian Revolution* (Macmillan – now Palgrave Macmillan, London, 1966), presents a double reaction to the phenomenon by the 1980 Nobel Laureate in Economics, first as student in the 1940s, then as a leading academic practitioner in the 1960s. Articles on the subject by Murray Milgate, Don Patinkin and Laurie Tarshis in the *New Palgrave Dictionary of Economics* (Macmillan – now Palgrave Macmillan, London, 1987, III, pp. 10–41, 42–46, 47–50) present further useful insights into a complex phenomenon in a leading economics reference work. Another interesting prospective is given by G.L.S. Shackle, *The Years of High Theory 1926–1939* (Cambridge University Press, Cambridge, 1967, chs 11–14, esp. ch. 12). A fine overview of the economics of effective demand is in Luigi Pasinetti, *Growth and Distribution*, Cambridge University Press, Cambridge, 1974, ch. 2).

Section I

The First Generation

18
John Stuart Mill, 1806–73: a Figure of Transition

John Stuart Mill was born in 1806, the first son of James Mill. His youthful education was rigorous, and by the age of fourteen, Mill was learning political economy during long walks with his father. By 1823 his education was completed and he joined the East India office, from which he retired in 1857. His work left him leisure for writing and during his years at the India Office, he wrote and published his two major works: *A System of Logic* (1843), and *Principles of Political Economy with Some of Their Applications to Social Philosophy* (1848), following *Essays on Some Unsettled Questions in Political Economy* (written during 1829/30, published in 1844). In 1851 he married Harriet Taylor, claiming later to have been strongly influenced by her when writing *On Liberty* (1859), *Representative Government* (1861), *Utilitarianism* (1863), and *The Subjection of Women* (1869) as well as the final chapter of Book IV of his *Principles*, 'On the probable Futurity of the Labouring Classes'. He was a Member of Parliament (1865–68), supporting Disraeli's 1867 reform bill and land reform. In 1869, he recanted his mechanical view of the wages fund doctrine, following criticism by his friend and colleague, William Thornton. He died in France in 1873. Mill's essays on socialism were posthumously published in 1879 in the *Fortnightly Review*.

Mill's *Principles of Political Economy* enjoyed an enormous success. It went through seven editions during his lifetime and dominated economic discussion for much of the second half of the nineteenth century. Jevons denounced Mill's 'noxious authority'; Marshall learned his initial economics from careful study of this book, while Marx described it as a schizophrenic exercise in which Mill managed to maintain simultaneously the views of his father and the opposite view. There is much that is novel in Mill's work. Its influence on Jevons (largely negative) and on Marshall (positive) make it appropriate to describe him as a figure of transition to the new economics. A brief reader's guide to his *Principles* provides useful background to the detailed discussion of his value and distribution theory which follows.

Reader's guide to the *Principles*

Its preface declared 'the work similar in its object and general conception to that of Adam Smith, but adapted to . . . the present age' (Mill, 1848, 1965, I, p. xcii). Abstract theory hence combined with social philosophy, in this discourse of production, distribution and exchange of wealth, Mill's definition of the scope of political economy. The work is divided into five books:

Book I: Production. After presenting definitions of land, labour and capital, Mill treats the factors influencing their productivity, in the process enunciating the laws of returns. Mill's treatment of capital embodies Senior's notion of abstinence and Rae's discussion of the time element in production. It contains four propositions on capital the most famous of which is the statement that demand for commodities is not demand for labour. Labour productivity is discussed in terms of machinery, the division of labour and the impact of education. Land involves diminishing returns; large scale industry may induce increasing returns; internal and external economies are recognised as is the possibility of diseconomies of scale for very large firms.

Book II: Distribution ('the static theory', as Marshall called it). A discussion of the nature of private property introduces the classes among whom the product is distributed, the role of competition and custom in distribution, and the forms of production and land tenure (slavery, peasant proprietorship, cottiers, métayage) as influences on distribution. Chapters on wages, profits and rent are the core of the static theory. Wages are discussed from a strict wages fund perspective, which is supplemented by chapters on remedies for low wages and the theory of differential wages. Profits and rents are discussed in a single chapter.

Book III: Exchange. The first six chapters deal with the theory of value. The next seven chapters cover domestic monetary theory. Single chapters follow on overproduction and gluts, the measure of value, and peculiar cases in the theory of value (including joint production). Pure international trade theory is discussed in chapters 17 and 18, followed by international monetary theory (four chapters), and chapters on the rate of interest, central banking policy, international competition, and a discussion of distribution as it is affected by exchange, thereby connecting Book III to Book IV.

Book IV: Influence of Progress on Production and Distribution (the 'dynamic theory' of distribution in Marshall's words)
Its seven chapters cover the nature of a progressive society, the influence of progress on prices and values, on population, on distributive shares (with special reference to the tendency of the rate of profit to fall), the nature of a stationary state and, finally, 'The Probable Futurity of the Labouring Classes'.

Book V: Government and Public Finance. The first long section on public finance in a book of general principles since the *Wealth of Nations* contains on the revenue side a long discussion of taxation (in general and in terms of particular types of taxes) and the national debt. Discussion of the functions of government represents a fascinating qualified general *laissez-faire* position, which is usefully studied in conjunction with Mill's *Representative Government*.

Mill's *Principles* is well worth reading, in small doses. The monetary theory is particularly fascinating (demonstrating Marx's diagnosis of schizophrenia since it upholds both currency and banking school positions), as is the theory of international trade and much of the public finance material. The following discussion, however, concentrates on aspects of Books II to IV on value and distribution. This more clearly illustrates the transitory nature of Mill's economics relative to both the classical system as expounded by Ricardo and the work of some early marginalists, especially that of Marshall.

The theory of value

'Happily, there is nothing in the laws of value which remains for the present or any future writers to clear up; the theory of the subject is complete; the only difficulty to be overcome is of so stating it as to solve by anticipation the chief perplexities which occur in applying it . . .' (Book III, Ch. I, § 1). This frequently quoted statement is interesting from various points of view. Relative to Ricardo, it appears nonsensical. Mill failed to grasp the link between value and distribution theory which had worried Ricardo until the time of his death, and simply transformed Ricardo's theory into a cost of production theory. Jevons, the first English marginalist, made great sport with the statement since his transformation of value into utility theory was the foundation for a new economic theory. Marx only saw confusion in Mill's value theory, particularly important for him because Mill confounded profit and surplus value. Only Marshall agreed significantly with Mill, because he had produced an essentially correct foundation in value theory, which only had to be completed and clarified. These comparisons reveal Mill as a figure of transition in economics.

The development of Mill's theory of value in the *Principles*

The opening chapter of Book III also elucidates some preliminary problems in the theory of value. The distinction between use value and exchange value raised by Smith disappears when use value is shorn of moral and philosophical implications. All economic goods with exchange value, must be useful. The distinction between value and price is simply stated. Value is the real phenomenon; price is value expressed in terms of the monetary unit. Hence the theory of prices is the quantity theory of money.

Supply and demand are introduced in chapter II. The preliminary statement is greatly influenced by arguments derived from De Quincey's *Logic of Political Economy* (1844) and Samuel Bailey's *Critical Dissertation on the Nature, Measures and Causes of Value* (1825). The law of value as generally conceived in terms of costs (and sometimes labour costs), applies only to freely reproducible commodities under conditions of competition (as Ricardo had argued).

Other aspects of supply and demand, covered by Mill in later chapters, can be mentioned now. Chapter 16 analyses the difficult case of joint-costs as a peculiar case in the theory of value. Mill clearly formulates the problem of joint-production and presents a correct solution for the fixed proportions joint products case:

(i)   prices of the products must equal joint costs;
(ii) the price of each product is determined in equilibrium by the equality of quantity supplied and quantity demanded.

The concepts of supply and demand are further refined by Mill in the context of international values. The notion of reciprocal demand curves are there so neatly described, that they can virtually be visualised (for a Marshall steeped in Euclidean geometry, they were easily transformed into diagrams). Mill's discussion also clearly indicated what was already implicit in the previous discussion of Book III, chapter 2; he regarded supply and demand as functions, namely as functions of price.

In addition, Mill seems to have clearly recognised the notion of *elasticity* of demand, when considering three different types of influence of cheapness (low price) on demand:

(i)   demand increases at a greater rate than cheapness, what would now be called, elastic demand;
(ii) demand increases at the same rate as cheapness, what would now be called unitary elasticity;
(iii) demand increases at a slower rate than cheapness, what would now be called inelastic demand.

Cost–price concepts are constructed from the Smithian distinction between natural and market price. Two propositions follow: (i) natural price is the equivalent of cost of production, that is, the sum of the wages, profits and rent, which need to be paid to bring a commodity to market; (ii) in equilibrium, when demand equals supply, market price equals natural price (cost of production).

Mill is also aware of the concept of alternative cost. This justifies his inclusion of rent into cost of production, as had earlier been done by Smith. Where land has alternative uses, that land will have a price. No-rent-land in corn production may have a positive rent in the production of hops, or turnips, or from its use as a grouse-shooting moor.

Finally, Mill introduces a variant of real cost doctrine, which was subsequently popularised by Marshall. All commodities, generally speaking, in their production, incur two real, human costs. One is the painful exertion of labour, the other the exercise of abstinence of painfully refraining from consumption. The work of nature does not entail such real costs, which by definition necessitate human exertion. Abstinence had been introduced in Mill's discussion of capital and thrift. His development of such concepts once again illustrates Mill's economics as that of an economics in transition.

Mill's version of the labour theory is discussed in chapter IV. The theory is correctly stated as implying the proportionality of cost of production to the quantity of labour embodied in production. Mill's list of modifications to this proposition is longer (and seemingly more significant) than Ricardo's three qualifications, hence giving the impression that using units of labour embodied as a proximate measure of value, cannot be practically entertained.

Mill's modifications to the labour-proportionality rule are as follows: (1) Wages may affect value if there are differential wage rates for different types of employment, that is, rejection of Ricardo's homogeneous labour assumption; (2) profit may affect value if there are differential rates of profit due to risk and like factors (rejection of the uniform profit rate assumption); (3) commodities have different capital intensity, or a different time period of production. (Mill discussed in this context the special case of wine in the cellar and oak in the forest, which had plagued his father in the *Elements* as well as the more general difficulties raised by Ricardo); (4) there can be artificial additions to value and cost of production through the imposition of taxes which (in the language of Ricardo and Sraffa's *Production of Commodities by Means of Commodities*) affect relative values if they affect basic commodities: (5) rent may enter cost of production as either a scarcity value or (in the manner already discussed) as an alternative cost. Hence Mill effectively rejects the notion of a labour theory of value. This has no real consequences for his analysis of distribution, unlike the case of Ricardo.

Mill's final chapter on value criticises Ricardo's abstraction of rent from influencing exchange value, suggests that the theory as stated applies only to the 'present', capitalist organisation of society. Value relationships are different in slave societies, in a subsistence economy or under the potential social arrangements associated with cooperative socialism, the form of socialism which Mill preferred.

In short, Mill's theory of value is essentially a supply and demand theory. Only in long-term competitive equilibrium under constant returns, does cost of production, broadly conceived, determine value. The classical trappings of a labour theory of value and the dichotomy of natural and market price, are submerged by this supply and demand approach. Mill's book therefore greatly enhanced more general acceptance of supply and demand analysis, reinforcing that which came with the marginal revolution from the 1870s.

The static theory of distribution from Book II

Mill's theory of distribution is based on a three class analysis. Landlords, capitalists and labourers share in the product in the form of rent, profits and wages. The contents of Book II discuss the determination these income shares. Mill warns that the class structure of society need not be permanent, because it depends on the prevailing property relations Hence, his distribution analysis only applies to contemporary, British society.

The theory of wages

Mill's theory of wages in Book II is a simple wages fund theory. The wages fund for a society consists of the wage goods accumulated at any point of time. In a closed economy, this is fixed after the harvest. In the short run, the supply of labour is also given, because the population principle is inoperative. Wages are then determined by the competition of the given supply of workers for the given wages fund, i.e.:

$$w = W/L$$

where w is the wage rate; W, the wage fund and L the given labour supply.

The following quote from the opening paragraph of the chapter on wages (Book II, chapter 11) illustrates the supreme simplicity of this theory:

> Wages, then, depend mainly upon the demand and supply of labour; or as it is often expressed, on the proportion between population and capital. By population is here meant the number only of the labouring classes, or rather of those who work for hire; and by capital only circulating capital, and not even the whole of that, but the part which is expended in the direct purchase of labour. To this, however must be added the funds which, without forming a part of capital, are paid in exchange for labour, such as the wages of soldiers, domestic servants, and all other unproductive labourers. There is unfortunately no mode of expressing by one familiar term, the aggregate of what has been called the wages-fund of a country; and as the wages of productive labour form nearly the whole of that fund, it is usual to overlook the smaller and less

important part, and to say that wages depend on population and capital. It will be convenient to employ this expression, remembering however, to consider it as elliptical, and not as a literal statement of the entire truth.

With these limitations of the terms, wages not only depend upon the relative amount of capital and population, but cannot, under the rule of competition, be affected by anything else. Wages (meaning, of course, the general rate) cannot rise, but by an increase of the aggregate funds employed in hiring labourers, or a diminution in the number of the competitors for hire; nor fall, except either by a diminution of the funds devoted to paying labour, or by an increase in the number of labourers to be paid.

(Mill, 1965, pp. 337–8)

The theory provides few avenues to wage earners for improving their lot. They cannot control or influence the size of the wages fund; they can, however, reduce the supply of workmen competing for the given fund. Two remedies for low wages which operate via a reduction of labour supply are considered by Mill:

(a) emigration to underpopulated countries like Australia, Canada or the United States;
(b) artificial limitation of the labour supply through restrictions on family size by various means including contraception.

Creating a minimum wage (above the wage fixed by the available wage fund) would be useless. Strikes to secure sectional wage increases in the wage fund from accumulation or from the importation of food and other wages could also raise wages but these are only treated two Books later in the dynamic discussion of distribution. A flexible wage fund destroys the one equation wage determination model which made the wages fund theory so attractive.

The wages fund doctrine also gives the clue to why for Mill, demand for commodities was not demand for labour. Demand for labour came from the wages fund, and this, in a closed economy, could only be increased by accumulation or thrift, that is, the abstention from consuming or demanding commodities.

The theory of profits

John Stuart Mill's discussion of profits greatly resembles that of Ricardo. Profits are treated as a residual after wages and rent have been determined, but these are *gross* profits, not *net* profits or the minimum supply price of capital.

Gross profits are divided into three parts: interest, or the net profit category; depreciation of capital; and wages of superintendence and the risk premium. *Depreciation* is determined by the technical considerations of using the fixed capital in the production process, which regulate the proportion of that fixed capital which needs to be replaced. *Wages of superintendence* are determined by the customary level in the industry. The *risk premium* in gross profits depends on the degree of risk associated with the enterprise which can vary substantially and resembles an insurance premium paid out to cover the risk. Hence net profit or interest remains to be determined.

The latter is explained as follows. The minimum or net rate of profit is determined by the compensation necessary to induce the capitalist to invest his capital in an undertaking, that is, it is the minimum supply price of that capital. This in turn is determined by interest or the price of abstinence, which is a function of the degree of time preference in society. Competition only ensures the equalisation of net profit in all industries. Gross profit rates needs to be equalised, given differences in the risk premium and the relative importance of wages of superintendence. Mill therefore presents a dual theory of profits, the Ricardian residual theory and the Senior abstinence/time preference theory explaining net profit or the interest component of profit.

The theory of rent

Rent is explained very much as in Ricardo's theory. It arises from the difference in cost of production on marginal land at both the intensive and the extensive margin and the cost of production on intra-marginal land. This difference is appropriated by the landlord as rent, in order to equalise the rate of profit in agricultural production.

The dynamic theory of distribution

This is presented in Book IV. Mill himself used the word dynamic to describe his argument on what happens to profits, wages and rent in a growing society. An analysis of the influence of progress on value and price is presented as background to the discussion. Here it is shown that agricultural produce and raw materials, subject to diminishing returns, will tend to rise in price over time, as will, consequently, those industrial commodities where raw material costs form a large proportion of total costs. For the remainder of industry (by far the greater part), increasing returns are said to apply from the effects on productivity of large scale production and technical progress. Hence, similar to Smith's analysis in the digression of silver, there is a dual movement in prices. Price of most manufactured goods have a tendency to fall with progress, agricultural goods or goods whose inputs have a sizeable agricultural content have a tendency to rise in price. This in turn affects the distribution of the product over time. Wages are largely paid in agricultural produce which exhibits rising prices over time.

The progress of rent

With economic progress, that is, as capital accumulation and population increases, agriculture becomes more capital intensive and is forced onto inferior land. This augments both the intensive and extensive margins of cultivation, thereby raising rents. Such a rise in rents can be postponed in two ways. First are land saving improvements and which therefore delay the pressure on the intensive and extensive margins. The second is the importation of foodstuffs and raw materials from countries rich in agricultural land, a possibility available to Britain after the repeal of the Corn Laws in 1846. However, in the long run, *rents must rise* as improvements cannot be expected to continue forever, and the importation of cheap produce is limited as new agricultural countries themselves develop and grow.

The progress of wages

Book IV replaces the wages fund theory of Book II with a dynamic supply and demand theory. In this account, wages are determined by the relative movements in capital accumulation and population growth (the classical theory of Smith and Ricardo). This in turn is influenced by trends in the productivity of labour. In a progressive society, especially if labour productivity is high, capital accumulation will be fast and wages will rise. Moreover, food, that food which is subject to higher prices from development, will become less important in worker's budgets, providing further impetus for rising real wages. If, in addition, population growth is restrained, growth in real wages has even greater scope.

The demand factor of accumulation is limited in this model by the effect thereon of the profit rate which, according to Mill, has a tendency to fall (see below). Eventually, the profit rate falls to a level at which further accumulation becomes unprofitable, and only replacement investment is undertaken. Population growth will slowly catch up at this stage, and real wages fall back to subsistence level. Technical progress and the other counter-tendencies to falls in the profit rate may postpone the time by which zero net accumulation is reached (which Mill calls the stationary state) but cannot do so indefinitely.

Mill argues that the stationary state need not be a state of gloom and poverty. If population is limited (hence the emphasis on birth control and emigration in his system), then real wage levels remain relatively high. Furthermore, the increased leisure possibilities in a stationary state provide greater opportunities of education and moral improvement. The stationary state can therefore be seen as a state of bliss.

In addition, and this is the crux of the chapter on the 'futurity of the labouring classes', there are other ways in which the lot of the workers may improve and class differences may be reduced. These arise from possibilities for social reorganisation of production such as profit sharing arrangements which make capitalism more humane and give labourers a wider interest in industry or, more importantly, from cooperative enterprises of the Owenite type, particularly exciting in the area of production. Mill's detailed discussion of the various forms of cooperative organisation and profit sharing arrangements in England and France shows how serious he was about these strategies for ameliorating working class conditions. The final section of the chapter sings the praises of competition as an essential feature of working class improvement. Not only does it provide the most effective system of quality control over production, it also ensures higher wages than would otherwise be the case when population is suitably restrained.

The progress of profit: the falling rate of profit

Mill explains the falling rate of profit partly in terms of diminished agricultural productivity *à la* Ricardo, but given his position on the prospects for the long run wage rate discussed above, Mill's use of the Ricardo mechanism needs to be qualified. As a further explanation of the falling profit rate, Mill therefore relies on the Smith–Malthus mechanism of the competition of capitals (or on analysing the effects of capital accumulation on the profitable opportunities of investment).

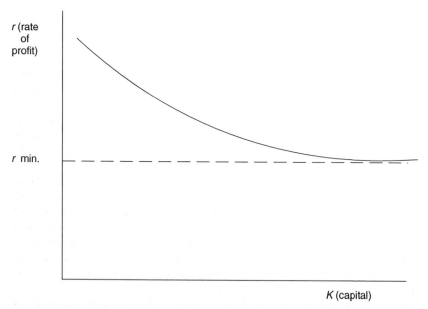

Figure 18.1   The falling rate of profit

Figure 18.1 illustrates the tendency of profits to fall as capital accumulates over time. Limited investment possibilities at various rates of profit explain the downward slope of the profitability of investment curve. As capital increases, investment opportunities are used up in order of profitability until reaching the specific rate of profit which eliminates incentive for further accumulation. When, at this profit rate, the rate of accumulation falls to zero, society reaches the stationary state. There are, however, as in the case of Smith and Marx, a number of countervailing tendencies which postpone the fall of the profit rate to the rate at which positive accumulation is no longer sustainable. Mill listed the following factors: (1) the waste of capital through faulty investment and speculation, especially in boom periods such as the 1840s railway boom; (2) technical progress and innovation which lift the general profitability of investment (shifting the curve of Figure 18.1 upwards to the right); (3) cutting marginal costs and wage costs through importation of cheap materials and foodstuffs from abroad; and (4) exportation of capital for foreign investment. The last was a phenomenon of increasing importance in Britain from the mid-nineteenth century onwards, when British capital financed much loan expenditure in Russia, in Latin America, in the United States, and in the British dominions of Canada and Australia. Together, Mill suggested, these factors would considerably delay the fall of the rate of profit to its minimum at which positive accumulation ceased. Nevertheless, he held that sooner or later, a situation of zero accumulation and growth would be reached, inaugurating the stationary state.

Conclusions

As a figure of transition, Mill transformed much of Ricardo's analysis with respect to value and distribution, thereby presenting the types of argument which were being developed after the 1870s by economists such as Marshall. His contributions to supply and demand theory as a more general explanation of price and value, despite its shortcoming, was one step in this direction. His supply and demand approach to distribution when analysed dynamically, was another. Other aspects of his theory, such as the discredited wages fund approach to (static) wage determination and his seeming defence of cost of production theories in its old labour form, attracted attention of the new economics which sprang up in the 1870s with Jevons's work (discussed in the next chapter). However, Mill's political economy is often innovative and produced a great many new insights (the classification of demand responses to price changes, the treatment of the falling rate of profit and, not discussed here, the reciprocal demand analysis of international values and the sophisticated discussion of monetary theory and policy in the light of increasingly serious business fluctuations).

Notes for further reading

As earlier indicated, a reading of Mill's major work, the *Principles of Political Economy*, is strongly recommended, specifically its Book I, chapters V and IX; Book II, chapters XI, XV and XVI, Book III chapters I–VI, XIV–XVIII though the material on money and fluctuations is also well worth reading; Book IV (all chapters) and Book V, especially, chapter XI. The introduction by Bladen to the variorum edition of the *Principles* in Mill's *Collected Works* (Toronto University Press, Toronto, 1965) is also worth studying. This is the edition used here. George Stigler's essay 'The Nature and Role of Originality in Scientific Progress', *Essays in the History of Economic Thought* (Chicago University Press, Chicago, 1965, esp. pp. 6–11) gives a useful assessment of Mill's originality; Neil de Marchi, 'John Stuart Mill Interpretation since Schumpeter' in (*Classical Political Economy*, edited by William O. Thweatt (Kluwer Academic Publishers, Boston, 1988) gives a useful survey of Mill's scholarship and a bibliography; Hollander's massive *The Economics of John Stuart Mill* (Blackwell, Oxford, 1985) two volumes, is a veritable reference book on Mill's economics, although not conducive to detecting the Millian wood among the trees depicted in all their detail by Hollander. Peter Groenewegen ('Was John Stuart Mill a Classical Economist?', *History of Economics Review*, 13(3), 2005, pp. 9–32) discusses in more detail some of the views on the position of J.S. Mill raised in Chapter 18.

19
William Stanley Jevons, 1835–82: Utilitarianism and Economics

Jevons was born in Liverpool, the ninth child in a solid, unitarian middle-class family. His father was an iron merchant and engineer, whose firm's bankruptcy placed the family in financial hardship from 1848. During the early 1850s Jevons attended University College, London, studying chemistry and mathematics, but without taking his degree. In 1853, he accepted appointment in the newly established Sydney Mint. He stayed in Australia for the five years from 1854 to 1859, developing an interest in the social sciences including economics. On his return to England, he completed his London degree (1860). He then unsuccessfully tried to earn his living from journalism and writing. In 1863 his academic career commenced with his appointment as general tutor at Owen College, Manchester. His work on logic and scientific method, as well as writings on applied economic questions (in particular, *The Coal Question*, 1865) brought him national recognition as an important scientist. In 1866 he became Professor of Political Economy at Owen College, in 1876 at University College, London. In 1872 he was elected Fellow of the Royal Society. He retired in 1880 to have more time for research and writing, an expectation cut short by his untimely death in a swimming accident in 1882.

Jevons's contemporary claim to fame rests on the publication of his *Theory of Political Economy* in 1871 (second edition, 1879), which tried to establish the foundations of economics on the principle of utility. This contribution had been foreshadowed in a paper of 1862, 'Brief Account of General Mathematical Theory of Political Economy' read before Sector F of the British Association. In 1863 he published *A Serious Fall in the Value of Gold*. Neither work attracted much attention. Jevons published a successful textbook on *Money and the Mechanism of Exchange* in 1875, and a final book, *The State in Relation to Labour*, appeared shortly after his death in 1882. Other posthumous editions of his work followed: a volume of essays, *Methods of Social Reform*, edited by his widow (1883), *Investigations in Currency and Finance* (1884) edited by Foxwell (this not only reprinted his *A Serious Fall in the Value of Gold*, but many monetary essays and his work on commercial fluctuations) and in 1905, a fragment of a treatise on the *Principles of Economics*, together with several early papers. Between 1972 and 1981 the Royal Economic Society published Jevons's correspondence and other associated, miscellaneous papers in seven volumes, edited by R.D. Collison Black.

This section concentrates on Jevons' development of utility as the foundation of economics, thereby neglecting his many rich other contributions to economics and related subjects, particularly in monetary economics, taxation and business fluctuations.

Utilitarianism and economics

Jevons attempted in his *Theory of Political Economy* 'to treat economy as a calculus of pleasure and pain' or an endeavour to solve what he described as a major problem in economics:

> *Given, a certain population, with various needs and powers of production, in possession of certain lands and other sources of material: required, the mode of employing their labour which will maximise the utility of the produce.*
>
> Jevons, 1862, 1911, p. 267 (italics in the original)

The 1871 book developed the view which Jevons had unsuccessfully presented to the British Association 1862: 'A true theory of economy can only be attained by going back to the great spirit of human action, the feelings of pleasure and pain' (Jevons, 1862, 1911, p. 304). This embodied a theory of *utility* which elaborated on the pleasure obtained from certain activities such as the consumption of a good. It also included a theory of labour, firstly as a means by which pleasure is obtained; secondly, as something which is invariably accompanied by 'painful exertion', increasing with both the intensity and the duration of labour. These basic principles of pleasure/pain calculus enabled novel results in the theory of value, exchange and cost. Moreover, they acted as a veritable prolegomena to detailed economics covering the 'effects of money, of credit, of combination of labour, of the risk or understanding of undertakings, and of bankruptcy . . . [as well as] the determination of the rate of wages, or the produce of labour after deduction of rent, interest, profit, insurance and taxation.' (Jevons, 1862, 1911, p. 314).

Much of this detailed economics was only fragmentarily covered in Jevons's economic writings. It was intended to be treated more systematically in his *Principles of Economics* of which the outline by chapter-headings and draft of about a dozen chapters were published in 1905. There is therefore an enormous consistency in the bold outline for a new economics sketched by Jevons as a young unknown (aged 27) in 1862 and the major works which he constructed, or intended to construct over the subsequent

20 years of his short life time as economist. This also suggests that the text of Jevons's 1871 *Theory* was designed to present no more than the novel kernel of an extensive system of economics conceived in terms of pleasure and pain, utility and labour.

The mathematical theory of value

The first half of Jevons's *Theory of Political Economy* is concerned with the elucidation of the principle of utility. This is applied to the theory of allocation, exchange and the analysis of labour (or cost). Jevons's introduction argued that economics is an exact, mathematical science and that it is only deficiencies in statistics which make many of the economic variables immeasurable. Even individual feelings are indirectly measurable, since they can be estimated in terms of the price which has to be paid in order to obtain a certain pleasure. Jevons is, however, careful to qualify this statement by indicating that the whole pleasure to be obtained from a specific commodity can never be so measured, and that pleasures for different persons are incomparable.

The second chapter takes up the theory of pleasure and pain, largely from where Bentham had left it, since economics for Jevons consists of the application of this theory to economic problems. Goods confer pleasure; discommodities confer pain. From experience, it is easily argued that as the quantity of a commodity is increased, the pleasure derived from it gradually decreases in intensity; while as a quantity of discommodity is increased, the pain derived from it gradually increases. Figure 19.1 illustrates this fundamental relationship.

Jevons argued that a discommodity (negative utility) curve could start from the origin (a zero quantity of discommodity implied zero utility). However, the utility function could not be completely drawn since initial small quantities of a commodity, particularly when it was essential for life, commanded infinite utility. This explains why the total pleasure derived from a commodity is impossible to measure. Jevons elucidated the general law of pleasure and pain by elaborating on the time factor involved, uncertainty, and possibilities of discontinuity in the variables. From this he developed the theory of utility in relation to value, price, allocation and exchange.

Chapter 3 of the *Theory* elaborates the general attributes of utility. It is not an intrinsic quality of the commodity; it simply expresses the quantitative relationship between the user of the commodity and the commodity itself. Total utility, degree of utility and final degree of utility must be carefully distinguished. Total utility is the utility of the whole quantity consumed. The degree of utility is the utility associated with the consumption of a small portion of the commodity. Final utility is associated with the utility of the last unit of the commodity consumed. Disutility is negative utility (as

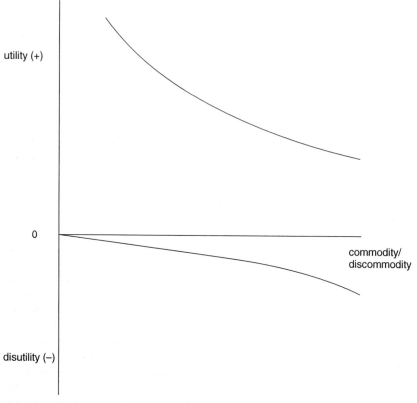

Figure 19.1   Positive and negative utility

implied in Figure 19.1). Actual utility is the utility of a commodity ready for use; prospective utility is the utility of something which is expected to be ready for use in the foreseeable future; potential utility is the utility of something which may be expected to be used at some conceivable but indefinite period of time.

Jevons illustrates the applicability of the concept of final utility for solving economic problems by using it in a rule designed to ensure maximum utility from the allocation of a given stock of a resource among its various alternative uses. This optimal allocation will occur when the final degree of utility is equated for all these various uses. This is intuitively the best possible use of the resource stock since if final degrees of utility of various uses were not equalised, a person could increase utility by transferring a fragment of the good from a use with a low, to that with a higher, degree of final utility.

The theory of exchange

The theory of exchange is developed in the fourth and longest chapter of the *Theory of Political Economy*. Exchange is described as one of the most basic problems in economics since nearly all economic activity can be argued to involve some form of exchange. Value is intimately connected with the theory of exchange, as is indicated by the phrase, exchange value, developed, for example, by Adam Smith. Exchange value is a ratio and expresses the quantity of one commodity which has to be given up in order to obtain a specific quantity of another commodity. Jevons indicates that three usages of the word 'value' should be distinguished, making it at best an ambiguous term. Value in use (as used by Adam Smith in Jevons's view) equals total utility; esteem value equals final utility; exchange value (or exchange ratio) equals the purchasing power of the commodity in terms of another.

The definition of market is also important for the theory of exchange. 'By a market I shall mean two or more persons dealing in two or more commodities, whose stocks of those commodities and intentions of exchanging are known to all. It is also essential that the ratio of exchange should be known to all others.' With such requirements for disclosed information, Jevons's assumed market situation approaches that of perfect competition. However, the fact that his analysis started with the case of two sellers made his initial analysis far more complex than he seems to have realised.

Jevons's theory of exchange itself is conducted in terms of trading bodies. 'By a trading body I mean, in the most general manner, a body either of buyers and sellers' either one or two, or thousands or millions. The device is used to handle problems of aggregation as Jevons quickly slips from the two individuals to a multi-individual case of exchange. In addition, Jevons introduced what he calls the 'law of indifference'. Where commodities are homogenous commodities, there can be only one price for the same type of commodity. Finally, it follows from the law of indifference 'that the last increments in an act of exchange must be exchanged in the same ratio as the whole quality is exchange'.

The key proposition in the theory of exchange is then the following. 'The ratio of exchange of any two commodities will be the reciprocal of the ratio of the final degrees of utility of the quantities of commodity available for consumption after the exchange is completed.' This follows from the proposition that in an exchange the final utility of the things exchanged must be equal in equilibrium for both parties. From there it is not difficult to arrive at the general neo-classical proposition for an optimal exchange in terms of proportionality between marginal utilities and prices, where prices are the exchange ratios expressed in terms of some *numéraire*.

Before discussing the allocation of labour, and the more formal relationship between utility and cost, Jevons presented a general argument of the relationship between his new value theory based on utility and the older, classical theory, based on costs. Since exchangeable value, as just explained, depended on final (or marginal) utility, where does cost of production fit in? Jevons answers this in terms of a famous causal chain of argument:

> Cost of production determines supply;
> supply determines final degree of utility;
> final degree of utility determines value.

The remainder of chapter IV then discusses the gains from trade in terms of utility, and the manner in which utility can be measured by price. The last comes from the relationship between final utility (MU_x) of commodity x, price of x (p_x) and the marginal utility of the money income of the buyer, provided it can be assumed that variations in prices do not affect the marginal utility of money income (which technically speaking cannot be the case, because price variations alter the purchasing power of that money income).

The theory of labour

Smith is quoted at the start of chapter V to link labour exertion with costs, that is, 'the painful exertion which we undergo to ward off pain of greater amount.' Using a diagram similar to Figure 19.1, it is not difficult to depict the pleasure (utility) produced from the product of labour over time, and the pain from the exertion of labour required to produce this flow of product. The horizontal axis measures quantities of labour time and product; the vertical axis positive (and negative) utility. The upper quadrant shows the positive (and declining) utility of the growing product from increased labour time; the lower quadrant the increasing pain (disutility) of labour after a certain amount of time has been worked (during which, as shown in the diagram, it is pleasurable). Pleasure from labour is maximised when the final utility of product and the final disutility of labour are equalised (UE = ED), which thereby determines the optimum amount of time worked (OE).

From there, Jevons developed the proposition that 'the ratio of exchange of commodities will conform in the long run to the ratio of productiveness, which is the reciprocal of the ratio of the cost of production' (but confined by Jevons in this context to simple labour costs). From this he showed that 'commodities will exchange in any market in the ratio of the quantities produced by the same quantities of labour' so that, under certain circumstances, Jevons's utility theory of value can be harmonised with a pure labour theory of exchange ratios. He then demonstrated a number of other propositions relating to joint production, overproduction (described as the complete accomplishment of 'the aim of the economist, which is to

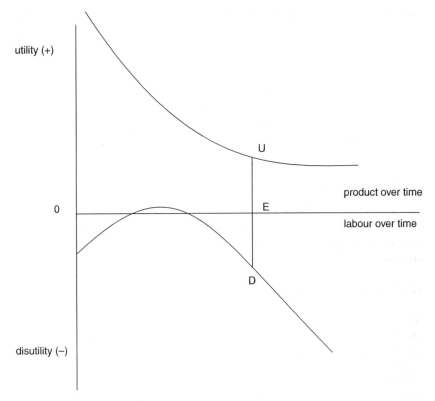

Figure 19.2   Allocation of labour

maximise the products of labour') and attempted to measure labour fatigue in terms of muscular exertion.

Jevons's theory of labour implicitly demonstrated that the reward for labour, or the price to be paid for the 'painful exertion' of labour in work, is the utility (value) of the product created by labour. Subsequent chapters on rent and interest attempt to do likewise for the reward to landowners and capitalists. A concluding chapter stresses other limitations of the distribution theory as developed in these chapters. It presents no real results, and explicitly omits issues of population. It likewise fails to present a real theory of supply and demand, of the firm, of the role of the entrepreneur, and so on. This is not surprising when Jevons's *Theory* was only an attempt to demonstrate how far it was possible in economics to reach solutions to problems on the basis of foundations laid by Bentham's calculus of pleasure and pain. The concluding chapter also criticised various aspects of the wages fund doctrine, of Ricardo's inverse relationship between wages and profit, ending on a warning note about the dangers of according excessive authority to writers in political economy. Jevons's *Theory of Political Economy* shows the potential for deriving a set of results from the basic tenets of late eighteenth century utilitarian doctrine.

Notes for further reading

For consolidation of the argument of this chapter, the whole of Jevons's *Theory of Political Economy* is clearly desirable. The text of the so-called fourth edition (Macmillan – now Palgrave Macmillan, London, 1911) provides useful auxiliary material including the 1862 account of a general mathematical theory of political economy. *Investigations into Currency and Finance* (Macmillan – now Palgrave Macmillan, London, 1885) collect Jevons's monetary writings and work on cyclical fluctuations, including his *A Serious Fall in the Value of Gold*. Examination of the unfinished *Principles of Economics* (Macmillan, London, 1905) gives an indication of what might have been. It reprints Jevons's celebrated essay on Cantillon and some of his innovative essays on taxation. The strength and variety of his applied work is shown in *The Method of Social Reform* (Macmillan – now Palgrave Macmillan, London, 1883) and in his *The Coal Question* (London: Macmillan 1865). A short insight into his economics can be obtained from his little text, *Political Economy*, in the series of Science Primers for Macmillan. Detailed information on Jevons's life and work can be found in the edition of his correspondence and associated documents by R.D. Collison Black (mentioned at the start of this section).

There is a vast mass of secondary material, some of it providing important new insights. Reference could usefully be made to the entries in the *New Palgrave* by Collison Black and Terry Peach; Keynes's biographical Memoir (in *Essays in Biography, Collected Works*, vol. X, Macmillan – now Palgrave Macmillan, London, for the Royal Economic Society) still makes interesting reading; Margaret Shabas, *A World Ruled by Numbers*, Sandra Peart, *The Economics of W.S. Jevons* and Harro Maas, *William Stanley Jevons and the Making of Modern Economics*, provide book length accounts of Jevon's life and work, including that on scientific method. Ian Steedman's 'Jevons's *Theory of Political Economy* and the "Marginalist Revolution" ', *European Journal of the History of Economic Thought*, 4 (1), spring, 1997: 43–65 provides a particularly neat discussion on a major concern of this section.

20

Carl Menger, 1840–1921: the Importance of Marginal Utility and the Economics of Scarcity

Carl Menger was born in February 1840 in Neu-Sandetz in Galicia, then part of the Austro-Hungarian Empire. His father was an attorney, his mother a landowner in Galicia. Menger studied law in Vienna and Prague. He gained his doctor's degree from the University of Cracow. He was therefore more or less self taught in economics, characteristic of many of the first generation of marginalist economists. He worked initially as a journalist, then entered the Press Department of the Prime Minister's office where he reported on economic matters. His demand-oriented outlook was argued to have been influenced by his stock exchange analysis since share prices follow demand rather than cost factors. In 1872 he passed his Habilitation in Economics at the University of Vienna with his *Principles of Economics*, published in 1871. He became Associate Professor in 1873 and full Professor in 1879. In 1893 he published *Investigations into the Method of the Social Sciences with Special Reference to Economics*, followed two years later by *Irrthumer des Historismus in der Deutschen Nationalokonomie*. These were followed by a *Kritik der politischen Okonomie*, and lengthy encyclopaedia articles on capital, money and the principles of classification in economic science, as well as a number of biographical articles on List, von Stein, Roscher, Mill and Böhm-Bawerk. His collected works were published by Hayek in 1935–36. He was actively involved in the Commission on Monetary Reform which prepared Austria for the gold standard in the early 1890s. In 1900, he became Life Peer in the Austrian Upper House. In 1903 he had to retire prematurely from his chair. He died in 1921.

Menger is famous for his role in the marginal revolution and his unique contribution in methodology as founder of the Austrian School. This has recently become more conscious of its Mengerian roots, appreciating the features of his published work in painstakingly analysing the principles of value and price determination, of monetary theory and of market process. Detailed study of Menger's work is therefore becoming more important.

This chapter confines the argument to aspects of his theory of goods, his theory of value and theory of exchange and price determination, as exposited in his *Principles*.

The importance of marginal utility

Ignoring discussion on the origin of money, the nature of the factors of production and the value of the productive services they render, Menger's *Principles of Economics* is devoted to elucidating the principle of utility in relation to value, exchange and price determination. Even factors of production and the pricing of their services, and the theory of money, are treated from the standpoint of the new theory of value. Menger's economics is therefore inseparable from his subjective approach to value theory, and many of the later Austrian economists make marginal utility the cornerstone of their analysis and refrain from any reliance on extraneous cost concepts. Menger's starting point is a detailed account of the general theory of goods.

The nature of goods

In order to acquire good characteristics, all things require the following four conditions: '1. A human need; 2. Such properties as render the thing capable of being brought into a causal connection with the satisfaction of that need; 3. Human knowledge of this causal connection; 4. Command of the thing sufficient to direct it to the satisfaction of the need' (*Principles*, p. 52).

Having defined a good in terms of its necessary and sufficient qualities, Menger then differentiates goods according to whether they satisfy immediate, or indirect (postponed), needs. Goods that satisfy immediate needs, consumption goods, are called 'goods of the first order'. Production goods which satisfy indirect needs are called goods of a higher order, the ranking dependent on the time which has to elapse before a higher goods matures into one ready for consumption. Factor services are hence immediately integrated into the theory of goods, and thereby into the theory of value. This follows from the fact that the character of goods of a higher order is derived from that of the good of the first order into which they gradually mature. (This matter is taken further in the context of von Wieser's economics, below in Chapter 24.)

Economy and economic goods

Goods become requirements of the economising individual. Everyone needs goods. Goods of the first order are required for life itself. Goods of a higher order are required to ensure in advance that the required goods of the first order will be available in sufficient quantities. The less myopic society is in its provision of goods of the first order, the more goods of higher orders rank in importance, since existence of the former requires the presence of the latter in the requisite quantities at some past period. The time element in production, and in want satisfaction, is therefore immediately stressed, as is the element of time preference in individual economising behaviour. The greater the quantity of higher order goods owned by a person, the better that person's future wants will be provided.

Goods become *economic goods* when requirements are larger than the quantities available. Hence in becoming economic or scarce, goods can acquire a value or price. Abundance of a good removes it from a person's economising behaviour. Whether or not goods are economic therefore depends on the circumstances and not on objective qualities. Higher order goods derive economic good characteristics from the first order goods to which they are related. Thus if A, an economic first order good, with respective goods of a higher order P, Q, R, S, T . . . become uneconomic, then P, Q, R, S, T . . . also become uneconomic goods unless they have alternative uses in connection with a good B which is economic.

The distinction is also used to distinguish wealth from property. Wealth is the sum of the economic goods in the ownership of an individual; property is the sum total of that individual's goods.

The nature and origin of value

The origin and nature of value depends on the relationship between persons and their economic goods. This is an entirely subjective relationship, depending on circumstances. For goods of the first order, the valuing process is as follows. The importance which goods have for individual persons and which is called value, is simply imputed. Basically, only satisfaction is of importance to people, because the maintenance of life and well-being depends on them. Logically, however, the importance is imputed to the goods which need to be available to be able to yield these satisfactions. The magnitudes of importance from different satisfactions of concrete needs tend to be unequal and measuring the importance of the separate acts of satisfaction that can be realised by means of individual goods flows from the degree of that importance for the maintenance of life and welfare. The magnitude of the importance of individual satisfaction imputed to goods is therefore also unequal and follows from the degree of importance that the satisfaction from the good in question has for that individual. For every particular case, from all the satisfaction assured by total quantity available of the good, only those that have the *least* importance to an economising individual are dependent on command of a given portion of the whole quantity. The value of a particular good, or of a given portion of the whole quantity of a good at the disposal of an economising individual, is therefore equal for that individual to the importance of the least important of the satisfactions assured by the whole available quantity and achievable by any equal portion. After all, the economising individual in question is dependent on the availability of the particular good, or a given quantity of the good, with respect to these least important degrees of satisfaction.

An illustration clarifies this ponderous chain of analysis. In the consumption of water or foodgrain, the first portion is of immense value, the second of lesser value, the last part, or the least important part consumed, determining value. In this manner Menger arrived at the concept of marginal utility without mentioning the term.

Because only goods of the first order are immediately involved with the satisfaction of wants, they have an immediate value. The value of goods of a higher order is imputed from the value of the goods of the first order with which they are associated. The problem of valuing productive services rendered by individual items of land, labour or capital, is therefore solved by imputing these values from the values of the goods of the first order which they help to produce.

The theory of exchange

The theory of value provides the basis of a theory of exchange. Exchange arises from the gains which people can make by parting with things to which they attribute little value at the margin in return for things to which they attribute a great deal of value. Or, as Menger put it (*Principles*, pp. 177–78), 'we encounter a case in which, if command of a certain amount of A's goods were transferred to B and if a certain amount of B's goods are transferred to A, the needs of both economising individuals could be better satisfied than would be the case in the absence of this reciprocal transfer.' If this motive for exchange is present, and there is nothing to prevent an exchange (such as distance, lack of information, or transport costs), exchange can take place.

The theory of price formation

The theory of price formation is treated next. Like Jevons, Menger starts with the case of isolated exchange. Unlike him, Menger does not argue that this has a determinate solution. The isolated exchange example is as follows:

A values 100 units of his wheat by 40 units of wine. He will therefore be willing to buy 40 units of wine for anything up to a hundred units of wheat. A's maximum price for wine is therefore the exchange ratio of 100:40. If A finds another person B to whom 80 units of wheat are the equivalent in value to 40 units of wine, a fruitful exchange between A and

B can take place, because B has a lower wheat price for wine than the maximum A is prepared to pay. Even if A pays 99 units of wheat for 40 of wine he will gain, while B will gain if he gets as little as 81 units of wheat for the 40 of wine. The limits of the exchange are therefore determined by the value ratios of A and B.

To determine the ratio at which exchange will actually take place a bargaining process has to be traced out. Menger argues, 'each of the two bargainers will attempt to acquire as large a portion as possible of the economic gain that can be derived from the exploitation of the exchange opportunity, and even if he were to try to obtain but a fair share of gain, he will be inclined to demand higher prices the less he knows the economic conditions of the other bargainer and the less he knows the extreme limit to which the other is prepared to go' (*Principles*, p. 195). The problem is artificially solved by special assumptions. 'Under the assumption of economically equally capable individuals, and equality of other circumstances, . . . he effort of the two bargainers to obtain the maximum possible gain will be mutually paralyzing, and the price will therefore be equally far from the two extremes between which it can be established' (*Principles*, p. 196). This yields an exchange rate of 90:40 between wheat and wine. Menger's problem of price formation in an isolated exchange is solved by assuming equality of situation in bargaining which yields an average of the two maximum prices or a midway solution.

Menger then offers a number of cases of exchange (price formation) under conditions of monopoly, from which he derived the following conclusions:

(1) When a monopolist sets the price of a unit of a monopolized good, the competitors for the monopolized good who are excluded from acquiring quantities of it are those for whom one unit of the monopolized good is the equivalent of a quantity of the good offered in exchange that is equal to, or less than, the price of the monopolized good.

(2) Competitors for quantities of a monopolized good for whom one unit of it is the equivalent of a quantity of the good offered in exchange that is larger than the price fixed by the monopolist will supply themselves with quantities of the monopolized good up to the limit at which one unit of it becomes for them the equivalent of an amount of the good offered in exchange that is equal to the monopoly price. The quantity of the monopolized good that will be acquired by each of these competitors at each price set by the monopolist is determined by the foundations for economic exchange operations existing for each individual at that price.

(3) The higher a monopolist sets the price of a unit of monopolized good, the larger will be the class of competitors for the monopolized

good who are excluded from acquiring it, the less completely will the other classes of the population be provided with it, and the smaller will be the sales of the monopolists. Opposite relationships hold in the reverse case.

(Principles, p. 210)

The solutions to the case of monopoly provide the framework or further examples of bilateral competition or the many individuals–two commodities cases. Just as the increase in the number of buyers in the case of monopoly raises the price of a commodity, so an increase in the number of sellers lowers the price. Where there are many buyers and sellers, the range between which the price lies is presumed to be approximately equivalent from the sellers' as from the buyers' prices and all of course will gain from the exchange. Prices will be lower than under monopoly. Although, as far as it goes, Menger's solution is correct, it lacks the elegance of a competitive price determination model using the apparatus of supply and demand. However, its emphasis on process in the individual bargaining cases is superior to many expositions of supply and demand analysis. Menger's detailed account of value, exchange and price determination together with his careful classificatory framework for the theory of goods, has still much to teach.

Notes for further reading

A useful introduction to Menger's life and work is Hayek's essay which introduces the reprint of Menger's *Principles of Economics* (New York University, New York; Press, 1981), the edition used here. The whole of Menger's *Principles of Economics* is worth reading, but read especially chapters 3, 4, 5. The same applies to Menger's *Investigations into the Methods of the Social Sciences* with special reference to economics (New York University Press, New York; 1985), esp. Book III.

Bruce J. Caldwell (editor), *Carl Menger and his Legacy in Economics* (Duke University Press, Durham, NC; 1990) presents the proceedings of a conference, of which Parts III and IV are particularly useful; Streissler's essay on 'Menger, Böhm-Bawerk and Wieser: the Origins of the Austrian School' (in Klaus Hennings and Warren Samuels (eds), *Neoclassical Economic Theory 1870–1930*; Kluwer, Boston; 1988) is useful reading, as is the collection edited by Sir John Hicks and Wilhelm Weber, *Carl Menger and the Austrian School of Economics* (Clarendon Press, Oxford; 1973). Karen Vaughn's entry on Menger in *The New Palgrave*, vol. 3, pp. 438–44, gives a useful summary introduction.

21
Léon Walras, 1834–1910: the Notion of General Equilibrium

Léon Walras, the founder of the modern theory of general equilibrium, was born in Evreux, a French market town. His father was a secondary school administrator with a penchant for economic studies; his mother the daughter of a notary. After completing his preliminary education at Caen and Douai, Walras entered the School of Mines at Paris in 1854 but abandoned its studies some years later for literature, art and philosophy. He published a novel in 1858, the year he also promised his father to continue his work in economics Miscellaneous employment followed while he searched for a university appointment in France. He worked as journalist, for a railway company, for a cooperative bank which failed and a private bank, and as a public lecturer for the cooperative movement. Participation in 1860 at an international congress on taxation at Lausanne (through the favourable impression he had made there on a local politician) secured his appointment in 1870 as Professor of Economics at its university. He retired in 1892 in order to complete his writing programme. In 1874 and 1877 he had published what became his best known work, *Elements d'économie politique pure*. Early retirement enabled publication of *Etudes d'économie sociale* (1896) and *Etudes d'économie politique appliquée* (1898) as collections of earlier work covering social justice, property, distributional issues, and monetary questions. The financial implications of the long illness of his first wife over the 1870s forced interruptions to his research through casual journalism and consultancies with an insurance company to make ends meet. Financial security only came with his second marriage in the 1880s and a legacy in the 1890s. He died in 1910.

Walras's reputation in the history of economics rests on his pioneering work on general equilibrium theory and mathematical economics. His work on utility developed that begun by his father, Antoine Walras, whose economics influenced other parts of Walras's economics as well. His work on mathematical economics gained much from Cournot's book, present in his father's library. Emphasis on general equilibrium distinguishes his contribution from those of Jevons and Menger, and especially from that of

Marshall (see below). Unlike them, Walras raised the question of what 'were the natural and necessary consequences of free competition on exchange and production'. More formally, he posed the problem in the following manner. Given certain predetermined quantities of productive services (land, labour and capital) and their distribution; the techniques of production (production functions) and the prevailing consumer preferences (utility functions), pure competition will inevitably ensure that, after an interval of time:

(a) certain definite quantities of various products will be produced;
(b) each of these products will have a definite price at each instant of time;
(c) each of the productive services will have a definite price at each instant of time.

The problem was to show how quantities of commodities, prices of commodities and prices of factor services were determined, given free competition and a fixed supply of factor services. Walras analysed this problem in two stages. First, by assuming commodities to be given, he determined their prices from the preferences (utility functions). Then, by integrating a theory of production and productive services into the general equilibrium theory of market price determination, he determined total output and its composition, and solved the distributive problem of the prices of productive services. In mathematical terms, Walras formulated the problem as, 'given the quantities of the commodities, formulate a system of equations of which the prices of the commodities are the roots'.

A simple exposition of the first part of Walras's problem follows. This enables illustration of the nature of his conception of general equilibrium in an elementary way. It unfortunately leaves out his analysis of production, of capital, of distribution, and the monetary aspects of his pure economics. Furthermore, it ignores his contributions to social and applied economics. The treatment of Walras's economics presented here thereby deliberately leaves out two of the three parts which, in Walras's scheme of things, together constitute social and political economy. These parts were (1) the study of the natural laws of value in exchange, of exchange and the theory of social wealth. These are called pure economics; (2) study of the most favourable conditions for agriculture, manufactures, trade, credit or the theory of the production of wealth, this is called applied political economy; (3) the study of the best state of property and taxation, or theory of the distribution of wealth. This is included in social economics. As already indicated, his early retirement enabled completion of all three parts in book form, though his social and applied economics were only published in a preliminary and incomplete form though reprinting previously published essays.

Walras's general equilibrium theory

Walras's preliminary analysis of market price determination is the starting point of his theory of general equilibrium. Its discussion enables basic features of the analysis to be sampled and some of its essentials illustrated.

Wealth and value

Definitions of wealth and value start Walras's analysis. Social wealth is defined as 'all things material or immaterial, that are scarce, that is to say, on the one hand, useful to us, and, on the other hand, only available to us in limited quantity.' (*Elements*, p. 65). Scarcity, the necessary attribute of social wealth, therefore implies both usefulness and limited quantity. Only social wealth has exchange value, since only social wealth has *rareté*, the term for utility used by Walras. Little space is devoted to the definitional subtleties of the subject. Walras immediately began analysing what he saw as its core, price determination in a two commodities case. Utility is not defined in much detail, though utility schedules are later derived and used in formulating the theorem of maximum satisfaction associated with a competitive general equilibrium situation.

The market and competition: exchange of two commodities

Commodities are defined as things that are valuable and exchangeable; the market is a place where commodities are exchanged. As buyers, traders make demands by outbidding one another. The meeting of buyers and sellers and the mutual bidding determines exchange values. The more buyers and sellers, the better competition works and the more rigorous is the manner of arriving at exchange value.

Assume a market in which some people hold commodity A, others hold commodity B. Holders of A want some B, holders of B some A. The bidding starts at the closing rate of the previous day, that is, one of the holders of B offers to give n units of B for m units of A. This bid embodies the equation of exchange, $mv_a = nv_b$ where v_a and v_b are defined as ratios of value of exchange or relative exchange values.

Hence:

$$p_a = \frac{v_a}{v_b} = \frac{1/m}{n} = \frac{1}{p}$$

indicating the non-monetary nature of the economy at this stage.

'Prices, or ratios of values in exchange are [therefore] equal to the inverse ratio of the quantities exchanged' and the price of any one commodity is the reciprocal of the price of the second commodity in terms of the first.

Offer and demand

Let D_a, O_a, D_b, O_b be the effective demand and offer of A and B respectively at their respective prices, $p_a = n/m$ and $p_b = m/n$. A basic relationship exists between quantities offered, quantities demanded and prices. From the definition of offer (any offer made of a definite amount of commodity at a definite price) and that of demand (any demand for a definite amount of commodity at a definite price) it follows that:

$$O_a = D_b \cdot p_b \quad O_b = D_a \cdot p_a$$

Likewise, when an owner of A offers O_a at p_a, his effective demand for B can be given as $D_b = O_a \, p_a$, while similarly, $D_a = O_b \, p_b$.

Only two of these equations are independent, say $O_a = D_b p_b$, $D_a = O_b p_b$. The other two equations follow from them and from the price relationship, $p_a \cdot p_b = 1$.

Equilibrium in the two commodity case

Assume that the offered quantities are determined by the quantities demanded, since no one can demand without offering at the same time (this is a simple statement of the law of markets under barter conditions). At prices p_a and p_b, D_a and D_b will be demanded, so that $O_a = D_b p_b$ and $O_b = D_a p_a$.

Let $D_a = \alpha O_a$ where α can be $= 1$, >1 or <1.

α in this case is of course equal to the ratio of the effective offer of B to the effective demand for B, that is, $\alpha = O_b/D_b$.

When $\alpha = 1$, $O_a = D_a$ and $O_b = D_b$ and the market will be cleared since at prices p_a and p_b the quantities offered and demanded of A and B are equal. If, for example, a > 1 then $D_a > O_a$ and $O_b > D_b$. In this case p_a will rise because of the excess demand for A, while p_b will fall given the excess supply of B. The rise in p_a increases O_a and lower D_a, the fall in p_b will lower O_b and raise D_b. This process will continue until $D_a = O_a$, $D_b = O_b$ ($\alpha = 1$) and the market has cleared. Walras showed that when $\alpha \gtrless 1$, excess demand for one of the commodities equals the excess supply of the other commodity, a statement which since then has been called Walras law.

From this, the following definition of equilibrium is derived:

> Given two commodities, for the market to be in equilibrium with respect to these commodities, or for the price of either commodity to be stationary in terms of the other, it is necessary and sufficient that the effective demand be equal the effective offer of each commodity. Where this equality does not obtain, in order to reach equilibrium price, the commodity having an effective demand greater than its effective offer

must rise in price, and the commodity having an effective offer greater than its effective demand must fall in price.

(*Elements*, Lesson 6, p. 106)

The theorem of maximum utility of commodities

After analysing price equilibrium in a two commodity market, Walras reintroduced the subject of utility (rareté) into the analysis in order to demonstrate that equilibrium prices which clear the market also ensure maximum utility for their owners, the parties to the exchange.

The utility function is shown in Figure 21.1. Note that the axes are reversed from the usual (Marshallian) way (see Chapter 22,below). Note also that utility remains finite on the grounds that all wants can be fully satisfied at a zero price.

Utility (total utility) is defined as a function of the quantity held, i.e. $u = \phi(q)$; effective utility (rareté or marginal utility) is the derivative of the utility function, i.e. $r = \phi'(q)$.

Walras demonstrates that the parties to an exchange will attempt to maximise their utility. This occurs when the ratio of utility of the two commodities is equal to that of their prices, that is, $r_a r_b = p_a p_b$. Until this equality is reached, a party to an exchange will find an advantage in selling the commodity the utility of which is smaller than its price multiplied by the utility of the other commodity and buy the commodity of which the utility is greater than the price multiplied by the utility of the other commodity. Equilibrium and maximum utility are assured when:

$$r_a = p_a \cdot r_b \text{ and } r_b = p_b \cdot r_a$$

Solution to the problem of exchange of more than two commodities: general equilibrium in the goods market

Walras extended the analysis first to a three commodity case where, through arbitrage (tâtonnement), the same general condition is established that certain prices can be found at which the market for the commodities is cleared. Instead of envisaging a single market, Walras assumes there are numerous markets. In the case of n commodities, there are n markets: one where A is traded against B, C, . . . N; one where B is traded against A, C, . . . N; one where C is traded against A, B, . . . N and the nth market where N is traded against A, B, C., . . . The demand functions are now no longer simple functions of a single price, but complex functions of all the prices, that is, $D_a = f(p_a, p_b, p_c, \ldots p_n)$; $D_b = f(p_b, p_a, p_c, p_d \ldots p_n)$; . . . and the offer functions can no longer be simply derived from them as in the simple, two commodities case. The solution to the problem of general equilibrium is found by solving a system of equations in the following manner.

Quantity

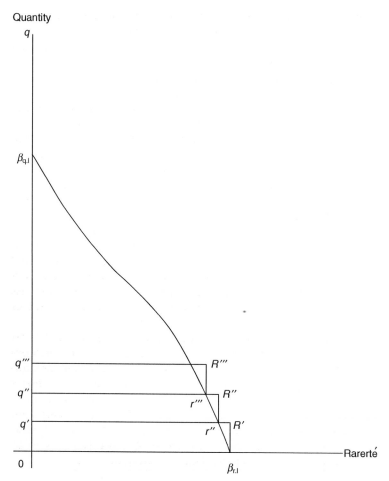

Figure 21.1   The Walrasian utility (*rareté*) function

For m commodities, there will be $m-1$ equations of exchange, which relate the demand for one commodity to the offers made for it in terms of the other commodities in the market at the prices ruling in the market; there will be a set of $m(m-1)$ equations of demand relating the demand for the m commodities to the prices ruling for each of them in terms of the other commodities in the markets in which it is traded; and there will be a set of $(m-1)(m-1)$ general equilibrium equations which show that the equilibrium prices ruling in the markets prevent profits being made from arbitrage transactions. The equilibrium prices are consistent, stable prices. This gives sufficient $(2m^2 - 2m)$ equations to solve for the $m(m-1)$ prices of the m commodities in terms of one another and the $m(m-1)$ total quantities of the *m* commodities which are exchanged for one another. The theorem of general equilibrium is then extended by Walras to show that this situation also leads to maximum utility for all parties to the exchanges, when price ratios and the utility ratios are equalised. This is the optimum condition for exchange under perfect competition and in this sense makes general equilibrium a position of maximum satisfaction.

At this stage, Walras's system already exhibits a number of peculiarities which need to be mentioned. Reaching equilibrium by the prices which he analysed requires 'tâtonnement', groping, trial and error, by an 'auctioneer' who manipulates the various prices where necessary to ensure that all markets are cleared by eliminating excess supply and excess demand. To hark back to the simple two commodity case discussed earlier, it requires someone to move p_a up and p_b down until the adjustment of offers and demands is such that it brings them into equality. If there is to be no trading at 'false' (non-equilibrium) prices, all transactions in the market places need to be finalised at equilibrium prices. This part of the process greatly worried Walras, and its explanations were continually altered during the various editions of the *Elements*. Nevertheless, Walras believed that this process of trial and error price adjustment to eliminate excess supply and demand provided a realistic solution to the problem of achieving a competitive general equilibrium in practice.

Secondly, the existence of a general equilibrium solution, which Walras perceived to have been proved by the equality of the number of independent equations and that of unknowns, in reality required much more stringent proof. Such a system may have no solution in practice, or many solutions, or only solutions which have no economic meaning such as negative prices. It was not until the 1930s that solutions for this problem were found and that a general equilibrium of the type envisaged by Walras could be said to exist. (The first of such demonstrations was published in German in 1936 by the mathematical economist, Abraham Wald.)

Factor markets and the equations of production

In subsequent sections of his *Elements*, Walras introduced the market for factor services and the equations of production, in order to demonstrate that with given factor services, there will be a set of factor prices which will lead to an allocation of these services to produce the requisite quantities of commodities which, when traded at equilibrium prices, will yield maximum utility. From these prices (akin to the marginal productivities of the factor services), Walras also derived the optimum conditions of production. This was achieved by the third edition of the *Elements*.

The theory of production, involving as it does the hiring of productive services in the appropriate quantities and combinations, introduces the notion of entrepreneurs into the analysis. As Walras explained in a letter to F.A. Walker, the American economist:

> The definition of entrepreneur is, in my opinion, the kernel of the whole economic science. I, for me, consider him exclusively as the person who buys the productive services at the market for services and sells the products at the market for products, thus making a benefit or a loss. If he possesses part of the land or of the capital goods productive in his firm, or if he takes part, in the quality of manager or otherwise, in the activities relating to the transformation of the services into products, he is, for that reason, landowner, capitalist or labourer, and cumulates his own function [i.e. that of entrepreneur] with other, different functions. In practice such a cumulation occurs frequently and may, in general, even be necessary; But I believe that theoretically it [i.e. that cumulation] should be discarded from the analysis.
>
> (Walras to F.A. Walker, 12 June 1887; Jaffé, 1965: letter 800).

In this description, the key feature of the entrepreneur is that of co-ordinator of the product market. The entrepreneur matches the requirements of productive services by the 'firms', to the output required in the market for goods which matches the demands and the preferences of the consumers. Profits and losses in this process are signs of disequilibrium, just as excess supply and demand are in the goods market. Hence in competitive equilibrium, profits are zero. The underlying theory of production is however not very detailed, but the analysis provides sufficient equations to solve the unknowns in terms of prices of productive services and the quantities of the goods produced.

Theories of the capital market and of money and circulation completed the general equilibrium model designed by Walras over the four editions of his *Elements*. The first introduced problems of determining the prices of land and personal services, as well as those associated with the relationship between savings and the market for capital goods. Prices of these capital goods are related to the prices of the services they yield, together with allowances for insurance for risk and depreciation (aspects of the problem which also enter the pricing of other productive services). Intermediation in the capital market is sometimes assumed away (savers invest their savings directly into physical capital) but is sometimes assumed to take place through the purchase of stock certificates representative of productive assets. Demand for capital goods comes from production, not savers. Competition equates the net rate of income derived for capital goods, the effective rate of interest in the system, which also acts to equate investment with aggregate savings. The money market enters via the need of consumers and entrepreneurs to have access to purchasing power (cash balances), hence introduces demand for cash balances which need to adjust to the available money supply (determined by the monetary authorities in a fiat money system, by the stock of available bullion in a commodity money system), with interest rate variations bringing demand and supply into balance, hence linking money and capital market.

Together, the analysis underlying the general equilibrium system with its four associated markets contributed much what lies at the core in contemporary neo-classical analysis in the theory of consumption, production, capital and money. Integrating this into a system of general equilibrium by means of a comprehensive set of simultaneous equations is the second major part of this contribution. Such a tremendous input into the research program of a large group of leading twentieth century economists makes it not surprising that Schumpeter and Hicks described Walras as the greatest economist ever, and that much of contemporary mainstream theory goes under the name of Walrasian economics. This success was achieved slowly. By the time he died in 1910, Walras had few staunch disciples who grasped the significance of what he had attempted to do. Among them were his successor at the chair of Lausanne, Vilfredo Pareto and several other Italian colleagues and friends, including Maffeo Pantaleoni and Enrico Barone. Schumpeter's praise and use of Walrasian theory came during the decade after Walras's death; Hicks both explained and developed his general equilibrium framework during the 1930s. General equilibrium theory itself did not begin to dominate the literature until after the Second World War, so that the essentials of Walras's contribution had a long wait before they came into their own. These developments also did much to differentiate Walras's work from systems with which it had been so frequently linked in the context of the marginal revolution.

Notes for further reading

A reading of at least part of the *Elements of Pure Economics* is obligatory. A study of its Part II (Lessons 5–10) enables following Walras for the part of his work which is summarised here in some detail. Study of Part VI on the theory of money and circulation is also strongly recommended, partly because of its significance in some of the early debates over Keynesian economics. At this stage, a look at Walras's other economic work requires an ability to read French, since neither of the two *Etudes* has been translated into English. William Jaffé, a leading commentator who edited and translated the *Elements*, also edited Walras's *Correspondence* in three volumes (North Holland, Amsterdam, 1965) much of it again untranslated from the languages into which the letters were originally written. A collected works of Walras (father and son) is in preparation by the Centre Auguste et Léon Walras at Lyon, of which a number of volumes have appeared.

The commentator literature is legion. Schumpeter's essay on Walras (*Ten Great Economists*, Allen and Unwin, London, 1952, pp. 74–79) and

Hicks's original tribute ('Léon Walras', in John Hicks, *Classics and Moderns, Collected Essays*, vol. 3 (Basil Blackwell, Oxford; 1982, pp. 85–95) are still worth reading but need to be supplemented by more contemporary appraisals. Jaffé's essays on Walras have been collected by Donald A. Walker (Cambridge University Press, Cambridge, 1983); Walker's entry on Walras in the *New Palgrave Dictionary of Economics* (vol. 3, pp. 852–3) is a superb introduction. In a different and broader vein, this also applies to Albert Jolink's study of *The Evolutionist Economics of Léon Walras* (Routledge, London, 1996) and his study, with Jan van Daal, of *The Equilibrium Economics of Léon Walras* (Routledge, London, 1993) which provides a step by-step discussion of Walras's theoretical system with appendices including a biographical sketch. An issue of *Economies et Sociétés* (October–November 1994) devoted to Walras gives a splendid overview of all aspects of his work by leading Walras specialists of the 1990s.

22
Alfred Marshall, 1842–1924: Partial Equilibrium and Useful Economics

Alfred Marshall was born in Bermondsey in 1842. He was educated at the Merchant Taylor's school in London, gaining a taste for mathematics. Subsequently, he completed the Cambridge Mathematical Tripos in 1865 and gained a fellowship at St John's College. He then gradually switched to the moral sciences moving from philosophical, ethical and psychological studies to political economy. In 1868 he became College Lecturer in the Moral Sciences, by the early 1870s he was concentrating on advanced political economy teaching and working on a book on international trade. He wrote his first book *Economics of Industry* (1879) jointly with his wife, and privately printed material from a foreign trade manuscript (on the pure theory of domestic and international values). In 1884 he became Cambridge Professor of Political Economy until 1908 when Pigou (see Chapter 28, below) was appointed as his successor. His major work, *Principles of Economics*, was published in 1890 (eighth, and definitive edition, 1920). During retirement he published supplementary volumes (*Industry and Trade* in 1919, *Money, Credit and Commerce* in 1923) instead of the projected second volume of the *Principles*, which was to have covered these and other (public finance, monopoly, combinations, the role of the state) topics.

Marshall is often somewhat misleadingly bracketed with Jevons, Menger and Walras as a founder of the marginal revolution. Marshall's initial price analysis, following that of Cournot and Mill, ignored utility considerations, only introduced in the context of analysing consumer surplus (see below). Secondly, Marshall failed to show the hostility to Ricardo and Mill revealed by Jevons. Marshall argued that their work was rarely incorrect, it needed to be completed (or reinforced) by aspects emphasised by the new economics, such as demand, consumption and certain allocative aspects conducive to the improvement of human welfare. For this reason, Veblen aptly described it as 'neo-classical'. Although aware of the relevance of general equilibrium considerations and the importance of interdependence between economic variables, Marshall preferred a partial equilibrium approach as more practical for solving economic questions. Never explicitly defined by him, it refers to essential abstraction and simplification in analysis or stripping an issue of those elements not required for a solution. Marshall saw economics as a useful subject geared to alleviating poverty and encouraging improvement. Marshall therefore also disliked indulgence in pure theory, particularly mathematical theory. At best, mathematics was an aid to analysis to be hidden when the problem was solved. Geometry was useful as a pedagogical device, but banished to footnotes in the *Principles*.

Utility theory and the derivation of demand curves

In his first paper on the theory of value, written circa 1870, price determination is simply analysed in terms of supply and demand, with the last constructed from hypothetical data relating prices to the specific amounts of the commodity which will be bought at these prices. Utility does not enter into this derivation. However, value in use (defined in terms of the amount of general purchasing power a buyer is willing to give up to obtain a specific quantity of a commodity can never be less, and generally speaking, is considerably more, than the price paid for it. This suggests the later notion of consumer surplus. This paper (reprinted in Whitaker, 1975, pp. 125–59) draws heavily on Cournot and Mill's demand analysis. The privately printed *Pure Theory of Domestic Value*, written some years later (though not published until 1879) derives the demand curve in similar manner. Its Chapter II introduces the notion of consumers' 'rent' or consumer surplus.

Book III of the *Principles*, from its first edition onwards, deliberately linked the derivation of the demand curve to the notion of marginal utility. This is almost certainly explained by the fact that Marshall by 1890 had become fully convinced of the potential usefulness for applied economics of the consumer surplus concept, an issue pursued here to illustrate some of the strengths and limitations of Marshall's partial equilibrium approach.

The shapes of marginal utility functions and demand functions intuitively show that the former can lead to the latter. This had to be the order of causality, since it is consumer preference which influences the demand for a product at a particular price. The derivation of demand functions from utility functions is most easily shown algebraically as Marshall himself did in note II of the mathematical appendix to the *Principles*. Start with the equilibrium condition for the consumption (purchase) of a commodity, x, which can be given as:

$$MU_x = p_x \cdot MU_m$$

where MU_x is the marginal utility of a commodity, p_x its price, and MU_m the marginal utility of the consumer's money income. This condition expresses the fact that since price (weighted by the utility of the consumer's command over general purchasing power) reflects the marginal utility to the consumer of that commodity, when marginal utility and weighted price are equal, incentives for further purchases of the commodity disappear.

The familiar condition for maximum consumer satisfaction is easily derived from this equilibrium condition:

$$\frac{MU_x}{p_x} = \frac{MU_y}{p_y} = \ldots\ldots \frac{MU_n}{p_n} = MU_m$$

From this, it is an easy step to the theory of demand. Take the equilibrium for the individual consumption good, x, which has just been stated. Assume a fall in the price of x, p_x. The former equality is then broken, since $MU_x > p_x \cdot MU_m$. To restore the equality, the consumer needs to lower MU_x, by purchasing more x, until once again $MU_x = p_x \cdot MU_m$. The fall in price raises the quantity demanded. When p_x rises, $MU_x < p_x \cdot MU_m$, MU_x has to increase so that less of commodity x will be demanded. The result only holds if MU_m remains constant when prices change. Any price change, however, affects the purchasing power of money income, price falls raising, and price rises lowering it. Hence MU_m is likely to be affected by what is now called the income effect of the price change. Since the income effect on MU_m is in the opposite direction to the substitution effect of the price change, it is possible that the income effect of a change in price precisely offsets the effect of the change in price itself, hence maintaining the equality ensuring consumer equilibrium. Marshall eliminated this problem by assuming that, generally speaking, the commodity in question is sufficiently minor in the consumer's spending pattern, to exert minimal income effect and hence a negligible influence on MU_m. This highlights the partial equilibrium nature of Marshall's demand analysis. Other *ceteris paribus* clauses need to be invoked if the demand for x is to be a simple function of p_x. Neither tastes, the prices of related goods, the prices of unrelated goods, nor expectations of future prices, are allowed to change. The derivation of the demand function of x as a simple function of p_x, requires that certain types of variation be abstracted from for the purpose of the analysis.

Dependent and independent variables: Marshall *versus* Walras

Those who have carefully absorbed the material on Walras, will have noted important differences between his and Marshall's analyses of demand. Marshall's approach starts with a price change which disturbs equilibrium in order to see how quantities purchased adjust to restore equilibrium. For Walras, as shown in Chapter 21, equilibrium in the market was disturbed when there was excess demand or excess supply (offers) in that market. Prices then change to eliminate the excess demand/supply and restore equilibrium. For Walras, prices are therefore the independent variable, Marshall treated prices as the dependent and quantities purchased as the independent, and adjusting variable. Marshall's approach has a number of implications. It fits in better with his emphasis on consumer surplus; inverting the axes also results in neater diagrams when supply curves or offer curves are introduced into the analysis.

The derivation of the Marshallian supply curve

Marshall laid the foundations for his supply curve in his theory of production (or output), presented in Book IV of his *Principles*. This demonstrated the role of the factors of production, land, labour, capital and organisation, as well as their quantitative growth and changes in their productivity. The latter introduced the laws of returns in which at least historically diminishing returns were associated with the use of land and increasing returns with superior organisation and large scale enterprise in much of manufacturing industry.

The operational form of Marshall's notion of the supply price of commodity is the sum of the costs of the various agents which help to produce it. Hence Marshall's notion of the real costs of production in terms of the labour costs of personal exertion and the capital costs of abstinence and waiting can only be given a realistic meaning in terms of the money costs of production. Marshall warned that the nature and type of these expenses of production is not independent of the scale of output. Furthermore, they are affected by the period of time to which the investigation of supply refers, a number of factors of production are of slow growth and decay and this affects the analysis.

On the basis of some simplifying assumptions to eliminate these difficulties, Marshall indicated how a notional short period supply curve can be constructed for a specific firm and a specific output level. Measuring supply price on the vertical axis and quantity 'supplied' of the commodity on the horizontal axis, for any quantity of product, say OM, the supply prices of the factors required to produce that quantity can be indicated separately with point P being the total supply price for quantity OM. As Marshall explained himself:

> Suppose for instance, that we classify the expenses of production of our representative firm, when an amount OM of cloth is being produced under the heads of (i) M_{p1}, the supply price of the wool and other circulating capital which would be consumed in making it, (ii) p_1p_2 the corresponding wear-and-tear and depreciation on buildings, machinery and other fixed capital, (iii) p_2p_3 the interest and insurance on all the

capital, (iv) p_3p_4 the wages of those who work in the factory, and (v) p_4P the gross earnings of management etc. of those who undertake the risks and direct the work. Thus as M moves from O towards the right p_1, p_2, p_3, p_4 will each trace out a curve and the ultimate supply curve traced out by P will be thus shown as obtained by superimposing the supply curve for the several factors of production of the cloth.

(Principles, p. 344 n)

The partial equilibrium nature of this analysis should be noted. The component parts of the supply price of a commodity are assumed to be given, hence the quantities required of these factors and their prices are assumed to be known. This is a legitimate assumption for the individual producer, particularly if the productive unit is small so that its output decisions cannot significantly affect input markets and prices. However, if the commodity produced required a substantial amount of a rather scarce imput for its production, changes in its output would raise its price so that the assumption of given supply prices for the inputs can no longer be sustained.

Marshall also warned that the rising supply curve shown in Figure 22.1 depended on the implicit assumption that costs rose more than proportionately as output increased, that is, the firm was operating in a situation

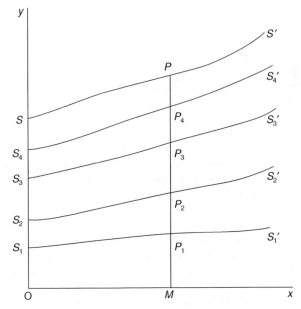

Figure 22.1 The Marshallian construction of the supply curve

of diminishing returns. However, where there are important increasing returns to scale present in the industry the supply curve may be a declining one as output increases, other supply curves may alternatively rise or fall, depending on the impact of the scale of production on costs.

Marshall's argument about the specific effects of time on the nature of supply, and his division of supply analysis into three distinct time periods, has passed fully into the accepted wisdom on price theory. In the market period, supply tends to be totally inelastic in an upward direction since time is too short for any increased supplies to reach the market (it can of course be lowered by dealers withholding stocks from sale). In the short period supply becomes a little more elastic, since new output can be produced from working the existing plant and equipment more intensively. Variable costs of labour, energy and materials alter. Only in the long period can plant and productive capacity be increased, hence making supply as elastic as possible. Fixed costs now become variable, new technologies can be introduced and there is potential for progress and growth.

Some aspects of Marshall's theory of progress

Marshall's hopes about the eventual elimination of poverty as the result of economic progress was mentioned in the introduction. The final chapter of his *Principles of Economics* discussed the issue of progress at some length in the context of its potential for lifting the standard of life. The last not only involved the presence of material progress in the form of higher wages and living standards. It invoked as well changes in attitude to improve consumption habits from the increased wealth together with better employment of the growing leisure time which came with the shorter working day and longer holidays economic progress brought in its wake. The state had a minor but significant role to play in this progress of improvement by its fiscal expenditures on education, better housing, town planning and transport and to a lesser extent by redistribution through the tax system, and by attempting to reduce the frequency and severity of periodic crises and the resultant unemployment and dislocation of industry. Trade unions needed to enhance their social responsibility by refraining from strike action and restrictive practices. Such actions lowered productivity growth and international competitiveness, thereby reducing the potential for progress.

More generally, Marshall's strong faith in the potential for improvements dispelled the more dismal picture painted by the earlier classical economists of a stationary state brought on by the impact of diminishing returns in agriculture on profits accumulation and wage rates. Marshall strikingly countered this spectre by emphasis on the immense potential for increasing returns. Moreover, he pointed to the benefits from technical progress in transport and communications, free trade, and the agricultural developments in the new worlds of North America and Australasia in delaying indefinitely the pessimistic forecasts about the possibilities for food production held by Ricardo and Malthus and their followers.

The major impetus for progress, growth and improvement in Marshall's scheme of things came through increasing returns from the superior organisation of industry which progress itself made possible. After all, the scope for the division of labour depended on the size of the market, as Adam Smith had indicated in 1776. This lesson about cumulative interaction in the growth process had been fully absorbed by Marshall and adapted to the industrial possibilities revealed during the final decades of the nineteenth century. Division of labour for Marshall included locational concentration of industry and, combined with technical progress, the growth of the size of the firm. The first gave rise to external economies of scale, the second to internal economies, stressing the cumulative aspects of economic growth and the growing interdependence of economic entities. Dynamic considerations therefore gain the focus.

External economies arise from the locational concentration of particular industries as well as from the growing size of the national and the world economy. The first are said to induce the developments of special skills and machinery as a specific consequence of this spatial aspect of the division of labour. The second encourages the growth of knowledge and progress of the arts which are said to be dependent on the aggregate volume of production in the whole world.

Few external economies are compatible with partial equilibrium. Marshall discussed internal economies in even more detail. These are ascribed to the growth of the firm, including its plant. Following Stigler (1941, pp. 77–78), they can be summarised as follows (page references in brackets in the quote are all to the eighth edition of the *Principles*:

(i)   Economy of materials, or the utilization of by-product, which is 'rapidly losing importance' (p. 278).
(ii) Economy of machinery (pp. 279–81).
(iii) Economy in the purchase and sale of materials (p. 282).
(iv) Economy of skill (pp. 283–4).
(v)   Economy of finances. It is frequently urged that the larger (and older) firm secures credit on easier terms (pp. 285, 315).

(Stigler, 1941, pp. 77–8)

The logical implications of massive internal economies for the growth of the size of the firm and the nature of competition are the potential monopolisation of the industry (see below, Chapter 29). Marshall countered such monopolistic consequences both empirically and theoretically. His extensive factory inspections and study of industrial data did not reveal the growth of monopoly on the requisite sale. The hypothesis of a life cycle of firms was posited by way of explication. Under individual or family ownership, a firm flourished, stagnated and died in three generations (a situation Marshall admitted to be less likely under the perpetual life of a joint stock company). Diseconomies of scale, in terms of growing management and marketing problems associated with size were said to effectively constrain the benefits from increasing returns achieved through growth. However, internal economies and their consequences could not be deleted from the economic agenda. They were too important a factor in growth, progress and the hopes for a better life for all. As tools of analysis, they therefore continue to be used in the economics of growth and development, another example of the many contributions Marshall made to economics.

Notes for further reading

Reading should start with perusal of the *Principles of Economics* (eighth edition, 1920) concentrating on Books III (consumption, demand, welfare), Book IV (production, growth and development) and parts of Book V (chs 1–5). Appendix H is also instructive reading as are Appendices A–D on the historical developments of competitive industry, economic doctrine and economic methodology. Marshall's *Industry and Trade* is an interesting pioneering international comparative study of industrial organisation and change in the context of developments in trade, marketing and government regulation.

The commentator literature on Marshall is massive. A full biography is available in Peter Groenewegen, *A Soaring Eagle. Alfred Marshall 1842–1924* (Edward Elgar, Aldershot, 1995). This also deals with the economics. Keynes's famous obituary memoir on Marshall remains a fine brief portrait (in *Essays in Biography, Collected Works*, Vol. 10). Whitaker has edited *Marshall's Early Economic Writings* (Macmillan – now Palgrave Macmillan, London, 1975) and *Marshall's Correspondence* (Cambridge University Press, Cambridge, 1996). A substantial number of the many articles on Marshall are reprinted in J.C. Wood (ed.), *Alfred Marshall: Critical Assessments* (Routledge, London, 1982, 1996) in 8 volumes. Pascal Bridel, *Cambridge Monetary Thought* (Macmillan, London, 1987) gives a handy introduction to Marshall's monetary analysis. Useful volumes on Marshall's economics were published in the context of the centenary celebrations of Marshall's *Principles* in 1990, especially John Whitaker (ed.), *Centenary Essays on Alfred Marshall* (Cambridge University Press, Cambridge, 1990) and the two volume issue of *Quaderni di storia dell'economia politica* vol. XI(2–3) 1991, Vol. X(1) 1992. Stigler's *Production and Distribution Theories. The Formative Period*, The Macmillan Company, New York, 1941, chapter 4, gives a critical survey of Marshall's theories of production and distribution, still worth reading. A useful overview of Marshall and his economics is *The Elgar Companion to Alfred Marshall*, edited by Tiziano Raffaelli, Giacomo Becattini and Marco Dardi (Edward Elgar, Cheltenham, 2006).

Section II

The Development of Marginalist Economics: Distribution and Capital Theory

23

J.B. Clark and P.H. Wicksteed: the Development of Marginal Productivity Theory

The application of the new marginalist theory to the theory of distribution was essentially the work of two men, J.B. Clark in the United States, and Philip Wicksteed in the United Kingdom, who coordinated the laws of distribution by a judicious use of Euler's theorem. Since Clark's analysis is logically preliminary to that of Wicksteed, this chapter starts with his account of the marginal productivity theory.

J.B. Clark, 1847–1938

J.B. Clark was born in Providence, Rhode Island. Academic studies at Amherst were twice interrupted, first by illness and then by the death of his father. He finally graduated in 1872, choosing economics, doing postgraduate work in Germany and Switzerland (1872–75). His first book, *The Philosophy of Wealth* (1886) shows the influence of his German studies and is sympathetic to Christian socialism. It independently developed the notion of marginal utility under the name, effective utility. It was followed ten years later by his magnum opus, *The Distribution of Wealth* (1899), a subject on which Clark had been working from the 1880s, particularly with reference to capital theory and to what became the road to his discovery of the marginal productivity principle, generalising the Ricardian theory of rent. Problems of maintaining competition dominated his subsequent work. His career was undoubtedly that of the first North American economist of international standing (the first of many), while his contributions to value and to distribution theory made him a leading participant in consolidating the sway of marginalist economics in the 'new world'. He was one of a small group of young American economists involved in creating the American Economic Association in 1885, which in turn has commemorated this contribution with the award of a biennial J.B. Clark Medal to a very promising, young economist.

A marginalist theory of distribution

Clark's *The Distribution of Wealth* (1899) synthesised the development towards a marginal productivity theory of distribution made previously in a number of journal articles and especially in his 'Distribution as determined by a Law of Rent' (*Quarterly Journal of Economics*, 1890–91, V: 289–318). The last clearly argued that rent is very much like earnings from other productive services than land and that, just as land rent (or the marginal product of land) can be derived from the experience of dosing a fixed quantity of land with variable units of labour (where the product associated with each increment of labour gradually declines as a result of diminishing returns) so interest of capital can be conceived as the marginal product of capital when a fixed fund of capital is dosed with variable units of labour likewise subject to diminishing returns. The same experiment can be conducted with labour as the fixed factor. In the experiments where labour is the variable factor service, 'The last man added . . . earns wages only', and with competition ensuring a uniform wage rate, the total wage bill (wage share) can be easily calculated. The argument is simply illustrated in Figure 23.1.

In Figure 23.1, AD represents units of labour successively applied to a fixed quantity (fund) of capital; the curve BC represents the declining marginal product of labour as more labour is applied (the assumption of diminishing returns), so that DC is the wage rate given by the marginal product of the

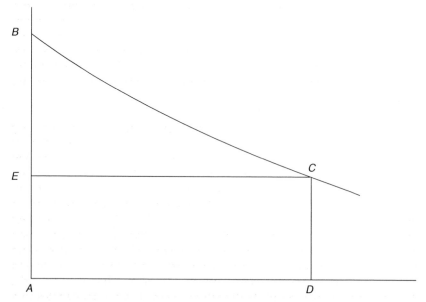

Figure 23.1   The J.B. Clark marginal productivity function

last unit of labour applied. The total wage bill is then ADCE and ECB is the product of the fixed factor, capital or its interest (if land was the fixed factor, then ECB equals the rent). Marginal productivity theory was therefore a simple generalisation of the traditional and widely accepted law of rent, as initially presented by Ricardo, Malthus, Torrens and West.

One important problem arising from this simple presentation of the marginal productivity theory was only addressed by Clark himself in terms of his definitions underlying the analysis. This problem is as follows. How can we be sure that ECB (the total interest share accruing to the fixed quantity of capital), allows individual units of capital to be paid exactly at a rate (of interest) equal to the marginal product of that capital. Clark (1899: 201) simply answered this question in the affirmative. Under perfect competition, each hired productive service (whether labour, land or capital is immaterial in this context) will be paid according to its marginal product (the product due to the last increment of the productive service applied under diminishing returns), any surplus over and above the total rent, interest or wage bill calculated according to the appropriate marginal product, goes to the entrepreneur who had hired and combined these productive services. However, under pure or perfect competition, entrepreneurial profits are zero by definition. Hence aggregate remuneration of land, labour and capital according to their respective marginal products, exactly exhaust the product.

One special aspect of Clark's marginal productivity theory should be noted. In *The Distribution of Wealth* (Clark, 1899, 7, 324n), Clark argued that payment of productive services according to marginal productivity not only explained how that remuneration was determined, but also demonstrated that this resulted in what agents deserved to be paid, assuring a *fair* distribution of income. Marginal productivity theory became therefore immediately intertwined with what Veblen called 'naive productivity ethics', which confused an analytical proposition and a moral prescription.

Capital theoretic aspects of Clark's distribution analysis

In 1962, Samuelson brought J.B. Clark's capital theory 'parable' explicitly into the Cambridge controversies in capital theory, arguing that Clark's distributional theory relying on fixed quantities (fund) of capital provided the foundation for the simple aggregate production version of capital theory around which the controversy had been started by Joan Robinson. Contemporary neo-classical theory, Samuelson contended, presented a more realistic approach with disaggregated capital rather than the 'fund' approach to a quantity of capital on which Clark's theory had been explicitly based. The more robust contemporary theory so Samuelson claimed, supported the distribution 'parables' (capital is paid according to its marginal product) of Clark's pioneering but simplistic analysis. Samuelson's discussion unintentionally brought the capital debates to a higher level. Garegnani's detailed examination of Samuelson's argument in

1970 led directly to the reswitching results and to the identification as an 'unobtrusive postulate' of the widely held inverse relationship between interest rates and the degree of capital intensity.

Further reading on Clark

Clark's *The Philosophy of Wealth* (1886) which reprinted a series of articles published during the previous decade, and *The Distribution of Wealth (1899)* are his major contributions to marginalist economics. A more readable version of his marginal productivity theory is his article, 'Distribution as determined by Law of Rent' (*Quarterly Journal of Economics*, April 1891, 289–318). Useful commentators include Stigler's (1941: 296–310) chapter on Clark and John Henry's, 'John Bates Clark and the Marginal Product' (*History of Political Economy*, 15 (3) 1983, 375–90). Tobin's centenary evaluation of Clark and neoclassical theory (*American Economic Review*, 75(6), December 1985; 29–32) needs to be supplemented by Harcourt's overview of the role of Clarkian theory in the capital controversies (G.C. Harcourt, *Some Cambridge Controversies in the Theory of Capital*, Cambridge University Press, Cambridge, 1972, esp. ch. 4).

P.H. Wicksteed, 1844–1927

Sraffa (1960, p.v) described Wicksteed as the 'purist' of marginalist theory, because he staunchly developed and defended the marginalist principles he had initially learned from Jevons's economics. Philip Wicksteed was born in Leeds. He studied Classics at London University and Manchester New College. Not until 1882 did he become interested in economics through studying Jevons's *Theory* (see Chapter 19, above,) and he has sometimes been described as Jevons's only disciple. His economic debut (1884) was a critique of Marx's value theory on Jevonian lines. Three books on economics followed. *The Alphabet of Economic Science*, intended for beginners appeared in 1888; it was followed by *An Essay on the Coordination of the Laws of Distribution* (the main concern of this section) in 1894 and in 1910 by a textbook, *The Common Sense of Political Economy*. A posthumous edition of the last by Lionel Robbins (in 1933) contains a splendid introduction to his work, In addition, it reprints Wicksteed's major economic papers and reviews (including that of Marx and his very important article on the 'Scope and Method of Political Economy').

The coordination of the laws of distribution

Like Clark, Wicksteed generalised the law of rent into a theory of distribution, solving problems associated with exhaustion of the product when factor services were paid according to marginal productivity principles, and the treatment in such a theory of entrepreneurial profits by invocation of Euler's theorem. The first of these, known as the 'adding-up' problem, can be formally stated that if A and B are the total factors employed in producing a product, P, and if $\delta P/\delta A$ and $\delta P/\delta B$ are the marginal products of A and B respectively then:

A. $\delta P/\delta A$ + B. $\delta P/\delta B = P$ in value terms

An auxiliary problem within the marginal productivity framework was the question of the determination of the profit of the entrepreneur. Constituting a single factor service in a particular production process, the entrepreneur was not easily assigned its marginal product. As Clark had suggested, under perfect competition this dilemma disappeared, since entrepreneurial profits were zero in this case. Hence, perfect competition became a crucial assumption to the generalised distribution theory.

Wicksteed's *Essay on the Coordination of the Laws of Distribution* developed the marginal productivity theory as a generalisation of a two factor case analogous to the classical (Ricardian) theory of rent, indicating it was a simple inference from the Jevonian law of value and price. Just as the marginal utility of a commodity determines its price, the marginal utility of a productive service determines the price of this service. If P is the product, and A the flow of productive services, then dP/dA is the marginal utility of that productive service in terms of its product or its marginal product. Wicksteed saw this as a truism. After all, entrepreneurs will only hire an additional factor so long as the return in terms of product of its service is greater than (or at the margin equal to) its cost. This was a simple application of the marginalist rules for efficient resource use.

The crucial problem for the theory was to show that the sum of the payments to each factor according to its marginal product exactly exhausts the product. For the general case of N factors contributing to the production of P, that is, for a production function:

$P = F(A, B, C, \ldots N)$

it must be shown that:

$P = A.\ \delta P/\delta A + B.\ \delta P/\delta B + C.\ \delta P/\delta C + \ldots + N \cdot \delta P/\delta N$

Wicksteed's own proof of this proposition was lengthy and rather clumsy. However, a review of his contribution in the *Economic Journal* by A.W. Flux, a former student of Marshall, argued that the proof could be greatly simplified by invoking Euler's theorem. This required that the production function;

$P = F(A, B, C, \ldots N)$

is homogenous and linear, that is, that

$mP = F(mA, mB, mC, \ldots mN)$

In that case, it followed automatically from Euler's theorem that

$$P = A. \; \delta P/\delta A + B. \; \delta P/\delta B + C. \; \delta P/\delta C + \ldots + N \cdot \delta P/\delta N$$

A linear and homogenous production function, implicitly assumed in Wicksteed's *Essay* (1894) ensured exhaustion of the product automatically via the application of Euler's theorem.

The appropriateness of this assumption about the nature of the production function was hotly debated. Wicksteed himself argued that if the product was conceived as physical product, constant returns to scale (the implication of a homogeneous and linear production function) secured the necessary condition almost immediately, since a proportional increase of all the factors will secure an equi-proportional increase in the product. If the factors are made sufficiently specific, this rules out increasing returns under static conditions. The last, however, may make nonsense of the notion of marginal product when this specifically implies large, indivisible factors included separately within the production function. If, alternatively the product is regarded as utility (value) product, a proposition Wicksteed entertained as a good Jevonian, the assumption of constant returns to scale can be maintained if factors of production include consumers of the product. When the product increases, the number of consumers is increased proportionately, and marginal utility (value) stays constant because product per individual consumer remains constant. Because the appropriate concept of product is commercial or revenue product, price has to remain constant for Euler's theorem to remain applicable, and marginal products become marginal revenue products. Under perfect competition where increased output the single entrepreneur cannot affect the price, this condition is fulfilled. This restriction of a perfectly elastic demand curve, the perfectly competitive firm, *not* the industry, made generalised marginal productivity theory utilising Euler's theorem only applicable to the firm when product is treated as revenue product. The imperfect competition revolution (see Chapter 29, below) therefore more or less destroyed the generalised marginal productivity theory as a theory of distribution.

The rigid nature of this assumption was quickly and extensively attacked. Pareto pointed out that the theory could not be applied to cases of monopoly, for reasons already stated. He also argued that Euler's theorem is inapplicable where there is interdependence between particular factor services, as is often the case in actual production processes, or in the equally likely case in practice, when there is no perfect substitutability between the factors, some coefficients of production being fixed, others variable. Wicksell stressed the implications of the constant returns assumption more precisely. If doubling the factors more than doubles the product (in other words, the important case of increasing returns to scale prevails), then total product will be greater than the sum of the factor shares calculated according to their respective marginal products; if doubling the factors less than doubles the product (diminishing returns to scale) then total product is insufficient to pay the factors according to their marginal products.

Wicksteed seemingly withdrew from the theorem in his *Common Sense* by acknowledging the validity of Pareto's and other criticisms. However, he nevertheless continued to maintain that, generally speaking, the production function was homogenous and linear, so that the essentials of applying Euler's theorem to the problem of distribution could be maintained. Robbins recounts that Wicksteed continued to profess the theory which he had developed within his *Essay of the Coordination of the Laws of Distribution* in his lectures.

Notes for further reading

Wicksteed's *The Alphabet of Economic Science* (1888) is the simplest way to gain the flavour of Wicksteed's style. *The Common Sense of Political Economy* is useful as a detailed treatment of the essentials of marginalist economics. The mathematically adept may wish to tackle the *Essay on the Coordination of the Laws of Distribution* (its reprint by Duckworth, London, 1987, containing a valuable introduction by Ian Steedman, whose comprehensive article on Wicksteed in the *New Palgrave* (1987, IV, 915–19) should also be consulted). Flux's original review of Wicksteed's *Essay* (in a combined review with Wicksell's *Value, Capital and Rent*) appeared in the *Economic Journal* (June 1894, vol. 4, 305–13) Stigler's (1941) chapter on Wicksteed and evaluation of Euler's theorem (Stigler, 1941, 38–60, 323–87) and Joan Robinson's 'Euler's Theorem and the problem of Distribution', *Economic Journal* (September, 1934, vol. 44, 398–414; reprinted in her *Collected Economic Papers*, Blackwell, Oxford, 1960: vol. 1, 1–19), remain valuable references. For a discussion of Flux as economist, see Peter Groenewegen, 'Alfred William Flux (1867–1942), A Mathematician Successfully Caught for Economics by Alfred Marshall', *History of Economics Review* No. 48, Summer 2008, pp. 63–77.

24
Von Wieser and Böhm-Bawerk: Austrian Versions of Capital and Distribution Theory

Carl Menger (see Chapter 20) left his two able pupils and colleagues, von Wieser and Böhm-Bawerk to work out details of his theory. Von Wieser did this by developing the theory of imputation as the Austrian version of distribution theory; Böhm-Bawerk developed the insights into capital theory of Menger into his own fundamental account. Together with Menger, von Wieser and Böhm-Bawerk therefore constitute the founders of the Austrian version of marginalist economics.

F. von Wieser, 1851–1926

Von Wieser was born in Vienna in 1851. He studied first at the prestigious Benedictine Schotten Gymnasium in Vienna (where Böhm-Bawerk was his fellow student) before together studying law (and economics) at the University of Vienna under Menger. On completion of their degree, they followed this with postgraduate studies in Germany under Knies, Roscher and Hildebrand (leading figures of the German historical school). Von Wieser was appointed in 1844 to his first academic position as associate professor to the University of Prague, becoming full professor in 1889. In 1903, he succeeded Menger at the University of Vienna, to be followed there a year later by Böhm-Bawerk. He entered the Austrian House of Lords on the death of his father, and was appointed Minister of Commerce from 1917 to 1918. He died in 1926.

In 1884, Wieser published *Ursprung und Hauptgesetz des wirtschaftlichen Werthes*, followed in 1889 with a book, *Natural Value*, which attempted to 'exhaust the entire sphere of the phenomenon of value without any exception'. He then turned to monetary theory and questions of public finance. In 1914 he published *Social Economics*. His last book, *Das Gesetz der Macht*, was published in 1926.

The theory of imputation

The theory of imputation is an extension of von Wieser's theory of natural value. It shows that the values of production goods (productive agents) are determined by the value of the goods they help to produce and can therefore be imputed from them. The argument implies that physical production functions with fixed coefficients of production are known and that the prices (exchange values) of the final products are given, and the entrepreneurs face an infinitely elastic demand so that they can sell all their output at this particular price. (This assumption limits the imputation theory to the operations of a single entrepreneur or firm under perfect competition, as was also the case for Wicksteed's theory as discussed in Chapter 23, above.) This problem can only be partly overcome in a general equilibrium analysis, where the prices of the products are determined at the same time as the price of factors, as shown in principle in Chapter 21, Walras's general equilibrium system. To highlight its similarity with Wicksteed theory more fully, the conditions for the theory to operate can be stated in an alternative way. The value of the productive agents is assumed to be equal to the value of the product, that is, product exhaustion is assumed at the outset, hence implying a linear and homogeneous production function. Secondly, the producer goods (productive agents) are combined in fixed proportions, which vary in the production of different commodities (in different industries).

Algebraically the imputation problem can then be solved through a system of simultaneous equations based on the given production functions. Assume three factors, X, Y and Z, which enter into the production of three different commodities in the following manner:

$$x + y = 100$$
$$2x + 3z = 290$$
$$4y + 5z = 590$$

The equations (production functions) are all expressed in value terms; x, y, z are the value of a unit of the factors of production X, Y, and Z; 100, 290 and 590 are the value of one unit of the three different commodities which X, Y, and Z help to produce. The values of the productive agents are determined by solving the three equations simultaneously. x, the value of a unit of X, = 40; y, the value of a unit of Y, = 60; z, the value of a unit of Z, = 70. These are, of course, the productive contributions of the factor to the production of the three commodities and it is implied in the solution that payment of the factors at these values must exhaust the value of the total product. The factor values obtained from solving the equations simultaneously implies that the values obtained for x, y and z can be substituted in the respective equations. For example, $x(40) + y(60) = 100$, to carry out this substitution for the first equation.

Wieser's theory of imputation shows that non-mathematicians can arrive at similar results as mathematicians, provided that their logic is sufficiently rigorous. However, such arithmetical proofs may not always disclose the precise analytical foundations of the theory, such as the nature of the production function assumed, and the type of market organisation required for the analysis. In this respect, von Wieser's theory of imputation greatly resembles the generalised marginal productivity theory where, (as shown in Chapter 23 above) it took some time before these assumptions were fully spelled out and the limitations of the theory realised.

A number of eminent economists in the period between the two world wars expressed a preference over the theory of imputation as compared with the generalised marginal productivity doctrine. F.M. Taylor (in his *Principles of Economics*, ninth edition, Ronald Press, New York, 1925, ch. 29; Part II, ch. 31) prefers the Austrian imputation theory of distribution because it is so much less mechanical than the use of Euler's theorem in deriving marginal products of factors from a generalised production function. Hicks (*The Theory of Wages*, second edition, Macmillan, London, 1964; pp. 11–19) defended his use of imputation theory in wage analysis on the ground that it is disaggregated analysis, utilising the different production functions of different commodities, yet at the same time yielding a wage rate for the economy as a whole on the assumption of homogeneous labour.

Notes for further reading

Von Wieser's writings can only be sampled in English from two of his books: *Natural Value* (translated by G.A. Malloch, Macmillan – now Palgrave Macmillan, London, 1893) and *Social Economics* (translated by A. Ford Hindrichs, Adelphi Company, New York, 1927). Book II of the first presents the theory of imputation in considerable detail. Stigler (1941: 158–78) has a useful chapter on von Wieser, including a detailed analysis of the theory of imputation; Schumpeter presents a portrait of his former teacher as one of his *Ten Great Economists* (Allen and Unwin, London, 1952, pp. 298–301); reference should also be made to Erich Streissler's article on von Wieser in the *New Palgrave* (IV, pp. 921–2), the reference list of which illustrates the paucity of the commentary literature.

E. von Böhm-Bawerk, 1851–1914

Born in Brünn (Moravia) on 12 February 1851, the youngest son of a distinguished civil servant, Böhm-Bawerk enjoyed a good education concluding with a law (and economics) degree at Vienna. During 1872–75 he worked in the Austrian fiscal administration, completed a doctorate of law (1875) which enabled him to obtain a grant for further study in Germany with his brother-in-law, von Wieser. Böhm-Bawerk then entered fiscal administration for some years, obtained his habilitation in 1880 and was appointed Professor at Innsbruck, a post he held until 1889. He published four books in this period. One dealt with the theory of goods, the second was the first volume of his work on *Capital and Interest (Critical History of Interest Theory)* in 1884, the third was a monograph on value theory (1886) and the fourth the second volume of *Capital and Interest*, called *The Positive Theory of Capital* (1889). He then returned to public service, becoming Minister of Finance in 1893, 1896 and in 1901–1904. In 1904 he also joined the University of Vienna, where his seminar attracted brilliant students (including Schumpeter, Hilferding and von Mises). The final decade of his life intermingled academic with government work. His academic research, on capital and interest, is the reason for which Böhm-Bawerk is now remembered. It was developed by Irving Fisher (see Chapter 26, below) and by Wicksell (see Chapter 25, below). Wicksell's account is often described as the standard account of Austrian capital theory and is therefore largely drawn upon in the subsequent discussion.

Böhm-Bawerk's conception of capital

Böhm-Bawerk indicates there are two ways of looking at capital. The first embodied a forward looking approach, that is, looking at how the investment over time in the use of original factors, land and labour, eventually yields a final output. This is essentially a cost approach to capital. The other way of looking at capital is prospectively in terms of its productiveness with respect to future consumption goods. This approach derived from Menger's classification of goods into higher order (production) goods and consumer (first order) goods, where higher order goods are depicted as slowly ripening (maturing) into final consumption goods. Both conceptions stress the element of time in production. Böhm-Bawerk's formal definitions imply these two approaches. 'Capital in general we shall call a group of products which serve as a means to the Acquisition of Goods. Under this general conception we shall put that of Social Capital as a narrower conception. Social Capital we shall call . . . a group of products destined to serve towards further production; or briefly a group of intermediate products . . .' (Böhm-Bawerk, 1889, 1959, p. 32). This definition emphasises the forward looking approach in terms of future product, where intermediate products can only refer to the product of primary, or original factors, land and labour. Alternatively 'We put forth our labour in all kinds of wise combinations with natural processes. Thus all that we get in production is the result of two and only two elementary productive powers – Nature and Labour. This is one of the most certain ideas in the theory of production . . . There is no place for any third primary sources' (Böhm-Bawerk, 1889, 1959, p. 80). This definition clearly expresses the cost side of capital in terms of primary factors invested over a specific time period.

Via the forward looking approach, Böhm-Bawerk introduced his notion of the time period of production through which he attempted to define the quantity of capital as an aggregate. The simplest example involves the continuous application of labour which, after a specific period of time, yields a specific quantity of output (what is known in the literature as the continuous input, point output case). This allows the calculation of an average period of production as illustrated in the following arithmetical example. It involves the investment of 5 units of labour in total, three units for two periods and two units for one period. The average time period of production can then be calculated by the expression

$$\frac{(3 \times 2) + (2 \times 1)}{5} = \frac{6 + 2}{5} = 1.6$$

This clearly gives considerable importance to the first period, which does not always make economic sense. Other issues are raised by this simple calculation. Why is the average period of production a simple, arithmetic average? Why is only labour used in this example, and not land and labour? Why is interest not included in the calculation, as would be done in any realistic example of capitalist production? Special difficulties arise from the second and third queries. Adding land and labour cannot be done in physical terms, valuation has to enter in order to turn land into labour units, or vice versa (a problem, it will be recalled from Part I, Chapter 4, above, going back to Sir William Petty's doctrine of the 'par'). The interest problem can be dealt with simply by introducing simple interest into the equation, which cancel out in the end result. When, more appropriately, compound interest is used in the calculation, the interest variable does not cancel out and the average period of production explicitly includes the rate of interest (with the implication that it cannot be used in determining the rate of interest without arguing in a circle).

Two other cases are frequently encountered in the literature. One is the case of wine in the cellar, or the point-input-point-output case. A quantity of land and labour put down as grape juice at a specific point in time gradually matures into wine of a higher value. The average time period of production here reflects the current rate of interest or the stock of capital available to the wine producers. Another, where labour is continuously applied for a number of years at a uniform rate, yields an average time period of production approximately to one half of the time period over which the labour is applied, provided this is relatively large.

The three grounds for a positive rate of interest

A main aspect for Böhm-Bawerk was the demonstration of the existence of interest, which required reasons why a positive rate of interest existed in a capital-using society. This demonstration had an ideological purpose, since it justified the existence of interest at a time when this type of income was under attack from Marxist social democracy, rapidly rising in numerical strength in Austria. Böhm-Bawerk's answer is surprisingly simple. Interest, according to him, is an *agio*, which arises in the exchange of present for future goods. Three grounds are necessary and sufficient to demonstrate the existence of this *agio* and a positive rate of interest. These are: (1) the justified expectation of an objectively more abundant satisfaction of future needs; (2) the subjective underestimation of future needs or overestimation of future resources, due to incorrect calculations or weakness of will which causes the apparent superiority of present over future goods; and (3) the technical superiority of present goods (including present productive goods) over those in the future. The first ground depends on the equalisation of time-income streams. In a growing society, where age distribution of the population is changing, this by itself can give rise to a rate of interest by inducing either borrowing (people expect higher living standards from future higher incomes and wish to anticipate this improved income status) or lending (people expect lower incomes after retirement and wish to maintain their future living standards through saving), so that whether the resulting rate is positive or negative depends on whether the first or the second reaction predominates. The second ground rests on the irrational over-estimation of present needs as against future resources owing to deficiency of imagination, limited will-power and the uncertainty of life. The third ground postulates that present goods can yield higher returns in both physical and value terms than can goods only available in the future, as shown by experience (people invested present goods and obtained a greater product). Fisher and Wicksell both criticised these grounds even though they generally were sympathetic to Böhm-Bawerk's approach. The three grounds resemble a supply and demand analysis, with the first two grounds, based on attitudes to saving, reflecting the supply side, and the third ground, involving the productivity of investment, the demand side. This type of reasoning was invariably rejected by Böhm-Bawerk who regarded his theory as far superior to a mere supply and demand analysis.

Determination of the rate of interest

As shown in the final book of his *Positive Theory of Capital*, the determination of the rate of interest depends on three propositions: (1) all capital consists of intermediate goods, in essence consumption goods for workers, landlords and entrepreneurs which are not immediately available but gradually become so in the future; (2) the product (yield) of extending the period of production is subject to diminishing returns; and (3) all increases in capital must be used for extending the period of production if labour supply is assumed to be fixed and all lengthening of the period of production requires increases in the capital stock (as Wicksell pointed out, this is not strictly necessary. An increase in capital by lowering the marginal product of capital, raises wages, so that only part of the increased capital can be used to extend the period of production, the other is required for the rising wages bill. This followed from the assumption of fixed labour supply). From these propositions it is easily shown that interest arises as a rationing device to distribute the existing capital among entrepreneurs, since, if there was no interest and capital was not scarce (the unobtrusive postulate), the time period of production could be indefinitely extended. With a fixed supply of capital, the rate of interest is limited and determined by the marginal productiveness of the last extension economically permissible.

Wicksell summarised Böhm-Bawerk's theory of interest determination, revealing its strengths and weaknesses. If land is a free good, so that there is only one original factor; the economy uses identical production functions or produces a single commodity; there is simple interest and no net profit, then interest can be simply determined with given factor supplies. Let s be the value of the final product, w the annual wage of a labourer, t the length of the period of production measured in years or fractions of years, z the interest rate and $s/t = p$ the annual product of labour, then total wages will be $t{\cdot}w$, and if the wages fund was borrowed at the start of the period, interest on the capital employed is $t^2{\cdot}w{\cdot}z$. It is, however, more economical to borrow capital as needed, and if the labour is uniformly applied over the production period, the average period of production is $^1/_2$ (as argued previously). The first equation relates product to wages plus interest on the capital:

$$s = t{\cdot}w{\cdot}\ (1 + zt/2) \tag{1}$$

Dividing both sides by t we obtain:

$$p = w(1 + zt/2) \tag{2}$$

which implies that the annual product of the labourer is equal to his wage plus the interest thereon.

For an entrepreneur–labourer, the problem is to obtain a maximum annual wage, a simple problem in the calculus since $p = F(t)$ and z is a known constant. A maximum w is secured when $dw/dt = 0$, that is

$$dp/dt = wz/2 \tag{3}$$

Solving (3) simultaneously with (2) we obtain the value of t for which w is maximum. For the individual entrepreneur, for which w is given, the problem is to find the t which maximises z. z is a maximum when $dp/dt = wz/2$ and solving (2) and (3) simultaneously gives the value for t which maximises z (w is now the given constant).

The theory demonstrates the interdependence of the period of production and relative factor prices and that one of the factor prices must be known, in order to make a rational resource allocation decision. To determine w, z and t simultaneously, further information is required. If the quantity of labour, A, and the total capital stock, K, are known, then a further equation is introduced which, together with equations (2) and (3), suffices to solve the problem. Each labourer requires $tw/2$ of capital, so that with full employment of the given resources of capital and labour:

$$K = \frac{A.w.t}{2} \tag{4}$$

Eliminating z from (2) and (3) we get,

$$w = p - t \cdot \mathrm{d}p/\mathrm{d}t \tag{5}$$

which gives (6) when substituted into (4)

$$\frac{K\,A.t.(p - \mathrm{d}p/\mathrm{d}t)}{2} \tag{6}$$

This equation has only one unknown, t, since p, and hence $\mathrm{d}p/\mathrm{d}t$, is a known function of t, as indicated previously.

Hence, with given factor supplies, as Böhm-Bawerk suggested in the final Book of his *Positive Theory of Capital*, and as Wicksell's rigorously proved, factor prices (w and z) and the optimum period of production (t) can be determined.

Notes for further reading

Böhm-Bawerk major work on *Capital and Interest*, that is, the three volumes *History and Critique of Interest Theories*, *Positive Theory of Capital* and *Further Essays on Capital and Interest* are available in a one volume edition (Illinois, South Holland, Libertarian Press, 1959) and are worth dipping into. Libertarian Press has also published a volume, *Shorter Classics of Böhm-Bawerk*. Böhm-Bawerk's polemical style is illustrated at its best in *Karl Marx and the Close of His System*, edited with an introduction and supplementary material by Paul Sweezy (Augustus M. Kelley, New York, 1966). Schumpeter's long essay on Böhm-Bawerk (*Ten Great Economists*, London, Allen and Unwin, 1952, pp. 143–90) provides a detailed introduction to the man and his work. Peter Groenewegen, 'Some Critical Perspectives on Böhm-Bawerk's *Capital and Interest*', *History of Economics Review* No. 50, Summer 2009, pp. 31–45, provides a critical overview of Böhm-Bawerk as historian of interest theory with special reference to Turgot, J.S. Mill and Jevons.

Section III
Pioneers of Macro-economics

25
Knut Wicksell, 1851–1926: Interest and Prices

Wicksell was born on 20 December 1851 in Stockholm, the youngest of six children. His parents died while he was still young but left sufficient funds to secure him a good education. He attended the University of Uppsala from 1869 to 1873 to study mathematics, physics and astronomy and in 1875 made himself eligible for doctoral studies in mathematics. By the early 1880s, he switched to the social sciences, spurred by a growing concern over social issues about population and drunkeness; earning his living from journalism and public lectures. In 1885–86 he visited London, to study economics, and became actively involved in the neo-Malthusian movement. The Lorèn Foundation in 1886 provided a grant to study economics in Germany and assisted with the publication of his early books: *Value, Capital and Rent* (1893), *Studies in the Theory of Public Finance* (1896) and *Interest and Prices* (1898). In 1901, he was appointed first as associate professor, and in 1904 as full professor, at the University of Lund. At this time, he prepared his *Lectures on Political Economy* for publication. These elaborated and improved on his earlier work on capital, production and distribution theory (vol. 1, published in 1901) and on monetary theory (vol. 2, published in 1906). His academic career was highly productive and controversial. Many articles, pamphlets and tracts on population, socialism, money, banking, taxation and international trade flowed from his pen. In 1910 he was sent to jail for blasphemy. The many fine students (among whom Sommarin, Lindahl, Ohlin, the Akerman brothers) he attracted, formed the influential Swedish school of the 1930s. He died suddenly in 1926, before the international acclaim his work obtained in the 1930s through Keynes and the English translation of some of his major books, the *Lectures* and *Interest and Prices*.

Some fundamental definitions of money

Wicksell divided the function of money as follows: (1) money is a measure of value; (2) money is a store of value; and (3) money is a medium of exchange. Other commodities may serve in these functions and acting as a medium of exchange is the most basic attribute of the moneyness of a commodity. Money facilitates exchange and production because it is widely accepted as a means of payment. It renders these services continuously, unlike consumer or production goods which neither render service so quickly nor to so many people. The turnover of money is termed velocity of circulation, and this, combined with the quantity of money, determines the efficiency of money (MV). The last is regarded as the crucial variable determining the exchange value of money since it measures monetary demand, the only way in which demand as a whole can be conceived in a monetary economy. This demand is applied to the flow of goods and services over a period of time (T), and these together determine the price level, $P \cdot (P = MV/T)$. Because V is liable to substantial fluctuations, this is not a simple relationship.

Monetary demand for Wicksell reflects the inverse of the velocity of circulation. On receipt, money need not be immediately paid for another transaction; occasionally, it is kept on hand, while at any point of time all money must be held as cash balances by individuals in the economy. Wicksell is fully aware that the proposition that every seller on the receipt of money for a commodity immediately becomes a buyer, does not hold true. He 'often remains a seller and leaves the market without buying anything for himself. The money he acquires then remains in his hand both as ready money for anticipated future purchases or payments, and as a reserve for unforeseen liabilities' (Wicksell, 1906: II 23). Demand for money balances is therefore a two-fold demand for Wicksell: a fully anticipated *transaction demand* and an imperfectly anticipated *precautionary demand*. Expectations therefore enter the analysis at the outset, and Wicksell admits these may not always be fulfilled.

The velocity of circulation, banking and credit

The crucial variable in Wicksell's analysis of the price level is velocity of circulation, because of its volatility. The money supply was simply given as the quantity of monetary gold in the hands of the public and the banking system (almost an institutional datum), the volume of transactions in a fully employed economy was not apt to vary greatly. Velocity was therefore exhaustively treated in chapter 6 of *Interest and Prices*, particularly because earlier treatments were often unsatisfactory. Wicksell defined velocity as 'the average number of times the available pieces of money change hands during the unit of time, say a year, in connection with buying and selling excluding lending' (Wicksell, 1898, 1936, p. 52). Equally important is its reciprocal or money's 'interval of rest', or, 'the mean interval which elapses between two purchases effected by means of the same sum of money [during which] the money lies idle in safe or coffer'. Since holding money idle has an interest and capital cost, increases in the velocity of circulation which lower the costly interval of rest are encouraged by the use of credit instruments and substitutes for metallic money. The introduction of paper money, bills of exchange, cheques or any other medium of credit produced by the banking system, therefore speeds up the velocity of circulation. On the other hand, any frictions and leakages in the credit system impair and reduce the influence of credit on velocity of circulation.

Wicksell's notion of a perfectly elastic credit system illustrates this. 'A system of simple, unorganised credit certainly does to some extent reduce the necessity of holding cash balances; but the necessity still exists, particularly in regard to those cash balances which serve as reserves against unforeseen payments. The velocity of circulation is now seen as a somewhat elastic quantity' (Wicksell, 1936, p. 61). Hence, if there was a fully developed, perfectly organised credit system, the necessity for holding cash balances virtually disappears, there is then no limit to the velocity of circulation and it may approach infinity as the need for cash balances disappears. With a perfectly elastic supply of money substitutes, the need for metallic money is virtually eliminated and the efficiency of money (MV) steadily approaches the value of V. The level of prices, or the exchange value of money, therefore increasingly becomes dependent on the velocity of circulation, and the quantity theory of money is transformed from a relationship between M and P into one between V and P. Emphasis on the velocity of circulation is one difference between Wicksell's theory and the conventional quantity theory. Another is Wicksell's deliberate attempt to explain the observed relationship between the rate of interest and the level of prices, which indicated that rising prices were associated with rising interest rates, and vice versa. This was contrary to the conventional quantity theory view which suggested an inverse relationship between the price level and interest rates following changes in the quantity of money, at least until equilibrium between prices and the money supply was re-established.

Wicksell's cumulative process

The cumulative inflationary process described by Wicksell is as follows. There are two countries, A and B, the first of which is gold producing. Assume the discovery of a goldmine in B, hence an increase in the supply of monetary gold in B, and a rise in its domestic price level. The initial effect of this discovery is the transmission of higher prices from B to A, since there will be increased demand for imports from A. This raises prices in A since its production is relatively fixed (with full employment). Gold will flow from B to A, initially reaching its banking system. This will make the bank's monetary reserves higher than necessary, encouraging them to increase credit, and to lower the discount rate. A fall in the discount rates will (1) discourage saving hence expanding demand for consumption goods; and (2) increase the demand for borrowing, since the gap between interest rate and the profitability of investment has widened, hence raising demand for investment goods. With production relatively fixed, this increased domestic demand can only raise the price level, and this situation continues so long as the discount rate remains below what Wicksell called the natural rate (or real rate of return on capital). Wicksell asks whether this process can continue indefinitely, or whether there are countervailing tendencies which bring the prices to a halt thereby restoring equilibrium. Wicksell provided two sets of answers: one related to a hypothetical pure credit economy where credit is perfectly elastic; the other, more realistic answer, concerned an economy where credit is limited by frictions in the banking system.

Wicksell argued that in a system where credit was perfectly elastic, the cumulative process would continue indefinitely. As prices rose, the real price charged for borrowed funds would decline continuously in the absence of any change in the discount rate and excess demand would remain an important feature in both the consumption and investment goods sectors. Moreover, individuals could maintain their real balances by increasing demand for money balances since the money (credit) supply was perfectly elastic. Positive action from the monetary authorities through raising the discount rate and restoring its normal relation with the natural rate, would halt the cumulative process. Excess demand for consumption goods would be eliminated through the positive impact of a higher discount rate on saving while excess demand for investment goods would be eliminated since equality between the discount and natural rates made entrepreneurial borrowing no longer profitable. With excess demand in the goods market eliminated, the inflationary process comes to a halt. The inflationary process is stopped through the active intervention on interest rates of the monetary authorities.

When credit is not perfectly elastic, automatic forces can bring the cumulative process to a halt. The start and initial progress of the inflationary process, is as described previously. As part of this process, the real value of money balances falls but their replenishment in order to maintain real balances, implies a reduction in bank reserves. Lowered bank reserves eventually force a change in the bank's discount policy by raising the discount rate. Ultimately therefore, discount and natural rates return to equality to eliminate the excess demand in the goods markets and bring the system back into balance.

Wicksell's revitalisation of the quantity theory, by elucidating more clearly the process by which prices rose following an increase in the quantity of money through an analysis of the impact of discount rate on demand in the goods market, also linked the real with the monetary economy. Wicksell's students elaborated the theory by making it more dynamic through the introduction of period analysis (Lindahl) and by introducing expectations into the process (Myrdal). This made the Swedes very receptive to the new ideas of Keynes in both his *Treatise* (1930) and *General Theory* (1936), discussed in Chapter 31 below.

Notes for further reading

The whole of *Interest and Prices* (1936) is well worth reading, together with the introduction by Bertil Ohlin to the reprint of the English translation (Augustus M. Kelley, New York, 1962). It can be supplemented by a reading of volume 2 of Wicksell's *Lectures* devoted to monetary subjects (Routledge, London, 1934). Volume 1 presents the theory of value, production and distribution in a non-monetary framework, developing the material of the earlier *Value, Capital and Rent* (1893). The last's English edition (Allen and Unwin, London, 1954) has an interesting introduction by G.L.S. Shackle. Various selections of Wicksell's many essays in economics are available; *Selected Papers in Economic Theory* (edited by Eric Lindahl, Allen and Unwin, London, 1958); *Selected Essays in Economics* (edited by Bo Sandelin, Routledge, London, 1997). Sandelin's *History of Swedish Economic Thought* includes a useful general chapter on Wicksell by Carl Uhr (Routledge, London, 1991, pp. 76–121). There is a splendid biography by Torsten Gårdlund, *The Life of Knut Wicksell* (Almqvist and Wicksell, Stockholm, 1959) which is highly recommended as providing a comprehensive portrait of the life of this economist, in all its fascinating aspects.

26
Irving Fisher, 1867–1947: Appreciation and Interest

Irving Fisher was born in New York in February 1867, the place where he also died, aged 81. Widely regarded as one of the major economists produced in America, his work is still at the root of contemporary neo-classical theory, particularly in the fields of capital and interest, money and prices. Fisher was, however, more than economist. He was an enthusiastic crusader for all sorts of causes ranging from prohibition to various aspects of hygienic living, induced by his bout with tuberculosis from 1898. He studied at Yale, staying at his alma mater for the rest of his career. There he worked eclectically at mathematics, physics, social sciences and philosophy. His doctoral dissertation, *Mathematical Investigations in the Theory of Value and Price* (1892) illustrates this wide ranging training, as do his many contributions to statistics and econometrics (with Ragnar Frisch and Charles Roos, he founded the Econometric Society in 1930). It also heralds the great mathematical economist who was later acclaimed as an independent discoverer of the core of general equilibrium analysis, indifference curves, and consumer choice theory in the light of problems with utility measurement (Schumpeter, 1952, pp. 224–6). Fisher followed on from this work with a substantial research program on capital and interest. *Appreciation and Interest* (1896) was the first fruit of this work, followed by *The Nature of Capital and Income* (1906) and *The Rate of Interest* (1907). Much of this material was amalgamated in 1930 in Fisher's *The Theory of Interest*. A third major, and abiding, research interest was the price level, tackled theoretically with a careful analysis which introduced the Fisherine form of the quantity equation, $MV = PT$, from its micro-economic foundations. The basic theoretical findings were published in *The Purchasing Power of Money* (1911), its statistical investigation followed with *The Making of Index Numbers* (1922), while monetary factors and price stability also greatly influenced his work on cyclical fluctuations and the 1930s depression. All these works, together with the many others he wrote (a bibliography compiled by his son includes some 2000 titles written by Fisher alone), were produced as an academic at Yale, where he commenced teaching from the early 1890s, became full professor in 1898 and from whence he retired in 1935.

Appreciation and Interest

The study of this title was published by the American Economic Association as a monograph in 1896, to repair the scant attention from economists this important topic had received (Preface, p. ix). It dealt exhaustively with the effects of deflation (appreciation in the value of the monetary standard) or of inflation on contracts between debtors and creditors, borrowers and lenders. The analysis was conducted in the background of the long term appreciation of the value of money which had been apparent over the final decades of the nineteenth century. The last had arisen from the shortage of gold in a world whose monetary systems were then increasingly becoming part of the gold standard, reversing the earlier depreciation of monetary values induced by the immense gold discoveries of the middle of the century.

In this analysis, Fisher distinguished between sudden fluctuations in the value of money – as had occurred in the United States in 1862 during the American Civil War – and long term phenomena which were therefore fairly fully expected, of which the great deflation commencing during the 1870s was a prime example. Loan contracts involving interest payments were particularly influenced by such gradual and persistent price changes, to the detriment of one of the parties to the contract and the advantage of the other. As Fisher stated the problem, 'If a debt is contracted optionally in either of two standards and one of them is expected to change with reference to the other, will the rate of interest be the same in both?', to which rhetorical question he emphatically replied, 'Most certainly not' (Fisher, 1896, p. 6).

Fisher illustrated the problem with a simple example of a one year loan contract in terms of a gold standard (with no change in the value of the standard over the year in question) and a wheat standard where wheat in terms of gold was expected to depreciate by four per cent ('a bushel of wheat worth a dollar today was expected to be worth 96 cents a year hence'). If the rate of interest in the gold standard contract is set at 8 per cent, what ought to be the rate set in the wheat standard given the expected depreciation of wheat? Repayment of the loan in dollar terms at the end of the year inclusive of interest will be $108, what is the equivalent of this in terms of wheat at its known depreciated money price? The solution is simple. Since at the end of the year, 96 cents gold will purchase 1 bushel of wheat, $108 is the equivalent of 108/0.96 or 112.5 bushels of wheat. A wheat rate of interest equivalent to the money rate of interest of 8 per cent under these changed circumstances needs to be 12.5 per cent, the difference reflecting precisely the depreciation of the value of wheat. Having demonstrated the problem and its solution in terms of simple arithmetic, Fisher then worked out a general algebraic formula for calculating variations in the rate of interest flowing from relative variations in different standards of value, first for the straight-forward case of a one year contract, and then for the more complex case of loan contracts of more than one year. Fisher subsequently discussed problems for fair loan contracts when interest rates varied as well as the standard of value.

The second part of Fisher's study was empirical since 'no study of the relation between appreciation and interest would be complete without verification by facts' (Fisher, 1896, p. 35). Detailed statistical analyses of the impact on interest rates from appreciation of one standard in terms of another were presented, using those of variations in the value of paper money in terms of gold, those of gold in terms of silver, and, more generally, of money in terms of commodity standards in various countries. The last used the then relatively novel device of index numbers, to the construction of which Fisher himself made important contributions. For example, a table relating London rates of interest to variations (rising and falling) of commodity prices showed how virtual interest rates in terms of commodities adjusted upwards to compensate for inflation and downwards for deflation including the instance of a negative rate of interest in commodities in 1871–73 of –2.7 per cent when prices deflated by a massive 6.2 per cent and market interest rates were a low 3.7 per cent (Fisher, 1896, p. 59). From this London experience, and comparative analyses for Berlin, Calcutta, Tokyo, Shanghai and New York for much shorter time frames, Fisher derived the following broad conclusions:

> (1) High and low prices are directly correlated with high and low rates of interest; (2) rising and falling prices and wages are directly correlated with high and low rates of interest; (3) the adjustment of interest to price (or wage) movements is inadequate; (4) this adjustment is more nearly adequate for long than for short periods.
>
> (Fisher, 1896, p. 75)

Fisher's work therefore demonstrated what Wicksell's analysis confirmed two years later (see Chapter 25, above). However, Fisher's explanation of the phenomenon focussed on expectations, arguing that poor actual adjustment of interest rates to reflect variations in the level of prices, resulted from poorly formulated expectations of such price changes and inadequate responses by borrowers to benefits from such poor adjustments. Fisher hypothesised a better response by borrowers than by lenders to such price changes, hence concluding that loans in periods of inflation tended to disadvantage lenders who did not adjust their interest rates sufficiently to compensate for the loss in value of the principal over the period of the loan. Losses incurred in such imbalances in loan contracts, Fisher argued, could be corrected by taking greater account of expected variations in the value of money in determining loan contracts through the use of index numbers. However, he warned that these were imprecise instruments given the impossibility of estimating a perfectly accurate index number. Even with perfect index numbers, there would not be a satisfactory measure of differences in the subjective (marginal utility) value of money faced by the parties in a loan contract. The question, Fisher (1895, p. 82) emphasised, is 'not one of appreciation of gold relative to commodities, or to labour, or any other standard, it is . . . exclusively a question of foresight and of the degree of adaptation of the rate of interest'. Fisher therefore also made a plea to return monetary issues to the analysis of interest rates from where they had been eliminated by many of the great eighteenth century economic writers, including Hume and Smith (Fisher, 1896, p. 88).

These topics continued to engage Fisher's attention in much of his subsequent work. His analysis of *The Purchasing Power of Money* indicated both the pitfalls and the advantages of index numbers and the many problems involved in their estimation. He was an early and authoritative advocate of the virtues of price stability and, in its absence, of the indexation of contracts to ensure fair outcomes for the respective parties to them. Likewise, his subsequent work on the rate of interest reflected the multiple character imparted thereon from the monetary factor as well as from the real aspects of productivity, time preference and thrift. The last was fully elaborated in his monumental, *The Rate of Interest* (1930), one of his final important contributions to economics. This book foreshadowed a major building block of Keynes's *General Theory*, the marginal efficiency of capital, as Keynes (1936, pp. 140–3) was all too ready to acknowledge. Friedman, subsequently, was influenced by Fisher's analysis of inflation and his call for the need for the introduction of indexation for many important contracts to safeguard economic agents from the ravages of price instability.

Notes for further reading

Fisher's *Appreciation and Interest* (1896) is well worth reading, as is its successor published towards the end of his life, *The Theory of Interest* (1930), and his careful evaluation of the conceptual problems associated with *Capital and Income* (1906). The last introduces Fisher's famous argument about the double taxation of saving under an income tax, foreshadowing the case for substituting a consumption expenditure tax (direct or indirect) for the income tax because of its advantages for thrift and accumulation. Fisher's monumental work on the quantity equation, *The Purchasing Power of Money* (1911) can also still be read with profit. Schumpeter (*Ten Great Economists*, Allen and Unwin, London, 1952, pp. 222–38) presents a neat evaluation of Fisher and his work, which can be updated by the more recent account of Tobin (*American Economic Review*, 75(6) December 1985, pp. 29–30, 32–7; *New Palgrave*, vol. II, pp. 369–76). Fisher's son, I.N. Fisher, has written an illuminating biography of his father, *My Father, Irving Fisher* (Comet Press, New York, 1956).

27

Joseph Alois Schumpeter, 1883–1950: Economic Development

Schumpeter was born in 1883 in Trisch in Moravia, then a province of the Austro-Hungarian Empire. In 1901 he entered the Faculty of Law in the University of Vienna, receiving his Doctorate of Law there in 1906. The study of economics was then part of the Law course at Vienna and Schumpeter attended seminars given by von Wieser, von Philippovich (which gave Schumpeter an enduring interest in the history of economics) and from 1904, Böhm-Bawerk. The last was made lively from the brilliance of Schumpeter's fellow students, von Mises, and the Austrian Marxists, Otto Bauer and Rudolf Hilferding. The experience gave Schumpeter a life-long interest in marxism and socialism. After graduation, he visited England (meeting Marshall and Edgeworth), and briefly took up a legal position in Cairo. In 1909, he began teaching at the University of Czernowicz, followed in 1911 (until 1918) at the University of Graz. In 1919 he became Finance Minister in the newly created Austrian Republic, he then worked in banking. He returned to academic work in 1924, first in Bonn, and then at Harvard from 1932. He stayed at Harvard until his death in 1950.

Schumpeter's economic writings are extensive. In 1906, he published an article, 'On the Mathematical Method in Theoretical Economics'; it was followed in 1908 by his first major book, *The Essence and Scope of Theoretical Economics*, an exposition of marginalist economic doctrine. In 1912, his celebrated *Theory of Economic Development* followed, the ideas in which were painstakingly elaborated in his *Business Cycles* (1939) and to a lesser extent, in his *Capitalism, Socialism and Democracy* (1942). In 1912, he published a brief survey of the history of economic thought, *Economic Doctrine and Method*, a far more polished and coherent account of the development of the subject than the unfinished and enormous *History of Economic Analysis* (1954). Other work includes *The Crisis of the Tax State* (1919): essays on *Imperialism and Social Classes* (1920), while his biographical contributions on economists were collected as *Ten Great Economists* (1952).

Schumpeter's work on economic development, which is the focus of this chapter, forms a bridge between the marginalist economics of Walras and of Böhm-Bawerk and the macro-economics of growth and cycles. Its starting point is a position of Walrasian general equilibrium, because it was an analysis of the social process as an indivisible whole. After all, the Walrasian analytical scheme brings together all the transactions of economic agents in an attempt to solve their major economic problems of consumption and production. Given the stock of available productive services, the techniques and coefficients of production, and a set of consumer preferences, aggregate social product can be determined from the given production functions, together with hire prices paid to the owners of the productive services and the commodity prices paid by the final consumers. Such a theory of general equilibrium therefore assumed that technology was unchanged and that consumer preferences did not alter, and hence could only provide the theory of a self-reproducing stationary state or, provided output grows at the same rate as the labour force (and the other necessary productive services), a system of balanced growth where total product increases without any change in its quality or its composition. The Walrasian theory is therefore inadequate for explaining the capitalist process of economic development because it cannot deal with change and innovation. Furthermore, crucial manifestations of the development process in the explanation of profit; of money, credit and the interest rate; and of the business cycle which Schumpeter saw as an essential part of the development process, are, of necessity, ignored. To capture the aspects which static equilibrium analysis cannot grasp (profits are zero in a competitive equilibrium, money and credit are not required to effect its exchange transactions which can be handled by barter, while business cycles and their problems as excluded as disequilibrium situations) Schumpeter's theory of economic development focussed on innovation and the innovating entrepreneur, incompatible with the unchanged techniques and given tastes of producers and consumers under general equilibrium analysis.

Innovations and economic development

Innovation and the innovating entrepreneur are therefore the key factors in Schumpeter's theory of economic development. This emphasises the *qualitative* nature of change in the development process, in contrast to the *quantitative* aspects underlying economic growth. Such qualitative changes by their very nature tend to be discontinuous unlike the quantitative changes of the balanced growth process which are continuous (self-producing) by definition. Nor should innovation be confused with technological progress or change, although this may be part of the process of innovation. Schumpeter in fact sees five different forms of innovation and therefore a manifold role for the innovating entrepreneur:

(1) the introduction of a new good, either one with which consumers are not yet familiar, or a new quality expanding the nature of an existing good;
(2) the introduction of a new method of production – implying a shift in the production function rather than movement along it – either suggesting a new method of production never been applied before (even if its scientific possibility was recognised well before) or a new method of handling a commodity commercially;
(3) the opening of a new market which may well be an existing market, its newness arising from it not having been entered before by the economic agents of the economy in question;
(4) the conquest or discovery of a new source of raw materials or semi-processed materials, again irrespective of whether this source already existed or whether it had to be discovered first;
(5) new organisation of industry either by creating a monopoly situation through establishing a trust or by the break-up of a previous monopoly situation.

These five types of innovations all have the same effect: they disturb an existing equilibrium situation. A frequently used phrase to describe innovation within Schumpeterian dynamics is 'creative destruction', because the new destroys and invigorates existing industrial structures as part of the dynamics of development. Moreover, Schumpeter argued that such innovations arose through entrepreneurial activity, manifested in the formation of new firms designed to take advantage of the innovation; that is, they do not originate within existing firms. This adds a further dimension to the discontinuity which is so marked a feature of Schumpeter's view of the development process. However, he altered this view in 1942, arguing that innovation could occur within existing enterprise and that this possibility would ultimately lead to the transformation of capitalism into some form of socialism.

In its original version, Schumpeter indicated that innovations also affected the market structure of industry with the growth of new combines breaking up the competitive nature of the economy. However, and simultaneously, the continuous threat of innovations by new comers to an existing industrial activity posed a never ending risk of vigorous competition and thereby maintained the basic competitive nature of capitalist enterprise. Obviously, this was not a restoration of something resembling the static nature of perfect competition but a dynamic analysis of a continual state of flux in industrial leadership through the process of innovation.

The Schumpeterian entrepreneur is vaguely and ambiguously defined. He is the innovator but need not be the capitalist, that is, control and own the means of production. Frequently in fact, the entrepreneur needs to obtain the resources for implementing his innovation through credit supplied by the banking system. In addition, the entrepreneur is the only economic agent in the Schumpeterian system entitled to profit, an income category which, according to him, can only arise from capitalist development.

Profits

Profits are defined as the difference between sales receipts and costs. Such differences can only be present in dynamic situations involving innovation which induce either higher product prices or lower costs. Profits are therefore also a temporary phenomenon, because the cost or price advantages from innovation tend to be competed away in the longer run. From this association between profit and innovation, Schumpeter drew some interesting conclusions about the nature of profit. Profit contains a strong monopolistic element; it is essentially a dynamic phenomenon. It is not a reward for risk bearing, since entrepreneurs generally do not risk their own, but only borrowed resources. Entrepreneurial profits do, however, contribute to accumulation and new savings; and, last but not least, entrepreneurial profits explain the existence of the very rich who make their fortunes very rapidly, generally consolidating their new wealth through substantial asset holdings in existing enterprises.

Banking and credit

Schumpeter denied an essential role for money in situations of general equilibrium or balanced growth; all what was then required was simply a medium of exchange growing in balanced proportions with real output. Under economic development, however, entrepreneurs need access to credit to finance their activities and develop their enterprises, and this is generally obtained via the banking system. Some startling conclusions flow from this analysis: (a) interest is essentially a monetary phenomenon, the price to be paid for borrowing to be repaid from the profits which the entrepreneur hopes to reap; (b) innovations cannot be financed from saving, which are non-existent or, at best, negligible in a stationary economy, but they create their own flow of savings from the profits they generate; and (c) innovations therefore induce situations of credit expansion and associated price rises because entrepreneurs have to bid away from their present owners the existing resources they need to start their own business activity. The discontinuities in the process of innovation therefore also create discontinuities within the credit system, an important part of the process of capitalist development.

The business cycle

The business cycle cannot arise in a situation of stationary equilibrium or of balanced growth. It is an essential and logical consequence of the discontinuity underlying Schumpeter's innovatory process of capitalist development. Schumpeter himself explained this concisely in his first work on the subject: 'Why is it that economic development in our sense does not proceed evenly but as it were jerkily . . . the answer is short and precise: the new combinations are not, as one would expect according to general principles of probability, evenly distributed through time but appear, if at all, discontinuously in groups or swarms' (Schumpeter, *The Theory of Economic Development*, translated by R. Opie, 1934, pp. 223).

The essentials of the Schumpetarian story of cyclical growth can then be summarised as follows. From a position of equilibrium, innovations induce an increase in the level of economic activity. This is accompanied by credit creation, raised profitability and investment, in a *primary wave* through the innovation(s) it(them)self(ves). The process then continues in secondary waves through something akin to the multiplier process. The phenomenon is far from simple. It can take a number of forms which have varying explanations. Schumpeter himself identified three dimensions to the phenomena. First, were the 60-year or Kondratieff cycles, of which Schumpeter in his research identified two completed ones (those of 1783–1842 and 1842–97). The second type of cycle was the decennial one analysed especially by Marx and Juglar; the third type or Kitching cycle lasted for about forty months. Schumpeter claimed that no simple general explanation could be found for these cycles; their primary waves were set by different events and were associated with different industries. The similarities in cyclical behaviour from which generalisations could be made arose during the secondary phase when the influence of the innovation(s) affected the whole of the economy. The uniqueness of the primary movement implied for Schumpeter that cycles had to be studied statistically, historically as well as theoretically, since the further common feature of cyclical behaviour was that the primary wave constituted a break from equilibrium. Some of these Schumpetarian prognostications came back into fashion to explain the end of the long boom of the 1970s and much of his work on the subject continues to be highly regarded by researchers of cyclical development. This arises from its emphasis on dynamics and its aims of trying to understand the laws of motion of capitalist society.

Notes for further reading

Schumpeter's *The Theory of Economic Development* (translated by Redvers Opie, Oxford University Press, New York, 1934) is an essential introduction to his development theory. It can be supplemented by a perusal of his two volume study, *Business Cycles* (McGraw Hill, New York, 1939), and by his *Capitalism, Socialism and Democracy* (Allen and Unwin, London, 1942). Schumpeter's short *Economic Doctrine and Method* (Allen and Unwin, London, 1954, translated from the 1912 German edition by R. Aris) is an interesting monograph sketching the four main phases of the development of economics from its early beginnings up to the historical school and the rise of the marginalists during the final decades of the nineteenth century. Schumpeter's *History of Economic Analysis* (Oxford University Press, New York, 1954) unfinished though it is, remains a valuable reference work. A selection of his *Economic Essays*, edited by Richard Clemence (Addison Wiley Press, Cambridge), appeared in 1951. Haberler's obituary essay in the *Quarterly Journal of Economics* (64, 1950, 333–72) provides a valuable overview of Schumpeter's life and work, as does the *New Palgrave* entry by Arnold Heertje (1987, IV, pp. 263–7) and the commemorative volume of his work, *Schumpeter in the History of Ideas* (edited Yuichi Shionoya and Mark Perlman, University of Michigan Press, Ann Arbor, 1994) issued for the Schumpeter Society. Sylos-Labini, 'The problem of economic growth in Marx and Schumpeter' (in *Italian Economics Past and Present*, edited Joseph Halevi and Peter Groenewegen, Sydney, 1983, pp. 129–66, esp. pp. 142–57) provides an instructive comparison of the work of these two major analysts of capitalist development. Reference can also be usefully made to Alessandro Roncaglia, *Schumpeter: E'possibile una teoria dello svilupo economico?* (Banca Populare dell' Etruria, Arezzo, 1987). There is an interesting biography by Richard Swedborg, *Joseph A. Schumpeter: His Life and Work* (Polity Press, Cambridge, 1991).

Section IV

Further Developments in Micro-economics

28
Pigou, Clapham and Sraffa: Wealth, Welfare and Cost Controversies

A.C. Pigou, 1877–1959

A.C. Pigou was born in Ryde on the Isle of Wight, in 1877. He was Head of School at Harrow, one of the great English public schools, won a scholarship for study at King's College, Cambridge, and subsequently gained first class honours, first in the History, and then in Part II of the Moral Sciences Tripos, which included much economics. He commenced teaching and writing economics not long thereafter and in 1908 succeeded Marshall as Professor of Economics, a position he held until 1943. During the First World War, Pigou avoided active military service as a conscientious objector, working as part of a team of ambulance drivers near the front during the long summer vacations. His war time experiences probably turned him into the recluse he became from the early 1920s. As he grew older, Pigou became the type of eccentric academic about whom legends are made and anecdotes abound. He was notoriously shy of the opposite sex as illustrated by his writing practice. He dictated his books from one of his college rooms, door half closed, to a stenographer in another room and expected her to return the finished product via the college mail service. Pigou was a good teacher. 'An attractive presence; complete clarity; great precision of thought and definition; a little, but not too much, geometry and algebra on the blackboard; an occasional joke to illustrate a proposition, never a note', was Dalton's (a later Chancellor of the Exchequer) impression of him in the classroom.

Pigou's economics is now largely remembered for two things. First, and negatively, for his quarrel with Keynes over the theory of employment caused by Keynes's devastating critique of Pigou's *The Theory of Unemployment* (1933) in the pages of his *General Theory* (1936: esp. chs 2, 19 and Appendix), followed by Pigou's hostile review of Keynes's book (*Economica*, May 1936, vol. 3, 115–32) and a number of subsequent studies ending with Pigou's 1950 monograph, *Keynes's General Theory: a Retrospective View*. More positively there is Pigou's path-breaking work on welfare economics. This originated with, and developed from, his *Wealth and Welfare* (1912) and spawned three separate works during the 1920s: the *Economics of Welfare* (1920), *Industrial Fluctuations* (1927) and *A Study in Public Finance* (1928). This major contribution, which is the subject of what follows, also fitted in neatly with Pigou's own view on the purpose of economics:

> The complicated analyses which economists endeavour to carry through are not mere gymnastics. They are instruments for the bettering of human life. The misery and squalor that surround us, the injurious luxury of some wealthy families, the terrible uncertainty overshadowing many families of the poor – these are evils too plain to be ignored. By the knowledge that our science seeks it is possible that they may be restrained. Out of the darkness light! To search for it is the task, to find it perhaps the prize, which the 'dismal science of political economy' offers to those who face its discipline.
>
> (Pigou, *The Economics of Welfare*, 1920, p. vii)

In this, as in many other respects, he was the loyal successor to Alfred Marshall, thereby assisting retention of the basic thrust of Marshall's economics as the hallmark of the Cambridge tradition.

Wealth and welfare

Pigou's work on welfare economics developed both from the Marshallian heritage of welfare economics and from the utilitarianism of Henry Sidgwick, which itself had taken an applied economics turning in the third part of his *Principles of Political Economy* (1887). Marshall's own propositions in welfare economics (*Principles of Economics*, 1961, Book V, ch. XIII) arose in the context of his analysis of objections to complete economic freedom, that is, more specifically, from the possibility of raising aggregate satisfactions under conditions of increasing returns by a suitable mix of tax/bounty policies; from the difference in the marginal utility of money income as between rich and poor, and from the possibility of multiple equilibrium positions under certain sets of economic conditions. These propositions, Pigou set out to develop further. He did this in a broad context of applied economic policy discussion using the Marshallian tools of consumers' and producers' surplus. The first version in which Pigou presented this material was called *Wealth and Welfare* from which, as already indicated, a number of separate studies developed. The one relevant to this discussion, is called *The Economics of Welfare*. It treated the national dividend (income) as the basic index of economic welfare on the grounds that welfare was likely to be raised if (1) *per capita* national income rose; (2) the share in national income going to the poor increased; and (3) both the national dividend and the share accruing to the poor, did not fluctuate too widely. Economic growth, distribution of income, business fluctuations, and employment opportunities, were therefore important topics in Pigou's welfare economics.

Although this seems straightforward, Pigou's analysis was in fact highly complex and quite controversial. The maximisation of national dividend for maximum welfare referred strictly speaking only to *net* dividend, that is, the dividend remaining after capital was preserved in tact, a proposition that got Pigou into controversy with von Hayek over issues of depreciation. The operational definition of national dividend used by Pigou was the sum of the goods and services produced over a period of time (generally a year), *less* the required depreciation (that is, the goods and services needed to maintain the national capital stock in the same physical state). More generally, and in line with Marshall's approach which had followed that of the Commissioner of Taxation, Pigou defined it in terms of national expenditure on goods and services from money income but including the services from an owner-occupied dwelling. In making comparisons of national dividend over time, Pigou was fully aware of the index number problem (associated with changed tastes, distribution and so on) but he failed to appreciate Hayek's criticism that a precise concept of depreciation involved the valuation of capital and was therefore part of a pricing process (and inappropriate in what was presented as a physical measure).

Pigou's analysis of the benefits for welfare from a more equal income distribution, rested on the assumption of a declining marginal utility of money income applicable to all persons. A shift of income from the rich, or well-to-do, to the poor would then automatically raise welfare as measured by the aggregate utility derived from the resources available to the community, defined as the sum of its individual members. Given diminishing utility of money income, the utility lost by subtracting income from the rich would be greatly outweighed by the gain in utility when that income was given to the poor, indicating a net increase in total utility, or welfare, from the income redistribution. Pigou therefore argued that progressive income taxation was a welfare improving measure, a consequence further enhanced when the revenue of that taxation was spent on activities of greater benefit to the poor. However, Pigou was adamant that such redistributive policies should not reduce the national dividend. The last could arise if steeply progressive income taxation significantly impaired incentives to work or to save, and if social subsidies to the poor substantially lowered their incentives to work. Pigou's preferred areas of public, redistributive endeavours were therefore education, industrial training and public health, all investments designed to raise the productive powers of individuals and hence, generally positive in their effects on the national dividend. Likewise, the provision of public goods which did not encourage idleness, such as public parks, tended to gain Pigou's approval.

Externalities and returns

Both externalities and the laws of returns raised issues for Pigou about the maximisation of output and welfare through the reallocation of resources. For Pigou, externalities arose when, 'a person A, in the course of rendering some service for which payment is made, to a second person B, incidentally also renders services or disservices to other persons, C, D, E, of such a sort that payment cannot be extracted from the benefited parties, or compensation enforced on behalf of the injured parties.' (Pigou, *Economics of Welfare*, 1920, p. 159). The existence of such externalities clearly has the potential for distorting the direct impact of a particular type of resource use, and hence makes the association between the national dividend and social welfare more problematic. For example, the negative externality of a smoke stack needs to be offset against the national dividend (and welfare) it helps to create; a similar problem can arise when a tenant farmer at the end of his lease tries to get as much as possible out of the land thereby lowering the yield of the land over some future period for his successors as tenants to the farm (Pigou, *Economics of Welfare*, 1920, pp. 150–2). Such situations make compensation arrangements almost impossible to arrange.

Another classic case of potential detrimental consequences for national dividend and economic welfare from a resource allocation which seems optimal to the individual agents involves the output decisions for firms subject to increasing and diminishing returns. As Marshall had initially argued, welfare could be improved if firms subject to diminishing returns were encouraged to reduce their output by say, the imposition of a special tax; while output of increasing returns industries could be encouraged to expand by means of a bounty. The consequences of this policy included the following. First of all, it would lower the real resource cost of aggregate output. Furthermore, it would increase the aggregate level of satisfaction. Expansion of output in the increasing returns industries (where desire for the product is enhanced as it becomes more common) raises aggregate satisfaction, while curtailment of output in diminishing returns industries (where satisfaction is raised as the output becomes less common) likewise raises aggregate satisfaction, satisfaction being measured in terms of consumers' surpluses (Pigou, *Economics of Welfare*, 1920, Part II, ch. VIII).

Pigou's welfare analysis therefore relied on both interpersonal comparisons of utility (essential for deriving his conclusions on the benefits of a progressive income tax) and on the measurability and additivity of utility (or satisfaction). Without such assumptions, he tended to argue, it would be difficult to make welfare economics a practical subject, capable of assisting the poor and underprivileged. As Myint (1948, p. 235) has noted in his classic *Theories of Welfare Economics*, this position accepts that 'ultimately economic theory can only justify its existence by practical application, and in the sphere of practical social policy the economist . . . must make his own value judgment . . .'. Pigou's work in the field of welfare economics was therefore pioneering for a variety of reasons.

As already mentioned, Pigou's conception of welfare economics included the study of business fluctuations and unemployment, because these affected national income and its distribution. Pigou's 1912 contribution to the subject, *Wealth and Welfare* had dealt with employment, unemployment, the associated business fluctuations as well as public finance. During the 1920s Pigou reworked these segments of his welfare economics into separate volumes devoted to welfare economics proper, to industrial fluctuations, to public finance and, in 1934, to a book devoted to unemployment as the most pressing welfare problem of the day. This last contribution is now given some brief discussion in the context of this survey of Pigou's most famous work, because it has strong links with the material on Keynes' *General Theory* in Chapter 31, below.

Pigou's 1934 *Theory of Unemployment* meticulously refined the 'classical' theory of employment as part of the general theory of value and distribution, using real demand functions for labour and real wage rates as the key determinants of employment and unemployment levels. From this analysis, he concluded, *ceterus paribus*, that downward real wage adjustments could remedy unemployment given demand for labour functions and the requisite elasticity of these functions. If there is a certain number of would-be-workers who, given a specific labour demand function, would be fully employed at a wage rate w, but actual real wage rates are at a higher level, w', then fewer labourers will be employed relative to those seeking work. In short, there will be unemployment. The remedy for such unemployment immediately flowed from this analysis. If real wage rates, w', were reduced to their full employment level, w, then full employment would be effected. Pigou's analysis ignored the income effect of this employment policy: real wage reductions lowered workers' incomes any hence their demand for goods and services, the real determinant of employment levels in Keynes' later analysis (Chapter 31). Moreover, Pigou's analysis somewhat obfuscated the complications introduced for an analysis conducted in terms of money wage rates, these being of course the reward for labour manipulable for policy reasons in the real world. Pigou's policy was extensively, and unsuccessfully, practised during the world depression of the 1930s; it was reduced by the now more customary demand management policies after the Keynesian Revolution (discussed in Chapter 31, below).

J.H. Clapham, 1872–1946

The cost controversies and the laws of returns

J.H. Clapham, a noted economic historian, and like Pigou, a fellow of King's College, was wary of the claims of economic theory from his interest in empirical research. In 1922, he published an amusing and devastating critique of the conceptions of increasing, diminishing and constant returns as devices by which to actually classify the production process of specific industries, hence attacking as nonsense the welfare enhancing measure of taxing diminishing returns industries and subsidising increasing returns industries (which was part of the Pigovian welfare theory). Part of Clapham's critique hinged on what he saw as a confusion between individual production units and an industry; part of it rested on his belief that economics was often too far removed from reality. This made much theorising irrelevant and, when dressed up as policy recommendations, potentially dangerous if, or when, such recommendations were taken up for actual implementation. Clapham's last criticism was explicitly directed at Pigou's *Economics of Welfare* which had in fact sponsored such a policy. Not surprisingly, Pigou immediately replied to his Cambridge and King's College colleague. This reply effectively started what later became known as the cost controversies. Initially, these raised issues about the relevance of economic theory and the need for economics to be strongly based on the facts of real life. More specifically, they induced in the pages of the *Economic Journal* to which they were largely confined, (a) a careful investigation of the meaning and role to be assigned to the laws of returns, and (b) an explicit discussion of the difficulties raised by increasing returns for competitive industry, a topic that had worried Cournot in the 1830s and, subsequently, Marshall (see Chapter 22, above). As discussed below (Chapter 29), these issues were also brought to bear on a theory of imperfect competition, with the aid of the discovery of the concept of marginal revenue and hence, as a by-product, to the clear enunciations of the meaning of perfect competition and the requirements for its existence.

Piero Sraffa, 1898–1983

The controversy was indirectly responsible for the entry of Piero Sraffa into British economics as a Cambridge academic. Edgeworth, then co-editor of the *Economic Journal* with Keynes, had read Sraffa's careful discussion of the laws of returns, 'Sulla relazione fra costa e quantità prodottà' (*Annali di economia*, 1925) and suggested Sraffa be invited to write a similar article for the *Economic Journal*. Sraffa by then was already quite well known in English economic circles. Following his graduation in Law (and Economics) at Turin in 1920, Sraffa had worked on currency and banking at the London School of Economics. Shortly afterwards he met Keynes (via Professor Salvemini and Mary Berenson, the wife of the art critic and historian of the Italian Renaissance). Keynes was greatly impressed with Sraffa's talents and invited him to write on Italian banking for the *Economic Journal* as well as for a Supplement he was editing for the *Manchester Guardian*. Sraffa also translated Keynes's *Tract on Monetary Reform* into Italian. In the meantime, Sraffa had lectured at Perugia (1923–26) and had been appointed Professor of Economics at Cagliari in 1927. The publication of his article on 'The Laws of Returns under Competitive Conditions' in the 1926 *Economic Journal* led to an offer of a lectureship at Cambridge, which Sraffa accepted. He lectured on the advanced theory of value for some years from 1927, but ceased teaching in 1930 at his own request, instead taking up the position of Marshall Librarian and Director of Research Students at Keynes's suggestion. In 1930, he also commenced work on a collected edition of Ricardo's works in ten volumes, which was published between 1951 and 1955 with the collaboration of Maurice Dobb. (A general index appeared in 1973.) In 1960, based on work commenced in the 1920s, Sraffa published his *Production of Commodities by Means of Commodities*, a prelude to a critique of economic theory, as it was subtitled. In less than one hundred pages, Sraffa set out to rehabilitate aspects of classical economics using new techniques of analysis.

The laws of returns

In his Italian contribution, Sraffa carefully distinguished and defined the various meanings in which the laws of returns, as a relationship between costs and the quantity produced, could be put forward. Such a clear statement was essential if the ambiguities and mis-statements of the 'laws' of returns were to be removed from the contemporary economic literature. Some of those arose from Marshall's diffuse treatment in the *Principles* which often interspersed historical and analytical statements of the laws; which frequently blended together dynamic and statical applications of these laws; which occasionally failed to explicitly distinguish average from marginal returns and, finally which did not differentiate explicitly between economies of scale (where factor proportions remained constant) and the consequences for product when factor proportions altered, as when (in the classical theory of rent, for example), one fixed factor (land) was dosed sequentially with homogeneous units of capital and labour. Sraffa's 1925 article to this day remains a model of clarity and definitional precision and, had its views been accepted and extensively practised by economists during the early 1920s and before, would have made Clapham's critical intervention on the subject redundant.

Sraffa quickly reiterated these differences in the 1926 *Economic Journal* article, stressing also that both time and the definition of an industry, influenced the matter. The wider the meaning of industry (for example, agriculture or the iron industry) the more likely it is that the forces making for diminishing returns tended to predominate; a narrow definition of industry, such as fruit or nails, left much greater room for the forces making for increasing returns. A parallel difficulty arose from considerations of the assumed time interval; the shorter the period allowed for adjustments, the greater the probability of diminishing returns; the longer the period for such an adjustment, the greater the likelihood for increasing returns (Sraffa, 1926, pp. 180–84).

The laws of returns and the supply curve

What especially concerned Sraffa in the 1926 article was the fact that supply curves based on these laws of returns, did not often meet the requirements of particular (partial) equilibrium analysis under competitive conditions. Thus, for instance, if in the increase of output of a particular industry, forces are exerted not only upon the costs of that industry but also upon the costs of other industries, the conditions for partial equilibrium were violated and the usual supply and demand determination of value breaks down. Likewise, external economies of scale in Marshall's terms (see Chapter 22, above), arising as they did from general progress in the industrial environment, were clearly inharmonious with partial equilibrium analysis. Moreover, reductions in costs from increased production associated with internal economies or with the spreading of overheads more widely, were not compatible with competitive conditions. Hence, only economies external from the point of view of the firm, and internal from the perspective of the industry, would violate neither competitive nor partial equilibrium conditions. Unfortunately, such economies were not easy to find in practice, so that a theory relying on them could not be very general. Sraffa concluded that 'in normal cases the cost of production of commodities produced competitively . . . must be regarded as constant in respect of small variations in the quantity produced. And so, as a simple way of approaching the problem of competitive value, the old and now obsolete theory which makes it dependent on the cost of production alone appears to hold its ground as the best available.' (Sraffa, 1926, pp. 186–7).

However, this return to the classical solution was only a first approximation, useful though it was. Other approximations were general equilibrium modelling instead of partial equilibrium analysis, a procedure which Sraffa rejected because of its complexity. The most promising alternative, however, for Sraffa, was departing from the perfect competition framework by moving the analysis of competitive value closer towards monopoly. Such a move had a distinct advantage because the 'imperfectly' competitive environment enabled the economist to deal with two former problems.

First, such a theory could explain the observed reality that individual producers may have access to diminishing costs (increasing returns) over the relevant output range, and, secondly, and likewise conforming to observed industrial behaviour, single producers could often affect their individual market to a significant extent through marketing expenses, advertising and other selling costs. Sraffa himself summarised the advantages of this alternative solution so concisely, that it can be quoted in full:

> Everyday experience shows that a very large number of undertakings –
> and the majority of those which produce manufactured consumers'
> goods – work under conditions of individual diminishing costs. Almost
> any producer of such goods, if he could rely upon the market in which

he sells his products being prepared to take any quantity of them from him at the current price, without any trouble on his part except that of producing them, would extend his business enormously. It is not easy in times of normal activity, to find an undertaking which systematically restricts its own production to an amount less than that which it could sell at the current price, and which is at the same time prevented by competition from exceeding that price. Business men, who regard themselves as being subject to competitive conditions, would consider absurd the assertion that the limit to their production is to be found in the internal conditions of production in their firm, which do not permit of the production of a greater quantity without an increase in cost. The chief obstacle against which they have to contend when they want gradually to increase their production does not lie in the cost of production – which, indeed, generally favours them in that direction – but in the difficulty of selling the larger quantity of goods without reducing the price, or, without having to face increased marketing expenses. This necessity of reducing prices in order to sell a larger quantity of one's own product is only an aspect of the usual descending demand curve, with the difference that instead of concerning the whole of a commodity, whatever its origin, it relates only to the goods produced by a particular firm; and the marketing expenses necessary for the extension of its market are merely costly efforts (in the form of advertising, commercial travellers, facilities to customers, etc.) to increase the willingness of the market to buy from it – that is, to raise that demand curve artificially.

(Sraffa, 1926: 189)

Apart from the advantages of this solution though its close conformity with reality, it benefited from the fact that it had been already recognised by Marshall's statement that 'the appropriate demand curve for most individual producers was the particular demand curve of his own special market' (Marshall, 1890, p. 459). Sraffa's suggestion was rapidly taken up in Cambridge, first in Kahn's Fellowship Dissertation, and then in Joan Robinson's book on *Imperfect Competition*. Once that had been done, the way was clear for the rigorous exposition of the conditions which were required for perfect competition (see Chapter 29, below).

Notes for further reading

Pigou has written an enormous amount of material, but for the purpose of this section it is enough that students familiarise themselves with the argument presented in *The Economics of Welfare* (Macmillan – now Palgrave Macmillan, London, 1920, esp. Part I, Part II, Chapters I, II and VIII. A very useful commentary on Pigou's welfare economics is Hla Myint, *Theories of*

Welfare Economics (Longmans, Green, London, 1948) esp. Part II chapter X, Part III chapter XII. A more extensive introduction to Pigou's economics is David Collard's essay, 'A.C. Pigou' (in *Pioneers of Modern Economics in Britain*, eds Denis O'Brien and John Presley, Macmillan – now Palgrave Macmillan, London, 1981, pp. 105–39) which also deals with his theory of unemployment and the debate thereon with Keynes. Two of Pigou's obituaries are likewise well worth reading. These are P.R. Brahmananda, 'A.C. Pigou (1877–1959)', *Indian Economic Journal* (Vol. 6, April 1959, 466–87); and H.G. Johnson, 'Arthur Cecil Pigou, 1877–1959', *Canadian Journal of Economics*, (Vol. 26, February 1960, 150–55).

Many of the more important articles on the cost controversy have been conveniently reprinted in *Readings in Price Theory*, edited by George Stigler and Kenneth Boulding (Allen and Unwin, London, 1953, for the American Economic Association, Part II) including Clapham's 'Of empty economic boxes', the replies thereto from Pigou and Robertson, and Sraffa's 1926 article on 'The laws of returns under competitive conditions'. G.L.S. Shackle, *The Years of High Theory* (Cambridge University Press, Cambridge, 1967) has a useful chapter dealing with Sraffa's contribution in its wider context. Andrea Maneschi had produced a comparison of Sraffa's 1925 and 1926 articles (*Cambridge Journal of Economics*, 1986, vol. 10, 1–12); reprinted in Mark Blaug (ed.), *Piero Sraffa (1898–1983)* (Edward Elgar, Aldershot, 1992), which presents a useful collection of articles on Sraffa's work more generally. *Essays on Piero Sraffa*, edited by Krishna Bharadwaj and Bertram Schefold (Allen and Unwin, London, 1990) does likewise (of particular interest for this section is the essay by Paolo Sylos-Labini, 'Sraffa's critique of the Marshallian theory of prices'). The same applies to *Critical Essays on Piero Sraffa's Legacy in Economics*, edited by Heinz Kurtz (Cambridge University Press, Cambridge, 2000) of which the first chapter provides a particularly useful overview of Sraffa's contributions to economics.

29

Joan Robinson, 1903–83 and Edward Chamberlin, 1899–1967: Theory of the Firm

The dilemma posed for competition and increasing returns could in principle be solved by Sraffa's suggestion that a theory of price determination was more appropriately situated in a world of monopolies than in one of pure competition (see Chapter 28, above). Sraffa's suggestion was taken up by Joan Robinson in her *Imperfect Competition*. Alternatively, it was possible to merge aspects of monopoly and competition in the manner of Marshall, concentrating on selling and marketing costs so essential when a firm faces a downward sloping demand curve, and hence arrive at a world of monopolistic competition. This was the rather different approach taken by Chamberlin at Cambridge, Massachusetts.

Joan Robinson was born into a Cambridge educated family of Maurices and studied economics at Cambridge in the 1920s. She married Austin Robinson in 1926, not long after graduating. Following a brief period in India, they returned to Cambridge in 1928. Shortly afterwards, Joan Robinson started teaching economics there, gradually moving from assistant lecturer (in 1931) to full professor (in 1965). She was an indefatigable traveller, enormously stimulating teacher and prolific writer, publishing numerous books and articles in the world's leading academic journals and working with her teachers (especially Keynes) and contemporaries (Sraffa, Kaldor, Kalecki and above all, Richard Kahn), thereby becoming the first woman among the truly great economists. Her book on *Imperfect Competition* (1933) was followed by books on *Employment* (1937), *Marxian Economics* (1942), *Accumulation of Capital* (1956), *Economic Growth* (1962) and *Economic Heresies* (1971) as well as 5 volumes of collected essays.

Edward Chamberlin had a far less spectacular life. He was born in La Conner, Washington in 1899 and died in Cambridge, Massachusetts in July 1967. He studied for his PhD at Harvard under Allyn Young, and eventually became full professor there from 1951 until his retirement in 1966. He edited the *Quarterly Journal of Economics* from 1948 to 1958. His *Theory of*

Monopolistic Competition, based on his PhD thesis, appeared in 1933 (the eighth and final edition in 1962); this was followed in 1957 with *Towards a More General Theory of Value* and an edited collection of *Monopoly and Competition and their Regulation* (1954). His life was devoted to industrial organisation theory and the theory of the firm, the topics he had pioneered with his doctoral research of the late 1920s.

Although there are differences between the work of Robinson and Chamberlin, to be discussed briefly in this chapter, the similarities are major, and the focus is on Joan Robinson's account. This is also easier to summarise, because the essentials are set out in the first two chapters of her *Imperfect Competition*. These include the necessary assumptions and provide the geometry required to prove the basic theorems of imperfect competitive equilibrium. This mechanical approach to the subject later led her to reject emphatically the worth of her 1933 *Imperfect Competition*. Moreover, its static equilibrium approach totally ignored time. However, it did have the merit of demolishing the simple association between maximum welfare and perfectly competitive equilibrium.

Assumptions

Underlying the theory is rational behaviour in price and output determination, that is profit maximisation. This is influenced by two factors: the demand curve over which the firm has no control (apart from advertising and other marketing costs, assumed away by Joan Robinson) and the firm's cost curves over which it has limited control (though not over the factor prices on which they are based.) The definitions which follow further illustrate her abstract approach. A commodity is a consumer good, arbitrarily demarcated; a firm is an enterprise producing a single commodity; an industry is a group of firms producing a single commodity; the demand curve is a list of prices at which various amounts of a commodity will be bought in a market during a given period of time; the supply curve represents the amount of output over a given period of time available at particular prices. The last is regarded as only realistic in the short period, and for all practical purposes is replaced by cost curves. The geometry of cost analysis is detailed in chapter 2 of her book on imperfect competition. Average and marginal costs are clearly defined under conditions of falling, constant and increasing costs. For the resulting U-shaped average cost (AC) curve, the marginal cost (MC) curve is shown as cutting the AC curve from below at its minimum point. The demand curve (or average revenue – AR) curve is defined in the usually downward slopping manner and its marginal counterpart, the marginal revenue (MR) curve, is discussed in detail. The MR curve was the real novelty in the new theory of the firm, essential to its theorems of profit maximisation. It was simply defined as the function which plotted the additions to revenue for each increment of output (product) sold. Joan Robinson then used geometry to prove a number of

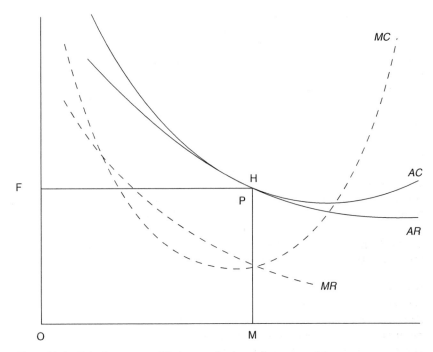

Figure 29.1 Price/output equilibrium under imperfect competition

properties of these curves, the most important one being that when the average curves are tangential, the marginal curves intersect (MC = MR) and profit is maximised at a price (AR) equal to its average cost (AC). This is illustrated in Figure 29.1 which, with U-shaped AR and MR functions, demonstrates maximum profit at output OM at which MC = MR (at *H*).

The remainder of the book is then devoted to proving an extensive set of theorems derived from this fundamental axiom of profit maximisation. These theorems deal with the implication of imperfect competition for distribution theory, for taxation, for price discrimination, for monopsony, for analysis of the demand for individual factors of production, and so on. The crucial innovation of the theory (which Robinson and Chamberlain shared) is the tangency of the AR and AC curves at which profit is maximised (MR = MC by definition.) This is *not* the point of minimum cost, hence equilibrium output maximises entrepreneurial profits rather than consumer welfare. Profit maximisation therefore required explicit formulation of the concept of marginal revenue, which occurred by the late 1920s, although both Cournot's and Marshall's analysis implied the concept in their discussion of profit maximisation for monopoly which required equality of the gradients of the total cost and total revenue curves.

Problems with the theory

As originally formulated, the theory induced a lot of debate and generated much qualification from both further theoretical and empirical work: (i) the notion of the commodity, the firm and the industry became more and more imprecise in a world where differentiated commodities predominated. The theory was transformed from one determining market prices of commodities into one seeking to explain the price and output decisions of individual firms. The stress on differential commodities favoured the Chamberlain version of the theory, which explicitly incorporated marketing and selling costs; (ii) partial equilibrium considerations became more difficult to handle with interdependence between cost curves of firms, since the output decisions of one firm affected the cost curves of other firms via the factor market. Demand curves likewise were not independent when differentiated commodities in an industry were close substitutes and there was vigorous marketing and advertising. In oligopoly theory with collusion, this produced an alternative theory altogether. Triffin tried to rescue what was left by incorporating imperfect competition into a general equilibrium framework; (iii) shapes of cost (AC) and demand (AR) curves became hotly debated, thereby inducing different approaches in theory. Examples are the kinked demand curve of oligopoly theory, and the identification of an L-shaped average cost curve, where costs remained constant over a long range; (iv) the analyses of profit maximisation via the marginalist (MR = MC) rule were criticised as unrealistic in terms of observed business behaviour and were replaced by full-cost, or normal cost, pricing variants emanating from Oxford (Hall and Hitch, P.W.S. Andrews), with full blown oligopoly theory initiated and developed by a range of theorists (including Sweezy, Stigler, Rothschild, Bain, Sylos-Labini, and Cyert), views in turn embodied in the 'micro-foundations' of post Keynesian analysis (Kalecki, Kregel and Eichner). Profit maximisation was also attacked as a realistic foundation for output and pricing decisions of firms: growth of the firm itself, maximisation of sales revenue, investment decisions and internal finance generation became prominent alternative rationales in the work of Berle and Means, Galbraith and Marris, among others; and (v) More generally, the new theories implied the destruction of a general theory of value or price in the classical manner because uniform principles of price determination designed to fit all cases were largely abandoned. What generality in the theory of value remained, can be summed up as follows: (a) the general equilibrium analysis of market prices, invariably under conditions of perfect competition, revitalised from the end of the 1930s (Hicks and Samuelson) and in the 1950s (Arrow, Debreu and Hahn); (b) partial equilibrium demand analyses of prices for raw materials and other, fairly homogeneous commodities while (c) and on a different plane of analysis, there was Sraffa's rehabilitation of classical price theory in his system of commodities produced by means of commodities where prices are determined under conditions of competition, a uniform profit rate and wage rate, and several other simplifying assumptions.

A final dividend

The debate over the appropriate theory of the firm generated by the development imperfect (and monopolistic) competition theory produced a further important result: a clear and concise definition of the conditions required for perfect competition as a pure, theoretical construct. Perfect competition with its simplifying assumptions so convenient for the application of marginalist techniques, remained in use particularly in the new welfare economics which was then also being developed (see Chapter 30, below). The substantial issues raised during the ongoing development of the theory of the firm clearly demonstrated its role as a theoretical artifact kept in analytical existence because of the powerful and elegant results derivable from its properties.

Notes for further reading

The starting point should be Joan Robinson, *The Economics of Imperfect Competition* (Macmillan – now Palgrave Macmillan, London, 1933), Books I and II; Edward Chamberlin, *The Theory of Monopolistic Competition* (Harvard University Press, Cambridge, Mass., 1933, eighth edition 1962, introduction, chs V–VII, Appendix H). Joan Robinson's articles, 'Imperfect competition revisited' and 'Imperfect competition today', reprinted in her *Collected Economic Papers* (Basil Blackwell, Oxford, 1964) Part III, are also useful. Rober Triffin, *Monopolistic Competition and General Equilibrium Theory* (Harvard University Press, Cambridge, Mass., 1942, pp. 19–48) presents handy summaries of Robinson's and Chamberlain's theories, as does G.L. Shackle, *The Years of High Theory* (Cambridge University Press, Cambridge, 1967, chs 4–5). *The Economics of Joan Robinson*, edited by Maria Marcuzzo, Luigi Pasinetti and Alessandro Roncaglia (Routledge, London, 1996) Part I, presents a more recent assessment of Joan Robinson's contribution.

30
Vilfredo Pareto, 1848–1923 and Lionel Robbins, 1898–1984: Critique and Decline of Utility theory

The marginal revolution of the 1870s had only one thing in common for the three economists with whom that revolution was associated (see Chapter 17 above). This was the development of a theory of value based on marginal utility. The essence of that revolution was the introduction of marginal analysis, particularly useful for the solution of resource allocation problems and used as well in the development of relative price theory, including that of factor prices. It was the *marginal* aspect which became important, not the utility aspect.

Dissatisfaction with utility theory came fairly quickly. Part of this arose from what were increasingly seen as the spurious psychological foundations of the theory. Furthermore, many economists were becoming embarrassed by its strong associations with utilitarianism and Bentham's felicific calculus of pleasure and pain. Others, such as Marshall (see Chapter 22, above) had become disillusioned with the operational value of utility-driven welfare concepts such as consumers' surplus. The measurability of utility, and its quantification, taken for granted by some of the pioneers of the new marginalist economics, were likewise gradually recognised as difficult to realise in a scientific manner. In the face of such difficulties, interpersonal comparisons of utility became increasingly suspect. Finally, with the possibility of deriving demand functions independently from utility functions, as had been done by Cournot and, initially, by Marshall, one aspect of utility's operational significance for economics had been conveniently removed.

Vilfredo Pareto, the successor to Walras's chair at Lausanne, was an early noted critic of utility theory, the analytical importance of which he successfully challenged in his *Manual of Political Economy* (1906). During the 1930s, Lionel Robbins in his very influential *Nature and Significance of Economic Science*, more pointedly criticised the assigned role of marginal utility in policy analysis. Their views have been largely responsible for the effective decline of utility theorising during the second half of the twentieth century, and are briefly examined in this section.

Vilfredo Pareto was born in 1848 in Paris, his early education in mathematical sciences prepared him for an engineering career. From the 1890s, he combined engineering work with strong public criticism of government intervention in economic activity, and vigorous vocal support for free trade, pacifism, anti-colonialism and radical democratic reform from a libertarian perspective. Two influential pieces criticising Italian economic policy and analysing the effects of protection, as well as claims about his growing status as a mathematical economist, induced an invitation to succeed Walras at Lausanne in 1892. He accepted and occupied this chair from 1893 to 1911. During this period he produced his major work: *Cours d'économie politique* (1896–97), *Les Systèmes socialistes* (1902–03) and *Manuale d'economia politica* (1906). The final decades of his life from the 1890s combined economic theory with sociological research, encapsulated in the immense *Trattata di Sociologia generale* (1916).

Pareto's critique of utility theory in the *Manuale*

Pareto's discussion of the general notion of economic equilibrium introduced his dissatisfaction with the notion of utility as conventionally used in economics. The term was not sufficiently rigorously defined, particularly with reference to the precise nature of the quality it was said to represent for a commodity. Utility also needed to be a quantity, but this was only achievable in the relatively rare case where utility depended on the quantity of a single good and was therefore independent of the quantities of other goods. Ordinal utility, or the ranking of degrees of satisfaction experienced, was fortunately all that was required for the construction of economic theory in Pareto's view. Such ranking could be achieved by the expedient of what amounted to revealed preference, making economics a science based on experience and experiment in line with the natural sciences.

Pareto then distinguished a variety of cases under which preferences could be revealed. One involved the construction of a notional price-quantity relationship which yielded a schedule of prices and the quantity of a commodity, strawberries to use Pareto's example, person would buy at each price. ('At thirty centimes a kilogram, I would buy ten kilograms, at 60 centimes, I would buy only 4 kilograms, at one franc I would not buy any'). A similar thought experiment yielded the notion of indifference as expressed by an individual for specific combinations of two commodities in his possession. In Pareto's words:

§52. Indifference lines of tastes. Take a man who allowed himself to be governed only by his tastes and who possesses 1 kilogram of bread and

1 kilogram of wine. His tastes being given, he is willing to obtain a little less bread and a little more wine, or vice versa. For example, he consents to having only 0.9 kilogram of bread provided he have 1.2 of wine. In other terms, this signifies that these two combinations, 1 kilogram of bread and 1 kilogram of wine or 0.9 kilogram of bread and 1.2 kilograms of wine, are equal for him; he does not prefer the second to the first, nor the first to the second; he would not know which to choose; possessing the one or the other of these combinations is *indifferent* to him.

Starting from that combination, 1 kilogram of bread and 1 kilogram of wine, we find a great number of others among which the choice is indifferent, and we have for example

Bread 1.6   1.4   1.2   1.0   0.8   0.6
Wine 0.7   0.8   0.9   1.0   1.4   1.8

We call this series, which could be extended indefinitely, *an indifferent series*.

(Pareto, Manual of Political Economy, p. 118)

Such data can be used in a graph to form indifference curves (see Figure 30.1). The curve *ns* posits the combinations which commenced with the ownership of one kilogram of bread and wine as tabulated in the quotation

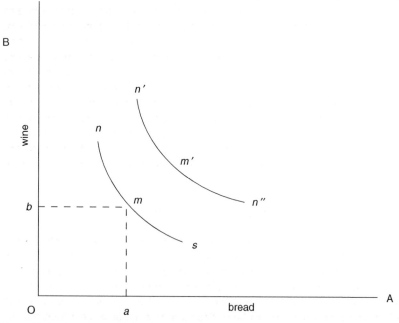

Figure 30.1   Paretian indifference curves

above (*m* reflects this original position, where O*a* and O*b* respectively make the original endowment of 1 kg of bread and wine). M', on the higher indifference curve, n'n" where m' reflects a higher endowment of, say, 1.1 kg of bread and wine, and any point on this curve indicates a different combination of the two commodities among which the individual in question is indifferent.

All the desired results for marginalist economic theory (competitive price equilibrium) can be derived on the basis of such indifference maps and do not need any knowledge of the utility surfaces of individual consumers. Instead of the absolute quantities of utility, all that needs to be known are the scales of preferences or the ordering of pairs of commodities in terms of their desiredness, in the manner just demonstrated. Demand curves can be derived from these data, and consumer behaviour can be explained in terms of such indifference maps. Knowledge about the slopes of the indifference curves, or the marginal rates of substitution between the two commodities (the equivalent of the ratio of the marginal utilities of the two commodities) was only required. Likewise, to reflect the notion of diminishing marginal utility as the general case, indifference curves need to be convex to the origin, a shape which facilitated simple geometrical proofs of competitive equilibrium. (This last paragraph draws on Hicks's elaboration of Pareto's analysis, formalised in his *Value and Capital*, 1938).

One important implication of Pareto's position can be mentioned here. With the abandonment of utility, attempts to measure aggregate welfare in terms of minimum net sacrifice or maximum utility become devoid of meaning. Pareto therefore substituted an alternative criterion of welfare: there is an unambiguous optimum with respect to consumption if, given certain quantities of the goods and given consumer preferences, it is impossible to improve the position of one individuals without worsening that of another; which since then has been called a Pareto optimum. For a production optimum, or more generally, efficient production, such an optimum exists when it is impossible to increase production of one good without reducing the production of other goods. These criteria implied scarcity of resources, including finished goods. They also implied the abandonment of distributional issues as part of welfare economics.

Lionel Robbins and the economic problem

During the early 1930s, Robbins systematised the new view of economics in terms of a definition which rapidly became accepted as a statement of the economic problem. Rejecting the former 'materialist' definitions of wealth which described economics as the science of wealth, (production, distribution and consumption of wealth), Robbins suggested the following definition as far more appropriate: 'Economics is the Science which studies human behaviour as a relationship between ends and scarce means which have alternative uses' (Robbins, *An Essay on the Nature and Significance of Economic Science*, Macmillan, London, second edition, 1935, p. 16). As a footnote to this definition indicated, its credentials were pure Austrian and reflected the allocation problem as treated, for example, by Menger (see Chapter 20, above).

Lionel Robbins was born in 1898 and for much of his life was an academic economist, concerned with theory and its application. He graduated from the London School of Economics, and except for brief periods at Oxford in the 1920s, made his academic career there, as full professor from 1928 to 1960. Apart from the book already mentioned, he contributed much work to applied economics (*The Great Depression*, 1934; *Economic Planning and International Order*, 1937; *The Economic Problem in Peace and War*, 1947) and to the history of economics (*The Theory of Economic Policy in English Classical Political Economy*, 1952, and *Robert Torrens and the Evolution of Classical Economics*, 1957). He also contributed much to policy making in England, particularly in higher education, in art administration, and through management of *The Financial Times*. He died in 1984. The implications of his formulation of the economic problem for utility theory and its application are the basic concern of this section.

One advantage Robbins claimed for his approach was that the division of ends and means he predicated, removed many value judgments from economics (given that politicians designed the ends). Furthermore, his concern over allocational matters (and implicit neglect of distributional issues) meant that notions such as the diminishing marginal utility of money income could be abandoned (and with it the case for progressive taxation as argued by economists like Pigou), because they implied 'unscientific' interpersonal comparisons of utility. For Robbins, the main virtue of his definition was that it turned economics into a positive science. Unfortunately, for him, that was exactly what it did not necessarily do. Jacob Viner pointed out in a review of the book that end and means were often difficult to separate in practice so that value judgements were not so easily eliminated from economic analysis. More importantly, the mass unemployment of the great depression of the 1930s had made resources far from scarce but plentiful, pointing to an economic problem additional to that posed by Robbins, the problem of unemployment and excess capacity. Some early solutions to this problem, are discussed in Section V below.

Developing a new welfare economics

The contributions discussed so far in this chapter contained an implicit invitation to construct a new welfare economics which rejected both the measurability of utility and the legitimacy of inter personal comparisons of utility, satisfaction or other simple welfare indices. The dilemmas of economic welfarism *à la* Pigou (see above, Chapter 28) were spelt out succinctly by John Hicks (1959). His preface and manifesto on the topic left an important role for the analysis of departures from the optimum likely to arise from a system of free enterprise, and in particular to use refined (rehabilitated) versions of consumer and producer surplus to this end. He himself has attempted such a rehabilitation (Hicks 1941) in which he tried to repair the damage inflicted on these notions of surplus by an older generation (Pareto, Nicholson and Cannan) and of what he called the younger generation (Robbins, Knight). Hicks' rationale was simple. Economics required solutions to a variety of problems (for example, the costs and benefits of advertising) in which these types of tools could still play a useful role.

Moreover, Hicks (1959) argued that the liberal economic case for non-interference under conditions of competition likewise needed a succinct analysis in which both the benefits of competition and the exceptions to its beneficial consequences were carefully demonstrated. Such optimum conditions of production and exchange had been constructed on the basis of perfect competition (for example, Reder, 1947) but their value as tools for policy makers has been rejected by critics of welfare economics (Little, 1950, 1957). Little's book examined in particular difficulties in applying the welfare criteria to specific issues. Examples included the pricing rules for public enterprises, as well as welfare aspects in the valuation of national income, assessing the welfare implications of international trade policy including tariffs, and, perhaps most interesting for historians of economics, assessing the implications of welfare theory for judging various political systems (socialism, *laissez-faire* capitalism). The last in turn gave rise to detailed discussions of the rationale behind group decision making; the problems of majority, and other styles of voting; assessing the costs and benefits of public enterprises, of public investment and, more generally, of public expenditure as a whole. These take the discussion into still very contemporary evaluations of the applications of welfare economics theory, as principal tools of economic policy and public finance.

Notes for further reading

On Pareto, a reading of his *Manual of Political Economy* (English translation by Ann S. Schwier, Macmillan – now Palgrave Macmillan, London, 1971, esp. chapter 3), is strongly recommended. A detailed history of utility theory is George Stigler, 'The development of utility theory', reprinted in his *Essays in the History of Economics* (Chicago University Press, Chicago, 1965) and with respect to the growth of the indifference curve, G.L.S. Shackle, *The Years of High Theory*, chapters 5 and 6. Busino's and Kirman's articles on Pareto in the *New Palgrave* (vol. 3, pp. 799–809) are a useful introduction to the man and his economics. A more detailed discussion are Luigino Bruno, *Vilfredo Pareto and the Birth of Micro-economics*

(Cheltenham: Edward Elgar, 2002) esp. chapter 1; Michael McLure, *Pareto, Economics and Society* (London: Routledge, 2001) and A. Kirman's chapter on Pareto in *Italian Economists of the Twentieth Century*, edited by F. Meacci (Edward Elgar, Aldershot, 1998, ch. 2). For Robbins, a reading of his *The Nature and Significance of Economic Science* (Macmillan – now Palgrave Macmillan, London, 1934, esp. chs 1, 2 and 6), is recommended. A fine commentary on this book is Claudio Napoleoni, *Economic Thought in the Twentieth Century* (Martin Robertson, London, 1972, ch. 2). Bernard Corry gives a useful overview of Robbins's life and work in his entry for the *New Palgrave* (vol. 4, pp. 206–8). A nice collection of the new welfare economics is that in the American Economic Association *Readings in Welfare Economics* (Allen and Unwin, London, 1969) which, among other things, reprints Hicks' 1959 'Manifesto for a new welfare economics' and his 1941 'Rehabilitation of consumer surplus'. It also reproduces classical contributions on public expenditure and public enterprise economics, on the economic analysis of politics and voting, and discussions of some of the foundations of welfare economics. M.W. Reder, *Studies in the Theory of Welfare Economics* (Columbia University Press, New York, 1947) and I.M.D. Little, *A Critique of Welfare Economics* (Oxford University Press, Oxford, first edition 1950, second edition, 1957) provide detailed overviews of immediate post-Second World War developments in welfare economics.

Section V

The Foundations of Modern Macro-economics

31
John Maynard Keynes, 1883–1946: a New General Theory of Employment, Interest and Money

John Maynard Keynes was born on 5 June 1883 (the same day and month as Adam Smith) in 6 Harvey Road, Cambridge. His father, John Neville Keynes, was a Cambridge don, teaching logic and political economy, and a close friend of Marshall. Keynes studied at Eton, then King's College, Cambridge, where he took first class honours in mathematics. Keynes was active in several undergraduate societies, including the Discussion Society, where he encountered the philosophers McTaggart, Bertrand Russell and G.E. Moore, and the 'Apostles' where life-long friendships were formed with Lytton Strachey and Leonard Woolf, and who, together with Leslie Stephen's brilliant daughters, Vanessa Bell and Virginia Woolf, were to form the core of the famous Bloomsbury Group. Keynes's interest in economics can be dated from 1905. Reading of Jevons and other major works combined with lectures from and classes with Marshall and Pigou. In 1907, Keynes joined the India Office, work which resulted in his first book on economics, *Indian Currency and Finance* (1913). In 1909 he became a Fellow of King's, with a dissertation on probability (more devoted to the theory of knowledge) and began teaching economics at Cambridge. The start of the First World War took him to Treasury and eventually as a participant in the peace negotiations at Versailles, an experience which generated two further books: *Economic Consequences of the Peace* (1919) and *Revision of the Treaty* (1922). His work on the international monetary mechanism over this period also induced private speculative activity in the foreign exchange market, which made him a fortune.

In 1919 Keynes resumed economics teaching at Cambridge as well as his editorial duties with the *Economic Journal* which had started in 1912. During the 1920s and 1930s involvement with business through company directorships grew to such an extent that Cambridge activities became confined to long weekends. In 1925, Keynes married the Russian ballerina, Lydia Lopokova, which further increased his involvement with the arts.

These decades were also very hectic ones in Cambridge economics, where effectively two revolutions in economic theory were in the making. One arose from the cost controversies, and developed into the imperfect competition revolution (see Chapters 28 and 29, above). The other arose from the developments in monetary, cycle and employment theory, in which Cambridge economists tried to come to grips with solutions to the economic problems caused initially by post-World War I reconstruction and later by the great depression initiated with the 1929 Wall Street crash. At first, these discussions remained very much confined to the Marshallian tradition, as is visible, for example, in Keynes's *Tract on Monetary Reform* (1923), but it was not long before these restrictive boundaries were breached under the pressure of growing unemployment and business recession and other problems of post-war adjustment, including the return to the gold standard. During these years Keynes produced a number of tracts for the time and from 1925 worked steadily on a major book, *The Treatise of Money* (1930). Its publication was surrounded by much debates within Cambridge (partly the famous 'Circus', or seminar composed of the younger generation of Cambridge economists, Richard Kahn, Piero Sraffa, Austin and Joan Robinson and James Meade) which gradually moved the focus away from the price level and price stability (the old, Marshallian focus) and towards the process of income (and employment) generation, which produced the *General Theory* in 1936. Keynes's defence and explication of this work was hampered by his first heart attack in 1937 and his enormous official work load during the Second World War. He died of a second heart attack in 1946, by then generally recognised as the greatest economist of the twentieth century.

From the *Treatise* to the *General Theory*

The gradual evolution of the *General Theory* from the debates over the *Treatise* as well as its basic contents, forms the focus for this section. This story is complex and still controversial. *The Treatise of Money* itself is a very peculiar book. Its long construction meant it exhibited various changes of mind and therefore never achieved a unity of clearly expressed ideas. Keynes admitted this in the preface where he candidly stated that the ideas with which the book finished were not those with which he had started out. The initial aim of the book had been to present an analysis of the price level (the theory of Volume I), the major problem of monetary theory and policy (the applied work of Volume II). It finished up as a book which did indeed analyse the price level by means of its fundamental equations but which also contained much criticism of the quantity equations, an incipient theory of output and a careful discussion of the investment cycle and its relationship with the business cycle. It also embodied, as part of the fundamental equations, a savings and investment theory. This, like the

General Theory was to do, separated savings and investment decisions as acts of different sets of people where differences (*ex-ante*) between decisions to save and to invest were described as a major factor in explaining instability in the price level. For much of this analysis, Keynes assumed constant output. Heated controversy in the years immediately following publication of the *Treatise* ensued about what Joan Robinson dubbed the 'buckets-in-the-well theory'. This referred to the decline in demand for consumption goods caused by an increase in saving which, via its effect in lowering the rate of interest, would lead to a compensatory increase in demand for investment goods. The constant output assumption of this analysis together with the use it made of conventional interest theory, effectively reintroduced Say's Law in another form to explain why saving would always equal investment. The analysis contained no theory of aggregate demand and, therefore, no real theory of output as a whole. Nevertheless, these debates produced what can be recognised as three important building blocks for the construction of the *General Theory*.

The first arose from debating what would happen if output was allowed to change. Then prices would follow changes in output, rather than the direction of savings-investment disequilibrium. Keynes had raised such matters as early as 1931 in his Harris Foundation Lectures, while they also arose in the increasing preoccupation in Cambridge discussions on the connection between the elasticity of the supply of goods and the effects of a monetary expansion on prices. Secondly, the *Treatise* steered inflation analysis away from quantity theory explanations towards income and demand inflation models. The critique of the quantity theory in the *Treatise* also highlighted the rate of interest as a monetary phenomenon, especially in its theory of bullishness and bearishness, which evolved into the liquidity preference theory.

This left the following five matters missing from what became *The General Theory*: (i) explicit formulation of the theory of aggregate demand; (ii) the multiplier; (iii) savings as a function of income rather than the rate of interest or the formulation of the consumption function; (iv) the aggregate supply function and its relation to the level of employment; and (v) a new theory of interest based on the foundations of liquidity preference.

The notion of aggregate supply and its analysis came first, arising as it did from the questioning by the 'Circus' of the implications of the constant output assumption of the *Treatise*. The early analysis of the multiplier (by Kahn) suggested elastic aggregate supply enabling the impetus of new investment to spend itself in generating output, rather than price rises. This initial multiplier analysis also induced the demonstration that new investment could be seen as self-financing via the leakages in consumption from the increased output in the form of savings on the dole, reductions in foreign investment (increase in excess of imports over exports), an increase in unspent profits and, the one negative influence, a reduction in saving due to rising prices. It was named Mr Meade's relationship, after its 'inventor', James Meade.

By the end of 1931 some of the missing parts had been supplied. A notion of the aggregate supply function had been developed, the elasticity of which determined whether an increase in aggregate demand (not yet explicitly formulated) led to a rise in output prices. An elastic supply curve ensured the demand stimulus resulted in rising activity levels. The multiplier was also largely developed. It showed that given a degree of elasticity in the supply curve, an increase in public investment would generate increased employment and via the additional consumption of domestically produced goods brought about by the new employment, would generate bursts of secondary employment. The amount of secondary employment generated depended on the proportion of the additional income spent on domestic consumption (or, inversely, on the leakages from that income in spending on imports, taxation and saving). Against the Treasury view which saw such public investment as useless for stimulating economic activity (because it would be offset by an equivalent private investment reduction), the new analysis was able to argue on the basis of Mr Meade's relation, that increases in public investment on the supply conditions postulated, would themselves generate the savings required to finance the investment.

The theory of effective demand, the key element in the Keynesian revolution, was probably developed by Keynes during the first half of 1933. Reasons for this dating are found in Bryce's notes of Keynes's lectures on the monetary theory of production given in 1932 and 1933 and from material which Keynes had added to his Malthus memoir when it was published in *Essays in Biography* (1933). Bryce's lecture notes show income as the sum of consumption and investment, consumption as a function of income, and investment as a function of the rate of interest. In a letter to Kahn (13 April 1934), the notion of aggregate supply and effective demand are clearly expressed, and the possibility of unemployment equilibrium is clearly stated:

> If W is the marginal prime cost of production when output = O, OW is aggregate supply. Let P be the expected selling price of this output, then OP is effective demand. The fundamental assumption of the classical 'supply created its own demand' is that OW = OP *whatever* the level of O; on *my* theory OW ≠ OP for all values of O and entrepreneurs have to choose the value of O for which it is equal . . . this is the real starting point of everything.

New drafts of the *General Theory* written in the middle of 1934 now contained chapters on effective demand, and more importantly, developed notions of the propensity to consume. Keynes explicitly argued in these drafts that savings had become less important to the argument than they were in the *Treatise* and that he now preferred to concentrate on consumption (the inverse of savings). A corollary was that causality shifted away from saving to concentrate on investment, a further departure from the analysis of the *Treatise*. New drafts also developed the notion of the propensity to consume (as a function of employment, the rate of interest and the level of expectations, showing how closely income and employment were intertwined for Keynes at this stage). They also showed how income acts as the equilibrating factor through the effects on saving of variations in income, while investment was shown to be determined by the rate of interest and the marginal efficiency of investment (a Marshallian conception of its profitability in terms of the expected future stream of quasi rents discounted to the present). Towards the end of 1934, Keynes could put his new theory together by arguing that given the propensity to spend on consumption, the rate of interest and the marginal efficiency of investment, the level of income (employment) was determined.

The argument needed a new theory of interest, created from the liquidity preference theory already present in the *Treatise*. A new interest theory was required because it had to determine the level of investment; the older, conventional loanable funds theory argued that interest was determined by investment and saving and therefore could not be used. As Pasinetti (1974) has argued, Keynes's theory required a rate of interest determined independently from savings and investment and with respect to the income determination process. It is the latter, dependent as it is on effective demand, which is the crucial contribution of Keynes's *General Theory*. As Keynes put it himself:

> As I have said above, the initial novelty lies in my maintaining that it is not the rate of interest, but the level of incomes which ensures equality between saving and investment. The arguments which lead up to his initial conclusion are independent of my subsequent theory of the rate of interest, and in fact I reached it before I had reached the latter theory. But the result of it was to leave the rate of interest in the air.
>
> (Keynes, *Collected Writings*, Vol. XIV, p. 212)

Putting it all together: the basic model of the *General Theory*

By the end of 1934 the basic elements of the new general theory of employment had all been discovered; 1935 was required to put them together into a coherent system and to round off the argument with introductory and concluding material. 1935 was also used to refine the argument and the manner in which it was to be presented. The last was needed to emphasise the novelty of the new theory, and to differentiate it sharply from earlier thought. This involved criticising the older generation directly, particularly, but not exclusively, as represented by Pigou. The preface of the book is signed December 1935, it came out in January 1936.

At the heart of the *General Theory* lies the principle of effective demand. At any stage in an economy there is a certain amount of productive capacity which determines the amount of output which can be produced from the given resources with the given state of techniques. This is the aggregate supply function which determines the potential output of economy up to the point of full employment. In earlier forms of society, full production potential was usually achieved, because individual enterprises produced as much as possible; with modern, industrial society, where the production process is geared to the market, the potential output of the given productive capacity will only eventuate if there is sufficient effective demand for that output, the effective demand being determined by the expectations of sales proceeds of the individual entrepreneurs who control the output decisions. The demand that entrepreneurs expect for their products therefore regulates their decisions about the degree of capacity utilisation (or the amount of employment they are willing to offer, as Keynes put it), and which thereby determines the level of output in the economy. Figure 31.1 illustrates this situation with a simple diagram portraying the supply curve as a 45° line. (This is often called a Hansen diagram, after the populariser of Keynes in the United States who first used it.)

The level of output is indicated along the horizontal axis, the expected sales proceeds from that output on the vertical axis, the dotted line is the

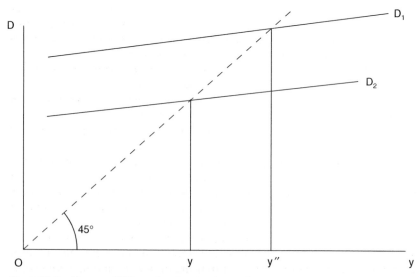

Figure 31.1   Hansen 45° line of aggregate demand

aggregate supply curve, the D_1, D_2 lines represent various levels of aggregate demand. Up to Y‴, the point of full capacity utilisation, the effect of an increase in D is on output, after Y‴ output cannot increase any further and additional aggregate demand raises money income only, that is, it raises the price level. The relevant range of the diagram is therefore the part to the left of Y‴, full capacity output. In this segment, entrepreneurs react to rises in aggregate demand by raising output and offering more employment. Pricing behaviour implicitly assumes a constant mark-up and the degree of competition, a situation where manufacturers raise output, costs rise, and then prices. A more subtle presentation of the aggregate supply function captures such matters better, and this is briefly given later in this chapter. A closed economy was also assumed.

The nature of effective demand

Aggregate demand is defined as the sum of demand for consumption and investment goods, and because it generates income, it can be written as $Y \equiv C + I$ where Y is income (output), C is consumption and I is investment. Aggregate demand therefore depends on the determination of consumption and investment. Consumption, Keynes argued, is a function of income, because consumers on the whole tend to spend a certain fraction of their income, a fraction which decreases as income rises. Keynes called this fraction the marginal propensity to consume, which is >0 and <1 and which has as its inverse the marginal propensity to save. This follows by definition, since $S \equiv Y - C$. Consumption in the short run depends largely on real disposable income, via the marginal propensity to consume.

For Keynes, investment is not determined by income (as in the accelerator mechanism) but by the marginal efficiency of investment (or expected profitability) and the interest rate. That is, $I = f(E, i)$ where E is the marginal efficiency of investment and i the interest rate.

If A (autonomous investment), c (the propensity to consume) and E (the marginal efficiency of investment schedule) are treated as givens in the system, the analysis of income (output, employment) determination has to be completed by a theory of the rate of interest (given the shape of the aggregate supply, provisionally left in this preliminary account as a 45° line, following Hansen). Keynes found his theory of interest in his analysis of the supply and demand for money, (liquidity preference). This demonstrated that i depends on a given liquidity preference schedule and a given quantity of money, that is, $i = f(L, M)$. This formally completes the Keynesian system of income determination since the four equations are sufficient to determine the four unknowns, Y, C, I and i.

The novelty of Keynes's analysis is that the level of effective demand which is determined by this system of equations, need not be the level yielding full capacity utilisation output or full employment. However, if there is unemployment at this level of effective demand, the remedy which suggests itself is additions to aggregate demand. Here the multiplier enters the picture, a relationship between an increment of income and an increment of investment (or government spending) which can be derived by substituting the consumption function into the aggregate demand function, yielding:

$$\Delta Y = \frac{1}{1-c} \cdot \Delta I$$

This form of the multiplier is the instantaneous multiplier which Keynes used in the *General Theory*, and not the lagged multiplier which Kahn had developed in his article in the *Economic Journal* for 1931, and which emphasised the dynamics of the manner in which a burst of new (public) investment generated additional income, output and employment. Keynes's static version illustrates the statical nature of much of the argument of the *General Theory*. However, Keynes's static presentation was sufficient to demonstrate how an increase in expenditure generated a proportionately greater increase in income, since the multiplier was > 1 given the value of c (by definition).

It may be noted that saving is explicitly left out of the picture. This is easily remedied. The consumption function implies that $S = F(Y)$ and that s, the marginal propensity to save equals $1 - c$. The passive adjustment of saving to investment via income determination is then easily demonstrated from the multiplier relationship:

$$\Delta Y = \frac{1}{1-c} \cdot \Delta I$$

which is equivalent to $\Delta Y = 1/s \cdot \Delta I$, so that $s \cdot \Delta Y = S = \Delta I$. The increased income from the increase in investment finances that investment by the saving it generates (in a dynamic statement of the multiplier only after a lag). Kahn's multiplier embodied Meade's relation, as previously indicated.

A system of equations of the causal type

Keynes's ordering of the material in the *General Theory* suggests that he saw his analysis as essentially one of causal, partial equilibrium analysis. It starts in Book I of the *General Theory* with the exposition of the principle of effective demand in terms of aggregate demand and supply analysis; Book II presents definitions and the importance of expectations in the theory of effective demand. Books III and IV then respectively discuss the components of aggregate demand: consumption and investment. The latter requires a *new* theory of the rate of interest and with its presentation the theory can be completed. Hence it can be re-stated in summary at the end of Book IV. Book V deals with qualifications and modifications (associated with money wages and the price level). The final book introduces miscellaneous material (notes on the trade cycle, notes on mercantilism and theories from the 'underworld of economics' which were claimed to resemble Keynes's perspective, and concluding remarks on the social philosophy to which the *General Theory* could lead). The book as a whole therefore presents no systematic trade cycle theory, and relatively little discussion of policy. On the latter, it implied that since there are only weak automatic forces to restore full employment equilibrium, government intervention is essential to secure full employment when the economy is in a state of recession or depression. This can be done through the direct stimulus of aggregate demand by government expenditure (consumption or, preferably, investment), an argument not explicitly conducted in the *General Theory*. Indirectly, the monetary authorities could stimulate investment by lowering the rate of interest through a monetary expansion, given the marginal efficiency of investment. The problematic nature of this policy is indicated by Keynes in a concise paragraph which also summarises the causal links from which the *General Theory* is constructed:

If, however, we are tempted to assert that money is the drink which stimulates the system to activity, we must remind ourselves that there may be several slips between the cup and the lip. For whilst an increase in the quantity of money may be expected, *cet. par.*, to reduce the rate of interest, this will not happen if the liquidity-preferences of the public are increasing more than the quantity of money and while a decline in the rate of interest may be expected, *cet par.*, to increase the volume of investment, this will not happen if the schedule of the marginal efficiency of capital is falling more rapidly than the rate of interest; and whilst an increase in the volume of investment may be expected, *cet. par.*, to increase employment, this may not happen if the propensity to consume is falling off. Finally, if employment increases, prices will rise in a degree partly governed by the shapes of the physical supply functions, and partly by the liability of the wage-unit to rise in terms of money. And when output has increased and prices have risen, the effect of this on liquidity preference will be to increase the quantity of money necessary to maintain a given rate of interest.

(Keynes, *General Theory*, p. 173)

The central message of the *General Theory* is that there is no market mechanism which ensures full employment.

Back to the supply function

Keynes's reluctance to use diagrams in the *General Theory*, meant that his vision of the aggregate supply function was never illustrated in a graph and that, therefore, by default as it were, the initial versions of the supply curve were the 45° lines pioneered by Hansen in his *Guide to Keynes* (1953). It seems more likely that this was not what Keynes had in mind, given the problems it causes for illustrating the potential inflation effects of increases in aggregate (and effective) demand. An alternative diagram suggested by Tarshis (1977, p. 59) fits the bill much better (Figure 31.2). It suggests rising inelasticity in supply as output rises, hence allowing for price rises to combine with growing output and employment, as a situation of full employment is approached. In addition, it has the merit to incorporate the imperfect competition arguments which were being so vigorously debated in Cambridge during the early 1930s, a fact which even arises in the simple 45° line expositions, as mentioned previously.

The diagram has the further merit of illustrating the generality of Keynes's *General Theory*. It provided not only a theory of output and employment, it provided a theory of inflation, in the case where increased aggregate demand encountered the near full capacity economy embodied in a highly (perfectly) inelastic aggregate supply curve. Shifts in the aggregate supply curve would likewise yield price as well as output changes. Keynes's theory was therefore not simply depression economics as it so often was described in the period following its publication; it had also policy prescriptions for situations of full capacity and employment, as those which appeared within four years of the publication of the *General Theory* during the early years of the Second World War. Keynes demonstrated this versatility of his theory in his little booklet, *How to Pay for the War*, which appeared in 1940.

The impact and meaning of the *General Theory* continues to be debated in the ever growing literature on Keynes and his revolution. This makes notes for further reading rather difficult to compile. The following can therefore only be a very general guide.

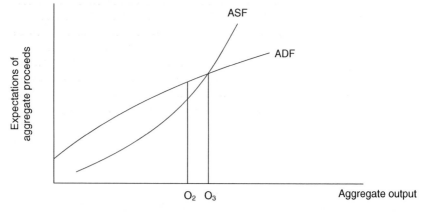

Figure 31.2   Aggregate demand/aggregrate supply analysis in Keynes's *General Theory*

Notes for further reading

A reading of at least part of Keynes's *General Theory* is essential to capture the atmosphere of the Book: read chapters 1–3, 5, 8–11, 13, 18, 24 as an introduction to some of the essentials. The commentaries are legion and should be historically sampled. Seymour Harris, *The New Economics*, is a large and useful collection of Keynes material published not long after his death, as is, in the wider setting of business cycle history, *Readings in Business Cycles and National Income*, edited by Alvin Hansen and Richard Clemence (Allen and Unwin, London, 1953). A more recent set of interpretations is *Keynes, Cambridge and the General Theory*, edited by Don Patinkin and J. Clark Leith (Macmillan – now Palgrave Macmillan, London, 1977) which includes the paper by Tarshis mentioned previously. *New Perspectives on Keynes*, edited by Allin Cottrell and Michael Lawlor (Duke University Press, Durham, NC, 1995) is one indication of the current state of research on Keynes and his economics; another is the two-volume *A Second Edition of the General Theory*, edited by G.C. Harcourt and P.A. Riach (Routledge, London, 1997). *The Impact of Keynes on Economics in the Twentieth Century*, edited by L.L. Pasinetti and B. Schefold (Elgar, Aldershot, 1999) presents a detailed overview of Keynes's general significance. Reference should also be made to *An Encyclopedia of Keynesian Economics*, edited by Thomas Cate (Edward Elgar, Aldershot, 1998). There are biographies a plenty, commencing with Harrod's *Life of Keynes* (Macmillan – now Palgrave Macmillan, London, 1951); D.E. Moggridge, *Maynard Keynes: an Economist's Biography* (Routledge, London, 1992) and the three-volume biography by Robert Skidelsky (Macmillan – now Palgrave Macmillan, London, 1983, 1992, 2000). Austin Robinson's obituary in the *Economic Journal* (1947, 57, 1–68) presents a marvellous portrait by a long time friend and colleague. Reviews of the *General Theory* are well worth reading. A handy collection, which includes second thoughts by many of the original reviewers, is Robert Lekachman, *Keynes's General Theory.' Reports of Three Decades* (Macmillan – now Palgrave Macmillan, London, 1964). A splendid historical sketch of the making of the *General Theory*: set in the context of British history, is Peter Clarke, *The Keynesian Revolution in the Making 1924–36* (Clarendon Press, Oxford, 1989). Don Patinkin's entry on John Maynard Keynes is a fine overview of the work by this controversial interpreter of Keynes (*The New Palgrave*, vol. 3, pp. 19–41) and contains a useful bibliography.

32
Michal Kalecki, 1898–1970: a New Macro-economics

Kalecki was born in Poland in June 1899 and died there in April 1970. He initially studied civil engineering, but had to give up his studies for financial reasons in 1923. In 1929 he became a member of the Institute of Research in Business Cycles and Prices in Warsaw, resigning in 1936 because of the dismissal of two colleagues for political reasons. He then went abroad, first to Sweden and then to England. There he established scholarly connections with Kahn, Sraffa and Joan Robinson. In 1940 he joined the Oxford Institute of Statistics and from 1945 worked for international organisations (the International Labor Office and the United Nations, for the last of which he prepared World Economic Reports). When McCarthyism reached great height in the United States, he returned to Poland (1955), working for the Planning Commission (1955–65) and teaching at the Polish Academy of Sciences (1955–61). From 1961 to 1970 he worked for the Central School of Planning and Statistics. His academic work spawned many publications. In 1939, he published *Essays in the Theory of Economic Fluctuations*, followed by *Studies in Dynamic Economics* (1943) and *Theory of Economic Dynamics* (1954). Most of his work tended to be published in journal articles. His early articles, many translated from the Polish were published as *Studies in the Theory of Business Cycles 1933–1939* (Blackwells, Oxford, 1966), while many of his essays were collected after his death in *Selected Essays in the Dynamics of the Capitalist Economy*, *Economic Growth of the Socialist and Mixed Economy*, and *Essays on Developing Economies* (Cambridge University Press, Cambridge, 1971, 1972 and Harvester Press, 1976). Kalecki is now particularly remembered as an economist who anticipated the essentials of the Keynesian Revolution from a Marxist departure point, in the process developing his own mathematical (and econometric) macro-economics of cycles and growth. His collected works have now been published in English, in Polish they have been available since 1986.

This section concentrates on Kalecki's early work on business cycles during the 1930s. A 1933 business cycle model by Kalecki is presented first, followed by a brief discussion of the role of international trade and the similarity between exports and investment in generating an upswing. Like Keynes, Kalecki developed the argument that investment generates its own savings to finance it through income changes, that interest is essentially a monetary phenomenon and that wage cuts cannot cure unemployment under the assumptions of the analysis. The discussion concludes with some comments as to why Kalecki was able to solve the problem of aggregate demand in such a simple way as compared with the long theoretical debate over the matter in Cambridge inspired by Keynes. This also indicates why, nevertheless, it remains valid to talk of the Keynesian rather than the Kaleckian revolution.

The business cycle model

Assume a closed economy, devoid of trends, so that the cycle is analysed in a non-growth economy. Income (Y) is defined in terms of the sum of wages (W) and profits (P), and as the sum of consumption (C) and accumulation, or investment, (A). Kalecki assumes that workers do not save, their savings propensity (S_w) = 0 so that wages equal consumption by workers (C_w). Hence $P = C_c + A$ where C_c is capitalist consumption and A, gross accumulation (investment). Assume that C_c contains a constant part, B_0, and a part determined by profits, λP, where λ is a small fraction (the propensity to consume of the capitalists):

$$\text{Then } P = B_0 + \lambda P + A = \frac{B_0 + A}{1 - \lambda}$$

where $1 - \lambda$ is the capitalists' propensity to save. In this way, the equation resembles that of the multiplier, except that the relationship here is that between profits and spending from profits on consumption and investment goods. Profits in fact are shown to be proportional to the constant part of capitalist consumption (C_c) and accumulation (A).

Gross accumulation equals the sum of investment goods produced and inventories. Because growth over the cycle is zero, gross accumulation equals replacement requirements, but in the upswing positive investment may of course be offset by negative investment in the downswing. Total inventories (working capital) are assumed to stand in a fixed relationship (γ) to capital stock.

Investment

Kalecki distinguished three stages in investment activity: (1) investment orders (I); (2) production of investment goods or gross accumulation (A); and (3) deliveries of finished equipment (D). Kalecki assumed a constant, average period of construction of capital equipment, v; this implies a simple relationship between D and I, deliveries (D) at time t denoted investment orders (I) at $t - v$. The relationship between A and I is more complicated. In any period of time, v, there is a portfolio of uncompleted investment orders (Z). At any point of time, therefore, the production of investment goods (A, gross accumulation) must be equal to Z/v (the portfolio of orders over time, v) that is, $A = Z/v$. With increasing investment orders over time at a constant rate at point of time, t, $D = A$ (at point of time $t - v/2$) and equals I (at point of time, $t - v$), while at point t, $I > A > D$. This indicates the simple proposition that in the upswing of the cycle, investment orders exceed the production of equipment which in turn exceeds the deliveries of investment goods, the size of the differences depending on the period of construction of investment, v. In the downswing, the opposite situation is applicable, because orders decline first as activity levels deteriorate. The increase in the capital stock depends not on deliveries of new equipment (D) but also on the volume of assets scrapped (U). The change of capital equipment over time, $\Delta K/\Delta t$, $= D - U$. Over the cycle as a whole, by assumption, $\Delta K/\Delta t = 0$, since $U = D = A = I$.

Kalecki assumes that investment orders are a function of gross profitability and the rate of interest. Furthermore, if it is assumed that the rate of interest, i, is an increasing function of the rate of profit, then investment orders are a simple function of profitability, P/K. (The significance of this is explained later.) Two subsidiary arguments qualify this position. First, investment orders should be considered relative to the capital stock, K, so that the functional relationship between investment orders and profitability should be written as

$$I/K = F(P/K)$$

Secondly, interest, which is negatively related to I, stands in a lagged relationship to P/K (the rate of profit), so that I/K on the whole is an increasing function of P/K. The relationship between i and M (the quantity of money) is explained in the context of the cycle where i is shown to rise in the upswing and fall in the downswing because demand for money, which is influenced by the level of economic activity, varies over the cycle.

The Kaleckian investment function

With I/K a function of P/K, and P proportionate to $B_0 + A$ by a constant factor $+ 1 \lambda$:

$$I/K = \frac{B_0 + A}{1 + \lambda}$$

and if it is assumed this is a linear function, then it can be rewritten as:

$$\frac{I}{K} = m \frac{B_0 + A}{K} - n$$

where m and n are positive (m, because F is an increasing function, and n, because the need for consistency with plausible values of B_o, A and I). Hence:

$$I = m(B_o + A) - nK$$

which shows that investment orders are an increasing function of gross accumulation (A) and a decreasing function of the capital stock (K).

The model of the cycle follows from the investment orders equation and from the time lag element built into the relationship between I, A, D and K which depends on the construction period.

Take an exogenous increase in investment orders. After an interval $v/2$, this raises A, which further increases I from the nature of the investment function. After an interval v, D starts to rise and, depending on the size of U (replacements) begins to increase the capital stock, K. Depending on the values of m and n, and the length of the construction period, v, the cumulative increase in K eventually outweighs the effect of rising I on A, so that investment orders start to fall. Once orders fall, this becomes cumulative, as decreases in I lead to further falls in A after an interval, $v/2$, and so on. Ultimately, the falls in I and A induce D to become less than U (replacements) at which point K starts to decline again. This ultimately will exert a positive influence on I and the cycle can start afresh. This is a picture of an investment cycle. However, it can be quickly extended into a general business cycle by introducing the two ways in which investment influences the level of aggregate activity.

First, increased investment production increases employment and hence the demand for consumption goods. Consumption goods production therefore rises with investment orders after a lag. Hence profits rise in both the investment and the consumption goods sector. Secondly, the rise in profit enhances capitalist consumption, thereby further increasing demand for consumption goods. Kalecki concluded, 'The aggregate production and the profit per unit of output will ultimately rise to such an extent as to assure an increment in real profits equal to that of production of investment goods and capitalist consumption.' (Kalecki, 1933, p. 14). This paradoxical result follows directly from the national income identity, $P = A + C_c$. Increased spending on consumption increases profits for capitalists as a class. Hence the statement is true that 'Workers spend what they get, and capitalists get what they spend'. (This paraphrases the initial assumptions, $s_w = 0$ and the identity $P \equiv C_c + A$ since $W = C_w$.)

Kalecki thereby demonstrated that investment creates its own savings, since rising investment orders ultimately raise profits to the level where the new investment is financed from the increased profits. It is his version of Keynes's paradox of thrift.

In an essay on foreign trade and domestic exports, Kalecki demonstrated the effects of an export surplus and a budget deficit on economic activity and on the level of profits. This flows from expanding the national income identities to incorporate the balance of trade and the balance of government sector transactions explicitly. P is therefore not just equal to $A + C_c$ but to

$$I + C_c + (E - M) + (G - T)$$

where E are exports, M imports, G government spending and T taxation. Kalecki reached three specific conclusions from this extension of the argument: (i) increased export surplus is as stimulatory to economic activity as increased investment orders; (ii) increased economic activity by raising the level of imports in a fixed proportion ensures that export surpluses cannot continue indefinitely; and (iii) rising government spending relative to taxation likewise stimulates economic activity.

Kalecki and Keynes

Some similarities between the two theories have already been mentioned, but the manner by which they are reached is quite different. This includes the argument Kalecki presents on the futility of wage cutting in stimulating employment. Wage cutting he argued, can only work if aggregate demand can be held constant, and this is not the case when wages are reduced. His main point is that only capitalist spending can alter economic activity, and there is no reason why such spending will change, unless it is argued that the anticipated increases in profits from wage cuts immediately stimulates capitalist spending, an eventuality he regarded as unlikely.

Joan Robinson has pointed out why Kalecki's theory is so much simpler than Keynes's. This simplicity arose from two factors: firstly, Kalecki did not know much orthodox theory and therefore did not have to unlearn any. He went straight to the point without having to bother with received ideas such as the quantity theory, savings-investment equilibrium and Say's Law. Secondly, Kalecki's background in Marxian economics made the underlying class analysis of his theory, such as the assumption that workers do not save and investment is financed from profits, quite automatic. His two sector modelling, not covered here, also benefited from his knowledge of Marx. However, Kalecki's achievement did in no way overshadow those of Keynes in the historical setting of the world economy in the 1930s. Kalecki himself could not have effectively made the revolution which Keynes made, his work was too easy to ignore, as it still is today to a large extent. It required a person with the stature of Keynes and with his diverse economic and intellectual background to (1) provide the critique of the conventional theory; (2) build the new theory in the light of the critique of the old; and (3) most importantly, secure a large audience for his views. Despite the similarities between the theories, as this chapter was able to demonstrate to a limited extent, the nomenclature of Keynesian revolution remains the correct description for the historical phenomenon. Kalecki, however, constructed a still very useful macro-economics of instability of growth, with applications to a wide variety of problems, and a detailed consideration of the underlying micro-economics. He also contributed extensively to the economics of planned, socialist societies, and to the economics of the developing world.

Notes for further reading

A study of essays included in Kalecki's *Studies in the Theory of Business Cycles 1933–1939* enables deeper insight into his early work on the business cycle than this section can give. A study of the contents of *Selected Essays on the Dynamics of the Capitalist Economy* is also highly recommended. Peter Kriesler and Bruce McFarlane, 'Michal Kalecki on Capitalism' (*Cambridge Journal of Economics*, 17 (2) June 1993, 215–34) is a splendid overview with a useful bibliography; Joan Robinson's 'Kalecki and Keynes' (*Collected Papers*, vol. 3, pp. 92–9) compares the work of these great economists; Peter Kriesler, 'Keynes, Kalecki and the *General Theory*' (in A *'Second Edition' of the General Theory*, Vol. 2, pp. 300–22) likewise reviews this relationship with a good, up-to-date, bibliography. K. Laski's entry on Kalecki in the *New Palgrave* (vol. 3, pp. 8–14) provides an interesting overview and bibliography. G.R. Feiwel's *The Intellectual Capital of Michal Kalecki* (University of Tennessee Press, Knoxville, 1975) is a detailed study of Kalecki's economics, well worth reading for those particularly interested in Kalecki's work.

33
R.F. Harrod, 1900–78 and E.D. Domar, 1914–99: Cycles and Growth

Roy Harrod was born in February 1900, completing his education by taking a first class honours degree in Classical Studies and Philosophy at Oxford (1919–22). This, together with a second, first class honours result in History (1923) gained him a tutorial fellowship at his College, Christ Church, to teach the then 'novel' subject of Economics at Oxford within its newly created honours school of Politics, Philosophy and Economics. Harrod was given two terms to prepare himself for the task (he had never studied Economics), doing so at Cambridge (partly with Keynes with whom he formed a strong friendship and of whom he became the first biographer) and later, at Oxford, with Edgeworth on micro-economics. His publications on economics began with articles on the topic of imperfect competition in the early 1930s (then all the rage, see Chapter 29 above), followed by a Cambridge Economic Handbook (1934) on *International Economics* (which, among other things, adapted Kahn's concept of the multiplier to international trade) and then a book on *The Trade Cycle* (1936). Harrod had been heavily involved in the lead-up to the *General Theory*, corresponding with Keynes on early drafts and he later helped in popularising its findings. Just before the Second World War, Harrod contributed an essay on dynamic theory to the *Economic Journal* (1939). This was developed into a booklet, *Towards a Dynamic Economics* (1948) and subsequently, *A Second Essay in Dynamic Theory* (1960). During the 1960s he wrote on economic policy. He died in 1978.

Harrod's growth model is the focus for this section. It greatly resembles the one independently constructed, but seven years later, by Domar at Harvard. Their work is, however, so frequently bracketed together, that it is almost invariably described as the Harrod-Domar growth model.

Domar was born in Lodz (then Russia) and settled permanently in the United States from 1936 where he pursued an active academic career until his retirement in 1984. His growth theory, structurally similar to Harrod's, was developed differently by incorporating the dynamic capacity changes caused from growing investment in order to demonstrate that steady-state capacity growth required investment to grow at a rate equal to the savings propensity multiplied by the implied capital output ratio. His work on growth originally published in journals, was collected in his *Essays on the Theory of Economic Growth*, published in 1957. As already indicated, the main focus of this chapter is Harrod's analysis.

The trade cycle, 1936

Harrod published his book on the *Trade Cycle* in the same year as Keynes published the *General Theory*. It introduced two novel arguments, developed and clarified in Harrod's later work on growth to which the material on the trade cycle turned out to be preliminary. The first, and more important, was the notion of a moving equilibrium growth path (what he called, the *warranted* rate of growth), which was grounded in the requirement for savings-investment equilibrium in the manner in which Keynes had presented this in his *General Theory*. In this work on the *Trade Cycle*, Harrod had used what he called the 'relation' (now called the 'Accelerator Principle') between the growth in output and the investment needed to produce that output, represented by the capital/output ratio. This relationship had not been used by Keynes in his *General Theory* (see Chapter 31, above), but was soon to become an important part of business cycle theory. Secondly, and more startling, Harrod claimed that if planned investment and saving ensured a higher actual rate of growth than the rate warranted, the system would embark on an ever-accelerating growth path which, once full employment had been reached, would generate spiralling inflation. Alternatively, if planned investment and saving yielded less than the warranted rate of growth, decelerating growth rates would result in an infinite downward spiral. Harrod's *Essay on the Trade Cycle* had presented this argument in a rather long-winded manner, and he was subsequently urged by Keynes to develop his view on growth more comprehensively. This was done in an 'Essay on Dynamic Theory', published in the *Economic Journal*, March 1939, and which, during its preparation, considerably benefited from Keynes's editorial advice.

An essay in dynamic theory

Harrod's 1939 essay in dynamic theory explicitly married the accelerator relationship to the multiplier, in order to develop three specific propositions: '(1) that the level of a community's income is the most important determinant of its supply of saving; (2) that the rate of increase of its income is an important determinant of its demand for saving, and (3) that demand is equal to supply' (Harrod, 1939, p. 201). The first proposition embodied a restatement of the multiplier principle; the second proposition related investment (as the demand for saving) to changes in income via the capital/output ratio; while the third simply expressed the condition of saving/investment equality as the condition for long-term growth equilibrium. Utilising these propositions, Harrod's formula for the warranted rate of growth given the marginal propensity to save and the capital/output rate, is then easily determined.

The saving-investment equilibrium condition, $S = I$ can be simply rewritten as $sY = \Delta K$. Dividing both sides by ΔY gives:

$$\frac{sY}{\Delta Y} = \frac{\Delta K}{\Delta Y}$$

which, given the fact that g, the growth rate can be written as $\Delta Y/Y$, and v, the capital/output rate equals $\Delta K/\Delta Y$ (the incremental capital/output ratio) on the assumption of fixed proportions between factors of production and output, can be easily re-arranged into $g = s/v$, Harrod's expression for the warranted rate of growth. (If s, the marginal propensity to save was 10 per cent and v, the capital/output ratio equalled 4, the warranted growth rate g, was set at $2\frac{1}{2}$ per cent.)

For growth without unemployment or, equally undesirable, overfull employment, the labour supply needed to grow in line with the warranted growth of output. Given Harrod's assumption of fixed proportions between inputs and outputs, this implied labour force growth equal to the rate of growth of output. Harrod used the natural growth rate to describe the growth of the labour force, arguing that stability requirements with respect to the employment level and the rate of inflation implied equality between the natural and the warranted rate of growth. In a free society, it is not easy to manage the natural rate of growth, so that for stability reasons, the warranted rate of growth, g (determined by s and v) needed to be adjusted to the natural rate. After all, if $g < n$, increasing unemployment results; while if $g > n$, there is increasing labour shortage and a tendency towards wage and price instability. Harrod's pessimistic conclusion from the analysis was the following. Since it was very unlikely that people's savings habits and the technical conditions of production determining the capital/output ratio would be so arranged that they matched the natural growth rate (determined by population increases), it would only be a fluke if stable growth, without labour market disequilibrium and price instability, would eventuate. This became known as the knife-edge theorem, since any actual departure from the warranted growth rate dictated by s and v would set up cumulatively worsening situations of instability in the form of either growing unemployment or rapidly rising inflation.

It is interesting to note that this type of result replicated research about the potential for equilibrium capital growth which had been conducted by Evsey Domar at Harvard and that, a similarly pessimistic expectation had been expressed by Marx on the bases of his models of expanded reproduction (see above, Chapter 16).

Some reactions to the Harrod/Domar analysis

Subsequent discussion of the Harrod/Domar results, such as those by Solow and Swan in 1956, suggested that it arose largely from the restrictive assumptions contained in the models, particularly that associated with fixed proportions of production. This failed to allow for substitution possibilities in production, as relative availability of capital and labour changed, which, on the basis of accepted theory, invariably generated changes in their relative prices. For example, if the natural rate of growth exceeded the warranted rate, the resulting unemployment (excess labour supply) would gradually lower wage rates (relative to the cost of scarce capital), thereby encouraging substitution towards more labour-using (less capital-using) methods of production, provided there was an adequate spectrum of techniques from which entrepreneurs could choose the factor mix between labour and capital appropriate to the circumstances. With factor price flexibility and a high degree of factor substitutability, market forces would equalise the demand for, and supply of, capital and labour, and stable, equilibrium growth would ensue. Since this effectively destroyed part of the impact of the Keynesian revolution (which claimed that unaided market forces could not restore full employment), this neo-classical growth theory of the 1950s was dubbed 'pre-Keynesian theory after Keynes' by Joan Robinson, a leading critic of the assumptions this 'revisionist' theory required.

The comfortable conclusions which could be derived from neo-classical growth theory became dominant among economists. They included that (1) the system was unstable in the short run, that is, the adjustment period when technical conditions via the changing factor prices adjusted to the labour supply; but in the long-run tended to be self-adjusting. (2) This emphasis on changes in technical conditions in response to changes in factor prices brought back some of the results from neo-classical production and distribution theory, that is, given a production function, $Y = f(K, L)$, distributive shares were determined by marginal products and factor quantities, that is, K. $\delta Y/\delta K$; L. $\delta Y/\delta L$. The new theory promoted by Solow and by Swan thereby combined aspects of Keynesian growth theory with neo-classical distribution theory.

However, these neo-classical versions of the Harrod/Domar models, which made the growth process self-adjusting through changes in relative factor prices (wage and profit rate) were attacked by many Keynesians as a counter-revolution against Keynes's stress on the importance of aggregate demand. After all, they constituted a return to the self-regulating equilibrium world of neo-classical economics, against which Keynes had so arduously fought. The use made in these arguments of aggregate production functions raised a number of capital theory puzzles. For example, the meaning of aggregate capital as used in aggregate production functions implied a unit by which heterogeneous capital was measured. If this was a value unit, then interest (or the profit rate) was involved, and hence the aggregate capital could not be used to determine the rate of interest (profit) without arguing in a circle. Nor was the meaning of the marginal product of capital very precise, given the peculiarities which could arise through reswitching of techniques and capital reversing. Such issues have still not been fully resolved.

Notes for further reading

Reference should be made to R.F. Harrod, *An Essay on the Trade Cycle* (Kelley, New York, 1965) and more importantly, to Harrod's 'An essay in dynamic theory', *Economic Journal* (March 1939, 14–33) and its full scale development in *Towards a Dynamic Economics* (Macmillan – now Palgrave Macmillan, London, 1948). Domar's *Essays in the Theory of Economic Growth* Oxford University Press, New York, 1957, should also be consulted, esp. *Essays*, 1, 3–5, 9, the last of which presents an interpretation of a Soviet Model of Growth by Feld'man. This demonstrates the similarity between Marx's growth theory and that of the Harrod–Domar models. Reference can also be usefully made to the entries on Harrod and Harrod–Domar growth model in the *New Palgrave*, vol. 2, pp. 595–604. R.M. Solow, 'A contribution to the theory of economic growth', *Quarterly Journal of Economics* (70, February 1956, pp. 65–94); T.W. Swan, 'Economic growth and capital accumulation', *Economic Record* (32(63), November 1956, 334–61), are prime examples of neo-classical responses to Harrod's growth dilemma. Joan Robinson, 'Mr. Harrod's dynamics' in *Economic Journal* (March 1949, Vol. 59, 68–85); G.C. Harcourt, *Some Cambridge Controversies in the Theory of Capital* (Cambridge University Press, Cambridge, 1972), esp. introduction and chapter 1 are useful guides to some of the Keynesian reactions, as are the overviews and developments presented by L.L. Pasinetti, *Growth and Income Distribution* (Cambridge University Press, Cambridge, 1974, chapter IV, esp. sections 4–6; VI, esp. sections 1–5).

34
Milton Friedman (1912–): Monetarism and its Critics

Monetarism is a doctrine which suggests that money has a major influence on both the level of economic activity and the price level, and that the objectives of monetary policy are best realised by targeting the rate of growth of money supply. As such, monetarism has strong affinities with the quantity theory of money, particularly as exposited by Wicksell (above, Chapter 25) and Irving Fisher (above, Chapter 26), but its modern variant is largely associated with the work of Milton Friedman. In 1976, this, and his other contributions to economics, gained him the Nobel Prize in Economics; his contributions to monetarism also made him one of the most controversial writers on economic policy in the post-Second World War period.

Milton Friedman was born in New York in 1912, in decidedly humble circumstances. He studied economics at Rutgers, Chicago and Columbia, worked in various research capacities, much of them statistically oriented (including work at the National Bureau of Economic Research) before turning to an academic career (at Chicago from 1946). He won his first academic laurels by writing on positive economics and the Marshallian demand curve (Friedman, 1953). His work on money which made him famous began in 1951, initially by testing and restating the quantity theory of money as a theory of the demand for money (Friedman, 1956). His *Monetary History of the United States 1867–1960* (Friedman and Schwartz, 1963) and much subsequent theoretical and empirical work developed arguments on the effects of variations in the quantity of money on national income, prices and output, together with their policy implications for both open, and closed, economies. The last involved analysis of the monetary effects of the balance of payments. Policy consequences of the monetarist position included analysis of the relative importance of fiscal and monetary policy (Friedman and Heller 1969); whether there was a trade-off between inflation and unemployment as postulated in the Phillips curve (Friedman 1968) and, arising from this, the development of a concept of the 'natural rate of unemployment', together with an armoury of policy propositions which made Friedman a major influence on Finance Ministers and Central Bankers especially during the 1970s and 1980s.

This is not to say that monetarism was solely Friedman's contribution. Henry Simons (1936), one of Friedman's teachers, had advocated control of money supply to achieve a stable price level; James Angell, some years previously, had advocated constant monetary growth as appropriate stabilisation policy, while Karl Brunner and Allan Melzer strongly advocated variants of monetarism in the post-Second World War era. In fact, Brunner coined the name, 'monetarism' for the phenomenon for reviving a quantity theory based monetary policy as an answer to Keynesian fiscal policies. This critical stance towards contemporary Keynesian policy thinking is a crucial aspect of monetarism as a guide to appropriate policy responses to price instability and unsatisfactory output and income levels. Monetarism has therefore been accurately described as a counter-revolution in economics designed to restore money supply as a key macro-economic policy variable, a position from which it had been displaced by the policy consequences inherent in Keynes's *General Theory* (above, Chapter 31).

As a revised statement of the quantity theory (Friedman 1956) to contradict Keynes's claim to have discredited it as a theory of income, employment and prices, monetarism had an explicit anti-Keynesian intent. Friedman's revision incorporated the notion that the quantity theory had to be interpreted as a theory of demand for money (an argument held by earlier quantity theorists as well) so that, as an explanation of changes in the price level (inflation), it needed to be supplemented with a theory of output and a theory of money supply. Friedman also reformulated the theory of monetary demand, making it dependent on interest rates and the rate of return on shares, the inflation rate (or incorporating a form of negative rate of return for financial assets), as well as wealth and other structural variables. This made the quantity theory resemble the Keynesian demand for money apparatus, although the policy implications Friedman drew from his analysis could not have been further removed from those drawn by the Keynesians. Friedman also indicated that the empirical evidence supported the view that his demand for money function was very stable, hence implying stability for the velocity of circulation of money or, as he occasionally described it, the 'monetary multiplier' since velocity of circulation, as Wicksell had shown, multiplied the effectiveness of the actual quantity of money. By contrast, Keynes's income multiplier was less stable, a hypothesis Friedman justified in terms of his 'permanent income' explanation of the consumption function. Friedman's view implied that monetary stimulus was more effective than manipulation of aggregate demand because it relied on the quantitatively more significant monetary multiplier.

This criticism of the effectiveness of the Keynesian aggregate demand approach to economic policy was reinforced by what became known as the 'crowding out effect', a view similar to the 'Treasury view' against which Keynes had so valiantly fought during the 1930s. If the money supply is given, changes in public spending from borrowing designed to stimulate economic activity, are offset by declines in private investment. Such countervailing decreases in private investment arose from the rises in interest rates induced by public borrowing in the absence of increases in money supply. A rise in money supply accompanying public borrowing, on the contrary, would stimulate economic activity and income levels, because it changed contractionary interest rate rises to the stimulus provided by declining interest rates. However, even though money supply changes in this way affected the real economy, the difficult to predict consequences of such monetary changes as a result of variable time lags made it difficult to use money supply variations as a discretionary tool for economic policy. Steady monetary growth determined by the long term growth rate of real output was the best solution for minimising unwanted fluctuations in economic activity, particularly since the competitive market frame work in any case was far better suited to make the necessary short term adjustments in price and output levels.

Monetarism in its original version by Friedman and the specific policy advice based thereon, did not survive for long in the ongoing debates over economic theory. The contests in the external development of economic theory included the Phillips curve model, with its trade-off between inflation and unemployment. This had introduced evidence on the role of expectations and the appropriate corrections brought to these models by the introduction of rational agents. Such considerations have further limited the general validity of the somewhat simplistic results of monetarist theory. These developments have generated room for wage and salary controls, and other forms of discretionary policy. They likewise suggest that consequences of stochastic disturbances of an extensive economic system can be eliminated by economic policy measures, the effects of which are unpredictable and unsystematic. This type of criticism has provided incentives to developing a theory of rational expectations, to analysing the real business cycle and to a large array of theoretical offshoots, which are still subject to discussion in contemporary economic literature and debate.

Money and equilibrium

It is also opportune to emphasise that monetarism in effect has a precise theoretical point of reference in Walrasian general economic equilibrium, or, more appropriately, in its modern version association with the work of Kenneth Arrow and Gerard Debreu. In this schema of general intertemporal equilibrium (see Arrow and Hahn, 1971), money is treated as a commodity like all other goods together with the existence of complete futures markets, let alone perfect information for the economic agents. These are able therefore to take all their consumption decisions in an instant initially also with respect to future time periods. Not only are they able to assume diverse future states of markets, secondly what is demonstrated or at least in any event determined, that there are overall contingent markets, precisely appropriate for each eventuality. In a world constructed in this way, there is no room for a Keynesian type of uncertainty, and thus no real room for money as 'a store of value'. The equilibrium which is established is of the Walrasian type with separate markets for each commodity which automatically eliminate excess supply and demand, thanks to the operation of the competitive mechanism indicated by the metaphor of the 'auctioneer'.

Under these conditions a dichotomy is re-established between the real economy (determining prices and quantities produced and traded) and a construction of a monetary economy which simply enables exchanges to take place at prices and quantities determined in the real part of the model. Models of general economic equilibrium do not, in general, leave any real room for the existence of money. Hence a genuine monetary economy is incompatible with such models. They are nevertheless appropriate to intertemporal equilibrium with its processes of automatic adjustment which justify a passive role for economic policy. General equilibrium models are therefore necessarily limited to ensuring a regular and steadfast flow of money as a means for circulating commodities.

The micro-foundations of macro-economics

Many, more critical, economists strongly disagree with the hypotheses inherent in a general intertemporal equilibrium model, which in fact has only concerned itself with non existing future markets and fully resolved contingencies and which, above all, is based on perfect information and knowledge about the future on the part of agents. This second consideration implies that actual markets are incompatable with models using an 'auctioneer'. The existence of non Walrasian equilibrium position is therefore possible, in which some goods remain unsold, and/or, particularly, some factors of production are not fully employed or, more precisely, can be unemployed (see Hahn, 1981). If there is no perfect information and hence no certainty about the future, significant room is made for analysing the behaviour of various economic agents and thereby raise the problem of the micro-foundations of macro economics. In particular, these attempt to show in what manner expectations about future economic magnitudes influence their determination. This type of argument has especially been applied to the labour market and to the expectations of workers and entrepreneurs about the dynamics of real wages and hence, money wages and prices. All of this has induced reinterpretation of the functioning of the labour market in transmitting the association, or to put it better, the *trade off* between price variations and unemployment rates, the inverse relationship of which was posited in the original Phillips curve.

Friedman himself has accepted the hypothesis that the labour market exhibits asymetrical information between entrepreneurs who not only know the value of money wages but also prices, and the workers who only know money wages, while only able to formulate expectations about prices and thus eventually about the real wage level. Nevertheless, the existence of asymetrical information does justify neither the use of fiscal policy for Friedman, nor, for that matter, the use of monetary policy to stimulate the economy. In fact, economic agents, particularly workers, learn from experience, that is, they have adapting expectations which ensure over time that their expectations will always be close to the real rate of inflation over the long period. The workers will also have certain information or perfect expectations realised for them in the sole magnitude which counts for anything in the labour market: real wages and not money wages. In the long run, the Phillips curve is perfectly stable and one in which the same level of unemployment rate, defined as the natural rate of unemployment, is compatible with any rate of inflation. Thus the level of equilibrium income is not influenced by monetary magnitudes, fiscal policy is totally ineffective and monetary policy exclusively determines the rate of inflation and not the size of any real variable in the economic system.

Friedman's conclusion about the ineffectiveness of expansionary fiscal policy has also been demonstrated by theoreticians from the new classical economics. They base this conclusion on a new conception of economic agents. Agents are now said to base their actions on rational expectations. To put it briefly, all economic agents, and not only workers, would know with any degree of certainty only the prices of goods being produced or sold, but would only be able to form such expectations about the state of other prices and thence about the general rate of inflation (see Lucas, 1972). Nevertheless, economic agents are rational in the sense that they utilise all available information about the functioning of the economic system. According to this school of thought, agents behave like true economic agents, they all have the same information available, and they are all aware how the model of the economy really works. Because opinions on that functioning are uniform, the expectations are automatically realised and everyone behaves fundamentally in the same way as the behavioural model suggests.

In such a situation, when every agent knows the behavioural mechanism of the economic system, economic policy becomes totally ineffective. The only remaining option for the monetary authorities is that of taking economic agents by surprise with an unforseen action and thereby randomly deceiving them. But this also will only have a temporary effect on the real part of the system and into the bargain would carry the risk of creating instability in the level of income rather than of the price level. It seems better therefore to follow simple and fixed rules in monetary policy, as Friedman had initially prescribed.

Notes for further reading

Those interested in learning more about Friedman's economics should consult his *Essays in Positive Economics* (Chicago University Press, Chicago, 1953); his 'The Quantity Theory of Money: A Restatement' in M. Friedman (ed.), *Studies in the Quantity Theory of Money* (Chicago University Press, Chicago, 1956); his 'The Role of Monetary Policy', *American Economic Review*, 58(1), March 1968, pp. 1–17; and his *A Monetary History of the United States 1867–1960* (with Anna Schwarz, Princeton University Press for the National Bureau of Economic Research, Princeton, 1963). A useful collection is Kurt B. Leube (ed.), *The Essence of Friedman* (Stanford University and Hoover Institution Press, Stanford, 1987) which reprints extracts from the works mentioned above as well as other work by Friedman. The monetary views of Friedman's teacher, Henry Simons, are contained in his 'Rules versus Authorities in Monetary Policy', *Journal of Political Economy*, 44(1) February 1936, pp. 1–30.

The literature on Friedman's monetary economics is immense. Useful introductions are M. Friedman and W. Heller, *Monetarism versus Fiscal Policy* (W.W. Norton, New York, 1969) and William Frazer, *Power and Ideas: Milton Friedman and the big U-turn* (Gulf/Atlantic Publishing, Gainesville, Florida, 1988). The original Phillips curve was presented in A.W. Phillips, 'The relation between unemployment and the rate of change in money wages', *Economica*, vol. 25, November 1958, pp. 283–99. The classic paper on rational expectations is R.E. Lucas, 'Expectations and the Neutrality of Money', *Journal of Economic Theory* 4(2), April 1972, pp. 103–24.

A general equilibrium critique of monetarism is F.E. Hahn, *Money and Inflation* (Blackwell, Oxford, 1981); the classic exposition of modern general equilibrium analysis is F.H. Hahn and K.J. Arrow, *General Competitive Analysis* (Oliver and Boyd, Edinburgh, 1971).

Epilogue

The final chapters of Part II (Chapters 33 and 34) have touched on issues still part of contemporary controversy and debate. In this way, the outline of the history of economic thought presented here is up to date, because it almost touches the present, and thereby converts the present into history. As explained in the Prologue, this is not the only reason why an understanding of the history of their subject is thought to be appropriate for practitioners of economics. It might be reiterated here that it is the whole history and development of the subject which is relevant in this way, not just the modern developments discussed in Part II of the book. Aspects of classical economics, for better or, in some cases, for worse, influence contemporary economic thinkers.

The book, by stressing the importance of background of the author by including a brief biographical sketch, also indicates that economics and its development are related to the environment from which it was created. Although the impact of environment on economic ideas can be overstated, it can never be ignored. Keynes' *General Theory*, to give a modern, important example is not simply depression economics – it presents a general theory – though it is not surprising that it was developed by its author to provide a more satisfactory response to the very significant problem of unemployment which the 'Great Depression' of the 1930s brought in its wake. As was mentioned at the end of Chapter 34 (p. 324), the policy response of much of the developed world to the 2008 World Financial Crisis saw a considerable return to using Keynes's aggregate demand approach in the stimulation of output and employment growth. Likewise, the early literature in favour of unregulated markets grew out of specific economic issues – legal abatement of interest, exclusive arrangement for particular trades – even if this type of response to such regulations was not the only response possible. The applied and practical nature of economics guides much of its research agenda.

Given the importance of environment in the shaping of economic ideas, it is also clear that the history of economics will be continually rewritten.

This does not imply that major figures in that history – Quesnay, Smith, Ricardo, Marx, Marshall, Walras, Keynes – will drop out from that history. Their classical work in the sense of influential work, will always be appreciated. Features stressed from their work can, however, easily change, and the major thrust of their books intended by their authors, is frequently identified in different ways. There is a subjective element in the interpretation of the specific significance of a particular work or to stress the obvious, there are numerous ways of reading and summarising a text. Such variation possibilities grow with the complexity of the economist's analytical system and the degree of clarity with which this system is explained.

In short, the outline history of economics here concluded cannot be the final word on the subject. What it has attempted is to provide a useful sketch on the development of economics from mercantilism to monetarism. Most strikingly, it has provided an overview of the variety of that development while the guides for further reading which accompany each chapter indicate the variety of interpretation to which this epilogue draws attention.

Bibliography
(to Part 1 only)

Appleby, J. (1978), *Economic Thought and Ideology in Seventeenth Century England*, Princeton University Press, Princeton.

Aspromourgos, A. (1986), 'Political economy and the social division of labour: the economics of Sir William Petty', *Scottish Journal of Political Economy*, 33 (1), February.

Aspromourgos, A. (1996), *On the Origins of Classical Political Economy. Distribution and Value from William Petty to Adam Smith*, Routledge, London.

Boisguilbert, Pierre le Pesant Seigneur de (1704), *Traité de la nature, culture, commerce, et intérêt des grains*, in *Economistes-Financiers du XVIII siècle*, E. Daire, ed., Guillaumin, Paris, vol. 1.

Boisguilbert, Pierre le Pesant Seigneur de (1707), *Dissertation sur la nature des richesses, de l'argent et des tributs*, ibid.

Cantillon, R. (1755), *Essay on the Nature of Commerce in General*, H. Higgs (ed.), Frank Cass, London, 1959.

Cartelier, J. (1976), *Surproduit et Réproduction*, Maspero, Paris.

Dobb, M. (1973), *Theories of Value and Distribution since Adam Smith*, Cambridge University Press, Cambridge.

Eltis, W. (1984), *The Classical Theory of Economic Growth*, Macmillan (now Palgrave Macmillan), London and Basingstoke.

Ferguson, 1767 *An Essay on the History of Civil Society*, reprinted Cambridge University Press, Cambridge, 1995.

Fox-Genovesi, E. (1976), *The Origins of Physiocracy*, Cornell University Press, Ithaca and London.

Galiani, F. (1770), *Dialogues sur le commerce des blés*, in *Mélanges d'économie politque*, E. Daire (ed.), Guillaum, Paris, vol. 2.

Garegnani, P. (1981), *Marx e gli economisti classici*, Einaudi, Turin.

Garegnani, P. (1983), 'The classical theory of wages and the role of demand schedules in the determination of relative prices', *American Economic Review*, vol 73, no. 2, May.

Giacomin, A. (1986), 'Un modello economico del ancien régime', *Ricerche economiche*, No. 1

Gilibert, G. (1972) 'Una formulazione algebreica del Tableau économique', *Studi economici*, ns. 1–6.

Groenewegen, P.D. (1969), 'Turgot and Adam Smith', *Scottish Journal of Political Economy*, vol. 16.

Groenewegen, P.D. (1971), 'A re-interpretation of Turgot's theory of capital and interest', *Economic Journal*, vol. 81, June.

Groenewegen, P.D. (1977), 'Adam Smith and the division of labour: a bi-centenary estimate', *Australian Economic Papers*, 16(29), December.

Groenewegen, P.D. (2002), *Eighteenth Century Economics. Turgot, Beccaria and Adam Smith and their contemporaries*, Routledge, London.

Groenewegen, P.D. (2002), *Classics and Moderns. Essays in nineteenth and twentieth century economics*, Routledge, London.

Hennings, K and Samuels, W. (eds.), *Neo-classical economic theory 1870–1930*, Kluwer Academic Publishers, Boston, Dordrecht, London.
Herlitz, L. (1988), 'Ideas of capital and development in pre-classical economic thought, *Economic History Report 7*, Goteborg.
Hischman, A.O. (1977), *The Passions and the Interest*, Princeton University Press, Princeton.
Hollander, S. (1973), *The Economics of Adam Smith*, Heinemann, London.
Hollander, S. (1979), *The Economics of David Ricardo*, Heinemann, London.
Hollander, S. (1985), *The Economics of John Stuart Mill*, Blackwells, London, 2 vols.
Hollander, S. (1997), *The Economics of Thomas Robert Malthus*, University of Toronto Press, Toronto.
Hutchison, T.W. (1953), *A Review of Economic Doctrines 1870–1929*, Clarendon Press, Oxford.
Hutchison, T.W. (1978), *On Revolutions and Progress in Economic Knowledge*, Cambridge University Press, Cambridge.
Hutchison, T.W. (1988), *Before Adam Smith*, Blackwell, Oxford.
Hoselitz, B.F. (1968), 'Agrarian Capitalism and the Natural Order of Things: François Quesnay', *Kyklos*, No. 4
Koch, P. (1958), 'Ferdinando Galiani: Dialogues entre M Marquis de Ronquemaure et Ms. le Chevalier Zanobi', *Romanische Forschungen*, vols 21–24, V. Klosterman, Frankfurt am Main.
I.N.E.D. (1989), *Boisguilbert parmi nous: actes du colloque international de Rouen*, Jacqueline Hecht (ed.), Institut national d'études démographiques, Paris.
Leontief, W.W. (1951), *The Structure of the American Economy 1919–1939*, second edition, Oxford University Press, New York.
Lunghini, G., (ed.), (1993), *Valore, Prezzi*, VTET, Turin.
Marget, A.W. (1935), *The Theory of Prices*, P.S. King, London.
Màtyàs, A. (1985), *History of modern, non-Marxian economics*, Macmillan (now Palgrave Macmillan), London.
Meek, R.L. (1954), 'Adam Smith and the Classical Theory of Profit', *Scottish Journal of Political Economy*, vol. 1.
Meek, R.L. (1962), *The Economics of Physiocracy*, Allen and Unwin, London.
Meek, R.L. (1973), introduction to *Turgot on Progress, Sociology and Economics*, Cambridge University Press, Cambridge.
Mirabeau, V.R. (1760), *Théorie de l'impôt*, Benjamin Gibert, The Hague, reprinted by Scientia verlag, Aalen, 1972.
Mirabeau, V.R. (1764), *Philosophie rurale ou économie générale et politique de l'agriculture*, chez les libraires associées, Amsterdam, reprinted Scientia Verlag, Aalen.
Mirabeau, V.R. (1769), 'Suite de la seizième lettre de M.B.A.M.***', *Ephémérides du Citoyen*, vol. II.
Mun, T. (1621), *A Discourse of Trade*, Nicholas Okes, London, reprinted Augustus M. Kelley, New York, 1971.
Mun, T. (1623?), *England's Treasure by Forraign Trade*, Thomas Clark, London, 1664, reprinted Augustus M. Kelley, New York, 1968.
Murphy, A.E. (1986), *Richard Cantillon: Entrepreneur and Economist*, Clarendon Press, Oxford.
Murphy, A.E. (1997), *John Law*, Clarendon Press, Oxford.
Myint, H. (1946), 'The Classical View of the Economic Problem', *Economica*, vol. 13.
Myint, H. (1948), *Theories of Welfare Economics*, Longman Green, London.
Myint, H. (1977), 'Adam Smith's theory of international trade in the perspective of economic development', *Economica*, vol. 44.

O'Brien, D.P. (1975), *The Classical Economists*, Clarendon Press, Oxford.

O'Brien, D.P. and Presley, J.R., (eds.), (1981), *Pioneers of Modern Economics in Britain*, Macmillan (now Palgrave Macmillan), London.

O'Donnell, R. (1990), *Adam Smith's Theory of Value and Distribution – A Reappraisal*, Macmillan (now Palgrave Macmillan), Basingstoke.

Pack, S.J. (1991), *Capitalism as a Moral System – Adam Smith's Critique of the Free Market Economy*, Edward Elgar, Aldershot.

Passinetti, L.L. and Schefold, B. (eds), (1999), *The Impact of Keynes on Economics in the Twentieth Century*, Edward Elgar, Aldershot.

Perrotta, C. (1988), *Produzione e Lavoro produttivo nel Mercantilismo e nell'Illuminismo*, Congedo editore, Galatina.

Perrotta, C. (1991), 'Is the mercantilist theory of the balance of trade really erroneous', *History of Political Economy*, vol. 23, n. 2.

Petty, Sir W. (1662), *A Treatise of Taxes and Contributions*, Brooke, London, in *The Economic Writings of Sir William Petty*, C.H. Hull (ed.), Cambridge University Press, Cambridge, 1899.

Petty, Sir W. (1676), *Political Arithmetick*, Clavel and Mortlock, London, in *The Economic Writings of Sir William Petty*, C.H. Hull (ed.), Cambridge University Press, Cambridge, 1899.

Quesnay, F. (1756), 'Fermiers', in *François Quesnay et la Physiocratie*, Institut national d'études démographiques, Paris, 1958, vol. II.

Quesnay, F. (1757) 'Hommes' in *François Quesnay et la Physiocratie*, Institut national d'études démographiques, Paris, 1958, vol. II.

Quesnay, F. (1766), 'Analysis of the arithmetic formula of the Tableau économique', in R.L. Meek, *The Economics of Physiocracy*, Allen and Unwin, London, 1962.

Rashid, S. (1986), 'Adam Smith and the division of labour', *Scottish Journal of Political Economy*, vol. 33.

Robbins, L.C. (1934), *An Essay on the Nature and Significance of Economic Science*, Macmillan (now Palgrave Macmillan), London.

Routh, G. (1975), *The Origin of Economic Ideas*, Macmillan (now Palgrave Macmillan), London and Basingstoke.

Schumpeter, J.A. (1954), *History of Economic Analysis*, Allen and Unwin, London.

Schumpeter, J.A. (1956), *Ten Great Economists*, Allen and Unwin, London.

Sewall, E. (1901), *The Theory of Value before Adam Smith*, American Economic Association publications, Baltimore, vol. 3, third series.

Skinner, A.S. (1982), 'A Scottish contribution to marxist sociology', in M. Bradley and J. Howard (eds), *Classical and Marxian Political Economy*, Macmillan (now Palgrave Macmillan), London.

Skinner, A.S. (1992), 'Adam Smith: ethics and self-love', in P. Jones and A. Skinner (eds), *Adam Smith Reviewed*, Edinburgh University Press, Edinburgh.

Skinner, A.S. (1993), 'Adam Smith and the role of the state: education as a public service', Associazione Italiana di storia del pensiero economico, Modena, mimeo.

Smith, A. (1748?), *Lectures on Rhetoric and Belles Lettres* (LRBL), J.C. Brice (ed.), Oxford University Press, Oxford, 1983.

Smith, A. (1759), *The Theory of Moral Sentiments* (TMS), D.D. Raphael and A.L. Macfied (eds), Oxford University Press, Oxford, 1976.

Smith, A. (1762–3/1766), *Lectures on Jurisprudence* (LJ), R.L. Meek, D.D. Raphael and P.G. Stein (eds), Oxford University Press, Oxford, 1978.

Smith, A. (1776), *An Inquiry into the Nature and Causes of the Wealth of Nations* (WN), R.H. Campbell, A.S. Skinner and W.B. Todd (eds), Oxford University Press, Oxford, 1976.

Smith, A. (1795), *Essays on Philosophical Subjects* (EPS), W.P.D. Wightman, J.C. Brice and I.S. Ross (eds), Oxford University Press, Oxford, 1980.

Saraffa, p. (1951) 'Introduction' to *The Works and Correspondence of David Ricardo*, The University Press, Cambridge, Volume 1, pp. xiii–lxiii.

Sraffa, P. (1960), *Production of Commodities by Means of Commodities*, The University Press, Cambridge.

Stewart, D. (1793), *Account of the Life and Writings of Adam Smith, L.L.D.*, in Smith (1795).

Stigler, G.J. (1941), *Production and Distribution Theories. The Formative Period*, Macmillan (now Palgrave Macmillan), New York.

Stigler, G.J. (1965), *Essays in the History of Economics*, Chicago University Press, Chicago.

Sylos-Labini, P. (1976), 'Competition: the product markets', in *The Market and the State*, T. Wilson and A.S. Skinner (eds), Oxford University Press, Oxford.

Sylos-Labini, P. (1984), *The Forces of Economic Growth and Decline*, MIT Press, Cambridge, Massachusetts.

Taylor, O.H. (1930), 'Economics and the Idea of *Jus naturale*', *Quarterly Journal of Economics*, vol. 44.

Vaggi, G. (1987), *The Economics of François Quesnay*, Macmillan (now Palgrave Macmillan), London.

Vaggi, G. (1990), 'The classical concept of profit revisited', in *Perspectives on the History of Economic Thought*, D.E. Moggridge (ed.), Edward Elgar, Aldershot, vol. 3.

Vaggi, G. (1995), 'The Limits of Physiocracy and Smith's Fortune', *Economies et Sociétés*, série oeconomia, histoire de la pensée économique, P.E. nos 22–23, no. 1–2.

Viner, Jacob (1991), *Essays in the Intellectual Tradition of Economics*, Princeton University Press, Princeton.

Weulersse, G. (1910), *Le Mouvement physiocratique en France de 1756 à 1770*, Alcan, Paris, reprinted Mouton, Paris, 1968.

Winch, D. (1969), *Economics and Policy. A Historical Survey*, Collins-Fontana, London.

Winch, D. (1971), *The Emergence of Economics as a Science 1750–1870*, in *The Fontana History of Europe*, Fontana-Collins, London, Vol. 3, section 9.

Winch, D. (1983), 'Adam Smith's enduring particular result: a political and cosmopolitan perspective', in I. Hont and M. Ignatief (eds), *Wealth and Virtue*, Cambridge University Press, Cambridge.

Winch, D. (1991), 'Adam Smith: the prophet of free enterprise', *History of Economics Review* No. 16, summer.

Winch, D. (1996), *Riches and Poverty – an intellectual history of political economy in Britain 1750–1834*, Cambridge University Press, Cambridge.

Index